FRAYING FABRIC

THE WORKING CLASS IN AMERICAN HISTORY

A list of books in the series appears at the end of this book.

FRAYING FABRIC

How Trade Policy and Industrial Decline Transformed America

JAMES C. BENTON

UNIVERSITY OF ILLINOIS PRESS
Urbana, Chicago, and Springfield

1 2 3 4 5 C P 5 4 3 2 1
∞ This book is printed on acid-free paper.

Library of Congress Cataloging-in-Publication Data
Names: Benton, James C., author.
Title: Fraying fabric : how trade policy and industrial decline transformed America / James C. Benton.
Description: Urbana : University of Illinois Press, [2022] | Series: The working class in american history | Includes bibliographical references and index.
Identifiers: LCCN 2022015970 (print) | LCCN 2022015971 (ebook) | ISBN 9780252044656 (cloth) | ISBN 9780252086724 (paperback) | ISBN 9780252053665 (ebook)
Subjects: LCSH: Textile industry—United States—History—20th century. | Clothing trade—United States—History—20th century. | Deindustrialization—United States—History—20th century. | United States—Commercial policy—History—20th century.
Classification: LCC HD9855 .B35 2022 (print) | LCC HD9855 (ebook) | DDC 338.4/767700973—dc23/eng/20220615
LC record available at https://lccn.loc.gov/2022015970
LC ebook record available at https://lccn.loc.gov/2022015971

CONTENTS

ACKNOWLEDGMENTS

Writing a book is never an individual effort, and this book certainly owes its existence to a sizable cast working over the years with me.

Tracking a sprawling issue like trade over years in what was once one of the largest manufacturing sectors of the United States is a daunting challenge. Simply put, you would not be reading this work were it not for the helpful and timely guidance of dozens of archivists and librarians.

I thank this significant cast, including Jennifer Boettcher, Maura Seale, and the circulation and interlibrary loan staff at the Joseph Mark Lauinger Memorial Library, Georgetown University; Louise Sandberg, Lawrence (Massachusetts) Free Public Library; Lynda DeLoach, George Meany Memorial Archives, National Labor College; Timothy Meagher and Jane Stoeffler, American Catholic History Research Center, Catholic University of America; Traci JoLeigh Drummond and Hal Hansen, Southern Labor Archive, Georgia State University; Tab Lewis, National Archives II, College Park, Maryland; Karen Adler Abramson and Steve Plotkin, John F. Kennedy Presidential Library and Museum; Allen Fisher, Lyndon B. Johnson Presidential Library; Roger Horowitz, Carol Lockman and Lucas Clawson, Hagley Museum and Library; Elizabeth Druga, Gerald R. Ford Presidential Library; Harry Miller, State Historical Society of Wisconsin; Patrizia Sione and Steven Calco, Kheel Center for Labor-Management Documentation and Archives, Cornell University; Kristen Chinery, Walter P. Reuther Library, Wayne State University; and Jim Quigel, Historical Collections and Labor Archives, Special Collections Library, Pennsylvania State University. A host of other, unnamed archivists deserve recognition for their assistance at the Library of Congress; the Special Collections and University Archives, University of Massachusetts at Amherst; the Southern Historical Collection, Wilson Library, University of North Carolina at Chapel Hill; the David M. Rubenstein Rare Book and Manuscript Library, Perkins Library, Duke University; the Kannapolis branch of the Cabarrus County (North Carolina) Public Library; and the main branch of the Cherokee County (S.C.) Public Library in Gaffney.

This book got its start at Georgetown University. I appreciate the efforts of many kind and talented academics along the way. In the liberal studies program, the late Phyllis O'Callaghan opened the door to a new pathway to learning, with Judith Sablosky, Ralph Nurnberger, Betty and Richard Duke, Anne Ridder, and Nikki Castle guiding me along the way. In the history department, I learned and contemplated things to include in this narrative with the help of exposure to ideas from professors such as Michael Kazin, Maurice Jackson, Chandra Manning, Marcia Chatelain, John Tutino, David Painter, Erick Langer, and Katie Benton-Cohen. I am especially grateful to Joe McCartin, my dissertation adviser and now a colleague at the Kalmanovitz Initiative for Labor and the Working Poor, for accepting me into his research seminar as a student with an MA but who was not enrolled in a degree program at the time. That decision has led to a working relationship that has lasted for nearly fifteen years. His assistance, for which I'm grateful, was particularly helpful in the path I took to become a historian.

As this work proceeded, it benefited from comments and suggestions arising from presentations before groups and conferences at Georgia State University, Louisiana State University, the City University of New York, the Social Science History Association, Georgetown University, George Washington University, and Wayne State University. I also thank members of the Washington, DC, Labor History Reading Group, housed at George Washington University, for their enthusiasm and questions, as well as a small student reading group in the Department of History at Georgetown that included Kelly Hammond, Graham Pitts, and Elizabeth Williams.

This work also benefited from research fellowships offered by a variety of foundations. I thank the Roosevelt Foundation; the JFK Presidential Library Foundation; the Lyndon B. Johnson Library Foundation; the Gerald R. Ford Library Foundation; the Cosmos Club of Washington, DC; the Southern Labor Archives' Reed-Fink Award; the Hagley Museum & Library; and HealthTank, LLC. The Department of History at Georgetown, through its Piepho research fellowship, its Dorothy Brown Teaching Award, and its Davis Teaching Fellowship, offered several opportunities at critical junctures to continue research.

Joe McCartin, Michael Kazin, and David Painter, as members of my dissertation committee, helped me along and were always there to assist with letters of recommendation or gestures of support. I thank the Labor and Working-Class History Association, which awarded an earlier version of this work its Herbert

Gutman Prize, and the journal *Labour* for its top international dissertation prize. (This work was also a finalist for the Glassman dissertation award, offered by Georgetown's Graduate School of Arts and Sciences.)

This work took on additional editing and revisions as I joined the office of President John J. DeGioia to assist Georgetown in its work to move forward and reckon with the university's connection to slavery via the Maryland Province of the Society of Jesus, which established plantations throughout the Chesapeake region and the college that would later become Georgetown University. I thank Dr. DeGioia and his chief of staff, Dr. Joe Ferrara, for their trust in me on such a crucial project and for the support of the job that helped make the revisions and additional research possible. I also offer a special thanks to Carole Sargent, director of Georgetown's Office of Scholarly Publications, for her suggestions and our brainstorming conversations during my revision process, as well as for her camaraderie over the years.

At the Kalmanovitz Initiative, I am fortunate to be part of an inspiring environment as part of a group devoted to respecting the dignity of workers and improving conditions for working people. Alongside fellow labor historians, including Leon Fink, Lane Windham, Patrick Dixon, and Clayton Sinyai, colleagues like Jessica Chilin-Hernández, Juan Belmán Guerrero, Sara Myklebust, and Lily Ryan, and students who come to us each semester, we work to create a unique space where academic research joins with activism in service to working-class people in Washington, DC, across the United States, and around the world.

At the University of Illinois Press, editors James Engelhardt and Alison Syring were helpful as I cut a rather unwieldy dissertation into the work you are now reading. The critical suggestions of a trio of readers—Gerald Jaynes, Will Jones, and Jarod Roll—also gave useful guidance in shaping the final product, for which I am grateful.

I thank my son, Julian, and his mom, Ann, for their support and patience over the years, as well as my mother, Shirley H. Benton, and other close relatives and personal friends who offered encouragement, listened to my seemingly endless anecdotes about research and writing, and expressed interest over the many years this work took to be finalized.

I wish to remember several special individuals I encountered along the way but who did not live to see the end result: Linda Golz, a colleague from my newspaper days in northeast Ohio; Evan A. North, a graduate school colleague whose interests in economic history were intersecting with my research ideas before his sudden passing; Philoine Fried, the daughter of Sidney and Bessie Abramowitz Hillman, who in the last year of a long, productive life opened her home and talked with me about the Amalgamated Clothing Workers of America as well as the experiences of women in the garment industry; and my father, Claude Benton Jr., who sharecropped into early adulthood with his family and my mother; in his older years he saw me start my academic research on the industry that focused on the cotton he once grew and picked.

This story is one of failure and decline thus far; the final analysis remains to be written. Yet it's also a story of people who saw problems with trade when the United States was relatively stronger economically, and who tried to do something to alter the course of history for their families, their workplaces, their communities, and their nation. I dedicate this work to the working women and men in this book—and the voices of those workers awaiting discovery in the archives—for their realization of the problems with the nation's trade policies from the 1930s onward. Their warnings, if heeded, might have led the nation into a much different, and better, place: one in which a more equitable balance of power between workers and managers existed, and one in which labor, capital, and the state structured an industrial policy that was more balanced and helped workers and communities affected by import competition. As contemporary workers across the United States and around the world seek a greater share of power as we labor under the COVID-19 pandemic, the warnings of their predecessors on trade offer a compelling reason that workers' voice is essential in building workplace democracy.

ABBREVIATIONS

AAA	Agricultural Adjustment Administration
ACMA	American Cotton Manufacturers' Association (1903–49)
ACMI	American Cotton Manufacturers' Institute (1949–62)
ACTWU	Amalgamated Clothing and Textile Workers' Union
ACWA	Amalgamated Clothing Workers of America
AFL	American Federation of Labor
ARA	Area Redevelopment Act of 1961
ATC	World Trade Organization Agreement on Textiles and Clothing
ATMI	American Textile Manufacturers' Institute (1962–2004)
BLS	Bureau of Labor Statistics, US Department of Labor
CEA	Council of Economic Advisers
CETA	Comprehensive Employment and Training Act
CFP	Commission on Foreign Economic Policy
CIO	Committee for Industrial Organization (1935–38); Congress of Industrial Organizations (1938–present)
CRI	Committee for Reciprocity Information
CTI	Cotton-Textile Institute
ECA	Economic Cooperation Administration
ECAT	Emergency Committee for American Trade
EEC	European Economic Community
EEOC	Equal Employment Opportunity Commission
EFTA	European Free Trade Association
ERISA	Employee Retirement Income Security Act of 1974
ERP	European Recovery Program
FERA	Federal Emergency Relief Administration

FFACT	Fiber, Fabric, and Apparel Coalition for Trade
FLSA	Fair Labor Standards Act of 1938
FTA	Food, Tobacco, Agricultural and Allied Workers of America–CIO
GATT	General Agreement on Tariffs and Trade
IAM	International Association of Machinists
ILGWU	International Ladies' Garment Workers' Union
ILO	International Labor Organization
ITAC	Interagency Textile Administrative Committee
ITGWF	International Textile and Garment Workers Federation
JFTW	Japanese Federation of Textile Workers
JTPA	Job Training Partnership Act of 1982
LTA	Long-Term Arrangement Governing Trade in Cotton Textiles
MDTA	Manpower Development and Training Act of 1962
MFA	Multifiber Arrangement, also known as the Arrangement regarding International Trade in Textiles
MFN	Most Favored Nation
MSA	Mutual Security Agency
NAACP	National Association for the Advancement of Colored People
NAFTA	North American Free Trade Agreement
NAM	National Association of Manufacturers
NEP	New Economic Plan
NIRA	National Industrial Recovery Act of 1933
NLB	National Labor Board
NLRA	National Labor Relations Act of 1935
NLRB	National Labor Relations Board
NRA	National Recovery Administration
NWLB	National War Labor Board
OECD	Organization for Economic Co-operation and Development
PNTR	Permanent Normal Trading Relations
RTAA	Reciprocal Trade Agreements Act of 1934
RTAP	Reciprocal Trade Agreements Program
STA	Short-Term Arrangement Governing Trade in Cotton Textiles
SWOC	Steel Workers Organizing Committee
SYE	Square Yards Equivalent
TAA	Trade Adjustment Assistance
TEA	Trade Expansion Act of 1962
TLRB	Textile Labor Relations Board
TPP	Trans-Pacific Partnership
TTIP	Transatlantic Trade and Investment Partnership
TWOC	Textile Workers Organizing Committee

TWUA	Textile Workers' Union of America
UAW	United Auto Workers
UFCW	United Food and Commercial Workers
UMWA	United Mine Workers of America
UNITE	Union of Needletrades, Industrial, and Textile Employees
URW	United Rubber Workers
USWA	United Steelworkers of America
UTWA	United Textile Workers of America
WARN	Worker Adjustment and Retraining Notification Act of 1988
WTO	World Trade Organization

FRAYING FABRIC

INTRODUCTION

In the past five decades, US manufacturing has declined significantly. As the nation's workforce more than doubled, from 81.9 million in January 1970 to 164.5 million in February 2020, manufacturing employment dropped 30.2 percent, from 18.4 million to 12.9 million.[1] The tremendous shift was due in part to capital mobility, deindustrialization, and a political economy favoring lower barriers to trade, part of an overly optimistic belief that broad-based, positive economic benefits would result from a greater volume of foreign trade.

Across the United States, however, international trade and economic change combined to accelerate the decline of industries and manufacturing communities that failed to adjust. Such was the case in textiles and apparel, which had been challenged for decades. Between January 1990 and February 2020, domestic textile and apparel employment plummeted 85.4 percent, from 1.44 million to 210,700.[2] The economic deterioration, in turn, laid the groundwork for an economic populism that factored into the 2016 presidential election and contributed to a politics of resentment that is drastically reshaping the nation's course.

This book uses the textile and apparel industries—one of the nation's oldest manufacturing sectors and at one point one of its largest—to demonstrate how shortcomings in trade policy by labor, business, and government from the 1930s to the 2010s delivered the nation to this point. In the late 1960s, as the collapse approached, these industries employed nearly one in seven US manufacturing workers. They toiled in New York, Chicago, and Los Angeles and small towns from New England and the Midwest to Appalachia, the South, and the Southwest. They produced fabric, yarn, clothing, bedding, towels, and other items for consumers in the United States and worldwide.

The increase in deindustrialization and the resultant backlash contributed to the election of a president who vowed a radically different approach to trade. In its first eighteen months in office, the Trump administration took policy positions that diverged from those of its predecessors—imposing tariffs on steel imports, withdrawing from trade agreements, hectoring Canada and Mexico into renegotiating NAFTA, and raising tariffs on Chinese goods, leading China to close its market to US soybeans and other agricultural exports. The flurry of actions led a historian of trade to note in 2018 that US observers were "present at the unraveling" of trade policy, recalling former Secretary of State Dean Acheson's phrase as he guided the creation of a post–World War II global order.[3]

The idea that led to this book originated in the abrupt end to the textile and apparel manufacturing sector. For decades, economists, sociologists, and historians sought to explain the variables that combined to produce deindustrialization by looking at taxation, investment, and trade policies. But there was more to the story. How did workers, unions, and companies in the textile and apparel industries view trade and foreign competition? While their voices populated many works on deindustrialization, they were largely missing from times when these industries were relatively healthy.

In compiling this work, I have sought to locate the views of workers, businesses, and federal officials on trade policy from the 1930s, when the current framework was first implemented under Secretary of State Cordell Hull. Their collective views reflect a desire to increase global trade amid international competition they saw as insignificant, until that competition threatened domestic manufacturing.

Chapter 1 begins with the years from 1974 to the present, in which new agreements encouraged greater trade, contributing to the decline of US manufacturing and fueling a populist response as trade captured the attention of larger swaths of the public. Yet several social factors related to cultural, social, and economic shifts also contributed to the 2016 election, the fifth in US history in which the candidate with the majority of votes lost the Electoral College.

The remaining chapters cover the years from 1933 to 1974, outlining the rise and weakening of modern US trade policy. Chapter 2, encompassing the years of the Franklin Roosevelt administration, explores part of the New Deal—its ambitious yet uneven attempt to fully advance workers' rights and expand international trade as part of the recovery from the Great Depression. The outcome of this effort, promoting trade while leaving workers' rights vulnerable, would ultimately affect US trade policy.

Chapter 3, covering the years from 1946 to 1960, shows how challenges like import competition and automation became increasingly apparent to textile and apparel workers and their unions. Labor representatives at times engaged in work that put them in touch with their industrial counterparts worldwide.

But labor faced challenges at home, including fights for policies to help workers and communities affected by trade. As a result, import competition received comparatively little attention during these years.

A coordinated federal program to aid the industries came into existence during John F. Kennedy's presidency, covered in chapter 4. This effort, rooted in Kennedy's work in Congress to preserve New England's shrinking textile and apparel industries, also marked an attempt to aid several key constituencies for Kennedy: organized labor, textile executives, and southern voters.

From 1964 to 1969, the years covered in chapter 5, satisfaction with trade policy quickly turned to discontent as imports of textiles and apparel surged. Some nations used their industries to produce low-cost goods for sale in export markets. Meanwhile, Mexico established tariff-free *maquiladora* zones through its 1965 Border Industrialization Program. The growth of low-cost textile manufacturing sectors and tariff-free zones for garment manufacturing or finishing quickly jeopardized hundreds of thousands of US textile and garment manufacturing jobs.

By 1969, the AFL-CIO finally began to follow the lead of its textile and apparel unions in questioning the federation's support of trade policy. In this momentous year, covered in chapter 6, textile and apparel unions organized to raise awareness of the effect of imports on jobs, livelihoods, and communities. Their protests succeeded in galvanizing the attention of lawmakers and the general public, placing renewed pressure on Congress to impose import quotas through legislation. The protests also attracted the attention of President Richard Nixon, who, like Kennedy, relied on textile manufacturers' support in his successful run for the White House.

Between 1970 and 1974, as the nation's balance of trade switched from surplus to deficit, labor and business squared off on trade policy. In these years, covered in chapter 7, textile and apparel unions waged two unsuccessful attempts to win import quota legislation. They met opposition from supporters of lower trade barriers, including public officials and multinational corporations that stood to benefit. Supporters of more foreign trade won a measure—the Trade Act of 1974—accelerating the lowering of trade barriers rather than curbing imports.

The story offers clues to which paths the nation, in the third decade of the twenty-first century, can take and what kind of economic future it will choose. In an effort to create a new world of peace and prosperity after the deprivation of the Great Depression and the destruction of World War II, the United States ultimately failed to secure the security and prosperity of its own citizens. If the nation is now to create an economy in which workers can attain meaningful economic security, it is critical to learn well the lessons of stories like this one.

1

FROM FREE TRADE TO POPULISM

How Did We Get Here? 1974–2016

Trade and a New Phase of Industrial Decline

Textile and apparel unions in the United States by 1974 had succeeded, with the help of other unions, in convincing much of the US labor movement and the general public of the harm that imports and lower trade barriers posed to US manufacturing jobs, community vitality, and the nation's economy. They did so despite waging a losing battle against companies and presidential administrations on the dangers of imports. Through informational pickets, protests, and lobbying, their efforts made trade and industrial decline increasingly important in US politics.

Success, however, came too late. They couldn't reverse a downward trend for the textile and apparel industries that was decades in the making. Between 1974 and 2019, textile and apparel employment in the United States had dropped by more than 90 percent.[1] One big reason, in the eyes of Evelyn Dubrow, longtime lobbyist for the International Ladies' Garment Workers' Union (ILGWU), came from the failure of international trade agreements like the Multifiber Arrangement (MFA) to protect US textile jobs. In effect between 1974 and 2004, the MFA was an international arrangement among textile- and garment-producing nations to limit exports from developing nations to developed ones, so that developed nations with more mature textile sectors could adjust to import competition. But, as with the Short-Term Arrangement Governing Trade in Cotton Textiles (STA) and Long-Term Arrangement Governing Trade in Cotton Textiles (LTA) in the 1960s and 1970s, nations could not adequately police trade patterns as they originally hoped. The MFA restricted growth of foreign textile imports in the United States to 6 percent a year, but participating nations found loopholes to evade this limit. The agreement also did not include some textile-producing nations, which encouraged further evasion.[2] The agreement was doomed. Despite the MFA and other attempts to manage the international textile trade, the dollar value of annual imports to the United States increased 428 percent between 1965 and 1984 (from $795 million to $4.2 billion). Imports grew at an annual rate between 7 and 10 percent, far outstripping the 2–3 percent growth in US consumer demand for textiles.[3]

While textile imports grew rapidly, the US industry failed to export its products, except during economic slowdowns when the domestic market was less able to absorb the industry's output. When US firms made no sustained effort to increase exports, preventing potential foreign buyers from developing long-term relationships with US textile firms, foreign producers stepped in, building bonds with these buyers while setting their sights on the United States as an export market.[4]

International competition, new technologies, new production methods, and marketing methods all posed steep challenges to the domestic textile industry. In a move reminiscent of their plight in the 1930s, manufacturers increased production, hoping economies of scale could keep them competitive. But increased production could not keep pace with changing market demands or the lower labor costs experienced abroad. Plant closings increased, production decreased, and automation advanced, further weakening the industry.[5]

As the US textile and apparel industries continued their decline, their unions were forced to change with the times. In 1976 the Textile Workers Union of America (TWUA) and Amalgamated Clothing Workers of America (ACWA), under Presidents Sol Stetin and Murray Finley, respectively, merged to create the Amalgamated Clothing and Textile Workers Union (ACTWU).[6] The new union's signature early act was a campaign to win union representation at J. P. Stevens and Company, organizing drives and product boycotts. The campaign also inspired the Oscar-winning *Norma Rae* (1979), loosely based on Crystal Lee Sutton, a J. P. Stevens worker in Roanoke Rapids, North Carolina, arrested and fired for organizing coworkers. The campaign culminated in a 1980 settlement in which the union won bargaining rights at plants it organized, in exchange for ACTWU dropping its boycott against Stevens.[7] Yet, at the point when organized labor finally cracked the door of one of the South's largest textile manufacturers, inspiring other southern textile companies to organize, the industry was declining. Against this backdrop, ACTWU continued to press for protection against imports, alerting the public to the continual deterioration of the nation's textile industry by import competition.[8]

The ACTWU's limited success in the South revealed a tragic irony. From the 1940s to the 1960s, when the textile and apparel industries' health had strengthened from earlier in the century, executives, especially in the South, largely succeeded in keeping labor out, often appealing to jingoism or racial, ethnic, and religious bias. But the victory was a short-lived and Pyrrhic one for the companies. In keeping out unions, textile executives had also denied themselves the opportunity to ally with labor, then at the peak of its power within the New Deal political coalition. They also missed the possibility of winning a trade regime that went further to protect the interests of workers in import-sensitive industries. By shunning labor, executives also blocked the development of an independent worker voice—one that could have joined with labor union officials, textile executives, their counterparts in other, similarly affected industries, and politicians at all levels concerned about the effects of imports on workers, industries, and local economies. Had labor and management teamed up to address import competition in the 1940s and 1950s, when textile labor began to notice increases in wool and cotton imports, they might have won meaningful trade policies long before the Kennedy administration embarked on its ultimately inadequate seven-point plan.

Furthermore, by keeping labor out of southern plants, the textile and apparel industries denied the ACWA, ILGWU, TWUA, and United Textile Workers of America (UTWA) stronger voices within the AFL-CIO and in counterpoint to unions favoring lower trade barriers. Had these four unions been able to organize and form a powerful base in the southern textile and apparel industries, they might have forced labor federations to seriously address import competition and question their support of trade policy. Because of their lack of presence in the southern industries, labor could not amass enough power within the New Deal coalition to influence trade policy to better protect workers' interests. For example, during George McGovern's 1972 campaign, they could have pushed the Democratic Party to address import competition, Nixon's wage and price controls, and unemployment issues. Instead, McGovern eschewed economic issues and focused on the Vietnam War. In the process, the Democrats lost the support of the AFL-CIO—which offered no presidential endorsement—and embarked on a futile attempt to win the "disaffected Americans" who had turned to George Wallace in 1968 without offering an economic program to address that faction's fears.[9]

Labor's improving fortunes in the South between the 1970s and the end of the twentieth century began to instill hope among workers that better pay and working conditions were finally within reach. But the steady erosion of textile and apparel employment in the region undercut those hopes. In a cruel twist of fate, textile and apparel jobs began to disappear just after successful efforts by civil-rights groups and the Equal Employment Opportunity Commission (EEOC), aided by Title VII of the Civil Rights Act, opened the southern textile industry to African Americans. The loss of jobs proved especially crushing, not only for African American workers who had been excluded for decades from the region's largest industry, but also for unions: Black workers often were more willing to organize than their white counterparts. Nevertheless, the continual loss of textile and apparel jobs strengthened the hands of employers who resisted unionization because many workers, regardless of race, who might have favored organizing began to worry that a union's arrival might spell a plant's closure.

Accelerating Decline: Economic and Social Changes and the Weakening of Labor

Ongoing US commitment to lowering trade barriers, global mobility of capital, and neoliberalism—a belief that markets, and not government, solve problems—set the stage for further social changes. The end of the Vietnam War in 1975 coincided with a combination of rising domestic unemployment, inflation, and stagnating wages. As prices rose, consumers found US-made goods undercut by cheap imports from low-wage nations and imports of better quality from other nations. The combination led to a public notion that other countries were passing up the United States in their competitiveness and production of consumer goods.

Larger societal shifts were also at play. The oil shocks of the 1970s that produced gas rationing, 55-miles-per-hour speed limits, and a short-lived expansion of Daylight Savings Time continued the unraveling of the postwar international economic system. The Vietnam War and the Watergate scandal also increased public skepticism about civil society institutions and their capacity for accomplishment, bringing a societal shift emphasizing individual effort over collective responsibility for the individual's well-being. It also produced a shift in corporate behavior—away from acting as a moderating force for broad economic progress to serving its interests first. At roughly the same time, a focus on shareholder returns led to rapidly increasing compensation for business leaders that far outstripped worker wage growth.[10]

With the passage of the Trade Act of 1974, one of the foundations of the nation's contemporary trade policy, the United States continued to promote lower trade barriers as the textile and apparel industries, unions, and politicians pushed for import quotas—a goal that other industries and agricultural producers sought as they faced increasing international competition. As they had done in past decades, textile and apparel industries resumed their push for import quotas through the 1990s. A 1978 measure in Congress, sponsored by Senator Ernest "Fritz" Hollings of South Carolina, exempted the textile industry from tariff reductions sought by Jimmy Carter, who vetoed it, fearing international trade retaliation. The veto, the administration's failure to end a Senate filibuster of a 1978 labor law reform

ILGWU Locals 23–25 protest imports during parade, New York, 1980s. (George Colon, ILGWU Photographs, Kheel Center for Labor-Management Documentation and Archives, Cornell University Library, Ithaca, New York.)

bill, and its embrace of legislation to deregulate the nation's airlines and trucking industry, all combined to demonstrate the enduring attractiveness of lower trade barriers to the elite within the Democratic Party. The actions also signaled that the party was continuing its retreat from organized labor and its embrace of neoliberal economic policies.[11]

As the nation's textile and apparel industries continued to shrink, industrial decline continued to spread to other industries. From the 1970s on, steel mills, automobile assembly plants and electronics facilities, among others, shut their doors and laid off millions. The number of US manufacturing workers, which had rebounded from 1970s recessions to peak at 19.5 million in June 1979, dropped to 16.7 million by December 1982, after twin recessions in 1980 and 1982. Plant closings were so widespread that the phenomenon earned a new moniker: "deindustrialization," coined by Barry Bluestone and Bennett Harrison.[12]

The economic downturn between 1979 and 1982 hit the textile industry especially hard, triggering new rounds of plant closings, layoffs, and short workweeks for workers. By early 1983, with textile unemployment in North Carolina and elsewhere as high as 16 percent, the industry again sought protection from imports. This time, manufacturers and unions joined forces, forming the Fiber, Fabric, and Apparel Coalition for Trade (FFACT). FFACT persuaded Congress to pass textile and apparel import quota bills in 1985 and 1987. Yet they failed to sway presidents who were open to their concerns but supported lower trade barriers. Like Kennedy and Nixon, Reagan courted southern politicians and textile manufacturers on the campaign trail. In 1980 he promised to protect the industries, but a year later he declared free trade "critical to ensuring a strong economy." In 1985 and 1987 he vetoed both bills, citing opposition from retailers, consumer groups, and exporters and fears that import controls would anger trading partners or raise consumer prices. Efforts to override the vetoes in Congress fell short.

Despite his vetoes, the Reagan administration often used negotiations instead of legislation to help the textile, automobile, and steel industries and agricultural producers win some protection from foreign competition. But the vetoes also conveyed a devotion to free trade that, paired with lack of concern for worker security, helped turn the tide against workers in the 1980s. His firing of eleven thousand air-traffic controllers in 1981 effectively transformed US labor-management relations, removing the strike as a weapon for workers and encouraging employers to expand the use of lockouts or replacement workers to turn back labor strife.[13]

The weakening of labor unions, accelerated after the air-traffic-controller strike, converged with the decline of US industrial economy from the 1970s and the advent of the New Right and neoliberal economic policies. These events turned the nation toward service and technology jobs to replace manufacturing jobs. The country's disadvantages against its industrialized competitors in its weaker safety net and its failure to commit to any industrial policy, meant the shift would be especially problematic for manufacturing workers or others whose jobs might be lost to trade deals. In 1981, after a billion-dollar outlay for Trade Adjustment Assistance (TAA) and the discovery that laborers, particularly unemployed United Auto Workers (UAW) members, were using TAA payments to supplement unemployment insurance, the federal government cut funding for TAA. The following year, Reagan eliminated the Comprehensive Employment and Training Act (CETA),which funded a Nixon-era program to promote job training and public service employment. Reagan replaced CETA with the Job Training Partnership Act of 1982 (JTPA), another program designed to promote, among other things, job training for displaced workers, though its effectiveness was later questioned.[14]

Reagan's vetoes were not the only signs of trouble for textiles and apparel. In 1987 a congressional report documented intensified international competition from a developing global textile industry. For nations with mature textile and

ILGWU/ACTWU protest urging Congress to override President Ronald Reagan's veto of textile import restrictions at US Capitol, 1986. (George Meany Memorial AFL-CIO Archives, University of Maryland–College Park.)

North Carolina AFL-CIO import protest, Charlotte, 1985. (George Meany Memorial AFL-CIO Archives, University of Maryland–College Park.)

apparel sectors where wages were higher and modernization lagged, as in the United States, the competition meant further industrial deterioration. Nevertheless, FFACT tried once again in 1990 to pass textile and apparel import quota legislation. As was the case in 1985 and 1987, the bill passed Congress, but President George H. W. Bush vetoed it. These three high-profile defeats highlighted the weakness of the textile and apparel industries, and their constituent unions, in shaping trade policy.[15]

Shifting Powers, Rising Protests: American Trade Policy in a New Era of Globalization

Just as labor and business struggled with import competition in the 1980s, the federal government struggled with the international agreements intended to regulate international trade in textiles and apparel. Nowhere was this clearer than in the administration of the MFA, which despite updates was quickly outpaced by a changing international textile and apparel sector. Developed nations hoping to preserve their textile and apparel sectors believed the MFA favored developing nations; conversely, the developing nations that were driving the growth in textile exports felt the MFA provisions were too restrictive. In December 1993 participants from 117 nations agreed to drop the MFA and end all trade barriers in the textile and apparel industries, including the politically popular import quotas that administrations had repeatedly rejected. The agreement, called the World Trade Organization Agreement on Textiles and Clothing (ATC), reduced tariff levels by 51 percentage points in three phases between 1997 and 2004, phasing out all remaining tariffs by the start of 2005. The ATC succeeded the General Agreement on Tariffs and Trade (GATT) at the end of the 1986–1994 Uruguay Round, and the World Trade Organization (WTO) monitored the ATC. In the United States, the agreement's effects included marked increases in apparel imports, lower prices for exports, and, most consequentially, a drastic reduction of US textile and apparel jobs. When the ATC took effect in January 1995, the industries together employed 1,307,100 people. By January 2005, when all import protections ended, in line with ATC provisions, US textile and apparel employment stood at 491,200. By January 2022 (and factoring in a rebound in employment during the COVID-19 pandemic) just 194,600 workers remained in the textile and apparel industries—an 85.1 percent decline in the number of workers in twenty-seven years.[16]

While the North American Free Trade Agreement (NAFTA) opened up Mexico as a tariff-free trading partner for the United States, the ATC accelerated the pace of change in the global textile trade, allowing lower-cost nations to take full advantage of the elimination of tariffs. The phaseout of tariffs, in combination with competition from low-wage nations that offset American advantages in quality and productivity with lower wages and better technology, hastened the collapse of the domestic industries. As Congress noted in 1987, low-wage producers and emerging textile and apparel sectors had long been challenging mature sectors like those in the United States. The ATC accelerated that process by encouraging numerous low-wage nations to modernize their textile sectors and trade with developed countries.[17] Yet NAFTA—by virtue of its visibility in the 1992 US presidential election and the 1993 campaign for congressional ratification—remains connected in the mind of large sectors of the US public as the cause of the demise of both industries.

By the mid-1990s, textile and apparel unions engaged in another round of mergers in an effort to remain viable. The UTWA merged with the United Food and Commercial Workers (UFCW) in 1994; a year later, ACTWU and the ILGWU merged to create Union of Needletrades, Industrial, and Textile Employees (UNITE).[18]

The decision to end the MFA and adopt the ATC was vastly overshadowed by the implementation of NAFTA on January 1, 1994, creating a free-trade zone encompassing Canada, the United States, and Mexico. The agreement, originally negotiated and ratified in 1991 as a modification of a US-Canada trade pact to include Mexico, was a topic of fierce debate in the US presidential campaign of 1992 and faced bitter opposition from labor, especially in textile and apparel unions, although some producers favored NAFTA. Opponents worried whether Mexico could be integrated into the existing free-trade zone without further harming US industries. In 1993 a bitter campaign raged over legislation to allow NAFTA provisions to go into effect at the beginning of 1994. To secure passage of the bill, several "side agreements" were added to NAFTA dealing with issues including labor rights and environmental protections. Congress and the Clinton administration also instituted a new TAA program to help workers whose job loss was connected to the increase in trade with Canada or Mexico.[19]

The battle over NAFTA, while a triumph for the supporters of lower trade barriers and others opposed to protectionism, marked a defining moment for Bill Clinton's presidency, trade politics, and public opinion on trade. The ascendance of the New Right to power with Ronald Reagan's election in 1980 marked the end of the dominance of the New Deal coalition. For various New Deal coalition constituencies, the electoral triumphs of Reagan and George H. W. Bush (who negotiated NAFTA with Mexican President Carlos Salinas de Gortari and Canadian Prime Minister Brian Mulroney) forced the Democratic Party in the late 1980s and early 1990s to reexamine its aims and goals as a means of returning to power. Clinton embraced the approach of lower trade barriers to generate prosperity, which had been pioneered by Cordell Hull and his Reciprocal

Trade Agreements Act of 1934 (RTAA). Clinton, though, demonstrated far less commitment than President Franklin D. Roosevelt to the promotion of worker security. With the exception of John F. Kennedy's brief efforts to stabilize the textile industry in the early 1960s, the Democratic Party had continued to embrace lower trade barriers even as worker security diminished and workers' ability to utilize collective action eroded. By the 1990s, no one in the nation's political elite was prepared to simultaneously support lower trade barriers and safeguard US workers' standard of living or their right to organize to protect their interests. The only significant commitment to workers' security in this period would be a 1988 law, the Worker Adjustment and Retraining Notification (WARN) Act, which required only a sixty-day advance notice of plant closings or layoffs, which did nothing at all to prevent those plant closings.[20]

While economist Douglas Irwin argues that NAFTA implementation led to rapid growth in bilateral trade and a more integrated North American economy, the agreement itself did not greatly affect employment or job flows in trade-sensitive industries. For the rest of the 1990s, the US economy appeared to display healthy signs: low unemployment, stable manufacturing employment overall, rising wages, federal budget surpluses. But for large swaths of the US public, the vitriolic populist opposition to NAFTA marked a turning point in their views on trade.

Likewise, NAFTA marked a turning point in governance on trade policy. Democrats in Congress turned more protectionist as they increasingly represented constituents and areas challenged by deindustrialization. Simultaneously, more Republicans, representing areas seeking direct foreign investment and nonunion manufacturing jobs, came to increasingly support lower trade barriers. The 1994 takeover of the House of Representatives by a Republican majority more likely to rely on conflict than consensus also contributed to lower Democratic support for trade policy and less cooperation on trade and other issues that once led to consensus. Clinton was the answer in the New Democrats' attempt to reclaim the presidency, but infighting over NAFTA left him increasingly at odds with a growing segment of his own party on trade.[21]

Into the New Millennium: Trade and US Manufacturing Decline

By late 1999, concern and anger about trade surfaced in Seattle at a WTO ministerial meeting. Although the meeting produced no significant agreements, it was better known for the protests against government officials and other attendees from labor unions, environmental groups, anarchist organizations, and others angry at the negative effects of trade.[22]

The following year, another heavily contested trade battle in Congress ended when both houses voted to extend permanent normalized trading relations to China, a necessary step for China's admission to the WTO. After China received Permanent Normal Trading Relations (PNTR), its exports to the United States surged, and the number of US manufacturing jobs dropped again—17 percent between 2001 and 2003, even after factoring in a short 2001 recession.[23]

The decline in US textile and clothing production coincided with China's rise to become the world's largest exporter of textiles and clothing by 2003. In the five years ending in 2005, China's textile and clothing exports to the United States grew from $8 billion to $19 billion; its share of US textile and clothing imports grew in that period from 11 to 25 percent. In the first year after the MFA restrictions were phased out, China's textile and clothing exports to the United States increased another 50 percent, prompting textile manufacturers to call for, and President George W. Bush to institute, a three-year agreement in 2005 that imposed limits on textile and apparel exports to the United States.[24]

In much of the country, textile and apparel plants either closed, moved, or were dramatically restructured after the ATC went into effect. In the US South, well-known industrial giants disappeared between 2000 and 2011: Burlington Industries filed for bankruptcy in 2001; two years later, Pillowtex, the owner of the former Cannon Mills, followed suit. Cone Mills closed in 2004; South Carolina's Springs Mills relocated to South America in 2005, becoming Springs Global. In 2006, after Virginia's Dan River Mills closed, its machinery was packed up and shipped to India. Finally, J. P. Stevens, which had aggressively resisted unionization for decades, merged with West Point Manufacturing Company and Pepperell Manufacturing to become WestPoint Home.[25]

The manufacturing losses of the early 2000s were overshadowed by strong labor markets, housing boom, and falling unemployment, not to mention the start of the "gray war" against al-Qaida and the Taliban after the September 11, 2001, terrorist attacks, and the 2003–2011 Iraqi invasion and war. But opportunities for trade-displaced workers did not always mean better chances. A new technological revolution in manufacturing led to greater production of goods with less labor. The changes especially affected workers in low-skill, labor-intensive industries, such as textiles and apparel. They often lacked new skills or education to find new jobs in other industries and the mobility to move elsewhere for new work. Their options were limited to a number of difficult choices: take lower-paying service jobs, undertake new education or retraining at their own expense, apply for disability benefits to earn some income, or drop out of the labor market.[26]

The nation's transition from a manufacturing economy to one dominated by services and technology, and the shifts on trade policy that further integrated the world economy had deep social consequences for US society. A confluence of economic change, social upheaval, and political backlash yielded bitter resentments, especially among those who most recently had been locked out of the economy. The shifts produced an economy in flux, where stability for all became harder, but especially so for those at the bottom. In the neologism of sociologist Guy Standing, this new group became known as the precariat—a group for whom economic progress was unstable and unpredictable.[27]

The continuing decline of unions also translated into less upward pressure on wages. As economic inequality deepened from the 1970s, working-class Americans who faced a declining number of manufacturing jobs were increasingly in trouble, regardless of their race, ethnicity, gender, or region. Median household income, after steadily increasing in each decade after World War II, *decreased* 6.7 percent between 2000 and 2010, to $54,673. A service economy begat a technology economy and then a "gig economy" relying on independent contractors under the aegis of companies like FedEx, Uber, and Lyft. Over time, millions were forced to piece together a living from jobs with scant—if any—benefits. Millions of people who had expected jobs to progress into middle-class security instead were forced to lower their expectations. "My dream used to be to live better at age 50 than I am now at age 35," said one respondent in a survey of workers affected by plant closures. "Now my dream is simply to survive."[28]

The Rise of the "Overclass" and the Emergence of Trump

Between 1947 and 1973, economic inequality in the United States narrowed, only to reverse course. The economic, cultural, and social changes unfolding after 1974 were paired with a decline in public support of societal institutions, such as government, business, labor unions, the military, and the clergy. Simultaneously, widening income and wealth inequalities produced a wealthier, more influential, and yet largely stealthy segment of society. In 1995 *Newsweek* magazine called this group an "overclass"—a group with enough power to warp the public interest in realizing its whims and desires, while standing as "one of the most anguished and self-doubting oligarchies in history."[29]

The creation and rise of the US technology sector, and the aggressive economy between the mid-1980s and the end of the twentieth century, spawned a culture in the United States that expanded the ranks of the overclass. Seemingly overnight, new billionaires appeared who were celebrated like entertainers or athletes. They also had the means to pledge fractions of their wealth to programs of social good that attracted positive press coverage. One of the first such actions came in September 1997, when CNN founder Ted Turner donated $1 billion—which he described as the increase in his net worth since the beginning of that calendar year—to the United Nations.[30]

Turner encouraged wealthy people to emulate his example, and many did, including the new technology billionaires. Such efforts, however, were ill-equipped to address, much less change, the fundamental causes of the social problems they purportedly attacked. Furthermore, such projects also gave wealthy benefactors tax breaks or other advantages. As cultural critic Anand Giridharadas has stated, members of the overclass who undertake and personally benefit from the social-good projects they champion are akin to an arsonist now rebranded as a firefighter.[31]

As manufacturing continued its decline after the 1970s, the pursuit of trade deals continued to outweigh workers' concerns. The struggles came to a head in 1992–93, as NAFTA loomed large both in the 1992 presidential campaign and in a congressional battle over legislation to implement the agreement. As previously explored, the struggle was repeated in 2000 over extending PNTR to China.

The political battles over NAFTA and PNTR only deepened public anger against trade among those who stood to lose jobs from import competition. Yet the push for new trade deals and lower trade barriers continued. As president, George W. Bush sought trade agreements in the face of the significant manufacturing decline after the extension of PNTR to China. Likewise, Barack Obama sought new trade agreements with the European Union (Transatlantic Trade and Investment Partnership; TTIP) and Asian nations (Trans-Pacific Partnership; TPP) in the 2010s, as manufacturing continued a slow recovery from the Great Recession of 2007–09.

By 2014, the nation's economic recovery from the Great Recession had been underway for five years. Yet millions of Americans, whether shut out of manufacturing work or living lives of precarity, did not share in the sense that a recovery was at hand. For them, trade remained a systemic failure in US society, joining taxes, healthcare, wars, infrastructure, race relations, and social program spending. Anger at elites was building once more, but this time it was paired with the growing radicalization of some working-class whites who not only felt left behind economically but also sensed they were being bypassed by other groups—immigrants, people of color, LGBTQ people—that they had long felt ranked below or behind them in social status. The system was ripe for someone new to tap into that anger, someone who Giridharadas said "correctly understood an intuition that other Americans had, that the system was rigged and elites in government and business were sort of in cahoots with each other and didn't care about regular people as much as they proclaimed."[32]

While some politicians sought trade deals despite the rising public anger over trade, several others since the 1970s tried to tap into that anger by way of populist appeals. In 1984 and 1988, Rev. Jesse Jackson's presidential campaign won support from economically strapped farmers and displaced manufacturing workers as he sought, with limited success, to pick up the mantle of Martin Luther King Jr.'s "beloved community" through electoral politics. In 1992 Republican candidate Pat Buchanan, who challenged Bush from the right in the primaries, opposed NAFTA. In the general election, businessperson and independent presidential candidate H. Ross Perot won the support of nearly 20 million voters (19 percent of the electorate) in part through his warning that NAFTA would create a "giant sucking sound" of jobs fleeing the United States. Perot would run again in 1996 as the candidate of the Reform Party, winning just 8.4 percent of the vote despite echoing many of the populist themes he'd sounded four years earlier. And, in 2004, Howard Dean's presidential campaign won a boost from his proposal to renegotiate NAFTA, showing that trade was still a vital issue for Americans struggling to make a living as a new gilded age arose around them.[33] By the 2010s, however, things would be different when populist anger arose out of economic desperation. A member of the overclass read this intuition and took on the mantle of rescuer but would institute another tactic.

Enter Donald Trump. From June 15, 2015, the day he announced his candidacy at his New York offices, he spoke the language of fear, resentment, anger, and bitterness that found purchase among an odd coalition: the dispossessed segments of the white working class and well-off workers who earned more than $75,000 a year. But his variety of populism—anger at the elites, paired with a strain of nativism and conservative and evangelical theology, strongly influenced by white nationalist philosophy—was connected to the desires of the overclass.

Trump's populism produced a resurgence of mean-spirited class politics that largely blamed women, immigrants, Muslims, African Americans, and marginalized populations, and elites across the board, for the travails of so-called "regular people"—even as his populism took pains to cater to the needs of wealthier Americans. These politics found favor with a subset of white Americans who felt they no longer enjoyed the social mobility of their forebears—many times at the expense of people of color. Some of this group, as Arlie Russell Hochschild's study of Tea Party supporters in rural Louisiana showed, also were fearful of the dramatically changing cultural landscape they were witnessing and felt left behind, or even pushed aside to allow people from other subgroups to get ahead of them.[34]

Trump's populism overshadowed a presidential campaign that had been expected to have historical overtones. Some of that overshadowing, no doubt, came from the documented interference of Russian interests in the 2016 election by way of social media and from infiltrating electoral systems.[35]

Nevertheless, the Democratic nominee and presumptive frontrunner, Hillary Rodham Clinton, struggled to reach voters—some of whom were wary of her as a candidate, while others remembered Bill Clinton's presidency and his support of both NAFTA and PNTR. Hillary Clinton's views on trade—which included a sober defense of trade agreements and a plan on trade that many industrial workers found uninspiring—opened the door for Trump's appeals to capture the attention of downwardly mobile, largely white, voters. His description of myriad problems in the United States at the 2016 Republican convention and his offer, spoken in terms of the overclass, to bring his private-sector expertise to government—"I alone can fix it," he famously claimed in his nomination speech—won over voters all too willing to overlook his personal conduct, his overt calls for Russian intervention on his behalf in the election, his bankruptcies, and his refusal to pay vendors, contractors, and subcontractors for work on his projects. Those voters also overlooked the warning Obama offered days later as Hillary Clinton was formally nominated: "Does anyone really believe that a guy who's spent his 70 years on this earth showing no regard for working people is suddenly going to be your champion, your voice?" he asked.[36]

A Bitter Harvest of Discontent: US Workers and the 2016 Election

By 2016, the fears and resentments of a segment of the US working class had finally boiled over, half a century after an infamous AFL-CIO survey that uncovered a rising backlash within the labor movement. For decades, successive presidential administrations sought trade deals while working-class Americans experienced little benefit from them. The Great Recession of 2007–9 robbed many of their jobs, homes, and retirement savings. In response, the economic recovery plan put in place by Presidents George W. Bush and Barack Obama offered bailouts for financial institutions and automakers, but Obama's economic stimulus was hamstrung by politics. Adding to the frustrations, homeowners received little more than faulty mortgage modifications and the working class was forced to endure a slow economic recovery as the fortunes of professional and white-collar workers improved much faster. Workers received only some tax breaks and unemployment insurance extensions in the 2009 stimulus package, as well as reauthorizations of TAA in 2009, 2011, and 2015.[37]

Their frustrations culminated in the rise of the Tea Party, a conservative political effort that spawned grassroots support from people opposed to the Obama administration's policies. But the Republican Party base was divided among members of the Tea Party, who saw "big government" in Obama's policies; moderate Republicans who differed with Obama on economic policies; and evangelical Republicans concerned about social issues. Traditional differences over policy that were to be expected as part of a presidential administration's legislative program were combined with conspiratorial fears that the Obama presidency would represent big government and would build a Democratic majority to carry out an agenda some opponents felt was too radical. Racial fears also contributed: in a 2013 study of key Republican constituencies, three Democratic pollsters reported that Republicans felt aware "of being white in a country that is increasingly minority" and worried that Democrats were using government programs to build dependency and political support among people of color.[38]

These fears, and resentment of the Democratic Party amid the weak economic recovery and enactment of the Affordable Care Act, sparked a political backlash in 2010. In the midterm elections that fall, Republicans regained control of the House of Representatives, picking up sixty-three seats. Voters also returned control of eleven state legislatures to the Republicans.[39]

In these states where legislative control shifted—which included Wisconsin, Michigan, Ohio, Pennsylvania, and North Carolina—legislators and governors wielded power in drastically different ways. Some efforts were immediately visible, like Wisconsin's push to end collective bargaining rights for state employees as a means of weakening organized labor. The move triggered massive protests and an unsuccessful recall effort against the governor, Scott Walker. Other efforts, like the 2010 round of redistricting, were less visible but had long-lasting effects. Lopsided partisan legislative and congressional majorities out of line with the partisan breakdown of the voting population emerged in states such as Wisconsin, Pennsylvania, Indiana, and North Carolina. Laws placing restrictions on voting eligibility in ways that disproportionately affected people of color and voting blocs who tended to vote Democratic, accelerated after 2013 when the US Supreme Court, in *Shelby County v. Holder*, struck down a section of the Voting Rights Act of 1965.[40]

By 2016, a segment of the working class was ready for change. To them, Hillary Clinton—whose husband was linked with NAFTA, among other reasons—was not the candidate to support. The workers in the white working class who went for Donald Trump were people who had long been turned off by domestic trade policies and who heard in his campaign promises to restore manufacturing—a hint of stopping the changes that threatened to tear their world apart. To them, Hillary Clinton was the person who would continue to act on behalf of the overclass at the expense of the working class, while Trump spoke their language, leading many to believe he would fight for them.

The continued involvement of African Americans in the labor movement, and growing unionization in the public sector, boosted the fortunes of organized labor. But challenges came with this growth. As labor continued to respond to the concerns of their new constituents, especially on issues like civil rights, a new feeling of alienation emerged among white blue-collar workers. One scholar, reflecting on her father-in-law's path from an impoverished childhood to a middle-class lifestyle, saw the disdain he had for organized labor. To him, unions had become more than simply "a bunch of jokers who took your money and never gave you anything in return."[41] These "jokers," by engaging in civil-rights advocacy, were actively playing a zero-sum game in which many whites equated advancement for their African American, Latino, and Asian contemporaries with loss of their own status.

To disaffected white working-class voters, trade mirrored civil rights on a different scale. Just as some whites perceived the extension of equality under the law to black and brown people as a denial of their civil rights, trade deals historically made to assist developing nations increasingly came to be seen as taking away from US interests. This perception is reflected in the sentiment of decades of letters and petitions from workers to government or labor leaders. Or, as UTWA President George Baldanzi bluntly stated in 1967, "What the hell good are we doing for this country or for world peace by exporting jobs to Taiwan or Hong Kong?"[42] When US politicians, executives, and labor leaders could not answer that question, much less build a security net to better help those whose jobs were lost from trade, they collectively allowed a bitter political backlash to take root and build.

Beginning in the late 1970s, the New Right represented a reaction against economic difficulties as well as civil rights; voter support for politicians in this coalition (including the "Reagan Democrats," who included laborers in places like suburban Detroit) opened the door to further assaults on labor rights, but not any relief for workers concerned about trade. When "third way" centrist Democratic politics challenged the New Right, a small expansion for economic growth and civil rights returned, but little progress on trade came for workers, especially among US manufacturing workers, who had hoped to maintain some relevance in the changing economy. The Russian influence in the 2016 election—whether through the sharing of intelligence between high-ranking Russian officials and the Trump campaign, or through efforts to use social media to instigate partisan demonstrations or spread lies about candidates—also played a role. Whether motivated by policy or prejudice, or both, white voters turned out in 2016. But turnout fell among African American and Latino working-class voters, an effect of both the voter suppression and voter ID laws placed in effect after *Shelby County v. Holder*.

Thus, the results of eighty-plus years of trade policy, decades of deindustrialization, working-class frustration, and increasing income and wealth inequality made itself evident over a tense three-and-a-half-hour period on the night of November 8, 2016. At 2:29 a.m. on November 9, the verdict was rendered in an Associated Press flash: Trump had won Wisconsin, and with it, the electoral votes needed for the presidency. A man whose glaring lack of qualifications and reliance on Russia made him a liability to US security nevertheless used his populist rage on the campaign trail to strike a nerve with enough workers, some of whom had been battered by the negative effects of trade and by an economy that seemed to offer no place for them.

That disaffected electorate turned to a member of the overclass who made people feel elite conventional wisdom demanded an unconventional answer. Decades of system failure in trade and industrial decline, and the failure of politicians to heed the protests of US laborers documented in these pages, contributed to the politics of 2016. A candidate who promised in part to address the needs of the working class to "make America great again" captured the presidency amid wildly shifting electoral turnout and while losing the popular vote by 3 million votes.[43]

The idea, much trumpeted by analysts and media outlets, of a working-class shift for Trump in 2016 in Pennsylvania, Ohio, Michigan, and Wisconsin, points to an overlooked division among working class voters. In the four states, Trump won between 53 and 62 percent of the white vote in Pennsylvania, Ohio, Michigan, and Wisconsin. But he overwhelmingly lost the African American and Latino vote in all four states. Only between 6–8 percent of African Americans in those states voted for Trump, while Latinos in those states offered Trump only between 22–38 percent. As people of color now comprise a growing share of the US working class, the difference in rates of support begs the question: Why did white working-class voters turn to Trump when their African American and Latino counterparts voted heavily for Clinton? A deeper look at exit poll results from the 2016 election offers context. On trade, a majority of Trump voters believed trade took away jobs, while a majority of Clinton voters believed that trade created jobs. Yet while voters in all states believed Clinton was better equipped to manage the economy, and overwhelming majorities favored Clinton over Trump in terms of personal qualities such as experience and judgment, an overwhelming number of respondents believed Trump was more likely to bring change.

In turn, economic precarity between the 1970s and 2010s yielded a radicalization of some working-class whites, though some are relative newcomers to a situation historically faced by working-class people of color who have faced extensive structural barriers to good jobs in even the best economies of the postwar period. For these whites, though, the feeling of being "left behind" or passed economically coincides with the presidency of Barack Obama to produce a backlash borne of panic. The real wages of work are declining, and the "psychological wage" of whiteness W.E.B. Du Bois famously described does not offer enough to foster a sense of security or status atop the US racial caste system.[44]

Indeed, the term "working class," as currently used, itself connotes a subset of the nation's working class. Much of US society uses the term to describe a largely male, largely white, conservative-leaning, manufacturing worker who lives in the industrial Midwest. That term does not seem to extend to the African American and Latino workers, largely women, who lean Democratic (yet are open to more conservative policies), live throughout the Midwest and other regions, and who work mainly in service and public-sector jobs. Despite being part of the US working class, these voters receive a much different consideration in public imagination, discourse, and policies. Manufacturing workers are revered, while service and public-sector workers are openly reviled or denigrated; their jobs are considered unskilled or less skilled than their manufacturing counterparts. Manufacturing workers receive protection from imports in the form of TAA; that protection was extended only briefly to service workers in 2009 and to public-sector workers between 2009 and 2011. The austerity measures imposed over the past forty years by governments at all levels increasingly affect public-sector workers—the largest source of working-class employment for African Americans. Austerity politics also brings to mind Lee Atwater's famous 1981 interview on the evolution of Republicans' Southern Strategy, in which Atwater describes a party moving from blatant racist appeals to voters in 1968 to more abstract appeals underlying policies that win support from conservative voters while disproportionately harming African Americans.[45]

The discussion of so-called white working-class voters turning to Trump in 2016 overwhelmingly avoided discussion of their black and brown counterparts who expressed very different sentiments at the ballot box. It also ignored the significant decrease in African American and Latino turnout between 2012 and 2016 made possible by voter suppression, foreign interference, and dissatisfaction with Clinton's candidacy. Nor did this discussion of the white working class mention its alliance with upper middle class and higher-income voters who backed Trump. These latter groups received the benefits of the 2017 tax cut as their working-class counterparts sustained plant closures and tariffs that raised prices on consumer goods, cutting further into their incomes.

As with the case of the difference between segments of the working class, another error in analysis of the results of the 2016 election was the disproportionate focus on voters' economic anxiety and the extent that it played a role in the election. The repeated attention given to this phenomenon as a cause of the 2016 outcome ignores several factors. First, economic anxiety has long been evident in the United States. Second, as a factor in politics and public policy, the US version has always included racism or nationalism of some sort. As the present work will show, textile and apparel workers were long aware of foreign competition and sought unsuccessfully to limit it, using protests and patriotic appeals that sometimes slipped into racism and nationalism. Finally, the economic anxiety that existed in 2016 was largely a rebirth of previous incarnations. It simply coincided with a decline in manufacturing and the rise of the Chinese in the global economy, as well as demographic change that has many white Americans—normally accustomed to being in control—increasingly worried about being overtaken by fellow Americans from other racial and ethnic groups and by other nations. This fear has driven some white Americans to join a nationalist movement that's also emerging in other nations. In the United States, nationalism was stoked by a candidate who paired it with economic populism.

The initial analyses of the 2016 election focused on support from the white working class in the Midwest and, particularly, in 206 counties nationwide that supported Barack Obama's 2012 reelection but went for Trump four years later. Other analyses also focused on exit polls showing Trump won among whites without college degrees by the largest margin of any candidate since 1980.[46] Yet this explanation, while part of the equation, tends to be simplistic. Unemployment may be a factor, but feelings about the effects of trade and lost status in an increasingly diverse nation are driving this fear as well.

Another part of the tricky nature of the term "white working class" is, as journalist George Packer wrote, the way in which the racial descriptor hints at historic advantages among whites while the term "working class" now hints at social decline. Put bluntly, the term "has been mobilized to connote downwardly mobile, poor, even pathological people" and linked with ills previously associated, stereotypically, with the urban, African American poor.[47]

While globalization unfolded, weakening social institutions and inflicting social disruption on individuals and families, another social change took place. US workers were radicalized to support candidates who helped them voice resentment at their loss of economic, cultural, and social status. Forming the base of a populism born of anger, they base their grievances on feeling that they have been attacked by elites who take their money and continue to prosper but give little in return.

Notwithstanding the degree to which foreign interference affected the 2016 presidential election (a full recounting of this phenomenon awaits), the results of the election represented, in part, a backlash from a group of voters who have felt unheard, including a segment of the working class. The irony of the election, however, is that the person they chose to help in resurrecting US manufacturing was utterly unqualified to deliver on that promise.

The 2016 election seemed to bring white working-class discontent to the fore, as exemplified by the electoral results in Wisconsin, Michigan, and Pennsylvania that swung the election for Trump by a combined 77,744 votes. Yet, while public opinion continues to support free trade—likely because of the lower prices it brings consumers and the growth of exports—the dissatisfaction of the working class, and the anger of people who lose jobs because of import competition, has long been evident. To them, US trade policy since the 1930s has served the needs and desires of the wealthy over those of the poor, the corporation over the worker, and the information and technology sectors of the economy over the manufacturing sector. As this book will show, resistance to lower trade barriers among workers in the textile and apparel industries were present long before Cordell Hull had a chance to carry out his trade policies. Despite their resistance and concerns, the US administrative state restated its commitment to lower trade barriers without paying equivalent attention to the needs of affected workers.

It is no wonder, then, that as US manufacturing workers in sector after sector were hurt by foreign competition, they became disillusioned with what they saw as substantial political support for new trade deals while giving little corresponding attention to the needs of people affected by such deals. To the displaced manufacturing worker, the threat was less an issue of partisan politics than a sense of class warfare waged on the working class by a wealthier, more powerful elite increasingly disconnected from the difficulties that workers faced.

From Populism to Economic Revitalization

What's needed to change this equation and put an end to the split of the working class? For one, policymakers must, in addition to their work on trade, embrace a different approach to manufacturing policy that benefits workers and communities as well as companies. Such a move would require equal responsibilities and roles for labor, capital, and the state. Since the New Deal, labor and the state dominated power from the 1930s through the 1970s; since then, capital has held sway. A recalibration and balancing of these entities is essential to build a stable, productive, and profitable economy.

A more comprehensive effort—more than a tax incentive here or a job retraining program there—is needed to better restructure local economies. All three entities at the local, state, and national levels must work together in developing new industries and sectors while improving existing ones through new innovations to compete more directly with low-wage competition. New and existing sectors can offer employment to newly trained workers entering the workforce and also build additional opportunities for people at risk of losing their current jobs and careers.

The results of the 2016 presidential election marked a turning point for the United States and a logical outcome of its use of trade policy. Since 1934, when the executive branch won the power to directly influence trade policy, administrations have used trade to promote peace, fight communism during the Cold War, and aid multinational corporations in helping US businesses expand abroad. But these administrations also turned their back on another vital commitment forged during the New Deal: the promise to promote US workers' rights and security. From the late 1940s onward, as deindustrialization unfolded in the collapse of the domestic textile and apparel industries, and then spread to other basic manufacturing sectors, leaders in business, labor, and government heard but never fully understood the urgency reflected in the increasingly desperate lives of the working class. In November 2016, aided by other societal, economic, and political factors, enough of the precariat sent a message that the system wasn't working and needed replacing.

The US economy is now defined more by service, technical, and public-sector jobs than by manufacturing—a shift, decades in the making, that marks a key development in the nation's economic history. The nation reached this juncture by trading swaths of its manufacturing heritage for the allure of a postindustrial, technologically advanced age. While labor and government put together some policies and legislation to aid displaced workers and communities—such as the Area Redevelopment Act of 1961 (ARA), TAA, and job-training programs—the federal government did not make the sustained effort in this area that it did in service of lowering trade barriers.

There are many reasons why that did not happen. The assumption of a continuation of US manufacturing dominance, especially after World War II, was widespread, as was confidence in the private sector to always provide needed employment. The antistatist impulses of the US public, which gained power after World War II, likewise created a reluctance to involve government in private markets, especially in their business functions. As neoliberal politics and economics took more of a central role from the 1980s, politicians and businesses began to expect workers to take more responsibility for retraining and forwarding their careers. The expectation exposes an ironic philosophical argument: Workers affected in part by government policy are nonetheless required to retrain themselves following a political ideal based on individualism and laissez-faire economics, in which state involvement in the economic sector is discouraged. Whatever the reason, it is clear that the United States, while attempting to create a world of peace and prosperity after the Great Depression and World War II, ultimately failed to secure the security and prosperity of millions of its own people. As trade and economics were concerned, the election of November 2016 was not so much a shock as it was a revolt against decades of being left behind economically, compounded by racial and class fears, in an age marked by capital flight. The economic changes of the era—namely the decline of manufacturing and the rise of services, technology, and the creation and trade of increasingly complex financial instruments as wealth-building tools—also contributed.

Manufacturing's decline in the United States in the past half century was made possible in part because businesses and the federal government succeeded in silencing the voices of workers. Through labor laws like Taft-Hartley that made union organizing increasingly difficult, and the weakening of other labor laws that offered protection, workers had little chance to make their collective voices heard on important issues that affected their work. That was highly evident in the nation's textile and apparel industries, where southern workers were unionized at rates far lower than their counterparts in the Middle Atlantic, New England, the Midwest, or on the West Coast. Although unions like the ILGWU, the ACWA, and the TWUA were strong in those regions, and had political power, their relative lack of organization in the South meant textile and apparel workers did not have the strongest possible independent voice. The UTWA, meanwhile, was better organized in the South but was too small to have an impact. As a result, textile and apparel workers, in an industry that quickly experienced foreign competition after World War II, were often marginalized or ignored in the fight against imports because their unions could not counter the desires of either capital or the state in setting trade policy.

Furthermore, the textile and apparel unions' diminished presence in the South meant they lacked a strong institutional voice among their fellow industrial unions. But in its approach to trade after World War II, the US labor movement was not blameless either. Although textile and apparel unions started to notice an increase in imports as early as the 1940s, neither the AFL nor the CIO responded; after their 1955 merger, the federation faced a division between unions in industries that stood to benefit from the increase in trade and unions in sectors that could be harmed by it. Wedded to a staunch support of US foreign policy during the Cold War, the AFL-CIO did not squarely address the mounting costs of lowering trade barriers until 1969, when imports sharply increased in several industrial sectors. By then, it was too late for the US textile industry, whose trade deficit with the rest of the world exceeded $1 billion per year, or for the apparel industry, which faced import competition from the *maquiladoras* of northern Mexico as well as from Asia and Europe. It would also prove to be very late for other industries, such as electronics, automobiles, and steel, whose collapses in the 1970s were part of the first widespread public awareness of deindustrialization.

To be sure, the US labor movement won greater security for US workers—milestones such as the Social Security Act of 1935 and the Fair Labor Standards Act of 1938 (FLSA), the extension of Social Security and minimum wage protections to more workers, the enactment of the Employee Retirement Income Security Act (ERISA) in 1974, and the WARN Act in 1988. Its actions on behalf of women, African Americans, and Latinos were indispensable aids to the struggle for civil rights in the United States and abroad over much of the twentieth century. But by supporting US trade policy for as long as it did, the US labor movement also contributed to the wipeout of manufacturing jobs and undermined some of the hard-won economic advances it secured for workers.

If labor has a responsibility here, so, too, does industry—the antiunion managers in southern textiles, operators of runaway apparel shops fleeing New England and the mid-Atlantic states for nonunion locations, the managers of multinational corporations, and financial traders. In creating large international enterprises and maximizing profits by seeking lower labor costs or avoiding, overpowering, and outlasting labor unions, business leaders, by shutting out domestic manufacturing workers, also deprived themselves of an ally in the fight against imports.

There is no single thing labor, capital, or the state could have done to help manufacturing industries in the United States avoid the decline that has taken place in the past half-century. But a different outcome—one in which manufacturing could have survived better this painful era of downsizing and closures—would have required a fundamentally different approach than what occurred during and after the New Deal. In the 1930s the federal government under Franklin D. Roosevelt sought to advance both trade policies and worker security. Almost from the start, the collapse of the National Industrial Recovery Act, in contrast with the relative success of the Reciprocal Trade Agreements Program (RTAP), meant that the federal government failed to adequately guarantee worker empowerment or condition the pursuit of lower trade barriers on the preservation of economic security for US workers. From the start, the political will to protect workers' interests paled considerably alongside the push for an increase in global trade.

Trade policy, and the rise of neoliberal politics and economics in the United States after 1975, compounded the mistakes by business, labor, and government in the decades after World War II. As the twentieth century neared its end, these political and economic policies encouraged both the further weakening of the US organized labor movement—especially outside the public sector—and the slow dismantling of the administrative state. As labor and the state became weaker, the corporate sector gained power in its relationship with the federal government.

A fundamentally different system in which labor, capital, and the state cooperated to preserve workers' rights and expand trade might have yielded a different result for US manufacturing, organized labor, and the nation as a whole. Had such a system developed as an alternative to the neoliberal economics and politics that dominated much of US society after the mid-1970s, the outcome in communities might have been different. A system of industrial democracy and responsible regulation, in which labor, capital, and the state shared responsibilities and benefits, could have worked together to help rural areas, small towns, and major metropolitan areas nationwide avoid some of the effects of deindustrialization. Collaboration might have yielded new industries to replace the old and to provide employment with living wages and secure benefits. A different system might have produced economic adjustments that retooled closed factories and offered jobs of better quality to displaced workers than the jobs they lost. Instead, the choices made over decades separated workers' security from trade policy, placing the nation's textile mills and apparel shops alongside the automobile plants, steel mills, and other closed factories that introduced Americans to deindustrialization. The fraying social fabric that accompanied the decline of manufacturing in the United States represents an outcome of the neoliberal dystopia that, since the 1970s, has encompassed segments of US manufacturing, the organized labor movement, and the nation itself.

2

CLASHING AIMS

The New Deal, Labor, and Tariff Reform, 1933–45

In early 1938, as a recession threatened to halt the US recovery from the Great Depression, Walter Griffin traveled to Washington from Lawrence, Massachusetts, with a plea on behalf of his city. For the past few months, Griffin, the city's mayor, had led a local committee of workers, civic organizations, and businesses opposing a trade deal between the United States and the United Kingdom.

For decades, New Englanders had watched as their textile mills, representing part of the region's industrial identity and the rise of US industrialization, slowly moved south, drawn in part by cheaper labor. By the spring of 1938, a recession that threatened to pull the nation back into depression had prompted job cuts in textile mills. Residents worried that lower tariffs would further devastate the woolen industry that sustained Lawrence and neighboring communities in the Merrimack Valley of Massachusetts and New Hampshire. In this critical moment for their community and industry, they chose to fight back.[1]

In Washington, Griffin and a delegation of about fifty people joined hundreds of others from across the country, representing companies, trade groups, and civic organizations, who wanted to weigh in on the agreement. To accommodate everyone, federal officials had to schedule four separate panels. The Lawrence group joined the Massachusetts congressional delegation at the Raleigh Hotel, located between the White House and the Capitol on Pennsylvania Avenue.[2] There, on March 15, as he would do the following day in a White House appointment, Griffin laid out his concerns with the trade agreement before the Committee for Reciprocity Information (CRI), a board appointed by President Franklin Roosevelt to set tariff levels and approve trade deals. The picture Griffin described was stark: Of the twenty-eight thousand textile workers in Lawrence, eighteen thousand were jobless. Thousands more were working part-time, and people were fearful that the UK agreement would throw the city back into depression. "At the very least we do not want to be worse off than we are," Griffin said. CRI Chairman Henry Grady, a former head of a San Francisco labor board who was known as a friend of unions, told Griffin the committee sought to use lower tariffs to increase trade and thereby increase domestic employment. Endorsing Grady's intention, Griffin's response drew applause from the delegation: "If you have them coming to your office every day looking for work you will realize what a wonderful blessing it would be to put them back to work again."[3]

The exchange illustrated a conflict between two philosophical approaches in the New Deal. One approach, a shift on tariff policy and trade, reversed more than a century of US support for protective tariffs. The second approach—more closely associated with the New Deal itself—was a recovery program that included limited reforms implemented in part to protect workers' rights and give workers a voice on the job. Though labor unions had existed throughout US history, the New Deal marked the first time that most US workers had won the right to unionize—through Section 7(a) of the National Industrial Recovery Act (NIRA) of 1933, then by the National Labor Relations Act (NLRA) of 1935. Additional safety-net reforms included the Social Security Act of 1935 and the FLSA, which introduced old-age pensions, minimum wages, and maximum work hours, all increasing security to a growing number of the nation's workforce.[4]

Both approaches generated a positive response. Workers used the labor provisions in the NIRA and NLRA to gain for themselves a greater voice at work. Organizing during the New Deal and World War II, led largely by the CIO, injected a vigor into the US labor movement not seen in decades.

At the same time, Cordell Hull, Roosevelt's secretary of state, crafted a new tariff policy through the RTAA. That law gave the White House, rather than Congress, the power to negotiate trade deals with other nations. Hull and tariff reform supporters sought agreements to lower tariffs and, they hoped, expand US exports and trade. They also hoped the agreements would contribute to international alliances and lessen the potential for armed conflict.

At their inception, the New Deal trade and labor measures might seem to have complemented each other: growth in trade could have created more jobs and income in sectors of the US economy that would benefit from exports, notably agriculture and some manufacturing industries. Domestically, workers could have used union rights and safety-net protections to improve job conditions and boost their purchasing power through higher wages and enjoy a more secure retirement in their later years.

The new policies, along with others, helped bring workers into an electoral coalition that would dominate US politics into the 1970s. But the New Deal labor policies had a limited reach. While millions of industrial workers took advantage of the NIRA and Wagner Act to form unions, other workers—particularly those in the southern branch of the US textile industry—were shut out. The failure to organize this critical region of a major domestic industry has contributed to the contemporary crisis facing both US workers and the nation's organized labor movement.

Labor was not the only institution to mishandle New Deal policies. In the intervening decades, and using various rationales, presidential administrations and federal policy makers prioritized trade policy over labor rights with the support of businesses and, for a time, parts of the US labor movement. Businesses also moved away from collaborating with labor unions and adopted a more confrontational approach, eroding labor rights and other regulatory protections and giving businesses an overwhelming share of power in their dealings with workers.[5]

After World War II, as the world's economies recovered and strengthened, the prioritization of trade over labor rights would come back to haunt the US textile and apparel industries, both of which were increasingly vulnerable to import competition. Similar patterns emerged in other domestic industrial sectors as they, too, faced decline and import competition. By February 2022, despite the restoration of 1,184,000 manufacturing jobs that had been cut at the beginning of the COVID-19 pandemic, the Labor Department counted 12,607,000 US manufacturing workers—35.5 percent fewer than in June 1979, when 19,553,000 were employed in manufacturing. Meanwhile, the domestic textile and apparel industries, which comprised one-seventh of the nation's manufacturing workforce in the 1960s, dwindled to just 195,900 employees by February 2022.[6]

A Revolutionary Idea: Cordell Hull, Tariffs, and Reciprocal Trade

In the early decades of the twentieth century, as the UTWA, ILGWU, and the ACWA fought to establish themselves in the nation's textile and apparel industries, a member of Congress, Cordell Hull, was building his own reputation on Capitol Hill. His stock in trade—support of lower tariffs and the use of taxation to raise revenue for public expenditures—ran counter to the prevailing ideology at the time.

Born in 1871 in a rural section of central Tennessee, Hull got his start in politics early, winning election to the Tennessee House of Representatives in his twenties and also serving as a county judge. In 1906 he was elected to the US Congress, where he would serve for more than two decades.

Hull had held an interest in tariffs since his teenage years. During his tenure in Congress, he became an expert on the issue as a way of mastering taxation and public expenditures, which he called "the two biggest, dullest, most continuing problems of government." In his initial speech to Congress in March 1907, Hull attacked high tariff levels, called for a national income tax, and criticized President Theodore Roosevelt for what he considered lax prosecution of antitrust violations. Over the years, Hull would come to see lower tariffs in various ways: as a preventative measure against monopolies and trusts; as a tool to lower prices for manufactured goods and to increase farm exports; and, finally, as a mechanism to ease international rivalries.[7]

With his appointment to the House Ways and Means Committee, Hull applied a behind-the-scenes work ethic and became an expert in trade, finance, and economics. As part of a 1913 bill lowering tariffs, Hull wrote a provision in the bill that, with ratification of the Sixteenth Amendment, reinstated a federal income tax to make up for lost revenue. His role in establishing the modern-day income tax fixed his reputation as a force on Capitol Hill.[8]

Yet his congressional reputation failed to yield greater opportunities in national electoral politics. In 1920 Democrats considered Hull as a vice presidential candidate with James Cox before choosing Franklin Roosevelt. Losing his House seat in the elections that fall, Hull from 1921 to 1924 was chairman of the Democratic National Executive Committee, becoming one of the party's most prominent figures and earning consideration for the Democratic presidential nomination in 1924 and 1928. Hull was reelected to the House in 1922, but his rising political fortunes and knowledge of tariff policy mattered little. Public sentiment favored high tariffs; workers affiliated with AFL unions and leaders of industries vulnerable to import competition supported high tariffs and immigration restrictions. Laws like the Fordney-McCumber Tariff of 1922, which raised tariffs to their highest level in US history to that point, kept out imports. Simultaneously, immigration restrictions like the Johnson-Reed Act of 1924, which excluded Asians and lowered immigration levels from the rest of the world outside Europe, made for a tighter labor pool that benefited US workers. These factors, and Republican control of the White House and Congress in the 1920s, left Hull no chance to act.[9]

Although public satisfaction with the US economy in the mid-1920s remained high, new strains began to show. The textile industry entered a prolonged slump, and public support for high tariffs began to drop as workers became skeptical of Republican claims that high tariffs would yield prosperity. Hull and another Tennessean, State Department economist Wallace McClure, argued, to no avail, that lower tariffs could create an export-driven economy that would benefit US farmers and the nation's fledgling automobile industry.[10]

Some labor leaders began to question claims—largely advanced by the Republicans who had dominated national politics since the 1880s—that high tariffs would protect domestic industry from import competition. That skepticism grew stronger by 1928, as international trade slowed and the textile industry slump persisted. "The workers in the mills of our land have suffered as never before in our history" since the passage of the Fordney-McCumber tariff, UTWA President Thomas McMahon told delegates to the 1928 UTWA convention. "It is to be regretted that the spots in the industry are few where wages and working conditions are such that we cannot honestly say a kind word in defense of the present tariff act."[11]

On the presidential campaign trail, New York Governor Al Smith, who won the Democratic nomination for president over Hull, found similar sentiments in New England, in part through his appeals to working-class voters and his critique of Republican economic policy, including tariffs. In doing so, Smith forged a new political coalition—foreshadowing the New Deal coalition to come in the 1930s—of urban, ethnic, Catholic, and "wet" voters seeking to end Prohibition, as well as workers wary of economic change. Though Smith lost the election to Herbert Hoover, he won Massachusetts and Rhode Island, in part because of the sentiments of voters in the textile centers of the two states.[12]

Opinion on tariffs continued to shift with the nation's economic fortunes. The Great Depression began with the October 1929 stock market crash; months later, Congress, still supporting high tariffs, passed the Smoot-Hawley law that raised tariff levels and exacerbated the economic downturn in the process. In 1932, after emerging as the Democratic challenger to Hoover, Franklin D. Roosevelt began proposing changes in tariff policy. In his famed "New Deal" speech, in which he accepted the party's nomination for president, Roosevelt offered a vague description of a new tariff policy, saying only that people in business, manufacturing, and agriculture were all hurt by high tariffs and that the "people of America want work and security."[13]

During the 1932 campaign, Hull—who had forged alliances with Roosevelt, William Jennings Bryan, Bernard Baruch, and other Democratic leaders as Democratic National Committee (DNC) chair in the 1920s, emerged as one of Roosevelt's most prominent southern allies.[14] During the campaign, Roosevelt argued for lower tariffs as a tool for economic recovery. In an address that summer outlining the Democratic platform, and in at least two additional campaign speeches, Roosevelt charged that Republican economic policies harmed trade and caused other problems that "brought the Government to a state of financial distress unprecedented in times of peace." In a nod to Roosevelt's speeches, the Democratic platform adopted in June called for drastic changes that would return the United States to "financial, industrial, agricultural, and commercial leadership in the world."[15]

In regard to trade policy, Roosevelt called for the executive branch, rather than Congress, to set tariff levels. The move was seen as a way to end lobbyists' influence on members of Congress in setting tariff rates favorable to the lobbyists' clients, a practice known as "log rolling." Roosevelt also supported an international conference aimed at restoring international trade and pledged to pursue trade agreements with other nations. He also condemned Smoot-Hawley for provoking "retaliatory action by more than forty countries" that disrupted trade, international relations, and domestic production. Yet Roosevelt differed philosophically on tariff reductions from Hull, even as both favored lower tariffs. Hull saw the potential for expanded trade through lower tariffs, but Roosevelt also thought tariffs should be "high enough to maintain living standards which we set for ourselves" and implied support for tariff levels protecting US producers if necessary.[16]

After Roosevelt's landslide victory over Herbert Hoover, Hull moved a step closer to guiding tariff policy when the president-elect tapped him to be secretary of state. The nomination followed the presidential precedent of nominating a powerful partisan to the top cabinet position. In Hull, Roosevelt could count a representative of two important constituencies—southern Democrats and Wilsonian internationalists.[17]

Hull saw Roosevelt's inauguration in March 1933 as a sign that "the highway was now open" to introduce his low-tariff policy. Hull also had a political advantage: as the 1932 election placed both houses of Congress under Democratic control, the seniority system elevated a number of southern Democrats and longtime colleagues of Hull to committee chairmanships. For Hull's ideas to become law, he would have to win over members with whom he had built relationships over decades as a fellow legislator and party operative. More important, he would need to navigate Roosevelt's "Brain Trust," an inner circle of policy makers and aides who disagreed with Hull's approach to trade and opposed his cabinet nomination.[18]

Roosevelt's inaugural address prioritized domestic economic recovery over international trade; he called the latter "vastly important" but "secondary to the establishment of a sound national economy." Roosevelt's focus on domestic affairs and clashing philosophies between Hull and the Brain Trust on tariff reform yielded no legislation on that front. It also slowed the international conference on the depression that Roosevelt had proposed as a candidate. When representatives from sixty-six nations gathered in London for the conference in June 1933, the president did not allow Hull to discuss tariff reform or other proposed solutions; the conference foundered. Whatever internal differences on tariff existed had largely been solved by that November, as Roosevelt embraced Hull's ideas on trade after Latin American nations' favorable response at a conference in Montevideo, Uruguay.[19]

In short order, Hull drafted a tariff reform and trade agreement bill that placed authority to negotiate trade agreements with the executive branch, notably the State Department. The bill eliminated the need for Senate ratification and allowed negotiators to move faster on agreements. It gave trade negotiators the power to lower tariff rates by as much as 50 percent from levels established by the Smoot-Hawley Act in 1930, though negotiators could lower rates an unlimited number of times. The legislation adopted the principle of unconditional most-favored-nation (MFN) status, meaning that a trade benefit the United States extended to one nation automatically applied to all trading partners.[20]

The trade bill was introduced in Congress in March 1934 and met few problems in either chamber. It drew a warning from Agriculture Secretary Henry Wallace, who said during House committee testimony on the bill that federal officials should exercise caution when adjusting tariffs. While supporters anticipated the bill would help increase exports, aiding industries and farmers, Wallace warned that workers and industries could also be hurt by increasing imports. "Here are certain workers who have spent their whole lifetime working in a factory of this type, and if there is a rapid loss in markets for the goods produced through that factory . . . injustice might be done," he said. "It would seem to me that special efforts should be made to discover the kinds of goods that could be imported that would be noncompetitive."[21]

In the Senate, the bill met only minor opposition from chemical and steel industries. Countering that opposition, Hull invoked the Depression in testimony to the Senate Finance Committee, calling the bill "an emergency measure to deal with a dangerous and threatening emergency condition." On the evening of June 12, 1934, less than four months after it was introduced, Roosevelt signed the RTAA into law, linking the domestic recovery with foreign affairs. In doing so, he pointed out that nations had spent years raising trade barriers; restoring international trade would require patience "but progress should be sure from the beginning and should accelerate."[22]

The new policy was intended to help manufacturers and farmers who hoped to sell more of their products abroad, or simply regain markets they had lost. "In the industrial East there are producers of fine machines, of automobiles and of textiles who have been selling abroad for years; whose market was cut off in 1929, and who would like to recapture at least a part of that market," Brain Truster Adolf Berle wrote shortly after the RTAA was enacted. The new policy also aimed to reverse other trends from the Depression and Smoot-Hawley: the value of US exports plummeted from $5.1 billion in 1929 to $1.5 billion in 1932; other nations were entering trade deals that excluded the United States—more than two dozen since the beginning of 1933. No longer could the nation afford to remain isolated. Lowering trade barriers "is the entrance by America into the great game of handling trade currents," Berle wrote. "It is the end of an ostrich policy of staying out while the rest of the world arranged its affairs to its own advantage, without reference to us."[23]

New Deal Disorder: The Failure of the NIRA

In prioritizing the domestic recovery during his inaugural address, Roosevelt sought to respond to the economic crisis confronting the nation. By 1932, the Depression had reduced US manufacturing output to levels barely higher than in 1913, essentially eliminating economic gains associated with growth from World War I and the years since. The RTAA fit within an overall theme of recovery that Roosevelt pursued to get the nation out of the Depression.[24]

In his first hundred days in office, Roosevelt marshaled an unprecedented response to the nation's bank collapses, widespread hunger and destitution, and soaring unemployment and mortgage foreclosures. His response included a bank holiday and federal deposit insurance. The Civilian Conservation Corps put unemployed men to work creating conservation projects nationwide. The Federal Emergency Relief Administration (FERA) offered soup kitchens, childcare, and jobs in fields as varied as construction and the performing arts. For farmers, the Agricultural Adjustment Administration (AAA) introduced crop quotas and other measures to stabilize farm prices.

A key measure of Roosevelt's first months in office was the NIRA, enacted in June 1933. Both the NIRA and the RTAA were designed to aid in the nation's economic recovery—the NIRA, by balancing wage and price levels, was to stabilize industrial production; the RTAA, by lowering tariffs, was intended to encourage greater trade, promoting domestic production for export, as Hull had envisioned. But the failure of the NIRA to protect textile workers, in one of the most troubled industries at the time, would have enormous lasting consequences.

Roosevelt saw industrial recovery as a means by which to assist the estimated 15 million jobless Americans. No industry was in as dire need of help as the highly decentralized, low-profit textile industry. More than one million worked in all branches of the industry and the related garment industry; between four hundred thousand and four hundred fifty thousand were in the cotton textile branch alone. By 1934, following decades of southward migration, just one-third of the industry remained in New England.[25]

Roosevelt's plans to stabilize industry through the NIRA won support from an industry trade group, the Cotton-Textile Institute (CTI). It had sought greater stability in the industry since the 1929 strikes, largely through higher wages, modern machinery, industrial harmony, and a reduction in working hours. Tellingly, however, the CTI opposed labor's involvement in industry decisions, favoring management initiative and government regulation instead.[26]

To achieve its goals, the NIRA directed the development of industrial codes of conduct and suspended antitrust laws to allow industrywide collaboration on production levels. Workers received a minimum wage, an eight-hour day, and in

An ILGWU garment worker makes blouses for the Women's Army Auxiliary Corps during World War II. (Marjorie Collins, Farm Security Administration, Office of War Information Photo Collection, LC-DIG-fsa-8d24259, Library of Congress, Washington, DC.)

Workers in a New York garment shop, 1940s. (Photo by Sam Reiss, ACWA Photographs, Kheel Center for Labor-Management Documentation and Archives, Cornell University Library, Ithaca, New York.)

Section 7(a), the right to form independent unions and bargain collectively with employers. The NIRA appeared to satisfy all groups' needs. In the textile industry, workers could form unions to fight arbitrary job assignments and advocate for higher wages and better conditions. An industry plagued by wildly varying production levels could design a code to balance production with the federal government's blessing.[27]

Yet legislators overlooked the authority given industrial trade organizations, like the CTI, to control production. And textile workers who hoped the NIRA would yield better working conditions were frustrated before it had a chance to affect their jobs. Before the NIRA became law, textile mills ramped up production to stockpile goods. Once the cotton textile industry code took effect, three weeks after NIRA was enacted, manufacturers cut jobs and assigned greater responsibilities to the remaining workers—a procedure, known as the stretch-out, that had triggered southern textile strikes in the 1920s. Between August 1933 and August 1934, the US Bureau of Labor Statistics (BLS) reported that textile employment fell by 12.7 percent.[28]

Stretch-outs became a focal point of disputes between workers and manufacturers over whether the CTI, or the National Recovery Administration (NRA), the government agency administering the NIRA, could restrict the practice. A section of the industrial code for the textile industry originally addressed stretch-outs but was amended after manufacturers objected. Many textile workers believed the industry code banned stretch-outs, but neither the NRA nor the CTI was required to regulate them.[29]

Other disappointments with the code surfaced. Employers ignored the minimum wage of $13 per week for northern textile workers and $12 per week for their southern counterparts. Unskilled workers' pay rose, but semiskilled and skilled workers received pay cuts. Longtime employees were suddenly reclassified as learners—a new category under the NIRA—who earned 75 percent of the going wage. Recalcitrant managers ignored the code, threatening or firing employees who resisted or sought to organize or join unions. And the stretch-outs continued. Thousands of textile workers filed complaints with the code authority, unaware their complaints were going to the trade group representing the manufacturers they were protesting.[30]

Complaints to the Cotton Textile Code Authority, an understaffed, slow-moving bureaucracy, did not lead to quick resolutions. Anonymous complaints stymied other investigations and, in other instances, manufacturers received enough advance notice of a visiting investigator to hide evidence of noncompliance with the code. An employer found to be noncompliant, meanwhile, was more likely to be asked to improve conditions than to receive punishment.[31]

For all its problems, the NIRA offered some improvements. It ended the use of child labor, a goal of reformers and labor unions. It rejuvenated the ACWA,

ILGWU, and UTWA, all of whom seized the opportunity to organize workers. The ACWA issued pamphlets explaining the NIRA's and workers' right to organize and bargain collectively, free from employer coercion.[32] Another pamphlet, which exhorted workers to unionize "for a New Deal" and "for prosperity and security," directed workers not to sign "yellow-dog contracts," illegal under section 7(a), containing agreements to leave or avoid joining a union.[33]

The NIRA boosted trade union membership across the board. In 1929, 17 percent of the nation's labor force belonged to a union; by 1934, that figure reached 33 percent. The ACWA reached four hundred thousand members by 1934, regaining fifty thousand members it had lost between 1929 and 1933. The ILGWU, so destitute in 1933 that it had contemplated mortgaging its office equipment to pay debts, grew nearly tenfold by 1934, to two hundred thousand members. The UTWA also saw explosive growth; in 1934, it claimed a membership of two hundred seventy thousand, more than six times the forty thousand members it had in September 1933. Some UTWA locals formed in this period counted women as officials and organizers—reflecting their presence in union leadership throughout the UTWA's history—but African Americans who organized were relegated to racially segregated locals.[34] The new growth inspired by the NIRA seemingly set the UTWA on a path to grow even larger, possibly even organizing substantial portions of the southern textile industry. Had this happened, it would have been a stunning reversal from the 1929 strikes and related violence in Tennessee and North Carolina that effectively halted southern textile unionization. But it was not to be. Instead, mounting worker discontent with the NIRA overshadowed the UTWA's growth. The federal government and the textile industry, administering both the NRA and the cotton textile code, ignored workers and failed to improve conditions. Emboldened by the lack of enforcement, the CTI cut workers' wages on at least two occasions in 1933 and 1934. The code compliance boards were little to no help: industry representatives opposed worker representation on them.[35]

Industry-labor relations continued to deteriorate during 1934. In May the NRA announced, without a public hearing, a 25 percent reduction in operating hours that represented a pay cut. The UTWA responded by calling for a general strike; it was averted only by a settlement shortly afterward between the NRA and the UTWA. But NRA promises to investigate alleged code violations and include workers on code boards, and last-minute mediation efforts by the NRA's National Labor Board (NLB), failed to assuage workers' anger. Individual locals passed strike resolutions; despite a lack of preparation, UTWA Vice President Francis Gorman issued a strike call on August 30. At midnight on September 1, the start of the Labor Day weekend, more than four hundred thousand textile workers walked off the job. The work stoppage shut many of the nation's textile mills for nearly three weeks but won no lasting changes. Ironically, the strike benefited owners who closed mills: poor economic conditions at the time removed

An ILGWU trade union discussion, 1935. New Deal legislation revitalized unions like the ILGWU, which had suffered severely in the depths of the Great Depression. (Courtesy Cornell University Library, under Creative Commons 2.0 license.)

any incentive to keep mills operating. Other mills remained open with the help of the National Guard. Several strikers nationwide, including seven at the Chiquola Mill in Honea Path, South Carolina, were killed in conflicts with police or military, though no one was punished for strikers' deaths. Georgia Governor Eugene Talmadge declared martial law, under which police arrested thousands of strikers; more than one hundred were held under armed guard in a prison camp.[36]

The strike officially ended on October 3, almost two weeks after a board chaired by former New Hampshire Governor John Winant issued a report urging better enforcement of NIRA labor provisions. The Winant board, which had investigated the labor grievances that triggered the strike, also suggested a board to monitor and enforce those provisions. In response, Roosevelt appointed the three-person Textile Labor Relations Board (TLRB) under Executive Order 6858 shortly afterward. The UTWA claimed the strike made a difference, but the union suffered a total defeat: Mill operators gave no concessions to returning workers; numerous strikers were ostracized and blacklisted. The UTWA had no more influence with manufacturers after the strike than before. Furthermore, the TLRB was so severely understaffed and overworked that it sought help from the Cotton Textile Code Authority, which monitored the industry code with the CTI. The code authority loaned investigators to the TLRB, a move that failed to end any but the worst labor abuses.[37]

The general strike and the NIRA's glaring weakness with regard to ensuring labor peace in the textile industry highlighted a failure of the New Deal to deliver industrial stability. Intended to create a system in which labor, capital, and the state could jointly revitalize a key manufacturing sector, the federal government and textile industry instead shut out workers—ironically, at the very moment the NIRA gave workers a voice through Section 7(a). The execution of that law excluded workers: the Roosevelt administration and the CTI together imposed their will on the NIRA and administration of the cotton textile code. Workers, unable to end stretch-outs through the NIRA, turned to the AFL-affiliated UTWA, a relatively conservative union in the textile industry, and pushed it into the General Strike of 1934, from which it extracted no gains. Though the Winant Board tried to help labor after the strike, the damage had been done. The UTWA's weakness, despite its growth under the NIRA, and its inability to win anything for textile workers in 1934 represented a particularly crushing defeat for labor in the South. In the strikes of 1929, radicalism and union militancy had failed to change conditions for workers. Now, under a president who received adulation from much of the working class for his efforts to end the Depression, action by a more conciliatory union had also failed.

The Reciprocal Trade Program and the Rise of Foreign Competition

The domestic textile and apparel industries were particularly vulnerable to the negative effects of lower trade barriers that Henry Wallace had raised during congressional hearings on the RTAA. In 1935 Roosevelt convened a cabinet committee to diagnose the textile industry's health. The Roper Committee, named after its chairman, Commerce Secretary Daniel Roper, described a litany of problems that had lingered for decades and would continue to overshadow the industry: Demand for textiles during and after World War I, and the industry's continual shift to the US South, led to overcapacity as manufacturers built new plants and added equipment. Overproduction forced companies to close mills or shorten workweeks. Industry competition also contributed to instability, and other nations' development of their respective textile sectors closed off markets for US exports. Japan represented a key example of an aggressive competitor in the US market. Between the 1860s and 1940s, Japan experienced a rapid transition from an isolated, agrarian nation to a major industrial power. As the US textile industry languished in the 1920s, Japanese industrialization continued apace. A manufacturing index that placed Japanese industrial production at 100 between 1910 and 1914 reached 600 between 1935 and 1938, reflecting its intense industrialization during and after World War I.[38]

The Roper Committee warned against direct aid to the domestic industry. But it did suggest several federal initiatives: the purchase and scrapping of old machinery; hourly limits on equipment operation; and efforts to reduce Japanese textile exports to the United States.[39]

As Japan rapidly industrialized and began exporting its goods to other nations, US textile manufacturers were among the first targets. In 1923 Japan exported 10.8 million square yards of cloth to the United States, just 4.9 percent of total US cloth imports. Over the next dozen years, the rate of cloth imports from Japan exploded. In the first six months of 1935, Japan exported nearly twice as much cloth (21.5 million square yards) to the United States as it did for all of 1923. Japanese imports of cloth during that six-month period represented 59.6 percent of total US cloth imports. The expansion of Japanese exports rested on two factors: the collapse of the yen, which made its exports cheaper and eased their entry into foreign markets; and Japanese entry into new markets in connection with the nation's militarism at the time.[40]

Japan was eager to take advantage of the RTAA. Its diplomats repeatedly expressed interest in a trade agreement with the United States under the RTAP. Under the RTAP, the State Department negotiated trade agreements with other nations and brought the agreements to Washington. There, the CRI held public hearings on the agreements before their adoption. Despite the entreaties of the Japanese, the two nations would not reach a formal trade agreement until after World War II. In the early years of the RTAP, Japan still occupied a key role in trade agreements. Because of the MFN principle, Japan benefited from lower trade barriers between the United States and other nations. Repeatedly, in CRI hearings on the first RTAP agreements, reached with hemispheric neighbors of the United States or its European trading partners, opponents, including textile industry representatives, invoked the specter of being overtaken by the Japanese because of its cheap labor, aggressive market entry, and indirect benefits from the MFN trading principle.[41]

Workers and unions were largely missing from comment sessions on the early trade agreements of 1934–36, reflecting the lack of priority unions and workers gave to trade or the relatively weak state of labor in the textile and apparel industries. In contrast, textile manufacturers and exporters offered vocal opposition to the first trade agreements under RTAP, despite Roosevelt's assurances that the trade program did not "contemplate unduly large or harmful imports of foreign goods into this country."[42]

In August 1934, days after ratification of the first RTAP trade agreement with Cuba, US textile exporters objected to the agreement's lack of an import quota for textile goods. The quota they sought would not have restricted Cuban imports; rather, it would have restricted imports from other nations in proportion to the amount of goods those nations purchased from Cuba. This arrangement would have largely closed off Japanese textile exports to the United States because Japan did not conduct much trade with Cuba. Because the agreement lacked import quotas affecting Japan, the Cuba deal "would not help this country to sell an extra pound of cotton or to turn an additional spindle or loom."[43]

Industry opposition to the trade deals continued in 1935, when the State Department embarked on a yearlong negotiation of a trade agreement with France and most of its territories. When the agreement came before the CRI for approval, objections to tariff reductions on textile products generated the largest number of comments—more than on chemicals, agricultural products, metals, sundries, and ceramics.[44]

In these hearings, US textile manufacturers raised another warning about the Japanese: their exports were not only flooding the United States but were crowding out export markets for US textiles in the Caribbean and South America. The issue was first raised in a pair of October 1934 hearings on proposed agreements with Haiti and Colombia, on the heels of the General Strike of 1934. In the Haiti hearing, Henry G. F. Lauten, a cotton fabric manufacturer and exporter, called attention to the Japanese export phenomenon. In 1932, for instance, Haiti imported no Japanese textiles; by the first eight months of 1934, however, Haiti had imported fifteen thousand "packages" of Japanese cotton textiles. US exports of textile "packages" of undetermined size to Haiti, meanwhile, plummeted in the same period—from 13,859 in 1932 to 1,300 between January and August 1934. Declines in US exports of cloth, yarn, and hosiery to Central America and South America between 1925 and 1934 showed the US hold on those export markets was slipping and companies might have to shutter their export business if the new trade agreements could not help the domestic industry. "It has become self-evident that under these conditions there is absolutely no further hope for this US industry to compete in foreign markets with particularly Japan manufacturing on the lower standards of conditions, much lower wages," Lauten said.[45]

The greater Japanese presence also affected US textile exports to South America. William DeMin, a representative of the Textile Export Association, told the CRI that increased exports to Colombia were dislodging the US textile trade there. He said Colombian merchants feared the larger volume of Japanese imports would saturate their markets, lowering prices and eroding profits. "The bankers here do not welcome this Jap business but as long as they get the collections they do not mind where they come from. But they would like to [see] the white races keep their commerce in this country," he wrote. "If our Government is going to sit by and let other Governments help their business men to take the bread and butter out of our mouths then we might as well throw up the sponge and all we poor exporters go on the relief roll."[46]

As manufacturers' and exporters' concerns mounted, Japanese diplomats continued to approach Hull about the prospects for a trade agreement. Hull initially held out the possibility of an agreement with Japan. But in 1935, when Japan accused the United States of using its trade agreements with Latin American nations to interfere with Japanese exports, Hull refused to consider the idea further.[47]

A New Day for Labor: The Rise of the CIO and TWOC's Southern Failure

The General Strike of 1934 exposed both the UTWA's failure to organize the southern arm of the textile industry and the flaws within the NIRA, which was already facing court challenges. In May 1935, in *Schechter Poultry Corp. v. U.S.*, the Supreme Court struck down the NIRA, and with it, Section 7(a). By then, a new bill sponsored by Sen. Robert Wagner, a New York Democrat, that retained the language of Section 7(a) was nearing passage in the Senate. The new measure, known as the NLRA, aimed to improve enforcement of labor disputes that had plagued NIRA boards. Roosevelt signed the NLRA, also known as the Wagner Act, into law on July 5, 1935.[48]

The NLRA provided an opportunity for a massive nationwide labor-organizing drive targeting industrial workers. For much of its existence, the AFL organized mainly skilled craft workers, largely bypassing industrial workers. Some AFL unions, however, like the UTWA, did organize industrial workers, and others, like the United Mine Workers of America (UMWA), the ILGWU, and the ACWA, counted unskilled workers in its ranks, though that was not commonplace. In 1932 the UMWA started urging the AFL to organize industrial workers; three years later, unable to sway the federation, the UMWA left the AFL. By November 1935, seven unions, including the ACWA and UTWA, joined the UMWA to form the Committee for Industrial Organization (CIO). The new group set out in 1936 to organize workers in the rubber, steel, automotive, and radio manufacturing industries.[49] John L. Lewis, the longtime UMWA president who chaired the CIO, urged greater organizing among workers to usher in labor peace and economic security. "Not only the workers, but our nation and its entire population, will be the beneficiaries of this great movement," he said.[50]

The CIO drives also attracted the attention of Sidney Hillman, an ACWA founder and its longtime president. In the CIO drives he saw an opportunity to end decades of struggle to organize more than 1.2 million workers across different

John L. Lewis and leaders of several unions within the Committee for Industrial Organization announce a drive to organize the US textile industry, Washington, DC, 1937. (AP photograph.)

branches of the textile industry. In March 1937, with funding from the ACWA and ILGWU, the CIO created the Textile Workers Organizing Committee (TWOC).

The TWOC established six regional offices and prepared to send hundreds of organizers into the field to organize cotton, woolen, and silk textiles. Aided by the UTWA's Gorman, Hillman announced the TWOC's intent to organize large manufacturers. Yet the TWOC's big prize was a New England–based chain—the American Woolen Company—rather than a southern-based one. CIO officials described American Woolen as the "General Motors of the textile industry"—demonstrating that the TWOC expected a win similar to that achieved by the United Automobile Workers (UAW) after its sit-down strikes against General Motors in Flint, Michigan.[51]

The TWOC used the Wagner Act to encourage textile workers to join the labor movement. "U.S. is for US! Nothing can now stop the union drive of the Textile Workers Organizing Committee," read one of its leaflets issued after the Supreme Court upheld the Wagner Act's constitutionality in April 1937 in

National Labor Relations Board v. Jones and Laughlin Steel Corp. The ruling found that Congress could regulate labor relations using its powers under the Commerce Clause of the Constitution, clearing the way for workers to organize.[52]

But the TWOC could not break through in the South. It made critical organizing errors and badly miscalculated the region's antiunion and social sentiment. First, the TWOC allocated 70 percent of its organizers to New England and the Middle Atlantic, expecting organizing momentum there to roll southward. Second, in entering the South, the TWOC excluded communists from its organizing ranks, despite their successes in other CIO organizing drives. And, though appeals to interracial unionism succeeded in other industries, such as steel, the TWOC made a third error by attempting to downplay its support of interracial unionism, hoping to avoid a backlash from a mostly white and racially segregated workforce. The cautious approach didn't work: southern textile workers largely shunned the TWOC. They were too aware of how the federal government and the UTWA had failed to improve conditions before and after the General Strike of 1934 and of how striking workers had been blackballed.[53]

The results quickly became evident as the drive took shape. In New England, the TWOC signed contracts in the region with forty-eight mills covering some 18,000 workers during the first six weeks of the drive. Southern workers were much slower to join despite the TWOC's claim that it was "breaking the solid southern opposition and destroying the conspiracy to defeat organization."[54] By October 1937, TWOC claimed to have organized more than 450,000 members and reached union agreements with 905 firms employing 270,000 workers. But most of the new members and agreements came from outside the South.[55]

The TWOC's greatest gains, in New England and the Middle Atlantic, were in areas where the ACWA and ILGWU had been established and, not incidentally, where workers had witnessed textile mills moving south and were concerned about their own jobs following in short order. One of those gains was the organization of American Woolen, where 25,000 workers across New England ultimately joined the TWOC. But surviving TWOC organizing reports from April through October of 1937—a period during which the drive started and gained momentum—reflected the regional disparity. The TWOC reached fifty-nine agreements and organized sixty locals in the Middle Atlantic states of New York, New Jersey, Pennsylvania, Maryland, and West Virginia. In the six New England states, the TWOC organized fifty locals and reached thirty agreements. By comparison, the TWOC organized just eleven locals and reached but nine agreements in the nine southern states from Virginia to Louisiana.[56]

The TWOC's pains to avoid addressing race and radicalism in its southern organizing work had little effect in the face of industry and community opposition. Before the TWOC drive began, textile companies attempted to blunt the campaign by raising wages roughly 10 percent. Organizers and supporters faced

If the Textile Workers Organizing Committee's organizing drive was to succeed, it would have to win outside New England and in mills in numerous small southern towns and cities, as in the North Carolina plant pictured here. That strategy differed slightly from CIO drives targeting mass employers in the automotive, rubber, and steel industries. (Carolina Power and Light Collection, State Archives of North Carolina, Raleigh, North Carolina. Courtesy of Duke Energy Archives.)

harassment, including economic and physical threats from employers and antiunion workers. Employers fired activists and evicted TWOC supporters from company-owned housing; they persuaded police to arrest organizers and encouraged clergy to denounce them from the pulpit. Vigilantes assaulted organizers and expelled them from towns. TWOC organizers were shadowed in some areas by marches and cross burnings by the Ku Klux Klan, which morphed its traditionally anti-Black, anti-Semitic, and anti-Catholic prejudices into antilabor and anticommunist varieties. In Greenville, South Carolina, TWOC opponents placed hundreds of placards on telephone poles, billboards, and corners near the Brandon Mill: "C.I.O. Is Communism. Communism Will Not Be Tolerated. The Ku Klux Klan Rides Again."[57]

Despite these obstacles in the South, the TWOC still was the third-largest CIO union by October 1937, when the federation met in conference at Atlantic City, New Jersey. With 450,000 members, the TWOC trailed only the

600,000-member UMWA and the Steel Workers Organizing Committee (SWOC) with 525,000 workers. Another CIO union, the UAW, counted 375,000 members. All told, a year of CIO organizing had brought 3.8 million new workers into its unions.[58]

On one level, the TWOC's meager organizing results in the South reflected its own missteps and the power of southern textile managers in a region hostile to organized labor. But it also reflected workers' very real fear of ostracism, economic reprisals, and violence, which they had experienced in the strikes of 1929 and 1934. Moreover, workers learned clearly from the aftermath of the General Strike of 1934 that, while New Deal laws and agencies might allow workers to form unions, they offered little to no protection from abuse and retaliation. By 1937, southern workers were likely to be just as skeptical about their rights under the NLRA. The TWOC, like other CIO unions, attempted to use the law to call workers to organize. But southern textile workers who might have been receptive to the TWOC's organizing efforts understood that, law or no law, they would still have to face opposition from companies, community leaders, police, clergy, vigilantes, or the Ku Klux Klan, all ready to attack and shun workers open to unions or push them out of desperately needed mill jobs and housing. Burned by the memories of failure from 1929 and 1934, southern textile workers remained reluctant to organize under the Wagner Act.

The 1930s failure to organize southern textiles and apparel was a defeat that has hampered textile unions, and the US labor movement, ever since. When the CIO drives started, no other union—the UMW, the UAW, the SWOC, or the United Rubber Workers—covered an industry with the nationwide reach and numerical strength of the textile industry. While the ILGWU and ACWA opened up much of the nation's garment industry and had some limited successes in the South the lack of organizing among southern textile workers during the New Deal—first by the UTWA, then by the TWOC—denied workers a voice in this growing sector and shifted the balance of power more firmly into the hands of antilabor mill operators. In the South, where many millowners were also among the region's economic and political elites, failure to organize also took away textile workers' chance to challenge, let alone shape, the region's social, political, and economic status quo.

While social forces condemned the TWOC to failure in the South, its own tactical errors contributed. Its decision to start in New England and the Middle Atlantic, its choice not to involve radical organizers out of a reading of the overwhelmingly white workforce, and its deference to more conservative textile workers and managers, also play a role. It is also worth noting that, in comparison with the TWOC, other CIO organizers embraced militancy and built successful southern industrial unions.[59] In other southern industries with biracial workforces, such as tobacco and steel, various CIO unions found success in the South during this time by encouraging a biracial labor movement. An embrace of interracial unionism may not have helped the TWOC in the South, however, in an industry that was overwhelmingly white. In fact, that decision was likely a tragic, but prudent, choice because of the ethnic makeup of the southern textile workforce and openly anti-Black prejudice.

Even with the failures of 1929 and 1934 in the South, radicalism in 1937 might have offered southern textile workers a new reason to consider the labor movement. While it is debatable whether a radical approach would have succeeded, creating a space for southern textile workers among the region's elites, the TWOC's decisions condemned textile unionism to limited gains in the South and a reduced presence within the industrial labor movement.

The lack of a labor presence in the southern branch of the textile industry also affected debates on trade policy. In the agreements between 1934 and 1936, textile industry representatives, sellers, and companies, especially southern ones, offered testimony on how lower trade barriers would affect the industry. By the fall of 1937, that pattern would change. In proposed agreements with Czechoslovakia and the United Kingdom, which came up during the TWOC organizing drives, textile workers joined in to argue against the agreements. Public opposition to trade agreements during Roosevelt's second term was most pronounced in these agreements with Czechoslovakia and the United Kingdom, both negotiated during the 1937–38 recession. The UK agreement was the broadest agreement the Roosevelt administration had entered to date under the RTAP, while the Czechoslovak agreement held out the promise of revived trade between the two nations.[60] But woolen workers from New England, not cotton textile workers from the South, were opposing lower tariffs. In Massachusetts, where the cotton textile industry had been shrinking since the 1860s, the specter of additional low-wage international competition during the Depression offered New England woolen workers a chance to act in defense of their jobs, industries, and communities. Although northern textile workers considered their southern counterparts as economic rivals, these protests also sent a message that they saw lower-paid foreign workers in the same light.[61]

The TWOC offered New England textile workers an organization through which they could express their concerns about trade, independent of and alongside any effort by which the industry or elected officials could oppose lower tariffs. By comparison, southern textile workers, of whom 2 to 5 percent worked under union contracts at the time, were absent from CRI hearings and protests on RTAP trade agreements.[62]

Labor did protest some of the early RTAP agreements, but that protest came largely from labor officials at the local level—who were closer to their rank-and-file members—than from regional or national leaders. With the exception of Francis Gorman, national labor leaders like Hillman, David Dubinsky of the ILGWU, Lewis (now the CIO president), and AFL President William Green did not oppose the early reciprocal agreements. While thousands of woolen workers from the Merrimack Valley protested the UK agreement, national labor officials, such as John Brophy, a leading aide to Lewis, were more focused on the threat of low-paid southern workers to the increasingly unionized New England mills than they were on imports. Brophy favored eliminating wage differences between New England and the South to preserve the New England branch of the industry. He also believed a federal wages and hours bill (which became the FLSA) would equalize wages nationwide and possibly eliminate geographic differences that had promoted the textile industry's ongoing movement south.

The TWOC was involved in several other issues by early 1938. In addition to its organizing drive, it was fighting wage cuts unilaterally imposed by New England mills, suspending local leaders who accepted wage cuts without first consulting the TWOC leadership, and struggling to keep disgruntled TWOC members in the fold in areas of UTWA strength. Conflict between Gorman and Hillman and other TWOC leaders ultimately dashed hopes of the creation of a single, industrywide textile union. In early 1939, the TWOC formally expelled Gorman, who took a group of UTWA locals loyal to him back to the AFL. The UTWA locals that remained within the CIO merged with the TWOC in May 1939 to form the TWUA-CIO. Despite claiming 235,000 workers at its inception, the TWUA's top priority—organizing the South—reflected the daunting challenge: Just one-fifth of the South's 350,000 textile workers belonged to the TWUA.[63]

Imports and Opposition to Trade Agreements, 1937–38

In 1937 Congress reauthorized the RTAA for three years; later that year, the US cotton textile industry brokered a gentlemen's agreement with Japan to reduce Japanese textile exports. But not everyone agreed on lower trade barriers. A sharp economic slowdown beginning in late 1937 triggered intense opposition to the RTAP from textile workers, some labor officials, and the textile industry itself. The downturn began after Treasury Secretary Henry Morgenthau convinced Roosevelt to sharply reduce federal spending. Roosevelt wanted a balanced budget and hoped to signal that the Great Depression had been conquered. The move backfired. As 1938 began, rising unemployment and falling stock markets heralded what some called the "Roosevelt recession." In Washington, as Douglas Brinkley noted, a sense of "exhaustion and paralysis" set in as people within the administration felt the Depression had conquered the New Deal. Critics saw Roosevelt as worried and lacking courage and fight; others saw resemblances to

Herbert Hoover's presidency and wondered whether Roosevelt would leave office defeated by the Depression as his predecessor did.[64]

The economic downturn, coupled with textile executives' existing worries about how Japanese imports would grow under the extension of trade preferences with other countries, intensified opposition to lower trade barriers. Hull, aware of the concerns about Japan, sought agreements outside the RTAP to limit Japanese textile exports to the United States. In 1935 he reached an agreement with Japan to limit its textile exports to the Philippines, then a US possession, but could not negotiate a similar agreement applying to the United States. After negotiations collapsed in May 1936, Hull arranged for the nations' textile industries to negotiate a "voluntary export restraint" agreement that limited Japanese cotton textile exports to the United States to a total of 255 million square yards over the two-year period 1937–38. The export quota also applied to transshipments of Japanese cotton cloth to the United States via third countries and material manufactured from cotton, such as tablecloths, gloves, and bedspreads.[65]

As textile manufacturers expressed concern about Japanese cotton imports, the ILGWU during this time learned of the possibility of import competition from British clothing manufacturers. In October 1937 Merle Vincent, the ILGWU's Washington representative, and ILGWU research director Lazare Teper met with New York clothing manufacturers to discuss British imports. The manufacturers believed they had been injured by imports, noting that women's apparel imports from Great Britain had more than doubled, from £120,734 for the first eight months of 1935 to £249,185 for the corresponding period in 1937. But during the first eight months of 1937, the United States had exported $5,714,000 worth of clothing to Britain—nearly five times the amount imported.[66] While Vincent did not see a compelling case of injury, he conceded British imports had cost domestic manufacturers some business, a possibility unions needed to prepare for. "It is quite probable that this organization and other unions will find it necessary to adopt a tariff policy," he wrote.[67]

The economic downturn overshadowed both CRI hearings on the Czechoslovak and UK agreements. With unemployment rising, hearing participants repeatedly expressed concerns that lower tariffs would yield cheaper imports, costing US textile workers' jobs. "You will know that the US workman enjoys a plane of living which surpasses that of any other country in the world," said Rep. Edith Nourse Rogers, a Massachusetts Republican who represented Lowell, a woolen textile center, and opposed textile tariff reductions. "I do not believe that this committee wants to lower that standard of living."[68]

Rep. George Bates, a fellow Massachusetts Republican, testified that an average US textile worker earned 42 cents an hour in a forty-hour week; a corresponding Czechoslovak worker, meanwhile, earned 9 cents an hour in a forty-eight-hour week. To Bates, lower trade barriers invited "the influx of . . . more foreign-made goods, with the peon labor of Europe or later the peon labor of Asia" and an increase in domestic unemployment and social service costs.[69]

Representatives from the cotton textile industry, such as Claudius Murchison of the CTI, argued against lower tariffs because domestic competition between 1926 and 1935 had already forced manufacturers to sell to consumers at prices below production costs. Other industry representatives, such as J. G. Johnson from North Carolina's Cannon Mills, testified that Japanese producers had undercut domestic producers on price so deeply that Cannon had no export business left. "It is all gone practically," he said. "We export a little goods. It amounts to very little. We did have a very nice export." Despite opposition, the CRI ratified the Czechoslovak agreement in early March 1938.[70]

Two weeks later, hearings began on the UK agreement, the twentieth under RTAP. Hull considered the agreement a crowning achievement with a longtime ally and trading partner. It also marked the first time under RTAP that tariff schedules dealing with virtually all textile products had been opened for negotiations.[71]

Discussion of the agreement triggered a flood of testimony from workers and industry representatives. Petitions, postcards, telegrams, and telephone calls opposing tariff concessions flooded into the CRI—nearly fifty thousand comments on the agreement in the four months preceding the hearings; seventeen thousand came from Lawrence alone in the form of newspaper coupons. Nearly 1,700 of the 2,500 workers at American Woolen's Ayer Mill in Lawrence, worried their industry and community would be harmed, sent a separate letter to James Roosevelt and a protest petition to Hull. "We have had actual past experiences of low tariff theories and practices," wrote three signatories to the letter. "The results have always been disastrous, not only to the industry but to the communities. We fear the ruin that will be forced upon us, and question the benefits to the country."[72]

While about seventy-five participants testified on cotton textiles and another fifty on wool textiles, workers from other industries and regions joined in with petitions of their own opposing tariff reductions: eight thousand American Woolen employees from New England and New York state; two thousand Massachusetts furniture workers; thirteen hundred fluorspar workers from Illinois and Kentucky; aluminum workers in Pennsylvania, lace-curtain workers in New York, and teachers, merchants, and professional workers.[73]

The UK agreement came at a time when no fewer than eighty thousand textile workers were unemployed, with another three hundred eighty thousand working less than two-thirds of a full work week. Yet US textile workers still made as much as 145 percent of what their British counterparts earned. With such discrepancies, an industry official testified, the CRI should "leave inviolate the cotton-textile industry, not for the sake of the industry only, but in the future interest of our entire foreign trade policy."[74] Another industry representative, noting the distinction between average hourly wages for US textile workers (52.9 cents) and their counterparts in the United Kingdom (17.4 cents), Czechoslovakia (10 cents), and Japan (3 cents), wondered "what is going to be the fate of our workers when they are faced with competitive labor conditions."[75]

Fred Steele, a New Bedford, Massachusetts, textile manufacturer who estimated the city had seventeen thousand jobless textile workers, highlighted a long-standing divide over immigration in the labor movement. In contrast to the ACWA and the ILGWU, whose membership featured significant immigrant presence and rejected immigration limits, mindful of the travails they and others had faced fleeing economic deprivation or pogroms to come to the United States, Steele echoed the side of the UTWA and other AFL unions dominated by native-born white Americans. In the UK hearing, Steele told commissioners that lower tariffs would effectively circumvent the Immigration Restriction Act of 1924. That law "was to protect the US workman's job from cheap coollie [*sic*] labor, or worse," he said. "Now the proposal under this treaty is not to let cheap foreign labor in, but to let in the products of the cheap foreign labor which we believe will further take from our workmen their livelihood and from the people who have made the business possible, their investment."[76]

In contrast to opposition to tariff reductions from elected officials, workers, and business interests, a few labor officials offered widely differing opinions on the agreement. Solomon Barkin, an economist who had worked for the New Deal's Labor Advisory Board under the NIRA before becoming the TWOC's research director, offered a word of caution. He argued that tariffs needed to be maintained at levels adequate to protect US workers from imports because other nations were developing textile sectors. An AFL tariff organization called America's Wage Earners' Protective Conference, meanwhile, was more direct in its opposition. The group, founded in 1928, counted the ILGWU among its membership. It argued lower tariffs would make US workers and industries more vulnerable to low-wage competition—a view echoing the AFL's endorsement of a protective tariff in 1881.[77]

M. J. Flynn, the group's secretary, also questioned whether the trade agreements would help US workers who "are opposed to any policy the result of which transfers the job opportunities of US workers to workers in foreign countries." Under the previous trade agreements, Flynn said, workers had not benefited. The agreements instead favored "economic royalists" such as bankers, industrialists, and US manufacturers with plants in foreign countries. "The organized workers of America are alert to what is happening," Flynn said.[78]

Vincent, the ILGWU's Washington representative, presented a brief at the hearings asking for some tariff protection for the women's clothing industry and Gorman, of the UTWA, issued a statement opposing tariff reductions one week before the UK hearings. The UTWA saw an "extremely dangerous condition" in the industry with mass unemployment, its ongoing move to the largely unorganized South, and competition with cheap labor in other nations. Curiously, the ACWA did not appear to offer an opinion on the UK agreement or the trade program. Aside from the limited protest and widely divergent opinions, key labor leaders, like the AFL's William Green, would not directly address trade agreements and the RTAA until 1940.[79]

The 1938 protests ultimately did not stop ratification of the UK agreement that November. Where the RTAA allowed for tariff reductions of up to 50 percent, the new agreement reduced tariffs by an average of 25 percent on forty types of cotton textile products, including yarn, cloth, apparel, and lace curtains.[80] Yet the objections posed by some workers, labor officials, and businesses to the tariff cuts illustrated the concerns Henry Wallace had raised in the 1934 congressional hearings on the RTAA—that a policy designed to increase world trade and strengthen US producers could also place US jobs, industries, and communities at risk.

Labor's involvement in New Deal policy and Democratic politics, especially by the ACWA and ILGWU, had brought labor leaders and the Roosevelt administration closer over the years. Evidence of that rapprochement appeared in February 1940, when the RTAA was before Congress for another three-year reauthorization. The ILGWU, in a quiet break with the wage earners' conference—and with apparent coaching from Adolf Berle, an assistant secretary of state under Hull—offered support for the law. On February 5, the ILGWU's General Executive board adopted a statement of support for RTAA closely identical to a draft statement that Berle had sent Dubinsky three days earlier. The ILGWU switch was done so quietly that Matthew Woll, the head of the wage earners' conference, failed to note it a month later in congressional testimony when he placed the conference on record as against renewing RTAA.[81]

World War II: A Temporary Abatement for Industry and Labor

As international tensions increased, culminating in the start of World War II in September 1939, RTAP action slowed. The conflict had a transformative effect on the US textile and apparel industries and on the industrial labor movement. Demands for materiel skyrocketed with the beginning of the war, and again with the nation's entry into the war in December 1941.

In the textile industry, the convergence of wartime demand and the absence of millions of Americans from the civilian workforce ended many woes that had plagued the industry for years. "The war has had a spectacular effect on the volume of activity in the cotton textile industry," Murchison, of the CTI, reflected in 1943. An industry once pitied as sick was operating at maximum capacity; annual cotton consumption had jumped from roughly 6 million bales in 1939 to nearly twice that in 1942. The number of cotton textile workers had increased from 340,000 to 520,000, with women now making up about 60 percent of the workforce, as compared with 40 percent before the war.[82]

The underlying causes of the textile industry's weakness remained. The conflict did make the industry less susceptible to import competition, and destroyed the Japanese textile sector, which in the 1930s had vexed US manufacturers with its aggressive entry into the United States and Latin America. Other structural problems, however, had not disappeared: the old machinery still in use and a persistent wage differential, caused by the weak labor presence in the South that encouraged continuing the movement of industry to the region. In 1934 southern textile workers had averaged only 2.5 cents less per hour than their New England counterparts (30 cents vs. 32.5 cents). And 35.2 percent of southern textile workers that year earned below 32.5 cents an hour, in comparison with just 2.4 percent of New England textile workers. By 1945, the gap persisted despite federal attempts to close it. Southern textile workers' hourly minimum wage, at 40–50 cents, lagged their New England counterparts (52–55.5 cents).[83]

Even with these problems, the war improved the standing of many civilian industrial workers in the form of steady employment and higher wages. Industrial unions also benefited: CIO unions like the UAW, the United Steelworkers of America (USWA), and even the UMWA added an estimated 1 million members between June 1940 and December 1941. Labor extended its reach into new spaces: during this period, the UAW finally organized the Ford Motor Company in 1941, and the USWA organized "Little Steel" companies like Inland Steel, Bethlehem Steel, and Republic Steel. From 1939 to 1944, CIO union membership more than doubled, from 1.8 million to 3.9 million, a figure offset by the loss of 600,000 miners when Lewis withdrew the UMWA from the CIO in 1942 and rejoined the AFL.[84]

The war also gave labor an opportunity to deepen its ties to the Roosevelt administration through representation alongside business and government in various wartime agencies. Ten days after the United States entered World War II, labor and business leaders attended a conference convened by Roosevelt with the purpose of outlining wartime industrial cooperation. The conference yielded no-strike pledges from labor for the duration of the war and management vows not to lock out workers. The conference also led to creation of a new federal entity, the National War Labor Board (NWLB). Comprising a dozen individuals from labor, business, and the general public, the NWLB sought to address labor disagreements that could not be settled through normal channels. Labor's presence on the NWLB included AFL secretary-treasurer George Meany, UAW President R. J. Thomas, and TWUA President Emil Rieve, who served as an alternate. In addition, Hillman held posts in wartime organizations such as the National Defense Advisory Commission, the Office of Production Management, and the War Production Board.[85]

The surge in union membership offset whatever leverage industrial unions might have lost through its no-strike pledge. During this time, labor won the right to a "maintenance of membership" principle in contracts from the NWLB in a decision involving a contract between the TWUA and textile plants operated by Marshall Field and Company. Under the principle, new hires in plants where a union existed were automatically inducted into union membership, unless they opted out at the time of their hiring. Maintenance of membership helped swell the ranks of organized labor to 15 million workers at the end of the war. In industries outside textiles, manufacturers in this period tended to take less of a hard line toward labor, content to pass on the cost of union organizing and collective bargaining through cost-plus federal contracts.[86]

The wartime gains for union membership in mines, steel mills, automobile plants, and shipyards did not extend to their compatriots in textiles, however, especially in the South. By 1944, the TWUA claimed it had grown to 216,000 members, but that figure represented a decline of 19,000 members from the union's 1939 inception. The TWUA did see some growth in New England and the Middle Atlantic, and in sectors outside cotton textiles: carpets and rugs, synthetic yarns, silk and rayon, hosiery, dyeing and finishing plants, and woolen and worsted mills.[87]

Whereas most important cotton mills in New England were brought into the TWUA fold by the end of 1943, the union counted only 70,000 southern members by the end of the war, by then one-sixth of the region's cotton textile workers. Chains like Burlington, Cannon, Cone, and Deering-Milliken either resisted union organizing or gave minimal concessions that made organizing extremely difficult. The TWUA's largest breakthrough in the South during World War II came in 1942 at the Riverside and Dan River cotton mills in Danville, Virginia, where 13,500 workers joined the union in a campaign led by organizer George Baldanzi. Emboldened by this victory, the TWUA embarked on similar campaigns targeting 550,000 textile workers in the Carolinas, Georgia, and Alabama. But the familiar southern patterns of worker reluctance and mill resistance took their toll by the end of the war. Mills violated National War Labor Board (NWLB) edicts and National Labor Relations Board (NLRB) rulings or used their influence on wartime boards to minimize labor's wage increase requests. The TWUA campaign added just 25,000 workers across the four states, ensuring the union's concentration in New England and the Middle Atlantic.[88]

As was the case with the NIRA and the Wagner Act during the New Deal, weak federal labor protections continued during World War II, despite the presence of agencies with power to set industrial policy and issue government contracts.[89] This weakness contributed to labor's ongoing southern troubles. A clear illustration played out in the upstate South Carolina town of Gaffney, where the Gaffney Manufacturing Company, part of the New York–based Deering-Milliken chain, successfully repulsed both TWUA Local 269 and federal authorities.

During the war, workers at Gaffney Manufacturing organized TWUA Local 269, anticipating a contract to follow, assuming wartime conditions. But Deering-Milliken resisted. In 1944 management refused to accept an NWLB-endorsed contract with a dues-checkoff clause requiring the company to withhold union dues from its workers' paychecks and a "maintenance of membership" provision that included new and existing workers in Local 269 for the duration of the contract. In May 1945 President Harry S Truman issued Executive Order 9559, ordering the War Department to seize and operate the plant.[90]

Federal operation for three months under wartime powers did not end Deering-Milliken's resistance. At the end of the war in September 1945, Truman released the plant from federal control under Executive Order 9603. The underlying dispute surrounding the NWLB contract was still unsettled when Deering-Milliken formally resumed control of the plant. Shortly thereafter, Local 269 struck, attempting to enforce the contract.[91] Deering-Milliken closed the plant, reopening in April 1946 with the help of 180 strikebreakers who braved as many as 700 picketers outside the plant. Over the following year, the company slowly added strikebreakers until it could operate two shifts; by July 1947, the TWUA abandoned the strike and Local 269.[92]

The Gaffney strike revealed the dependency of southern textile unions on the power of the federal government and simultaneously the shortcomings of the federal government's ability to enforce labor laws. Without worker and government power, Gaffney Manufacturing and Deering-Milliken defied the NWLB, the NLRB, and even President Truman and the War Department with no repercussions. As part of a chain of mills, Deering-Milliken shifted production to other mills while closing Gaffney Manufacturing and obtained an injunction to limit picketing outside its gates. It then waited out striking workers before replacing them with strikebreakers, taking away the union's use of strikes as a tool to negotiate a settlement with management. The episode laid bare the weakness of the Wagner Act and the NLRB in checking antiunion activities and gave other textile companies and executives a blueprint for thwarting future organizing drives.

Conclusion

In the midst of the Great Depression, Cordell Hull sought to link the United States with its hemispheric and European allies through lower trade barriers. Hull accomplished his goal over the opposition of some workers and labor leaders in textiles and apparel and from politicians representing areas susceptible to imports. For supporters of trade in the administrations of Franklin D. Roosevelt and Harry S Truman, the conclusion of World War II marked an opportunity to speed an international economic recovery and prevent the potential for political unrest, rather than lift the United States from economic depression.

After 1938, the RTAP continued to operate despite continuing opposition from opponents of lower trade barriers. Its aims would shift with US involvement in World War II. Once an emergency program to generate "full and stable prosperity" and promote US "comfort and welfare," as Hull described RTAP in 1934, by the early 1940s it became a program to counterbalance any impulse to return to isolationism after the war and, as President Roosevelt stated, the "social and economic forces which have been mismanaged abroad until they have resulted in revolution, dictatorship and war." Hull, citing health problems, retired as secretary of state in November 1944; by May 1945, with Roosevelt dead and World War II concluded in Europe, the State Department would cite RTAP as an element of US foreign policy, demobilization, and postwar reconstruction.[93]

In a domestic industry as troubled as textiles, the war presented opportunities for recovery from the difficulties listed in the Roper Report of 1935. In winning the war, Allied forces devastated much of Japan's industrial sector. In 1933 the unstable cotton textile industry was marked as the first recipient of an industrial code under the NIRA. A few years later, war production stimulated textile production and employment. At the end of the war, the conversion to a peacetime economy, and the end of wartime rationing, held promise for the production of textile goods for civilian consumers.

The New Deal and World War II years concluded a decade of momentous change for industrial unionism. The schism within the AFL in 1935 that created the CIO, and the endorsement of unionization and collective bargaining, offered that same year by the Wagner Act, produced a surge in unionism, anchored largely in the nation's industries. Yet the General Strike of 1934 and overall hostility to southern labor organizing meant unionism failed to take hold in a critical branch of the textile industry and in much of the southern region's garment factories.

Those workers, unlike many counterparts elsewhere, had no independent voice to raise on issues of importance to their industries. Unbeknownst to triumphant manufacturers and unions alike, this lack of worker voice in a growing region of the United States, and the lack of an independent, militant force operating for workers, deprived companies and the labor movement of an ally they soon would need.

3

NEW CHALLENGES

Labor's Limits, International Recovery, and Industrial Decline, 1945–60

The period between the end of World War II and the start of the 1960s marked a transition for the nation and its organized labor movement. While the United States assumed a leadership role in seeking international economic recovery and built multilateral organizations aimed at preventing a global conflict, organized labor, especially in the textile and apparel industries, was experiencing a time of transition in which it was most powerful—union density peaked at 34.8 percent of wage and salaried employees in 1954—and yet began to encounter the limits of its power.[1] The United States contributed to these limits by continuing its commitment to trade policy with a goal of speeding postwar international recovery.

Meanwhile, the nation's commitment to labor rights continued to diminish. Wartime rules that aided labor's growth vanished. Backlash to a 1946 strike wave led to the 1947 Taft-Hartley Act, which greatly weakened the reach and effect of the Wagner Act. In the workplace, antiunion activities resumed and even intensified, thwarting a key CIO drive to organize southern workers.

International policies also led to significant challenges for labor. The rise of the Cold War and its concomitant emphasis on anticommunism devastated the CIO. In 1949 the federation purged thirteen unions suspected of harboring communist leadership, depriving the labor movement of some of its most radical, active, and creative members. Yet labor leaders participated in international exchanges designed to encourage the spread of (anticommunist) labor movements throughout the world. At home, the postwar era also heralded a return to the familiar, uneven pattern of economic growth and recession, only slightly alleviated by demands for the Korean War. Textile and apparel imports continued to grow in this period, adding more uncertainty to the boom-and-bust cycles.

Still, labor leaders sought to exercise power to improve conditions for workers in this period of limitations. As the AFL and CIO hammered out a 1955 merger that brought industrial and craft unions together, labor leaders were calling attention to import growth in an effort to win import restrictions. Others developed policies to aid workers and communities affected by plant closures and import competition. Their concerns about the economy show a powerful constituent within the New Deal political coalition working to use its influence for good.

Cycles of Boom and Bust: Textiles in the United States after World War II

The end of World War II led to a short-lived period of optimism, as evidenced by a letter the ACWA's Hillman received in October 1945 from President Truman. Inviting Hillman to represent the CIO in an upcoming labor-management conference, Truman spoke of an effort to create policies "which will make possible better labor and management relationships in American industry," setting the stage for what Truman hoped would be "the greatest era of industrial progress in the Nation's history." The conference instead yielded a stalemate between labor and capital over the balance of power in labor-management relations. The result outlined both the limits of labor's gains in wartime and the limits of its gains to follow.[2]

The domestic textile industry emerged from the war facing pent-up public demand for its products. With much of the industry's wartime production claimed for defense, the result was predictable when hostilities ceased. Once converted to civilian production, "the demand far exceeded the supply and for the three years following V-J Day all mills operated at full capacity," wrote a leading New England textile executive. In fact, prices for products were high enough that New England mills could profit even with cheaper southern competitors available.[3]

Worldwide shortages of cloth and US consumer demand for new clothes and home furnishings also contributed to the surge. In 1948 the TWUA reflected on "intense activity" in the industry in the preceding two years. Between January 1946 and November 1947, employment grew 10.6 percent, from 1,247,600 to 1,379,500 workers. Many plants operated around the clock on three shifts, and workers were more likely to maintain a forty-hour workweek. Domestic production of cotton broad woven goods rose from 8.7 billion linear yards in 1945 to an estimated 9.75 billion linear yards in 1947. "The diversion of more than 20 billion yards of cotton goods to war use and export from 1942 through 1945 left a backlog of consumer demand which has yet to be filled," the TWUA reported. "After two years of high-gear production most branches of the industry were still hard-pressed to satisfy the huge demand for their products."[4]

Consumer demand appeared to vanquish decades of fragility in the industry. In the 1930s the Roper Committee and the Winant Board reported overproduction, low wages, thin profit margins, and fragmented ownership as factors inviting both uneven business cycles and worker abuses. In contrast, the TWUA lauded textiles as "the nation's most prosperous industry" in a 1948 report on industrial economic performance between 1929 and 1947. In 1947 alone, the industry recorded pretax profits of $2 billion, nearly 11 times as great as in 1939 and equal to the industry's cumulative profits from 1929 to 1942. Pretax profits in textiles showed a return on investment of 47.6 percent, far outpacing the manufacturing sector's 28 percent return on investment.[5]

"You Won't Starve Me Again": Operation Dixie's Collapse in the South

After World War II, industrial unions hoped to build on their growth in the years since 1935 by mounting a massive organizing campaign. They targeted the South, the region that had long resisted unionizing, including the TWUA campaigns of World War II. In 1946 the Southern Organizing Campaign, also known as Operation Dixie, got underway with an eye to organize hundreds of thousands of textile, lumber, and tobacco workers.

Weakened by the passage of the Taft-Hartley Act over Truman's 1947 veto, the campaign won no major victories. In the textile industry, millowners blocked organizing by accusing unions of connections to communist and radical elements or devotion to civil rights. They sometimes painted labor leaders as outsiders who would create dissension between owners and employees. "Who are the men who run this union anyway?" wrote one North Carolina millowner to the white, Protestant workforce the CIO sought to organize in 1948. "I will name some of its chief officers to you—Baldanzi, Rieve, Chupka, Genis, Jabor, Knapik, Rosenberg. Where do you think these men come from? Are their backgrounds, their up-bringing, their viewpoints, their beliefs, their faith, their principles, anything like yours and mine?"[6]

In addition to facing red-baiting and race-baiting, organizers failed because they could not understand some southern workers' conception of religion. CIO organizers sometimes used religious-themed material to convince workers to join unions. One such pamphlet, "The Bible and the Working Man," chronicled a worker drawn to join the CIO after being shown religious parables that linked the dignity of workers, by association, with unionization. The theme failed to resonate with workers who were more likely to see religion as a vehicle by which people sought individual salvation than as a vehicle for collective action, as the pamphlet emphasized. Workers may likely have found the pamphlet's implied equation of a union with organized religion distasteful.

Operation Dixie also failed because it took place in an environment where unions were roundly criticized for the 1946 strike wave that preceded Taft-Hartley.

As with the UTWA in the 1900s and the TWOC in the 1930s, the CIO's Operation Dixie in the 1940s and 1950s largely failed to overcome opposition from managers, workers, and police to organize the southern branch of the textile industry. In this photograph, police arrest CIO organizers during Operation Dixie, in Gastonia, North Carolina, in 1947. (George Meany Memorial AFL-CIO Archives, University of Maryland–College Park.)

The industry's relative prosperity also prompted a feeling among many workers that they could thrive without joining a union. Eager to leave behind the disheartening failures of the 1930s, such as the Depression and the General Strike of 1934, memories of rough times left many mill workers targeted by Operation Dixie bitter and defiant. "I have been working here for 7 years and don't want any part of your union," wrote a self-described union hater from South Carolina. "You think I am going to help you keep up your dam high officials, that's all you want. I liked to starved to death at Brandon Mill in Greenville a good many years ago and you won't starve me again. . . . All you want is those dues and you are getting them from the ignorant people, not me any more."[7]

Operation Dixie would continue into the 1950s, but it was overshadowed by national economic weaknesses that appeared less than two years after the war's conclusion. In May 1947 New England TWUA members observed rising prices that outstripped consumer purchasing power, shrinking retail sales, and the failure of an anticipated housing boom to materialize. "Warning signs are even now evident in the textile industry, with 10,000 workers in soft woolen mills out on the streets and thinly-veiled indications of a let-down in the boom in cotton textiles," the members proclaimed in a resolution. The TWUA called for rollbacks of some price increases imposed by the Office of Price Administration (OPA) since June 1946, an increase in the hourly minimum wage from 40 cents to 75 cents, and extension of unemployment compensation to 14 million uncovered workers.[8]

In late 1948 the national economy was in recession for the first time since the war ended. The downturn set off a slump in the textile industry that lingered through October 1949; it also foreshadowed similar downturns after recessions in 1953, 1957, and 1960. The 1948 downturn marked a rapid turn of fortune for an industry the TWUA had lauded as profitable only months before. With lower prices and increasingly competitive markets, "curtailment became the rule, and unemployment mounted through the industry." In New England, thousands of workers were laid off as mills closed permanently.[9]

Mill consolidation by conglomerates also contributed to the downturn. Companies such as Textron, a conglomerate in Providence, Rhode Island, often saw greater value in a mill's discrete parts than in the mill operation itself. Originally founded as a textile manufacturer in 1923 and growing through World War II government contracts, Textron began to consolidate textile mills after the war. During a six-month period in 1948, Textron bought mills, sold off their equipment, and repurposed their buildings, eliminating nearly ten thousand jobs in the process.[10]

The economic devastation in textile centers soon caught the attention of elected officials. By the summer of 1949, the White House was asking federal officials to use their purchasing power in labor markets with unemployment rates of 12 percent or more.[11] Several areas were home to concentrations of textile companies: the Massachusetts cities of New Bedford, Worcester, and Lawrence; the Connecticut cities of Bridgeport and Waterbury; Cumberland, Maryland; Utica and Rome, New York; Scranton–Wilkes-Barre, Pennsylvania; and Knoxville, Tennessee. In New Bedford, where more than twenty thousand worked in cotton and rayon plants during World War II, industry employment levels shrank by half between 1948 and 1949 alone. The cause: a decline in government orders after an increase in minimum wages on federal contracts to 87.5 cents an hour, a level closer to southern minimum wages but still 10 cents below New Bedford's prevailing minimum wage. "In a city, where the total labor force is about 50,000 people, you can well imagine what happened when its leading industry is materially curtailed," wrote a local labor official, who suggested higher minimum wages for contract work and smaller contracts encouraging firms to share the work.[12] By the summer of 1950, with the Korean War underway, unemployment in New Bedford stood at 10.5 percent, with some 7,700 workers jobless. Other Massachusetts textile centers were similarly affected: unemployment in Lawrence was 16.6 percent, with nearly 11,000 jobless workers; in Lowell, unemployment stood at 10.9 percent, with 6,650 jobless; and in Fall River, at 9 percent, 6,000 were unemployed.[13]

The economy, a growing fear of communism, and continuous antilabor attitudes did not help labor in its effort to organize southern textiles. To make matters worse, the CIO purge and larger questions within the movement about radical and communist influence renewed internal feuds. One such feud, between the TWUA and the UTWA, which sought to paint itself as a less radical alternative to its larger rival, was rooted in conflicts arising from the TWOC drive of the 1930s.

Through the 1940s, in mill after mill through the South and New England, the unions fought each other to organize workers. Instead of addressing issues of critical importance facing the textile industry, personnel for both unions spent a significant amount of time and energy battling each other. In 1951 the feud produced a calamitous result. TWUA Vice President George Baldanzi, determined to maintain the union's presence at the Dan River mills he helped organize during World War II, called a five-week strike that ended with workers voting for representation by the UTWA instead. Thus ended the TWUA presence in the largest group of southern mills it had organized.[14]

The Dan River strike "was the last great gasp at being a big factor in the South," Barkin, the TWUA research director, later recalled. He claimed the TWUA did not lose anything from the strike but allowed that it clearly demonstrated the limits of the union's power. After that, "we never dreamt of the South as something you could take over, like Sherman marching through Georgia," he said. "We had to become piecemeal about it, and couldn't conceive it as a unified operation. . . . We were stopped, and the textile union never again could proceed."[15]

Economic Challenges at Home: The Textile Industry in the 1950s

The Korean War boosted domestic textile production slightly but did not alleviate long-standing problems affecting the industry. In the words of a New England textile executive, the industry in the region had declined since 1925 for several reasons: low rates of southern unionization, an average hourly wage differential of 9.5 cents between workers in New England ($1.065) and the South ($0.97), and productivity (as southern workers were likely to be assigned more work).

To solve these problems, the executive called for higher minimum wages in the South to close the regional difference.[16]

The economic downturn that affected the industry in the 1949 recession continued into the early 1950s. Employment fell from 1.28 million workers in 1948 to as low as 953,000 workers in July 1954, although the number had recovered slightly to 998,000 workers by December 1954. By 1955, Barkin was warning in congressional testimony that the industry "has been in a depressed state since 1951 and has not yet recovered." The CIO, meanwhile, was declaring "no indication that a return to full employment is in sight." At one point in 1953, industry output fell a staggering 22 percent in six months.[17]

By 1956, the TWUA believed the industry was recovering and that workers would soon benefit from higher sales and profits, but no recovery materialized.[18] Instead, the industry faced significant textile import growth from Japan and Hong Kong starting in 1955. A 1957 recession also hampered the industry, prompting labor leaders to worry once again about its viability. For new TWUA President William Pollock, who succeeded Rieve in 1956, the industry's precarious state was precipitated by an unresponsive federal government. "We are now in the sixth year of a severe textile depression," Pollock wrote in 1958. "Our basic problem lies in the fact that we work in a sick industry—an industry upon which the Eisenhower administration consistently turns its back." Between 1952 and 1958, more than 1,000 mills had closed and total industry employment had dropped to 800,000 from 1.2 million. Pollock asked the Eisenhower administration to investigate the industry's problems, including an "unnecessary and unsound" trade policy. "At best, it merely serves to aggravate the textile industry's problems," he wrote. "At worst, it leads to the destruction of basic American industries like textiles and the jobs of American workers. . . . We think the line should be drawn when our government's policy generates a one-way flow of goods that can wipe out domestic industry."[19]

Pollock asked for a range of initiatives to address trade and production issues and dislocated workers' needs. These included a freeze on tariff rates for textile imports; import quotas on all textile products; a 35-hour workweek, without reductions in pay, to stimulate production; and a federal agency to redevelop areas affected by industrial decline.[20]

Imports, recessions, and an increase in automation were shrinking textiles and apparel employment in the United States, although it remained one of the nation's largest manufacturing sectors. In 1959 a report by the six New England governors found the nation's textile and apparel workforce had shrunk by 31 percent since 1929—from 1,264,000 to 866,000. Meanwhile, the proportion of textile and apparel workers in the nation's manufacturing workforce also contracted—from 12 percent in 1929 to about 5 percent of the nation's 16 million manufacturing workers three decades later.[21]

"Trade, Not Aid": Labor Assists the Marshall Plan

The industry challenges at home came against a backdrop of US labor unions' participation in the postwar recovery process. Through the European Recovery Program (ERP) of the 1940s and 1950s, largely known as the Marshall Plan, unions such as the UTWA and the TWUA aided the federal agencies carrying out the plan—the Mutual Security Agency (MSA) and, after 1951, the Economic Cooperation Administration (ECA). Encouraging the spread of free unions throughout the world gave US unions a chance to burnish their anticommunist credentials during a period in which they were scrutinized at home for links to communists.[22]

Through the ERP, US laborers met with labor representatives from other nations to discuss the operations of US unions. In some circumstances, the ECA sent US labor-management groups abroad. The UTWA and the TWUA provided textile workers to work with industrial groups across Western Europe to share suggestions for improving productivity or to learn techniques and practices that could aid the US industry. Sometimes the US unions' participation was part of a larger goal of constructing an anticommunist trade union movement. Such was the case in France, where nearly two million trade unionists, aided by the US Central Intelligence Agency, left the communist-led General Confederation of Labor in 1947 to found a separate federation, CGT–Force Ouvrière ("workers' strength").[23]

On other occasions, US labor unions and textile companies hosted visiting foreign delegations.[24] Some labor representatives, after passing an FBI loyalty and security investigation, participated in international labor meetings alongside government and industry representatives to discuss textile issues on behalf of the US labor movement.[25]

The ECA also took particular interest in issues like trade.[26] Paul Hoffman, the head of the ERP, pointed to imports as an issue to watch during a June 1950 speech to the UTWA's biennial convention in New York, in which he called for Western Europe to boost its future by ending reliance on the ECA and by building trade with other nations. Under this "trade, not aid" approach, Hoffman estimated Europe needed to build its earnings by $1 billion by 1953, of which Hoffman guessed less than $400 million—"less than three-tenths of 1%" of the wholesale value of goods the United States produced in 1949—would come from additional exports.[27] The UTWA later adopted a resolution supporting the RTAP, stating that greater trade helped US industries buy and import raw materials more easily. Exporters abroad, meanwhile, could use access to the US market to sell their exports for dollars with which to purchase US-made goods. The UTWA resolution also noted that the trade program had not "brought

After World War II, US trade union representatives visited other nations to exchange information on operations with labor unions in those countries and offered training to workers. During a 1950 visit to France, US government and labor leaders studied the effectiveness of Marshall Plan programs and its effect on French workers. Here, TWUA Vice President William Belanger speaks at a worker's education school in St. Malo, operated by the Force Ouvrière labor federation. (Economic Cooperation Administration photo, Textile Workers' Union of America Papers, State Historical Society of Wisconsin, University of Wisconsin–Madison.)

about any flood of imports of any commodities" since its creation sixteen years earlier. Even with tariff reductions for textiles, imports of textiles in 1949 "were ridiculously insignificant" in comparison with domestic production, the UTWA resolution stated. "In fact, since the development of the program, the American textile industry has grown very prosperous, jobs have been more steady [*sic*] and wages for textile workers have reached their highest levels in our history."[28]

The UTWA was also involved in international programs with the State and Labor departments; the latter periodically sent workers abroad as advisers to textile companies in the hopes of improving productivity. One such initiative proposed sending three UTWA workers to Iran, where they would spend at least two years improving product quality and production levels. The Americans would train their Iranian counterparts on loom repair and improving textile processes such as carding (creating rough filaments from raw cotton fiber) and spinning (processing the filaments into yarn or thread). Workers chosen for this assignment would be paid about $10,000 a year, including a housing allowance.[29] The amount was nearly triple the $3,390 that a full-time manufacturing worker in the United States, earning the average hourly wage of $1.63, would earn in a year.[30] Despite interest from several UTWA members, the program was halted in July 1953. Weeks later, a coup d'état, led by the United States and the United Kingdom, removed the democratically elected government of Mohammed Mossadegh and placed Reza Pahlavi in power as the shah. "Write and tell [Baldanzi] that the project is temporarily held up on account of internal conditions in Iran," read a handwritten response on a letter drafted weeks before the coup. While the note itself does not support the assertion that unions were privy to any knowledge of an imminent coup, it at least illustrated close ties at that time between the US federal government and the US labor movement.[31]

International Textile Competition, Import Growth, and Foreign Policy

As textile unions struggled after World War II to respond to the ways their members and industry were being affected by economic downturns, mergers, and automation, yet another issue emerged. The war reduced the flow of textiles through the US market and also wiped out the industries of nations like Japan. Now, as nations rebuilt, imports to the United States began to grow again.

In the late 1940s, unions began taking note of rising imports, particularly in woolen textiles, but initially played down the issue. By the early 1950s, imports were increasingly challenging union members' jobs, in addition to mergers, recessions, and relocations, driven partly by the nonunion environment made possible by Taft-Hartley and the raft of state-level right-to-work laws it spawned.[32]

In 1948 textile imports comprised less than 1 percent of domestic production, according to the Northern Textile Association, a textile trade association in Boston that represented New England textile manufacturers. A decade later, with domestic production levels steady and a shrinking workforce, imports made up 3.5 percent of domestic production. Between 1958 and 1960, the proportion of imports more than doubled to 7.1 percent of domestic production, translating into a tenfold increase since 1948. Import growth was highest in cotton textiles, which increased 612.5 percent from 1948 (64 million square yards) to 1958 (456 million square yards). By 1960, imports in this category more than doubled again, reaching 1 billion square yards—a 1,462 percent increase over 1948. By comparison, import growth for other textiles—wool, velvet, synthetic fabrics, and silk—were less steep, but still significant, for the same period. Total textile imports grew 381 percent between 1948 and 1958, from 131 million square yards to 630 million square yards; by 1960, all textile imports reached 1.3 billion square yards, an 892 percent increase over 1948.[33]

The increase in imports during the 1950s steadily eroded the balance of trade between the United States and the rest of the world in the textile sector. The rapid increase between 1958 and 1960 alone entirely wiped out the nation's trade surplus in cotton textiles. Using an interpretation of Commerce Department data, a textile trade group reported the United States enjoyed a $14 million trade surplus in cotton textiles in 1957. In 1958 the balance of trade in cotton textiles entered a deficit, at $36 million. From there, the trade deficit widened to $202 million in 1959 and to $248 million in 1960.[34]

The growth in imports during the 1950s initially posed little concern to textile labor officials. They at first considered imports a small part of the overall textile trade and believed the trend was driven more by the economic downturn of the late 1940s. By early 1950, the TWUA observed some evidence of slow recovery and saw that the textile industry was "not sharing in the revival of business activity" as consumers opted to buy houses, automobiles, appliances, and televisions.[35]

The Korean War raised demand again, although nowhere near the levels of World War II. Still, military orders boosted domestic production, in some cases leading to manpower shortages. "We are no longer concerned with surpluses but with finding resources, capacity and people," the TWUA reported in the late summer of 1950. The situation was unlike that of World War II, however, in that war-related production this time continued to mask the growth in imports.[36]

For a short time at the start of the 1950s, the TWUA seemed more concerned about domestic overproduction than about import competition. In 1950 Barkin wrote that textile production was on pace to reach 13.9 billion square yards, exceeding the 13.2 billion square yards produced in 1942, and could quickly surpass 14 billion yards. Cotton textile production was anticipated to reach 2.6 billion linear yards, surpassing the postwar record of 2.58 billion linear yards in the first quarter of 1948.[37]

But imports quickly joined overproduction and the industry's health as areas of concern. "An expansion of textile imports would have a highly unfortunate effect" on workers, Rieve told the CRI in June 1950. He worried that lower tariffs and higher import volumes, combined with automation and the creation of new products, threatened to displace thousands of workers in a labor market "where few opportunities for alternative employment exist."[38]

The quick reconstruction or retooling of several nations' textile sectors after the war hinted at an intensifying international textile market. By the mid-1950s, Japan, which angered and concerned many in the 1930s CRI hearings, was poised to send more of its goods to the United States. In the decade since its surrender ended World War II, Japan, with US assistance, built a new, more efficient textile industry and sent wave after wave of goods into the US market. The burst of Japanese imports, combined with the domestic industry's slump through the 1950s, suddenly caught the attention of US textile workers and manufacturers alike.

Japanese imports also commanded interest in 1955 when the nation was admitted to the GATT, the US-led multilateral agreement governing international trade aimed at removing trade barriers. The GATT originated in October 1947 when twenty-three nations agreed to rules and principles governing tariff and nontariff trade barriers. It would guide world trade until 1994, when it was replaced by the WTO, which monitored trade agreements and settled trade disputes. GATT participants pledged to abide by the most-favored-nation principle and agreed to lists, or "schedules," of tariff concessions that were revised periodically. The number of nations admitted to the GATT grew in its first two decades; by 1967, seventy-two nations participated, agreeing to tariff concessions on more than seventy thousand items, more than half the world's trade. Through the use of multilateral negotiations, as well as nations' general adherence to its rules, the GATT was instrumental in lowering worldwide barriers to trade and in building an orderly international trade system in the postwar era.

GATT member nations also agreed on other principles. They could not impose internal taxes on imported goods (accomplishing the same effect as tariffs) but could impose limited duties on imports that threatened to harm domestic industries. Furthermore, nations could not impose quotas on imports, except under circumstances in which a nation needed to protect its currency reserves from devaluation or depletion. In some cases, where imports could harm a domestic industry producing similar goods, a nation could use an escape clause to suspend, modify, or withdraw tariff concessions, but only after consultation with the nation producing the products seen as the source of injury.[39]

When Japan was admitted to the GATT, its textile industry was poised to disrupt its US counterpart more dramatically than in the 1930s. Japan's modern machinery eliminated the productivity advantage the United States once held. Its new plants churned out goods "in huge volume, commensurate with her position as the foremost textile exporting nation in the world," a textile executive told business leaders in 1957. Japanese textile wages were \$.136 per hour—one-tenth the average US textile manufacturing wage of \$1.35. Japanese manufacturers also paid 25 percent less for raw US cotton than their US counterparts, thanks to a

A worker in the spinning department of a Japanese cotton textile mill. In the 1950s some nations with rebuilt textile and apparel manufacturing sectors, like Japan, began to challenge US dominance more sharply, thanks to new machinery, far lower wages, and in some cases access to subsidized US agricultural products. For Japan, the increase in exports in the 1950s was a continuation of its pattern through the early twentieth century. (Black Star photo, ACTWU Photographs, Kheel Center for Labor-Management Documentation and Archives, Cornell University Library, Ithaca, New York.)

subsidy in the Agricultural Adjustment Act of 1956 that lowered prices for raw US cotton exports.[40] "We have no fear of our ability to compete on approximately equal terms with anyone anywhere in the world," said one US textile executive of Japanese competition, who added it was not fair to compete with products made on similar machines by workers who earned much less.[41]

In addition to being a formidable competitor, Japan, by its example, also provided a blueprint for other nations and manufacturing sectors who wanted to benefit by increasing their exports. By using modern technology, excess production, and lower input costs, other sectors and nations could produce goods for export to wealthy markets like the United States, where lower prices yielded sales and profits for manufacturers and generated employee wages. Over time, it helped shift balances of trade in favor of exporting nations.

US textile industry observers soon became worried about the potential for greater imports. "The American cotton textile industry is much disturbed by the inflow of Japanese cotton fabrics," a TWUA official wrote in a 1956 letter to a Japanese textile industry representative, noting that cotton fabric imports in 1955 grew 117 percent over the previous year to 115 million square yards. Imports of other textiles—woolen and worsted cloth, specialty fabrics, and finished products such as towels, shirts, pillowcases, and blouses—also saw significant increases. Japanese pillowcase imports had exploded from 790,000 in 1953 to 11.7 million in 1955, exceeding the low end of the estimated 10 million to 20 million US pillowcases produced that year.[42]

While other nations' textile sectors came on line during the decade, increasing textile imports to the United States amid fluctuating domestic production, US textile exports fell. In 1947 the United States exported 1.5 billion square yards of cotton goods. That number fell 63.8 percent by 1955, to 542 million square yards. In early 1956 the TWUA anticipated further decline as Japanese exports displaced their US counterparts in Canada, the Philippines, and Latin America. Although imports were less than 2 percent of domestic production, the TWUA argued that Japan should not use exports to aid its postwar recovery while the United States allowed the displacement of "hundreds and possibly thousands of workers."[43]

Imports also became part of organized labor's political calculations in the 1956 presidential election. In a letter reminding its members of the election, the TWUA's New Bedford Joint Board placed imports on a list of its most important issues, alongside an increase in Social Security benefits, tax relief for individuals, and a repeal of the Taft-Hartley Act. "Restrictions must be placed on cheap Japanese textile goods, if we are to keep some textile jobs," the letter stated.[44]

As imports continued to increase through the remainder of the decade, textile unions, employees, and some elected officials began to question the foreign policy decisions at the center of the nation's trade policy. While generally supportive of US foreign policy, the questioners wondered why more was not being done to protect domestic industry beyond asking trading partners to voluntarily restrict exports to the United States. Some textile manufacturers also grasped that the domestic textile industry had entered a new era in which its manufacturers could no longer expect to dominate the domestic market or have greater exports than imports.

A speaker from one of the nation's largest textile companies realized the importance of a stronger Japan but also believed in protecting the US economy. "An industry employing 1,460,000 wage earners and another 1,150,000 in the apparel and finished textile products field must not sacrifice the welfare of its workers, no matter how meritorious the objective of strengthening the Japanese economy," he said. He suggested that the United States help develop other Southeast Asian nations so they could become export markets for Japanese and US producers.[45]

Allyn McIntyre, another textile executive remarked in 1956 that State Department and Eisenhower administration policies, including failed attempts to secure voluntary export restrictions, encouraged greater imports of textiles and apparel. "With the exception of alarmed members of Congress, no government official has made a positive move in the direction of bringing the problem of increasing and unrestricted importations under control," this executive said, adding that the process, though gradual, was underway and would lead to "contraction of the domestic industry, curtailment of employment and loss of investment."[46]

The New England governors' committee, led by Connecticut's Abraham Ribicoff, also questioned US foreign policy in discussing imports and their effect on the region's industry. "We realize the importance of exports for a country like Japan, for example, and other competitors of the textile industry," the committee reported in 1959. "We have held, however, that in its foreign trade policy the government should take into account all methods of helping friendly countries, not only the method of increased imports." The committee urged that the Cold War objective of defeating communism needed to be borne by taxpayers and investors instead of "a few weak industries . . . having serious problems of adjustment."[47]

The growth in imports had raised calls for protectionist measures such as higher tariffs, import quotas, and opposition to further tariff reductions. The committee urged the federal government to take action to help the industry. "Surely, when an industry is declining without any help from the government, it is rather unjustifiable policy for the federal government to accelerate the decline," the committee stated.[48]

A Disunited Front: Textile Labor and Industry Responds to Decline

The multiple challenges to the textile and apparel industries—automation, consolidation, geographic relocation, and imports—inspired efforts from several quarters to strengthen the industry or to help workers adjust to changes. Textile labor officials and industry executives proposed a range of solutions to reverse the decline. Yet no unified front to help the industry ever emerged in the 1950s among the ACWA, the TWUA, the ILGWU, or the UTWA. In the 1950s the TWUA and the ACWA began to discuss protection for the industry, and the TWUA in 1958 proposed protectionist measures to slow import growth. But such efforts in this period were short-lived.[49]

Some TWUA labor leaders pointed out that its members, particularly in the woolen branch of the industry, began to see increasing imports as early as the late 1940s but downplayed it because of the industrywide postwar prosperity. Imports became more of a critical issue in the 1950s, after the recession of 1949 and successive slow years for the industry. Mill consolidations and relocations to the South, driven by the Taft-Hartley Act's encouragement of right-to-work laws, further accelerated.[50]

Internal labor politics also contributed to the lack of cohesion. The TWUA officially claimed it was working with the ACWA and the ILGWU on fighting imports by the late 1950s and early 1960s, but disagreements over policy and philosophical differences among the unions left that assertion open to challenge. The TWUA and the ACWA, for instance, could not agree on which import—manufactured cloth or finished goods—was the greatest threat to fight.[51] "The clothing manufacturers wanted to bring in cheap manufactured cloth. Did the clothing workers' union and the garment workers' union go along? The answer is yes," said one TWUA official. The ILGWU and the ACWA later changed their stance when importers started importing finished fabric, "because then there was no work for them."[52] The TWUA and the UTWA, meanwhile, harmed by the Rieve-Baldanzi feud and the subsequent raids and competition to organize, were too often at war to find a cooperative voice on imports. When asked whether the two unions ever cooperated on the issue, Sol Stetin, the TWUA's last president, was firm: "Never. Never," Stetin said, his voice rising. "There was just no interest. . . . there was really no real cooperation."[53]

In addition to the lack of labor cooperation, companies and labor also failed to coordinate their efforts on imports in the period, most likely a result of the highly adversarial relationship between labor and management arising from the resistance that unions faced in trying to organize southern textiles or "runaway shops" in the garment industry. The outcome might have been different had organized labor succeeded in obtaining a foothold in the South, particularly in the textile industry. A familiarity with issues that could have been realized during collective bargaining and the execution of contract provisions on the job might have convinced labor and capital to build a common front on issues like imports. Yet, even in the more unionized garment industry, the persistence of nonunion employers inhibited the ability to build a united front. When ACWA President Jacob Potofsky was asked to meet with a trade group of US garment manufacturers in 1956 to discuss the threat of Japanese imports, Potofsky refused because the trade group included nonunion manufacturers who continued to fight the ACWA.[54] Employers who wanted protection from imports, and sought help from Potofsky or other union leaders, made no friends with labor and prevented effective alliances when they resisted union efforts to organize.

Feuds, Strikes, and Resistance: Labor's Diversions from Imports

While organized labor was concerned about imports in the 1950s, other issues and controversies diverted its energy away from import competition. On the eve of its 1955 merger with the AFL, the CIO could highlight its "steady, tremendous advances" through twenty years of militant action, advocacy, and collective bargaining that had brought improvements to millions of workers through better wages, hours, working conditions, pensions, social welfare programs, and civil rights.

Yet for the TWUA, which Sidney Hillman had once hoped to build into a million-worker force, the reality was different. The raids, internal feuding, and inhibitions imposed by Taft-Hartley and failed campaigns such as Operation Dixie took their toll. Through much of the 1950s, the TWUA bounced from campaign to campaign, finding little success in trying to organize the large chains in the region—Cannon Mills, Burlington Mills, and, finally, J. P. Stevens. The latter campaign stretched for more than two decades, lasting beyond the 1976 merger between the TWUA and ACWA to create the ACTWU.[55]

Despite the growth in imports and competing claims for TWUA efforts, leaders such as Rieve had supported the nation's trade policy. While Rieve said that support was likely to continue, it was not absolute. "Our position is not identical with that of employers," Rieve wrote in 1950 to a TWUA representative in a letter that hinted of an intensified international textile trade to come, even as imports remained at low levels. "They are outright protectionists whereas we have examined the direction of textile development in this country and throughout the world and have arrived at the conclusion that in the interest of our own and other people *it is well not to promote the expansion of international trade in textiles.* We are not inclined to support an across-the-board protectionist position" (emphasis added).[56]

But as imports grew and the textile industry became more precarious in the 1950s, the TWUA began to revisit its assumptions about trade policy. They gradually adopted a more protectionist position, placing them at odds with much of the general public, policy makers, and its fellow industrial unions. In a 1953 memorandum, Barkin alerted Rieve to these changes as Congress prepared to take up trade policy:

> CIO will presumably repeat the regular Hull reciprocal trade position. . . . Our Union will no doubt be constrained to move toward our independent position of protecting the textile industry in this country, particularly as the truly vulnerable areas such as wool, are the hardest hit in the country. The position is likely to be discussed shortly in CIO circles and I think that it should be made clear that we will not be able to go along on the above policy. An all-out reciprocal trade position

> appears completely unrealistic, since the present regulations have been amended by regulations which limit injury and volume of imports into this country."[57]

With the TWUA falling out of sync with CIO unions on trade, the most visible opponents of textile imports in this period were industry groups such as the ACMI, the product of a 1949 merger between the ACMA and the CTI (the latter of which helped administer the NIRA industry code in the 1930s and reached the 1936 gentlemen's agreement that led Japan to voluntarily reduce its textile exports to the United States). The ACMI featured powerful large manufacturers such as J. P. Stevens, Burlington Industries, Deering-Milliken, and Cannon Mills. Politically connected through campaigns, government service, and lobbying, they also benefited from government contracts to produce goods in wartime and peacetime. The manufacturers pushed for import curbs or quotas, often ignoring overtures from labor to join forces on fighting imports. Yet their efforts were far from uniform; some industrialists believed the textile and apparel industries were strong enough to withstand challenges from imports, a sentiment that grew when the domestic economy was relatively strong. "The U.S. textile industry cannot afford to be high-protectionist and isolationist," one executive said during one such period in 1956. He believed that existing US trade policy would open "great new horizons of textile consumption" that would benefit the industry, nation, and the free world.[58]

In 1954, however, the industry took its fight for protectionism to Congress, demanding some form of government assistance to counter what it called rapid growth in cotton textile imports. It marked a significant step for an industry in which its leading producers had largely opposed government intervention in the marketplace. The domestic textile industry was particularly vulnerable to imports at the time; it also faced overproduction and growing numbers of displaced workers. The ACMI request initially failed, but the ACMI ultimately held up RTAA reauthorization. In fighting for additional protection, Claudius Murchison, an economist and ACMI adviser who had warned for decades of the weakness of the domestic textile industry, argued that further tariff cuts "might be completely destructive" for some industries, like textiles. The Eisenhower administration's response did not give the industry all the protection it sought but promised to use tariff laws more vigorously to protect domestic industries.[59] The ACMI lobbied Congress for curbs on imports of Japanese textiles, which appeared to succeed when, in late 1955, the Japanese government announced voluntary restrictions on cotton textile exports to the United States.[60] The move did not placate some textile manufacturers; the following year, they unsuccessfully requested that Congress impose import quotas on Japanese textiles. The Japanese move to reduce exports had failed to produce any relief because Hong

Kong, another source of textile imports, refused to enter into a voluntary export restriction agreement with the United States. Eventually, imports from Hong Kong replaced their Japanese counterparts.[61]

Also in 1955, the ACMI rebuffed a TWUA proposal that the two groups join forces to fight import competition. "We have followed the efforts of your Institute to secure Congressional support for limitations on imports," the TWUA wrote in requesting a joint effort. "We have lent a helping hand in these projects. . . . A more extensive program is essential to provide long-term protection for this industry." After the ACMI refused, the TWUA was reduced to expressing its disappointment while asking the ACMI to consider some future action.[62]

The ACMI's rejection of the TWUA's overtures was not a surprise; in fact, Barkin had pointed out that the domestic cotton textile industry was most concerned that imports would grow as a result of the agricultural subsidy on cotton exports. Yet the textile manufacturers had long shunned any type of joint effort with labor unions on fighting imports. Instead, Barkin argued, textile manufacturers seeking protection from imports were more interested in programs "designed to maintain their profits" than in preserving jobs.[63]

In September 1956 the United States began seeking additional trade concessions from Japan. After the Japanese resisted, Eisenhower limited wool imports from Japan and raised tariffs on wool cloth—decisions that appeared retaliatory but had been sought by domestic wool producers for years. In January 1957 the Japanese agreed to a five-year restriction on textile exports to the United States.[64]

As was the case with the 1956 agreement, the 1957 export restriction agreement with Japan opened the door to additional imports from Hong Kong. In 1958 the US textile industry began to push Hong Kong to restrict its exports. Negotiations with Hong Kong were more difficult, in part because Hong Kong had strategic and historic alliances as a British colony. Furthermore, any negotiations over import limits had the potential to strain relations with the United Kingdom; drive Hong Kong exports to Europe, possibly antagonizing American allies there; or even risk efforts to build a strategic alliance in Asia with Hong Kong. More than two years of negotiations failed to produce an agreement.[65]

The TWUA sought to point out the lack of cooperative effort between labor and management to fight imports. In 1959, after the ACMI argued that textile industry wages were "not satisfactory in the eyes of either management or the workers," the union tried and failed to place ads critical of the statement in an unidentified "southern textile trade paper," in the words of the TWUA's publicity department. The TWUA later circulated the ad directly to industry managers, stating that labor and management shared "many areas of common interest"—including a quota system for imports and an end to the subsidy for raw cotton exports.[66]

It was not surprising that labor and management in the textile industry could not work together to fight imports. While appearing to share common interests, short-term views and power took precedence over long-range views and financial issues. Industry and some labor officials seemed to share views opposing the use of trade instead of foreign aid to help economies recover. In 1953, for instance, the ACMI had criticized a proposed policy of the Eisenhower administration to lower tariffs and generate greater imports into the United States. The organization agreed that sustaining exports was important, but "rejects the notion that it can be accomplished by a program destructive of vital segments of American industry and agriculture." It asked Congress to reappraise international trade more closely and successfully pushed for a one-year renewal of the RTAA, instead of its customary three years.[67]

Barkin, of the TWUA, also opposed such "trade, not aid" policies for international economic revitalization. In a 1955 statement, Barkin agreed in principle with the idea of stable economies in the free world but disagreed with the timing of lowering trade barriers and about its significance as a tool of US foreign policy, especially when the nation's economic health needed attention. "The maintenance of a less than full employment economy in the United States will be injurious to us and will sharply curtail our capacity for absorbing imports," he wrote. "A liberal import policy is no substitute for a full employment economy even for the purpose of promoting a high level of imports."[68]

Barkin was not the only labor figure in this period trying to aid imperiled workers who were losing jobs. In 1953 USWA President David McDonald proposed a program to aid workers who had lost their jobs through the increase in foreign competition. The proposal, Trade Adjustment Assistance (TAA), would offer a range of benefits—unemployment to affected workers; job training and worker relocation allowances; compensation for dismissed workers; and early eligibility for full retirement benefits. Communities and industries could apply for grants to retool plants or redevelop industrial areas.[69]

In another proposal, forwarded by Barkin, the Commerce Department would extend grants, loans, and technical assistance to economically distressed cities and regions. Beginning in 1955, Barkin and the TWUA joined legislators like Senator Paul Douglas, an Illinois Democrat, in seeking "area redevelopment" legislation that high-unemployment regions could use to train workers and attract industry. Such legislation was inspired by the Employment Act of 1946, which aspired to "promote maximum employment, production, and purchasing power." Nonetheless, political parties, organized labor, and trade associations like the US Chamber of Commerce and the National Association of Manufacturers fought the legislation for six years. Despite nearly 180 economically distressed metropolitan areas nationwide, measured by declines in textile, aircraft, and agricultural production, area redevelopment legislation failed in Congress in 1956, 1958, and 1960. In 1956 Douglas's bill met opposition from the Eisenhower administration, which introduced a competing measure. Douglas's measure passed the Senate but stalled in the House until just before Congress adjourned. In both 1958 and 1960, amid the recessions of 1957–58 and 1960–61, new versions of Douglas's bill passed both houses of Congress, only to have Eisenhower veto both. Barkin, who built support for the legislation among the AFL-CIO, industrial unions, and local and state development officials, was one of the leading voices in taking up the issue of area redevelopment to combat the disinvestment and industrial decline he saw in textile communities. The legislative fight contributed to Republican losses in Congress in 1956, 1958, and 1960, and Richard Nixon claimed that voters' perceptions that the GOP was not attuned to their needs, especially in distressed areas, contributed to his defeat in the 1960 presidential race.[70]

By 1958, general concern over the state of the textile industry, compounded by the ongoing recession, prompted the Senate Commerce Committee to form a six-member subcommittee to study problems of the textile industry. The hearings, chaired by Senator John Pastore, a Rhode Island Democrat and one of the Senate's leading experts on the textile industry, featured testimony from more than two hundred people representing business, labor, importers and exporters, and elected officials.[71]

The Pastore Committee, as it was known, held twelve days of hearings in New England, the Mid-Atlantic region, and the South. From more than two thousand pages of testimony, a clear picture of decline emerged: While the nation's industrial production increased 45 percent between 1947 and 1957, textile industry production in that period declined 2 percent. The industry also experienced declines in production, profits, investment, and wages. Across the industry, employment across all industry branches decreased 24 percent, from 1.3 million to 1 million. The textile industry alone lost 438,000 jobs, a decline of 32 percent. Textile employment plummeted 55 percent in New England (158,000 jobs), 41 percent in the Mid-Atlantic region (126,000 jobs), 39 percent in the Midwest (12,700 jobs), and 15 percent in the South (102,000 jobs).[72] Imports at that time equaled just 3 percent of domestic production, yet the domestic textile industry was losing its export markets. Furthermore, the growing presence of imported goods, produced by workers making one-tenth to one-half the hourly wages of their US counterparts, undercut domestic mills and placed additional downward pressure on prices.[73]

The TWUA circulated the Pastore Committee report to its locals, joint boards, and staff, urging people to learn about the union's recommendations to Congress: a textile development agency to research new products, and a Textile Labor Relations Act, patterned after the Railway Labor Act of 1926, to govern industry labor relations. Congress took no action on either recommendation.[74]

By 1960, the TWUA was openly calling for import quotas on textile products, frustrated with the industry's decline and the slow pace of change. Import limits would place the United States in line with other countries, which the Pastore Committee found to be raising trade barriers as the United States lowered its own. But the TWUA's support of import quotas placed the union at odds with the AFL-CIO executive council, which in 1957 went on record in support of the RTAA as a means of promoting economic cooperation to counter "the growing challenge of Soviet imperialism." While supporting RTAA renewal, the executive council asked Congress and the Eisenhower administration to promote "fair labor standards in international trade" as a fundamental trade policy objective. The council believed that establishing and maintaining fair labor standards in trade agreements would equalize international competition by making other countries raise wages and improve working conditions closer to US standards. The executive council also asked Congress to pass TAA legislation for workers, communities, and firms affected by imports.[75]

The TWUA also called for expanding the use of quotas beyond GATT guidelines. The union wanted new trade rules allowing nations to use import quotas to protect their respective textile sectors. "We are witnessing the results of the U.S. Government's failure to come to grips with the problem of foreign trade in textiles," the TWUA executive board declared in 1960, summing up its frustrations at a decade of industry decline. "To leave the American market open to this developing invasion is to invite the destruction of the domestic textile industry."[76]

Conclusion

The years immediately after World War II began with promises that prosperity would accompany a newfound peace. Yet, by the conclusion of the 1950s, the US textile industry, which had recovered during the war, was again in decline. Increases in productivity gave way to employment declines, rising import competition, and decaying textile centers nationwide. In this period, organized labor recognized the limits of its power as its influence and presence in US society reached its twentieth-century peak. While imports grew, labor unions could not grow their base or make significant inroads in southern textiles. Feuds among textile unions, a lack of collaboration between textile and apparel unions on the import problem, and a near-total lack of labor-management collaboration meant little action on imports in this critical period. Still, labor leaders like Barkin and McDonald continued to search for answers to help workers, businesses, and communities affected by declines in manufacturing. At the beginning of the 1960s, greater action was needed to help fight imports. That action would come from a politician who knew about the departure of large swaths of his state's textile industry.

4

NEW DOMESTIC AND INTERNATIONAL FRONTIERS

John F. Kennedy, Labor, and Trade, 1961–63

When the closest presidential election in the nation's history came to an end in November 1960, US Senator John F. Kennedy of Massachusetts stood as the victor by just 0.1 of a percentage point over Vice President Richard Nixon. The win capped a meteoric rise for Kennedy as a politician. Just fourteen years before, in the election where Republicans regained control of Congress for the first time since 1932, Kennedy was a gaunt twenty-nine-year-old campaigning on the phrase "The New Generation Offers a Leader" and winning the open seat from the Eleventh Congressional District of Massachusetts left by retiring James Michael Curley, who had opted to run for mayor of Boston.[1]

Despite his patrician roots, Kennedy built a track record in the House and Senate reflecting the working-class nature in parts of his district. On domestic matters, he became a reliable—if not always stalwart—friend of labor. In his first term, he criticized unions for excesses "that have caused this country great discomfort and concern" but ultimately opposed the Taft-Hartley Act, which became law over President Truman's veto in 1947, as a measure that would threaten union shops and collective bargaining. "It destroys with high-sounding words the power of labor unions to bargain equally with the employers," he said. "It will if passed in its present form bring not peace but labor war—a war bitter and dangerous."[2]

While Kennedy sought to establish his interests in the areas of foreign policy at the dawn of the Cold War, the 1949 recession and textile industry consolidation quickly demanded his attention. In a speech, Kennedy cited an unemployed textile worker from Maynard, just west of Boston, who worried about lack of work and a federal government more interested in foreign affairs than its unemployed citizens. "We have been thrown out of work here the last three winters from five to six months at a time," the worker said. "It is cruel what they have done to the people of Maynard. Most of them are too old to do anything else. . . . This country has billions for over across but not a dime for here."[3]

Kennedy began to propose solutions to aid the industry and meet with labor groups to discuss their concerns. He also urged establishment of a congressional New England caucus to address the region's common interests and, during the Korean War, promoted labor-management cooperation to aid the defense effort and asked federal agencies to award defense contracts in distressed areas of the region to ease unemployment.[4]

It was likely that awareness of the precarious nature of the Massachusetts textile industry, gained through speeches and meetings with voters around the commonwealth, that propelled him into a Senate race in 1952 against the incumbent, Henry Cabot Lodge Jr. Shortly before entering the race, Kennedy, whose Boston-area district had little to no textile manufacturing, called for action to aid the New England branch of the industry.[5]

A tight Senate race ensued, with Kennedy defeating Lodge by just over 70,000 votes out of 2.3 million votes cast statewide. Massachusetts textile centers provided the difference. In Bristol County, home to New Bedford, Fall River, and Taunton, Kennedy won with 110,000 votes, running well ahead of the 66,000 votes that David Walsh, the Democratic candidate in 1946, received in losing to Lodge in 1946. While Kennedy lost both Middlesex County (Lowell) and Essex County (Lawrence) in 1952, Kennedy nearly doubled in each the vote totals that Walsh had received. Lodge, who had won both counties with more than 60 percent of the vote in 1946, barely cleared 50 percent in either county in 1952.[6] Kennedy's performance points to his skill in using textile and labor issues to demonstrate interest in helping Massachusetts textile workers and their communities. He used these issues to introduce himself to communities outside his district while signaling an intention to preserve the industry and workers' jobs.

In the Senate, Kennedy sought protection for the textile industry, its workers, and the communities that had been affected by industrial decline. He asked the Eisenhower administration to pursue voluntary agreements with Japan and Italy to restrict both nations' cotton textile exports to the United States and limit wool textile imports, which it did. He cosponsored area-development legislation with his Senate colleague, Paul Douglas, backing the legislation that the TWUA had developed and that was supported by other industrial unions and the AFL-CIO. He also supported expanded minimum wage coverage and stronger regulations governing federal contracts for manufacturing. He did, however, lose an effort to restrict cotton textile exports from nations aided by the Marshall Plan. Nevertheless, Kennedy felt that his efforts had largely succeeded. "While there has been a serious decline in the New England segment of the industry, the over-all rate of decline seems to have been arrested," he wrote in a 1957 memorandum to supporters and constituents.[7]

By the time Kennedy emerged as the Democratic nominee for president in 1960, after a rough primary season and an equally tumultuous convention in Los Angeles, the health of the textile industry nationwide was a concern. As imports increased, the nation's textile industry operatives were emerging as crucial constituencies for Kennedy and Nixon. An industry trade publication, *America's Textile Reporter*, published a front-page editorial asking both candidates to outline their policies on imports.[8]

Both Kennedy and Nixon met with textile executives in the summer of 1960 to seek their support and to promise help. "I believe that I have some appreciation of the problem faced by the textile industry as a result of increased imports," Kennedy wrote one executive, Robert Stevens, adding that his party's platform supported "practical measures" to help industries and communities hurt by imports.[9] He also produced statements on his background in aiding the industry as a senator and vowed to shape foreign trade policy in ways to help the industry. The textile and apparel industries, he wrote, "are international, and both are peculiarly susceptible to competitive pressures, particularly from low-wage countries. . . . A comprehensive, industry-wide remedy is necessary."[10]

The attention Kennedy paid textile executives was not lost on Gov. Ernest F. "Fritz" Hollings of South Carolina, one of the largest textile-producing states. On August 30, 1960, Kennedy and Hollings met in Washington to talk over solutions to the industry's problems, with Hollings providing textile import data compiled by Gordon McCabe, a J. P. Stevens vice president. The next day, Kennedy released a letter to Hollings in which he agreed with the findings of the Pastore Committee that an industrywide effort was needed to help the industry; he promised to "explore and work out solutions within the framework of our foreign trade policies" for textiles and apparel as president.[11] Hollings made the letter public in South Carolina, and Robert Jackson, the executive vice president of the ACMI, circulated it to the institute's fifteen hundred members. Media response to the letter disappointed Hollings, yet Kennedy's sentiments found an encouraging reception among textile executives. "This group publicly are all Republican, but a few of the individual members are beginning to break over," Hollings reported to the Kennedy campaign in late October. "We are still working on them."[12]

During the final month of the presidential campaign, a fellow New England senator, Styles Bridges, a New Hampshire Republican, proposed a program to aid the textile industry, not unlike the program that Kennedy had suggested in 1952. Bridges's program, released in mid-October, was highly protectionist. It proposed twelve changes, including import quotas based on nation of origin and specific textile categories, tax changes, and adjustments to foreign aid budgets to prevent other nations' expansion of their textile sectors. Bridges also called for area-development legislation and suggested the federal government encourage other countries to build export trade in industrial sectors where US counterparts could better withstand international competition.[13]

Kennedy's narrow win in 1960 came during a crucial period in which US commitment to lower trade barriers and an increase in trade was strengthening and worker protections were being eroded. Import growth and its effects were concerns of labor figures like Solomon Barkin and David McDonald, industry representatives like J. P. Stevens and the ACMI, and policy makers like Kennedy and Hollings. Kennedy's victory represented a win also for textile labor, who supported him. Even after the enactment of Taft-Hartley and overall failures to organize southern textiles, as exhibited in this period by Operation Dixie and subsequent drives at other textile companies, Kennedy's election also hinted at a possibility that unions could see some progress in their agenda: fighting imports, establishing TAA, and enacting area-redevelopment legislation. For textile officials, especially the southerners he had pursued for political support, Kennedy was an unknown quantity on import protection. Yet labor and capital hoped that the new president, who'd voiced support for import quotas, would follow through.

Kennedy's inaugural address on January 20, 1961, ushered in his New Frontier program. Although some critics found the young president's speech bombastic, much of the US public was enthusiastic about Kennedy's energy. The new president also found a favorable response in his call to action to promote US ideals around the world, a sentiment made evident in his oft-quoted admonition: "Ask not what your country can do for you; ask what you can do for your country."[14]

Yet domestic affairs were almost completely absent from the inaugural address. Kennedy, who had dabbled in international issues during his time in Congress while paying attention to his Massachusetts constituents, was now far more interested in the international arena; in fact, during the drafting of the inaugural address, Kennedy had directed Ted Sorensen, his speechwriter, to "drop the domestic stuff altogether."[15] On another occasion—a conversation with Nixon after the election—Kennedy was blunter: "Foreign affairs is the only important issue for a President to handle, isn't it?" Kennedy asked Nixon. "I mean, who gives a shit if the minimum wage is $1.15 or $1.25, compared to something like Cuba?"[16]

Lasting less than three full years, Kennedy's administration was mostly known for its actions in dealing with the Soviet Union and Cuba by way of the Bay of Pigs and the Cuban Missile Crisis and with domestic issues such as civil rights. Yet for all the attention these events received, Kennedy's actions on trade—which included a new bill to rework the nation's trade apparatus in the face of greater competition from the European Economic Community (EEC) and Cold War tensions, as well as an effort to aid the US textile industry—underscore the difficult nature of trade in domestic and international policy. Indeed, trade intersected with international issues, repeatedly forcing Kennedy to navigate among some core constituencies.

Textile workers were acutely aware of the importance of trade to their jobs, and they did not hesitate to tell Kennedy, who had helped Massachusetts textile workers and mills challenged by southern and international competition. From New England to the Deep South, textile workers told the thirty-fifth president that trade was not an abstract issue of political calculations or international relations. For them, Kennedy's efforts to reduce imports and put the US textile industry on a sound footing meant the difference between holding a job to provide for their families and facing joblessness and an uncertain future.

The stakes were high for both international and domestic affairs, but Kennedy's efforts at the outset of his presidency were complicated by his lack of interest in domestic policy. He also faced a suspicious Congress, whose key committees were controlled by southern Democrats. As his presidency aligned with the intensifying civil-rights movement, Kennedy found difficulties in surmounting the opposition to civil rights by the southern wing of his own party, even as he worked with them to save the region's largest industry. Nor did Kennedy benefit from the presence of his vice president, Lyndon Johnson, a southern Democrat who knew well, and had wielded skillfully, the levers of power in the Senate as its majority leader. As journalist Robert Caro has noted, a mutual mistrust among Johnson, the new president, and the president's brother, Robert Kennedy, poisoned the well of goodwill and shackled Johnson's ability to accomplish anything of significance in Congress on the president's behalf.[17] In such an environment, it took Kennedy some time to convince critics that he sought to address trade competition.

Trade issues had certainly taken on new importance for textiles and apparel, one of the nation's largest manufacturing sectors in the 1960s. Threatened by the severe downturn of the Great Depression, the industry had roared back to life during the 1940s, thanks to World War II and a short-lived postwar economic recovery that followed. But familiar strains resurfaced during the 1950s. Alongside repeated recessions during the decade, a new wave of competition arose from Asia. New producers from Japan and Hong Kong paired low-wage workers and technologically advanced machinery to provide a formidable challenge to the domestic industry. In 1947, during the postwar recovery, 2.3 million US workers held jobs in the textile and apparel sectors. By 1961, thanks to import competition, economic downturns, and modernization, the number of US textile and apparel workers had fallen 9.7 percent, to just under 2.1 million workers.[18]

The shrinking US textile and apparel workforce commanded the attention of labor and executives in both sectors. Unions, in particular, were concerned about the effect of plant closures on the communities where they were located.

In response, Kennedy took far-reaching efforts to aid these industries and attempted simultaneously to shift the nation's trade policy: his administration hammered out a pair of international trade pacts that sought to guard against increases in imports in cotton textiles to avert lasting damage to an industry that was politically important to him, and his party, in both New England and the South. At the same time, to continue the nation's efforts at lowering trade barriers, Kennedy set the first new baselines in nearly three decades for a new round of tariff reductions. Simply put, Kennedy was forced to use trade as an issue in both international and domestic contexts like no other administration since the end of World War II.

The Kennedy presidency began amid a recovery from a recession that began in late 1959 and overshadowed much of the 1960 presidential campaign. For the domestic textile industry, that recession dovetailed with a 1959–60 surge in imports that nearly eliminated the US foreign trade surplus in textiles. In 1955 the United States exported $195 million more of cotton, wool, and synthetic textiles than it imported; by 1960, that surplus was just $20 million.[19]

Kennedy hoped to achieve the goals of domestic economic recovery and international trade expansion for the textile industry without cutting off trading partners' access to US markets and upending the international trade regime the United States had nurtured since the 1930s. Hence, Kennedy sought to impose protectionist measures on the global textile trade and offer incentives, like tax breaks for new investment or accelerated depreciation on old machinery, to help the domestic textile and apparel industries modernize and compete with the increases in other nations' production. He sought to use domestic and international economic negotiations, and limited, temporary measures to aid the industry. But he rejected import quotas, a popular request of manufacturers, labor unions, and workers. His stance represented a shift from Kennedy's time in Congress, when he had supported import quotas. Kennedy's actions to save the domestic textile and apparel industries addressed the common concerns among textile operatives (by now dominated by southerners) and organized labor officials (mostly ethnics) of the Northeast. Both groups enjoyed access to the Kennedy administration. That access arguably represented the high-water mark of textile labor's influence with both a presidential administration and the New Deal political coalition.

Unraveling the Color Barrier: JFK, Southern Textiles, and Civil Rights

For southern textile manufacturers, Kennedy's aid to the industry represented a paradox. Textile executives who might otherwise have opposed federal involvement in business affairs welcomed the industry assistance Kennedy extended through federal agencies. Yet on civil rights—an issue on which the administration asserted itself more frequently and forcefully as African Americans intensified demonstrations for full political and economic inclusion—white southerners in general and textile executives in particular were less welcoming.

Civil rights closely shadowed the 1960 election and, at times, intertwined with economic concerns triggered by the recession and import competition. The late winter and spring of 1960 saw the rise of a sit-in movement, spurred largely by college students across the South, that culminated in the creation of the Student Nonviolent Coordinating Committee. Later in the year, as Kennedy and South Carolina Governor Fritz Hollings campaigned for the support of southern textile executives, civil rights intervened again: in October, Martin Luther King Jr., arrested during an Atlanta sit-in, was transferred to prison in the dead of night on a probation violation. A week later, responding to concerns from King's family that his safety and life were in danger, the Kennedys—previously reluctant to campaign much among African Americans—stepped in. Senator Kennedy called Coretta Scott King to offer assurance and support while Robert Kennedy publicly berated the judge involved in the case. A day later, King was released from prison.[20]

Once Kennedy was in office, the textile industry's fears of intervention on civil rights were quickly realized. Southern textile executives resisted Kennedy's first antidiscrimination effort, Executive Order 10925, which the president signed on March 6, 1961. The order, banning racial discrimination among government contractors, affected textile companies who entered federal contracts to provide cloth and yarn for the military or for other agencies. The federal antidiscrimination efforts continued past Kennedy's presidency, including the Civil Rights Act of 1964 and federal lawsuits aimed at opening up the textile industry's hiring practices from the 1960s onward.[21]

Civil-rights organizations were also active in seeking an end to discriminatory hiring practices in the southern branch of the textile industry. In April 1961, before the administration had established the President's Committee on Equal Employment Opportunity called for in Executive Order 10925, the National Association for the Advancement of Colored People (NAACP) lodged employment discrimination charges against several textile manufacturers. In July 1961 NAACP legal secretary Herbert Hill alleged in affidavits that hiring practices at textile companies, where African Americans comprised less than 2 percent of the southern workforce, mounted to exclusion of African Americans from the region's "basic manufacturing industry." From 1961 through 1964, the NAACP filed more than eighty discrimination complaints against southern textile companies with the President's Committee on Equal Employment Opportunity, the forerunner of the EEOC.[22]

The new federal action on civil rights threatened to undo decades-long hiring patterns in southern textiles, where mills employed an overwhelmingly white workforce. White southerners, by and large, were especially opposed to federal civil-rights intervention in local affairs. Such federal actions could reverse local segregation practices or end racially biased patterns in the dispensation of federal resources. Textile manufacturers in the South were particularly exposed to these antidiscrimination efforts, as they ran an industry that virtually excluded African Americans from its workforce and shunned even private desegregation efforts. Federal efforts to desegregate the industry caused great concern to southern textile executives, even as the same government sought to help their companies compete in the face of foreign import competition.[23]

Kennedy's efforts to save the industry, rooted in his years of representing Massachusetts in Congress, could also determine his party's electoral success and his own political prospects. As a New England politician who had selected a Texan, Lyndon Johnson, as his running mate, and through his overtures in 1960 to executives, Kennedy understood the importance of the South in electoral politics and the industry's importance to that region. Acting to preserve the industry's existence, then, could serve at least three purposes: aiding the economy of New England, Kennedy's home region; preserving the industry in the South; and making future Democratic candidates politically attractive to the South. The forcefulness with which the administration handled civil rights, however, threatened to overshadow its work supporting the textile industry.

Partners in Aiding the Economy: Organized Labor and Kennedy

As the US economy recovered from the recessions of the 1950s, organized labor representatives suggested changes they felt were essential for helping workers and the overall economy. As with civil rights (and Cold War politics), the economy was a constant issue in the 1960 election. Organized labor offered its support for Kennedy. Indeed, the TWUA became the first labor union to endorse Kennedy at its convention in Chicago in June 1960.[24]

In a memorandum shortly after the 1960 election, AFL-CIO research director Stanley Ruttenberg described a nation besieged by imports, accelerating economic decline in cities and regions during much of the 1950s. He argued that this development called for a public role alongside private enterprise if affected regions were to recover. Ruttenberg also outlined a government role in tackling economic problems caused by slow economic growth and structural factors, like industry migration, automation, and fluctuating productivity among economic sectors. "The impact of imports on specific segments of industries and on particular communities is similar to the problems posed by technological change and distressed areas," Ruttenberg wrote. "Here, too, the problems cannot be solved by the efforts of private groups, alone."[25]

Three weeks before Kennedy took office, members of the AFL-CIO's economic policy committee gathered in Washington to plan their advocacy for policies to address the ongoing recession. The committee decided to wait until February to discuss the nation's balance-of-payments problem, as the United States was beginning to show deficits in overall payments with several nations. David Dubinsky, the president of the ILGWU, and Joseph Keenan, the president of the International Brotherhood of Electrical Workers (IBEW), also urged the committee to mention import competition along with the balance-of-payments issue "in order to show that while we are against over-all restrictive practices, against imports, there are certain domestic industries that are confronted by import competition, and therefore must be handled on a particular basis."[26]

Whether seeking legislation to extend federal aid to communities suffering job loss at the hands of foreign competition or urging tax and policy changes to boost the economy, labor representatives were not reticent about engaging anyone. Economist Nat Goldfinger, the AFL-CIO's chief researcher, demonstrated as much in a letter to an Illinois business representative noting the efforts of organized labor to seek programs to boost the economy by stimulating employment and business sales.[27]

Textile labor's assertiveness in this period was indicative of the significance of organized labor as part of the New Deal coalition. Yet textile labor's weakness within the organized labor movement afforded brief glimpses of the influence it could have exercised in the Kennedy administration. Kennedy's New England background meant he was from the region where textile unions were the strongest, as opposed to the region—the South—where much of the industry lay. Nonetheless, the TWUA's longtime research director, Solomon Barkin, recognized the potential for textile and apparel unions to exercise its influence with the White House and federal policy makers at a level they arguably had not enjoyed since Sidney Hillman and the ACWA wielded their legendary influence with Franklin Roosevelt. "I believe that we are witnessing the recreation of an atmosphere in Washington which resembles the one we experienced in the days of the Roosevelt Administration," Barkin wrote in an early 1962 memorandum to TWUA President William Pollock, in which he urged the TWUA to capitalize on the administration's broad knowledge of, and support for, the goals of the labor movement. Barkin worried that the labor movement was missing a chance to advance its priorities and the Kennedy administration was failing to set its policy agenda, despite several advantages the movement had: an advantageous position from which to offer advice and technical assistance, a cadre of technicians and representatives to advise the administration, and programs to help the administration carry forth its agenda.[28]

Concern about the economy also prompted textile workers to write Kennedy directly to remind him of more immediate threats to their jobs: the fact that textile import levels had increased by 50 percent in 1959 and 1960. "I believe it is safe to quote other men in the textile industry when I say, 'When imports go up, American jobs go down,'" said one textile worker from North Augusta, South Carolina.[29]

Other workers shared with the president their anxiety about the effects of imports on their jobs and work schedules. One, from Phenix City, Alabama, listed the trappings of a middle-class lifestyle he had enjoyed over the twenty-eight years he had worked in textile mills, most important among them being the achievement of "a fair standard of living" that allowed him to raise and educate his children and purchase a house. "I've seen textiles struggle during depression years, and I've seen the patriotic part they played during wartimes, but I've never seen textile conditions quite what they are now due to the flood of textile imports that furnish such unfair competition to our industry," he wrote.[30] "I have been working for Washington Mill's Company for a long time and this is the first time we have ever been on short time this long," a man from the Blue Ridge hamlet of Fries, Virginia, advised Kennedy.[31] "Won't you please do something about the foreign imports?" implored a woman from Statesville, North Carolina. "It has been almost four years since all of our looms have run."[32] Added a worker from Anderson, South Carolina: "I voted with millions of other workers for a Democratic government to do everything possible for America first. My wages have been cut $1500.00 per year because of these foreign imports. We help foreign workers to help themselves. Will they help us at any time? No."[33]

Other workers, already displaced by mill closures, worried about bleak futures and few employment options. "We were once proud and happy, especially on every pay day line. . . . But now when pay day rolls around all we do is hang our heads for we are no longer proud and happy," wrote Antone Viveiros, a forty-five-year-old from Fall River, Massachusetts. Jobless after twenty-two years' work in the mills, Viveiros poured out his pleas over three pages of rough-hewn poetry to his contemporary in the White House, describing a dystopian situation of abruptly unemployed men desperately seeking jobs.

Mr. President Kennedy
Can't you and Congress do something please
So we men can go back to work
To once again support our families . . .
I don't want to go on the welfare

I'm not asking for something for nothing
All I want is a job no matter how hard
A decent wage to support my family . . .[34]

The Administration Response and JFK's Seven-Point Plan

In the first month of his administration, Kennedy began to address issues related to textiles and trade. Building on his years of involvement on the subject in Congress, the Kennedy administration laid the groundwork for a broad range of solutions, starting with executive agencies that promised to stem the increase in imports that had attracted concern from industry and labor alike. On February 16, Kennedy established the Interagency Textile Administrative Committee (ITAC), filling it with five members of his cabinet: Commerce Secretary Luther Hodges, Agriculture Secretary Orville Freeman, Labor Secretary Arthur Goldberg, Treasury Secretary Douglas Dillon, and George Ball, undersecretary of state for economic affairs.[35]

The ITAC was charged with investigating the problems of the textile industry and proposing solutions. While the ITAC appointments encompassed labor, business, agricultural, and trade policy, the selection of Hodges as chairman was a nod to his southern origins (he was a former governor of North Carolina) and the textile industry. Before entering politics, Hodges had worked his way up from a millworker to an executive at one of the mills that later became part of the Marshall Field chain—a background that would find favor with industry executives. As governor, Hodges had also stood with manufacturers during a bitter textile strike—a detail that likely did not escape the notice of labor or the industry.[36]

Shortly after Kennedy appointed the ITAC, the AFL-CIO Executive Council issued a statement on international trade policy in which it noted its quarter-century of support for reciprocal trade and called for new policies to keep pace with international trade demands surfacing in the 1960s. Because trade had not kept pace with new demands, "the results have been a slowdown in trade expansion, no real help for specific industries and workers hurt by imports, and mounting threats to reverse the entire U.S. trade policy," the council wrote. The new policies, including an US effort to lower trade barriers, "must improve and expand trade relations with the free world while assuring practical, up-to-date flexible safeguards for certain US workers and industries against injury from import competition." The council called for the United States, other nations that were parties to the GATT, and the International Labor Organization (ILO) to seek "effective, multilateral solutions" to prevent disruptions in industrialized nations from sudden increases in imports from low-wage nations. Other suggestions included a program of TAA to help workers and communities affected by imports and changes in tax policy to reduce the incentives for US companies to invest abroad. "The American labor movement will continue to follow the trade union tradition of supporting the national interest, in international trade policy, as it has in other U.S. policies. . . . Labor has supported a liberal trade policy but we insist that gradual reduction of trade barriers must not entail a callous disregard for American workers displaced by imports."[37]

The AFL-CIO amplified its Executive Council's position later that year in a report on the nation's major manufacturing sectors. It found, with the exception of the textile and apparel industries, that virtually all US manufacturing sectors were strong across the board, exporting more goods than the United States imported from their foreign counterparts. The AFL-CIO report hinted at numerous challenges, such as the formation of the European Common Market and the European Free Trade Association (EFTA), as well as the Latin American Free Trade Association and the Central American Common Market in Latin America. These organizations were convincing both Europe and Latin America to eliminate their internal tariff barriers with each other and reduce their external tariff barriers faster than the United States, under RTAA, could reduce its tariff barriers with the individual nations or the new supranational bodies. In addition, the more rapid lowering of tariff barriers in Europe and Latin America had prompted US business to invest more heavily in both regions, getting "behind the tariff walls" and taking advantage of trade without having to contend with uncertainty connected to US tariffs. The AFL-CIO called for a new tariff-reduction program with the nation's foreign trading partners; policies to aid US industries, communities, and workers harmed by imports; and better monitoring of trade patterns via the GATT and the ILO.[38]

While the ITAC carried out its directives with the work of Hodges and White House aide Myer Feldman, Japanese labor leaders negotiated issues of importance involving international affairs and trade with a number of US government and labor officials during a goodwill trip to the United States between February 19 and March 10. The negotiations did not, apparently, include any public discussion of the controversial issue of imposing limits on exports to the United States. AFL-CIO President Meany, TWUA President Pollock, and George Harrison, the AFL-CIO international affairs committee chair, did discuss several issues with Minoru Takita, chairman of Zenro (the Japan Trade Union Congress) and president of Zensen Domei (the Japan Textile Workers Federation) during the visit. Meany and Takita reached six agreements, mainly centered on Cold War goals; one, however, was a promise to participate with the ILO and the GATT to find "more effective solutions to economic problems" and to seek trade liberalization where possible.[39]

As the ITAC drew up its plans to aid the textile industry, pressure mounted in Congress and in the US public for Kennedy to impose import quotas on textiles. The calls intensified after the Pastore Committee, whose 1958 hearings had focused attention on the state of the textile industry, resumed its work. Debates in both houses of Congress on problems facing the industry also ensued. And requests for import restrictions flowed into the White House. "Our jobs are mighty important to us and our families, and we believe you can help us through quotas," wrote a worker from upstate South Carolina.[40] The workers' requests joined similar calls from individual members of Congress, textile executives, and the congressional delegations of New Hampshire, the Carolinas, Georgia, and Alabama.[41] Kennedy himself had supported import quotas as a senator,[42] but now he was reluctant to follow through for fears of triggering an international trade war. Over the remainder of Kennedy's presidency, objections to the administration's efforts to aid the industry and a continual growth in imports triggered repeated calls for import quotas.[43]

While members of Congress and the public asked for import quotas, the ACWA took more direct action. In February its leadership voted to boycott cutting Japanese imported cloth after Japan refused to impose limits on the number of men's and boys' suits it exported to the United States. On March 9, a day after Kennedy discussed import competition and tried to downplay the ACWA's threat during a White House press conference, the ACWA announced its boycott would begin on May 1. ACWA President Jacob Potofsky called the boycott "an action taken with a grave sense of responsibility to hundreds of thousands of workers in the apparel industries of this country, whose livelihood has been placed in serious jeopardy by the failure thus far of our government to devise adequate means to meet our problem."[44]

Potofsky noted an explosive increase in imports of various apparel items in recent years: imports had increased to comprise 50 percent of knit gloves sold in the United States, as well as 10 percent of the volume of cotton sport shirts and 20 percent of that of trousers produced domestically. Furthermore, imports of shirts had increased from 2,400 per year to 23 million—all despite the ACWA's use of a variety of remedies designed to protect domestic markets from imports. "The President could not have been talking of the apparel industry when he spoke of imports as one or two per cent of the domestic market," Potofsky said. "We have watched item after item of apparel increasingly affected by rising imports. We have seen our shops close down and our workers thrown out of work by competition based on wages of 10 and 12 cents an hour and shocking work conditions." The issue that the textile and apparel industries had to confront, he concluded, was a "threat of death."[45]

The ACWA boycott declaration led to a flurry of exchanges between the union and the White House and a meeting at which Kennedy laid out his concern about the boycott: While the ACWA was concerned about the rapid increase in imports of Japanese apparel, pointing to a potential threat to its cloth-cutter members—as well as suit makers, the industry in which the ACWA got its start—the administration argued suit imports still comprised less than one-third of 1 percent of the 17 million suits produced in the United States. Furthermore, the United States enjoyed a $179 million trade surplus with Japan, and the White House argued allowing the ACWA boycott to proceed could inspire other unions to impose boycotts of their own against Japanese goods and even invite similar retaliation by Japan against US exports.[46] The ACWA called off the protest on April 18 at Kennedy's request, but not before the TWUA pledged its full support of the boycott and simultaneously called for all textile unions to put up a united front against import competition, apparently ignorant of a similar alliance the TWUA had entered a year earlier with the ACWA, the ILGWU, and the United Hatters, Cap and Millinery Workers, under Potofsky's direction, to fight imports from Japan and Hong Kong.[47] The ACWA also inspired a proposed boycott, to coincide with the ACWA action, from Chicago local 1031 of the International Brotherhood of Electrical Workers, which announced it would refuse to use Japanese electrical components. The IBEW local postponed its boycott in March to allow the administration to study import issues further.[48]

In May 1961, after Hodges and the ITAC had assembled proposals to aid the textile industry, Kennedy issued them in a seven-point plan that would involve several executive-branch agencies. The plan included approving a new depreciation schedule for textile companies, to promote modernization, and established an accelerated research schedule for textile products. The Kennedy administration also asked the Office of Emergency Planning to "determine whether national security requires limitation of imports of cotton textiles."[49] Finally, Kennedy directed the State Department to negotiate with other textile-producing nations and reach agreements to slow, at least temporarily, the pace of imports. The announcement of the industry plan intersected again with civil rights; this time, it was the Freedom Rides, in which an interracial group of protesters traveled through the South in an ultimately successful effort to force the desegregation of interstate transportation facilities.[50]

Responses to the Seven-Point Plan

Just as Kennedy found it difficult to placate civil-rights protesters without angering segregationists, his administration found difficulties in its efforts to aid the textile industry. The administration could not simultaneously please textile industry supporters in business and labor, who sought import quotas, and improve relations with other nations, who wanted unfettered access to the US market for their goods. Although the seven-point plan was generally well received, the textile industry and members of Congress were unhappy both with the administration's decision to negotiate with other nations and with the proposed import limits. Import quota supporters were unhappy, for instance, that the administration chose 1960 import and export levels as the baseline for negotiations with other countries. In that year, textile imports had already increased 64 percent over the previous year and imports of cotton goods had exceeded exports, as the South Carolina congressional delegation pointed out.[51]

Of specific concern was a decision in June 1961 by Ball, the undersecretary of state, to negotiate an initial international trade agreement outside the GATT framework that addressed only cotton textiles, leaving out wool, silk, and artificial fibers. The White House immediately reassured members of Congress that negotiations would cover all textile sectors.[52]

The State Department's proposed negotiations also would allow an increase in textile imports from Japan and give other participating nations an opportunity to increase textile and apparel exports to the United States. "It is the considered opinion of all of us in the House and Senate alike that Mr. Ball's program will insure the continued deterioration of the U.S. industry," Representative Carl Vinson, a Georgia Democrat, and Senator Pastore of Rhode Island wrote, adding that Ball's proposed negotiation was "a piecemeal and entirely inadequate program which is not in accord with your own pronouncements" and urging Kennedy to scrap Ball's proposal if it was the only effort the administration would attempt.[53] The White House responded that Ball's negotiations were but part of the effort to aid the industry and that the State Department had been asked to win import relief for all varieties of textiles.[54]

Textile executives poured out their dissatisfaction with the Kennedy White House and the State Department's role in carrying out parts of the seven-point plan and expressed their fears that State would undercut the textile industry. Nearly three decades after winning the power to negotiate trade agreements under the RTAA, State Department officials handled trade negotiations with a degree of secrecy that rankled textile executives accustomed to having access to cabinet secretaries and the White House.[55] At the same time, textile executives expressed confidence that they would receive favorable receptions with other executive branch agencies, such as the Office of Civil and Defense Mobilization. In April 1961 textile executives asked the office to designate the industry as vital to national security; the designation, which Kennedy requested in announcing the seven-point plan, would allow Kennedy additional latitude to curb imports.[56]

Members of Congress and textile executives were not the only ones worried that the State Department might place lower trade barriers and US foreign policy goals above supporting the domestic textile and apparel industries. The AFL-CIO, which supported the seven-point plan, was concerned about maintaining a 1956 "voluntary export restriction" arrangement between the United States and Japan. And while Japan had largely abided by that agreement, Japan also felt its textile sector had been harmed between 1956 and 1960 as US importers shifted some of their textile and apparel orders to Hong Kong. In response, Japanese officials wanted to negotiate higher import levels under the 1956 agreement. The State Department, hearing these concerns, granted Japan in late 1961 a 33.33 percent increase in the number of men's and women's trousers and shorts it could export to the United States and authorized an overall rise in the 1961 shipments of woven cotton apparel—agreements that, to the AFL-CIO Executive Council, were reached without consultation with labor and industry and in disregard for the disruption both might have on US apparel markets.[57]

With the 1956 agreement set to expire by the end of 1961, the United States made further concessions during bilateral negotiations with Japan governing woven and knit cotton apparel, prompting the AFL-CIO Executive Council to deride the agreement because it limited the ability of the United States to control market disruption, provided an abnormal increase in Japanese imports of knit and cotton garments (a 14 percent increase over 1960 levels and a 10 percent increase during 1961), and provided no adequate safeguards against a concentration of imports on one item. The Executive Council, in response, called for increases in Japanese imports to be offset with import reductions from Hong Kong and other nations.[58]

In an effort to argue for additional power to negotiate trade deals and allay fears that Ball would undermine the industry through his support of free trade in an effort to advance US foreign policy objectives, the Kennedy administration produced a memorandum in which it asserted its intent to both pursue liberal trade policies and offer protection to industries that needed it. While Ball was committed to liberal trade policies, they argued, he was also interested in the need to aid industries "which require Government assistance to maintain their health."[59] Furthermore, the administration argued, countering the claims of slow progress, that Kennedy was moving with sufficient speed on the seven-point plan: "Only 7 months have passed, and in that time, there has been a respectable series of Administration announcements. Never before has so much progress been made in so short a period of time."[60] The White House made sure to share the memorandum with at least one prominent textile executive, hoping to get the administration's arguments before the industry.[61]

Limiting Textile Trade outside GATT: The STA and LTA

During the summer of 1961, representatives of sixteen GATT nations, including the United States, convened in Geneva, Switzerland, to negotiate an agreement on limiting the growth of imports of cotton textiles. By July 26, participants had reached an agreement outside the GATT framework, meaning the agreement would apply only to the sixteen signatories and not all GATT member nations. The Short-Term Arrangement (STA), as it was called, would begin on October 1, 1961, and remain in place for a year. During that time, nations participating in the STA could reach agreements with other countries to reduce imports for more than sixty categories of cotton textile imports or take unilateral action to reduce imports in the absence of an agreement. In early 1962, nineteen textile-producing nations reached agreement on a five-year pact to succeed the STA. The Long-Term Arrangement (LTA) gave participants the option to limit imports against nations that did not join the agreement.

As negotiations proceeded on regulating the international textile trade, Kennedy resisted the widespread calls to impose unilateral import quotas on textiles. Instead, he sought to limit imports through the GATT and multilateral conferences, following the example of the 1961 Geneva conference that yielded the STA. By using multilateral conferences and the international trade framework, Kennedy sought to strike a trade compromise with other textile-producing countries; simultaneously, pursuit of this goal helped the president avoid a trade war, which the use of import quotas would likely cause because such a move would be seen by trading partners as aggressive. At the same time, negotiating through multilateral conferences allowed Kennedy to maintain his administration's commitment to greater trade liberalization.

Where Kennedy saw these moves as a way to limit imports without reverting to import quotas, concerned textile workers and executives saw quotas as a way for the United States to quickly squelch the threat of textile imports and save domestic jobs. The administration's view ignored various factors. First, according to the TWUA, textile industry productivity in 1960 was as high as in 1947. Yet the number of workers had declined by nearly 40 percent over that period, making plain the increase in the industry's use of automation.[62] Second, as other nations had rebuilt from World War II, US trade partners increasingly saw the US market as a source of consumers whose purchases provided currency that could be used to repay war debts or underwrite further industrialization. But while free trade supporters saw a balance of trade favorable to both the United States and US textile industry dominance, even as competing nations like Japan, Hong Kong, and Great Britain were closing the trade gap, manufacturers saw it as a threat to be contained.

Between the threat of economic disruption represented by imports and the potential for social and political disruption through the ongoing civil-rights movement, executives continued to press for import quotas to establish some security for the textile industry. "I believe, when the facts are known, you will realize that an overhaul of textile import quotas is sorely needed if we are to protect our industry and our working forces," wrote a manager of Tuscarora Cotton Mill in Mount Pleasant, North Carolina, where workers had been on a three-day workweek as a result of a rise in imports from 1960 to 1961.[63]

The Combed Yarn Spinners Association in North Carolina sent a resolution that decried the reduction of tariffs on textiles under the RTAA, the proliferation of foreign manufacturers using cheap cotton and cheap labor, and the explosion of cotton yarn imports (from 837,145 pounds in 1958 to 15,140,680 pounds in 1960). The association asked for protective tariffs and quotas on textiles to protect the domestic industry "toward the end that thousands of Americans shall not suffer for the sake of giving advantage to foreign competitors."[64] A director of Burlington Industries chimed in from New York, hailing the voluntary export restrictions reached with Japan in the late 1950s and suggesting import quotas as a "sound and logical approach" to protecting the 2 million Americans who worked in textiles and apparel.[65] And a local in Manchester, New Hampshire—which claimed Japanese imports were responsible for slashing employment at the city's Waumbec Mills from 1,350 workers in 1951 to 350 by 1961—passed a resolution urging Congress and Kennedy to impose import quotas and raise textile tariffs.[66]

With the revitalizing effect of World War II and the Korean War on the US textile industry, and industry executives' claims that textiles and apparel were essential to the nation's defense, it was little surprise that textile executives would attempt to make further connections between international issues and imports. One, from Alexander City, Alabama, noted that some observers had suggested that Japan and Hong Kong might take over textile manufacturing, citing economist Joseph Schumpeter's theories of creative destruction. While such a move might free up US mills to make other products, he cited the Cuban revolution and the nationalization of US business interests as an illustration of the possibility of a similar sudden loss of access to imported goods under this approach. "Where would we be if, when we do that, a Japanese Castro comes along?" he pondered, arguing for maintaining some domestic manufacturing presence.[67]

A Missed Opportunity: Organized Labor and the Politics of Trade

The push to save the domestic textile industry through Kennedy's seven-point plan was occurring within a larger debate in the labor movement about the direction of trade policy. The debate pitted unions from industries that were strong in exporting goods and that ran trade surpluses against unions fighting imports and representing industries with trade deficits. Sometimes trade was addressed only tangentially, as was the case on May 15, 1961, when the AFL-CIO's Ruttenberg appeared on a radio show dealing with labor issues. While he made no specific mention of trade issues—he urged a public works program and tax cut to boost the domestic economy—he discussed the Area Redevelopment Act. In doing so, he referred to a bill that the TWUA, as part of its response to industrial decline driven by import competition, had championed during the 1950s despite two vetoes from the Eisenhower administration. The bill passed both houses of Congress early in 1961, and Kennedy signed it into law on May 1. The act created a four-year program by which at least seven agencies provided about $300 million in assistance—including business loans, public infrastructure improvements, and workforce training—to communities with high unemployment.[68]

The debate among unions on supporting or challenging lower trade barriers surfaced again in a speech from Meany to the International Association of Machinists' (IAM's) inaugural conference on world trade in November 1961. Meany acknowledged a range of opinions on trade among member unions. To some, in the pottery, shoe, and garment industries, "foreign trade is a one-way street—all coming in. So from their point of view, the less goods that come in, the better they like it," he said. Other unions in industries that exported goods like trucks, agricultural implements, and machinery, supported trade expansion because it helped their members. And members in other unions could have divergent views, depending on how imports might affect their jobs.[69]

Meany, however, emphasized the dominance of US exports and argued that the concern about imports was overstated. Complaints about imports were directed at about one-third of US imports—roughly $5 billion of the $15 billion of goods entering the country at the time. The value of US exports, meanwhile, equaled the combined exports of Great Britain and West Germany. US export output was five times as high as Japan's and six times as great as Italy's. Further, he said, 2.5 million nonfarm US jobs, and another 600,000 farm jobs, depended on exports, while another 1.4 million jobs were created by imports, pointing up the importance of trade. "This country cannot prosper, or indeed, cannot even maintain itself, without imports from foreign countries," he said.[70]

By defending imports and delineating three distinct philosophies on trade among labor unions, Meany effectively consigned textile and apparel unions to the losing side of trade issues. Import-sensitive industries espoused one philosophy. Their unions were relatively weak, with the exception of one large industrial union—the Steelworkers, representing an industry in which opportunities for steel exports were declining.[71] The import-sensitive camp included the UMWA (who were concerned that a reduction in US industrial capacity would affect demand for coal) and small unions representing shoemakers, potters, and hatters.

Just as imports continued to diminish the textile and apparel industries, so, too, did its unions face diminishing influence. The movement of plants to nonunion locations, the failure of textile unions to organize the South, and overall manufacturer hostility to unions ultimately spelled a lower profile within the labor movement for textile and apparel unions on trade issues.

The group with the second philosophy outlined in Meany's speech were unions like the UAW and the International Union of Electrical, Radio, and Machine Workers, representing workers in industries that manufactured goods not widely available outside the United States; in contrast to workers in textiles, apparel, and steel, these workers stood to gain from a greater volume of trade.

The IAM would subscribe to the third philosophy and be allies of the Teamsters, whose leaders recognized its members would gain from expanded trade but were concerned, nevertheless, that declines in US industrial production could affect fellow workers in manufacturing unions.

Meany tried to bridge the divides by searching for a middle way in which the AFL-CIO could support lower trade barriers while sheltering its unions against the costs. "Now obviously some imports have caused a loss of jobs; otherwise we wouldn't have a problem," he said. "We think measures ought to be taken to make up for those losses." But Meany argued that imports equaled only 3 to 4 percent of the total national product and, of that amount, only 30 percent were competing with US goods. The result, Meany said, was that "the whole area in which damage may occur is limited to about 1% of your national product." Yet, he allowed, that narrow scope mattered little to workers made jobless because of imports.[72]

In his address, Meany set up a crude calculus to explain the need for lower trade barriers in the context of the Cold War. He argued that trade had economic importance and political implications as a defense against communism. Nations seeking to industrialize often started with industries with low barriers to entry, such as textiles. "If we and other developed countries do not buy from them, they won't have the money to buy from us. If we exclude their goods, they will be forced to exclude ours. And they will turn in desperation to the Soviet Union, even at the cost of becoming economic satellites."[73]

Meany made clear that the pursuit of an increase in trade was unsustainable without a strong and growing US economy that provided full employment. For this reason, labor proposed and supported policies that would expand the economy. Meany called for two changes in a proposed reauthorization of the RTAA to increase its effectiveness and diminish its harmful effects. First, he said, the president should have greater flexibility in negotiating tariff reductions, counter to efforts to limit presidential power in previous renewals of the RTAA. Second, the president needed greater power to act to limit the impact of imports without waiting for the US Tariff Commission to find injury before the president could raise tariffs or impose import quotas. Meany also called for the creation of a TAA program to aid workers who had lost their jobs as a result of an increase in imports.[74]

In addition to supporting free trade while conceding some of its flaws, Meany called for an expansionary monetary and fiscal policy to help the nation end what he termed "the rollercoaster of frequent recessions and incomplete recoveries" and strengthen the economy. Otherwise, the economy would be in danger of stalling, with unemployment increasing and plants idle. He supported a Keynesian approach that increased federal expenditures with the goal of a balanced budget during times of maximum manpower and production, expanded public works, followed a less restrictive monetary policy to ensure low interest rates, and made efforts to reduce long-term unemployment, such as a job retraining bill pending in Congress, which would become the Manpower Development and Training Act of 1962.[75]

While Meany placed his hopes with Kennedy's plans to expand the economy, other members of the AFL-CIO Executive Council, which included the ILGWU's Dubinsky and the ACWA's Potofsky, worried that imports were contributing to economic contraction. The Executive Council was becoming more aware about import competition and its potential effect on industries. In October 1961 the Executive Council declared, "large-scale influxes of imports from low-wage countries have adversely affected US domestic production and employment recently in such industries as textiles and apparel." At the behest of unions like the ACWA, ILGWU, and TWUA, the federal government asked GATT officials to consider the rapid influx of imports amid the 1958–59 recession as a "market disruption" that destabilized the domestic industry. Such pressure and constant deterioration in the textile and apparel industries had led to Kennedy's seven-point plan.[76] The Executive Council, nevertheless, regarded the seven-point plan favorably; furthermore, it considered the STA "a major advance in providing an internationally acceptable approach to the orderly marketing of cotton textiles and apparel."[77]

When trade issues surfaced in the Kennedy administration, imports were already an issue of importance for industries like textiles and apparel that faced challenges from lower-cost nations. Cold War considerations were also near the surface, as labor, business, and political figures recognized. Each had their own specific set of concerns to address: industry and labor were worried about low-cost competition, while textile unions, concerned about the decline of communities facing industrial losses, were still attempting to organize southern textile workers.

By the early 1960s, the million-member IAM, the fourth-largest union in the AFL-CIO, was hosting conferences on world trade, reflecting labor's concerns about the challenges they saw in the issue. The IAM hosted its inaugural trade conference, a two-day event in Washington in November 1961, attracting three hundred of its members and Labor Secretary Arthur Goldberg. Kennedy, who had been invited to speak, declined to address the conference.[78] Yet, in a statement to the IAM, Kennedy urged a new course in trade policy to keep pace with changes in international affairs. He cited the potential expansion of the EEC, trade expansion with less-developed nations, finding markets for Japanese exports, and the challenges of the Soviet Union as factors all requiring the attention of the United States "if we are to assure for ourselves and our free world partners the benefits of economic growth, expanding economic opportunity and the capacity to contend with Communist economic warfare in the years ahead."[79]

In placing textile and apparel unions on the side of workers who were likely to be affected by trade and import competition, Meany effectively, if inadvertently, consigned them to being losers in the context of labor's examination of trade in the early 1960s. Meany's argument in favor of trade aligned with Kennedy on foreign policy points while siding with unions in industries with strong export activity that stood to benefit from lower trade barriers. For workers in unions based in industries that were vulnerable to import competition, Meany and Ruttenberg envisioned expansionist economic policy to create jobs for them. For those who had lost their jobs, programs offered by the Area Redevelopment Act and the TAA program they envisioned would offer new opportunities and retraining. A stronger labor presence in the textile industry might have reshaped this balance of power in favor of a trade policy that assertively helped affected workers, but, for now, textile unions and their counterparts in import-sensitive industries could not alter the AFL-CIO's support of lower trade barriers.

Supranational Blocs, Taxes, and Trade: A Calculus of the 1960s

Kennedy's 1961 statement to the IAM augured a new chapter for trade in the postwar era. Whereas since the 1940s trade had been considered essential for international economic recovery from World War II, Kennedy now sought to place trade in a Cold War context of forging deeper international trade partnerships. Using a calculus similar to Meany's, Kennedy's argument for expanding trade in this period amounted to a call for greater trade with the rest of the world in order to keep other nations from establishing trade relations and closer ties with the Soviet Union. The supranational trading blocs forming in Western Europe and Latin America, Kennedy argued, demanded a response if the United States were to remain competitive.

The AFL-CIO also saw an economic challenge in the growth of the EEC and its steady removal of trade barriers. Between 1953 and 1960, the economic growth of the six EEC nations (West Germany, France, Italy, Belgium, Luxembourg, and the Netherlands) outstripped that of the United States: the EEC's real gross national product increased 45 percent, versus 19 percent for the United States. In that period, industrial productivity in the EEC grew 71 percent, nearly four times the 19 percent rate in the United States during that period. In 1961 the six EEC nations ended quotas on imports of industrial products within the EEC and equalized tariff rates for all six nations, effectively adopting a single common tariff. The policy was a direct challenge for the United States: as late as 1959, two-thirds of US exports to the EEC went to West Germany and the three Benelux nations. A lower EEC internal tariff and a higher external tariff for US goods threatened to reduce the volume of US exports to the EEC. "The Common Market growth is expected to continue," the AFL-CIO warned. "The U.S. has a problem. It must keep abreast and ahead of the growth of the EEC or lose its position of influence."[80]

In addition to the six EEC nations, seven others—Norway, Denmark, Sweden, Switzerland, Austria, Portugal, and the United Kingdom—had formed the EFTA and were interested in aligning with the EEC or joining it. Either move had the potential for the EEC to surpass the United States in population and economic power.[81]

The size and strength of the EEC (the "inner six") and the EFTA (the "outer seven") had vast implications for US trade. Europe was the largest single export market for US goods and services; in 1960 the United States exported $6 billion worth of goods to Europe (31 percent of US exports that year); in turn, Europe sold the United States $4 billion of goods, representing 27 percent of US import totals. And the $3.3 billion of exports to Europe in 1959–60 helped alleviate the woes of the US economy as it sought to recover from the recession that year.[82]

To the AFL-CIO, the pattern was clear: higher standards of living across Europe meant its people could buy more consumer goods, especially those made in the United States. President Kennedy's effort to update the RTAA would also lead to lower trade barriers with the EEC "and in so doing keep the markets of Europe open to American goods."[83]

The rapid growth of Europe's economy in comparison to that of the United States was also stimulating an outflow of dollars: US businesses increased their investment in the Inner Six and Outer Seven, from $4.3 billion in 1958 to $6.4 billion in 1960. Businesses were uncertain about whether tariffs between the United States and the EEC would be lowered as EEC nations lowered their internal tariffs, with an eye toward eliminating them altogether by 1969, and they established subsidiaries in Europe to take advantage of the lower internal EEC tariffs. The AFL-CIO, with its support for lower tariff barriers, called for ending tax deferrals given to US companies for their overseas subsidiary profits—initially part of a 1954 rewrite of the federal tax code—to help repatriate US income earned abroad. Such deferrals were increasingly seen as contributing to the US balance-of-payment and trade problems as US corporations increasingly entered world markets and established tax havens in other nations to which companies could divert profits, lowering their tax rates in the process. Kennedy and Congress had proposed ending deferrals in 1961 and 1962, ultimately succeeding with the enactment of Subpart F of the Revenue Act of 1962, which sought to reduce corporate tax avoidance through the use of tax havens.[84]

"One thing seems to be certain—that unless the [EEC] sees some signs of willingness on our part to lower tariffs, [its] continuing external tariff wall will mean serious problems for our domestic economy in terms of unemployment, idle plant and capacity, etc.," the AFL-CIO reported. Kennedy wanted the power to gradually eliminate all tariffs on goods in which the United States and the EEC supplied at least 80 percent of the world's trade (mainly industrial products), cut tariffs on other goods by up to 50 percent, and bargain on major categories of goods.[85]

To be sure, Meany and others in the AFL-CIO saw in these capital flows a move to depress union workers' wages in many manufacturing sectors while reaping higher profits through production of goods in low-wage nations by US multinationals for export to the United States: "Some of these companies, as you know, piously insist that they are 'forced' into this kind of operation because of 'high labor costs' here in America. And they use that argument as a weapon to beat down the wages and working conditions of the American workers they have left," Meany argued in his 1961 speech to the IAM. While wages abroad were often lower than for their US counterparts, low efficiency and more expensive fringe benefits often meant US unit labor costs were still lower. Meany argued that lower taxes, rather than labor costs, were the true motivator for US companies setting up shop abroad, because the foreign subsidiary did not owe taxes until the profits were repatriated and could also enjoy lower taxes in the new nation as well as concessions on US taxes. As a result, tax differences between the United States and other nations meant profits on earnings reinvested overseas "pile up twice as fast as they do here," Meany said, quoting a study from the American Management Association.[86]

Meany did not think any tax concessions could be "justified for companies that invest in other industrial countries, such as those in western Europe." He thought such concessions were outrageous when the overseas plant was "designed primarily to ship goods back to the U.S." He wondered why favors were extended to corporations that deliberately set out, "for the sake of extra profits, to rob Americans of their jobs." Meany suggested using tax incentives to help less-developed nations establish subsidiaries to manufacture goods for consumption there—but not for export. Such an arrangement, he argued, would provide an incentive that was likely "in the public interest."[87]

JFK's Trade Expansion Act: Response to a New World

Amid the growing challenge from Western Europe and Central America, as well as the overarching context of the Cold War, Kennedy opted not to simply push for a renewal of the RTAA. Rather, he proposed revamping the reciprocal trade program that Cordell Hull had set in place in 1934. Kennedy proposed a new trade program in addresses on consecutive nights in December 1961 to the National Association of Manufacturers and the AFL-CIO. The Trade Expansion Act (TEA), as Kennedy's trade proposal was known, would replace the RTAA by granting the president the authority to negotiate tariff reductions of up to 50 percent from 1962 tariff levels, replacing the 1930 Smoot-Hawley tariff levels that were the baseline for the RTAA.[88] By allowing further tariff reductions, the United States could lower its tariffs to rates that were competitive with the European and Latin American trade zones.

In speaking to the manufacturers, Kennedy acknowledged similarities in their goals despite their differences of opinion and approach. At the same time, he couched the TEA strictly in Cold War terminology—a competition between the United States and the Soviet Union for economic hegemony in Western Europe, Latin America, and the developing world. "Your organization and this Administration are both devoted to achieving a stronger, more prosperous America, in a world of free and peaceful states, making the most of our human and material resources and avoiding the most harmful effects and fluctuations of inflation and recession," he said. Noting the efforts of the "long-range drive" of communism to "impose its way of life on all the world," Kennedy emphasized the United States could take the initiative in economic policy, which would have a broader reach than defensive military and paramilitary efforts. Reminding his audience of the work done by the Marshall Plan, Point Four programs offering US-based technical assistance to developing nations, and the Alliance for Progress, Kennedy called the new trade legislation a "new long-range program to aid in the growth of the undeveloped and usually unaligned nations" that could yield further gains "not merely as a blow against Communism, but as a blow for freedom."[89]

Kennedy asserted the combination of the United States and Western Europe could serve as an economic check on the growing power of the Communist bloc. "But will our strength be combined and coordinated—or divided and self-defeating?" he asked. "Will we work together on problems of trade, payments and monetary reserves—or will our mutual strength be splintered by a network of tariff walls, exchange controls, and the pursuit of narrow self-interest in unrelated if not outright hostile policies on aid, trade, procurement, interest rates and currency?"[90]

Kennedy outlined a series of steps the United States needed to take to build a more favorable balance of payments, which included coordinating development aid; fiscal, debt management, monetary, and other policies through the Organization for Economic Co-operation and Development (OECD); new programs to attract foreign visitors and investment; removing artificial tax preferences for US investment in highly developed nations and loopholes for Americans investing in tax havens abroad; and a program to increase agricultural exports and larger loan guarantees through the Export-Import Bank to help manufacturers export more of their goods.[91]

In order for continued progress on exports, Kennedy called for "price and wage restraint by industry and labor, and responsible budget policies by government." He also referred to his seven-point plan for textiles, calling for accelerated depreciation schedules for textile machinery and possibly other kinds of equipment.[92]

While the general response to Kennedy's trade proposal was favorable, the reception was not as favorable on Capitol Hill, where textile-state representatives were still upset over the administration's closed deal making in crafting the STA and LTA in Geneva. By January 1962, Representative Carl Vinson, who served as the chairman of the House Textile Caucus, was warning the president that textile-state members of Congress were still worried the State Department, in ongoing negotiations on the LTA, would undermine the textile industry by eliminating all tariff barriers on cotton textiles. Such worries, Vinson wrote, would jeopardize the TEA and Kennedy's legislative agenda because "every Southern Congressman who has any cotton textiles in his District will have to oppose the program."[93]

But organized labor and the textile industry soon signed on in support of TEA. In March 1962 Meany offered the AFL-CIO's support in testimony to the House Ways and Means Committee. Meany said the federation supported the program specifically because it contained TAA for employers and workers adversely affected by imports. Meany also expressed his belief that expanded trade would increase, not reduce, job opportunities for US workers; were that to happen, TAA would not expand to "vast proportions":

> We support this program because we believe the time has come for a fundamental revision of our country's trade policy. It is no longer enough for Congress to extend, to amend and to patch up the reciprocal trade legislation that has been on the books since 1934. Times have changed, the world has changed, and this country's

> trade policy must be changed to meet these new conditions.... One of the most vigorous discussions at the [AFL-CIO] convention [in December 1961] was on the foreign trade resolution.... It is significant, I think, that some representatives of the unions that have been under the greatest pressure from imports, such as the textile unions, rose to support this resolution. They felt that if this kind of program had been undertaken some years ago, many of the difficulties they have faced could have been avoided.[94]

Meany acknowledged that imports did take jobs from US workers and contributed to the contraction and collapse of businesses, even as the labor movement supported TAA and TEA. "If we in the labor movement admit that imports can and do cause unemployment in some industries, why do we support this program? The answer is simple: Because we, and the nation, as a whole, will gain far more than we lose."[95]

Vinson campaigned among textile company executives to secure support for the trade package, meeting with a group in March 1962 that included Roger Milliken, Charles Cannon, and Robert Stevens, among others; the executives had long complained that the seven-point plan did not go far enough to aid the industry, and Cannon was especially vocal on the need to eliminate an 8.5-cent subsidy on raw cotton exports he saw as particularly detrimental to the domestic textile industry.[96] Stating that he believed Kennedy's trade bill would ultimately pass, Vinson outlined the seven-point plan and argued that no other industry had ever received such support in so short a time. He sought to assuage the complaints of textile executives over portions of the program yet to be carried out. The seven-point plan "places the textile industry in a unique, preferential, and beneficial position," Vinson wrote. "When I see what has now been accomplished for the textile industry, I, for one, am ready to quit while I am ahead." Vinson later told the White House he thought the overture went well and promised the White House he would "keep on fighting with these big people in the Textile Industry" to get their support. In late March, Vinson cautioned the members of the American Cotton Manufacturers Institute against seeking an amendment to the trade bill to favor the textile industry, noting it could jeopardize congressional and administration support for the seven-point plan.[97]

On March 31, the ACMI's members voted unanimously to support the TEA, pledging to help the Kennedy administration and Congress create a measure to expand international trade while preserving domestic textile production. With the ACMI's support now secured, Vinson believed the trade legislation at last could get through Congress.[98] Capital had joined labor in supporting the trade bill, even as the UTWA and several AFL-CIO unions continued to harbor reservations about it.[99]

The AFL-CIO, taking a page from Kennedy's addresses introducing the TEA, continued to press its support. It compiled at least two pamphlets and speeches to make the case that more trade would expand the economy and overcome fears of losing industrial sectors to import competition. One pamphlet, reprinting an essay by Meany that highlighted the role of trade in US history from colonial days to the 1960s, portrayed the EEC as similar in nature to the US republic. As the EEC had eliminated internal trade barriers, the Constitution, he argued, put an end to internal trade battles among individual colonies and placed the new nation under a uniform national policy, creating a "common market" not unlike the EEC. "This belated emulation of the US pattern has had spectacular results," he wrote. "The nations in the European Common Market are prosperous. Their economic growth-rate has been rapid. They enjoy virtually full employment; in some occupations there are even shortages of labor. In short, the concept of free trade, of the common market, is proving itself again in Europe as it proved itself for almost two centuries in the U.S." Meany went on to say that the AFL-CIO opposed any trade policy that allowed "all sorts of foreign goods, in any quantity whatsoever, to come pouring in, with no restrictions or safeguards whatever," but the federation supported more trade to produce greater prosperity, opportunity, and employment. In addition to an economic side to trade policy, Meany envisioned political calculations for trade connected to the Cold War. Trade could tilt the new nations of Africa and Asia toward the United States and the free world and away from the communist bloc, no matter the cost at home:

> In other words, if freedom is to survive and flourish in Africa and Asia—and in Latin America as well—the peoples of these continents must be convinced that the free way of life is for their material benefit as well as their spiritual salvation. *It might well be argued that if an expanded trade program meant nothing but grief for the U.S., it might still be necessary to insure the preservation of human liberty in new and needy nations* (emphasis added).[100]

Meany suggested continuing the reciprocity principle under the RTAA while giving the president greater leeway to adjust tariffs if a trade emergency were to arise. Also, Meany said, the bill needed to include safeguards that could soften the impact of imports on the national economy, as the RTAA was established with the assumption that greater trade would not yield harmful side effects or problems. US adherence to this principle "by many high-minded supporters of reciprocal trade handicapped the United States for years. It prevented the development of a program to assist communities, industries and workers who were adversely affected by imports; and it thereby drove some industries (and some unions) into the protectionist camp," Meany wrote, adding that Kennedy and the AFL-CIO rejected protectionist views. "Imports *do* take jobs away from US workers—even though many other jobs may be created. And imports *do* cause the contraction or collapse of certain business enterprises—even though many new business opportunities may be opened up. These facts must be faced realistically. They must be coped with, not ignored."[101]

While businesses bemoaned high wages and protectionists claimed cheaper foreign labor priced the United States out of world markets, Meany countered by arguing total labor costs per unit of production, rather than wages, was the proper comparison. By that standard, Meany contended, the United States was equal to or better than many other nations. "We are the world's No. 1 exporting country," he wrote. "We sell more goods outside our own borders than any other nation. We have been selling 59 percent more to Western Europe than we buy in return; 73 percent more to Japan than we buy," adding that the US labor movement was committed to narrowing the wage gap between it and other nations and was opposed to worker exploitation. The nation's foreign trade policy should "seek progress and security through expansion, not through efforts to preserve the status quo," he wrote.[102]

In an address to the ILGWU conference in Atlantic City in May 1962, Meany continued his portrayal of foreign trade as an economic weapon the United States could use during the Cold War. At the ILGWU conference, he joined a range of speakers, including Vice President Lyndon Johnson and Labor Secretary Arthur Goldberg. President Kennedy and New Jersey Gov. Richard J. Hughes did not attend but sent separate messages, reflecting the influence the union commanded among federal and state officials.

Though Meany pointedly ignored discussing import competition with the ILGWU delegates, he spoke of social, economic, and political problems facing Americans and trade unions, leading with a mention of the threat the Soviet Union posed to the United States. He then moved to portraying trade as a way to "deter aggression in the Far East, in Latin America, and other parts of the globe." Competition with the USSR was not merely military and political, he said. "It is also on the economic side. World trade has become a weapon in the Cold War."[103]

Meany lamented the nation's growth rate of approximately 2.5 percent per year for the previous decade, a rate placing it lower than any other industrial nation in the West, and the United States needed a growth rate between 4.25 percent and 4.5 percent to keep pace with its growing population. By comparison, France had a growth rate of 5 percent. While the United States had prosperity, much of it was concentrated at the top, away from the economic base that lay "in the hands of the great mass of workers at the bottom of the economic ladder. In other words, what we need are jobs for all of those who are able and willing to work." The slow growth rate was most evident in the higher unemployment rates preceding recent recessions and the slower recoveries from each. "What has this 2½% growth rate since 1950 meant to us?" he asked. "It has meant four recessions.

... The 2½% growth rate means that we are slipping back; we are not moving forward. What could it mean if we allow recession after recession to come, if we get to the point when 8, 10, and 12 percent of the workforce are unemployed?"[104]

Amid the push to secure Kennedy's trade program, organized labor continued to press its case for aiding the economic recovery. On June 14, Meany presented Kennedy with a memorandum on the economy in which he expressed concern about several trends and pressed the case for a tax cut: business spending had not picked up, while government spending was slow. Personal consumption had remained slow, and unemployment, while relatively low at 5.4 percent in May 1962, was higher than at similar points following the recessions of 1958, 1954, and 1949. Industry, meanwhile, was operating at 10 percent to 15 percent below optimum capacity. Demand among consumers, government, and business "is clearly not enough to keep the economy fully employed at present," Meany said in calling for a temporary tax cut targeted to the lowest individual tax bracket to avoid slowing economic growth, as opposed to lower corporate taxes and tax cuts for all income brackets, which he did not support. Meany also called for ending a series of temporary excise taxes imposed during the Korean War, which he said would provide a $900 million stimulus.[105]

Despite the slow recovery of the economy from the 1960 recession, the United States by 1962 enjoyed a positive balance of trade, exporting $5 billion more worth of goods than it imported. Even as officials in the ACWA and TWUA were complaining about being overwhelmed by imports, other organized labor officials held a more sanguine overall view of world trade. "We had a favorable balance of trade with every area of the world," said George Harrison, an AFL-CIO vice president and president of the Brotherhood of Railway Clerks, at a White House conference in May 1962. "So let's not push the panic button on this issue. We are not weak in world markets. We are strong. And we have nothing to fear from foreign competition. US workers and US business can and do produce a vast variety of goods that other peoples want and need and at prices they are willing to pay."[106]

In a separate address to a conference on trade policy, Harrison argued that labor supported reciprocal trade and lower trade barriers "because we recognize the importance of expanded trade for the nation at home and abroad." In December 1961, for instance, the AFL-CIO gave its support to Kennedy's call for the TEA. "Business gains, job opportunities, and political and economic strength are essential national goals," Harrison said. "Trade can help achieve them." Harrison also outlined an argument for TAA within the trade expansion bill: "Most of the bill merely modernizes the provisions of the past and brings them up to date. But something new has been added. The game of pretending that trade cannot hurt anybody is over."[107]

The Battle to Pass the TEA

Even with the efforts to portray the trade bill as an economic weapon in the Cold War, and despite support from organized labor, textile-state politicians, and industry executives, the TEA faced difficult odds in getting through Congress in 1962. The proposal to include a TAA package spurred opposition in Congress from conservative Democrats and Republicans who balked at giving additional aid to workers who had lost their jobs as a result of imports, rather than making it universally available to unemployed workers. Its passage was still in doubt by September 1962, when Kennedy taped an address to the Steelworkers during its Eleventh annual convention. "We are trying to pass legislation and we hope by the time this Congress ends, it will be substantially moved ahead," the president said, describing a laundry list of programs to aid workers, provide health care, and build public works, as well as a new tax bill.[108]

A successful White House campaign and the support of constituencies like organized labor finally succeeded in getting the TEA through Congress. Labor came on board to support the measure, as well as provisions to create the TAA program that USWA President David McDonald first envisioned in 1954. The program offered supplemental unemployment benefits to workers whose firms could certify with the US Tariff Commission that their jobs were lost as a result of import competition. In addition to their unemployment benefits, workers were eligible to receive up to 65 percent of their average weekly wage (up to $61 a week) for 52 weeks. Additional benefits were available: retraining workers and workers over the age of 60 qualified for up to a year and a half of additional benefits. Retraining workers also could receive travel allowances connected to their training expenses, as well as relocation allowances for up to two and a half times the average weekly manufacturing wage.[109]

Labor had supported a TAA program in the hopes it would help displaced manufacturing workers retrain for new jobs and give a boost to sectors not affected by import competition. The flurry of seemingly sudden activity had taken years to come to fruition—for instance, the TAA was first proposed in 1954 and the ARA was proposed in 1955.

Kennedy focused on the international aspects of the TEA when he signed it into law on October 11, calling it "the most important international piece of legislation . . . affecting economics since the passage of the Marshall plan." Though he spoke of the benefits of lowering tariff barriers in building strong economies, Kennedy described the trade law in Cold War terms, especially in opening new markets in Africa, Asia, and Latin America: "A vital expanding economy in the free world is a strong counter to the threat of the world Communist movement. This act is, therefore, an important new weapon to advance the cause of freedom."[110]

Five days later, the Cold War intervened once more, but not through trade policy. Rather, it was a thirteen-day showdown with the Soviets over its emplacement of missiles in Cuba that brought the superpowers to the brink of conflict. Kennedy may have seen a new economic sphere in formulating his arguments about trade and global economic competition, but the Cuban Missile Crisis was a stark reminder that military issues still drove the Cold War.

Labor and the Context of JFK's Final Year

As 1962 gave way to 1963, the AFL-CIO continued to voice its concerns that the US economy might be slipping back into recession, pointing to small increases in unemployment and idle plants and equipment, despite a $2.5 billion cut in business taxes the Kennedy administration put into effect in 1962. Meanwhile, driven by higher unemployment and shorter workweeks, consumer spending continued to lag. Housing starts were also slower at the end of 1962 than they were in the spring. Meany noted the economic trends pointed to either stagnation or decline in the first half of 1963—a "persistent increase of unemployment and idle productive capacity," as he put it, without federal action to expand the economy. Meany called for "prompt and decisive action" to that end, specifically a $10 billion tax cut aimed at low- and middle-income taxpayers that he argued would stimulate production and spending, and tax reforms that would close loopholes and lower overall tax rates.[111]

Though economic issues were of concern to organized labor, the upsurge in civil-rights issues during 1963 commanded the nation's and world's attention. Birmingham's Project C that spring, designed to produce a frontal assault on segregation in Alabama's largest city, brought shocking images of civil-rights protesters being attacked with fire hoses and police dogs. Faced with international outrage at the violence in Birmingham, Kennedy finally proposed a civil-rights bill to end segregation in public accommodations on June 11, only to be faced hours later with a new shock: the assassination of Medgar Evers, the NAACP's field director for Mississippi. Tensions continued throughout the summer, culminating with the March on Washington for Jobs and Freedom on August 28, an event with significant financial support from the UAW, but not the AFL-CIO, and the deaths of four girls eighteen days later in the bombing of Birmingham's Sixteenth Street Baptist Church.

As the year wound down, with Kennedy's civil-rights bill mired in Congress, the president again sought to focus on improving the nation's economy. On November 15, Kennedy traveled to New York to address delegates at the AFL-CIO convention. Though textile unions had not won the import quotas they sought, they and the rest of the labor movement had several reasons to support

Kennedy: during 1961, he had signed a minimum wage increase and the ARA, offering support to industrial cities affected by the loss of manufacturing jobs. His seven-point plan yielded, among other things, international pacts in the STA and LTA to stabilize the global trade in cotton textiles. In 1962 Kennedy had delivered a TAA package as part of the TEA, which was expected to help workers who had lost their jobs as a result of import competition. He also signed Executive Order 10988, allowing federal workers to collectively bargain, a move that had the unexpected effect of shoring up the US labor movement.

Now, despite the surge in civil-rights issues during the year—with emphasis on the need for economic access, inclusion, and access to public accommodations—Kennedy spoke to the AFL-CIO about a tax cut package he favored, as did the AFL-CIO, as the next element in the nation's continued economic recovery, attempting to square civil rights and economic growth. To Kennedy, it all started with "the right to have a job in this country in a time of prosperity in the United States That is the real right to work issue in 1963," he told the delegates, turning the phrase associated with Taft-Hartley and other antilabor legislation into an economic goal. "This issue of economic security, of jobs, is the basic issue facing the United States in 1963, and I wish we could get everybody talking about it," he said, adding that unemployed and underemployed workers cost the national economy 1 billion lost workdays, the equivalent of a three-week nationwide work stoppage.[112] "Civil rights legislation is important[,] but to make that legislation effective, we need more jobs in the United States," he continued. "If jobs are the most important domestic issue that this country faces, then clearly no single step can now be more important in sustaining the economy of the United States than the passage of our tax bill."[113]

President Kennedy's seven-point plan, the STA, LTA, and the TEA all portended a strengthening of both worker security and trade liberalization. Not since Franklin Roosevelt had a president put forth initiatives such as these to aid labor in the textile industry. Through the STA and LTA, the United States was negotiating bilateral trade agreements outside the GATT to slow the pace of cotton textile imports to the United States, giving the textile industry, workers, and communities an opportunity to recover. For those communities and workers for whom such aid came too late to save their jobs, the Kennedy administration offered the ARA to issue communities grants and loans to recover from the loss of manufacturing. In addition, workers and firms would have access to TAA through the TEA.

Yet this strengthening of the fabric of worker security and trade liberalization had limits: the overall weakness of textile unions and many of their counterparts from import-sensitive basic industries prevented them from convincing leaders like Meany of the downside of lower trade barriers. Meany, encouraged by prospects for export growth and staunchly anticommunist, saw in trade liberalization a path to uninterrupted economic dominance during the Cold War and to an expanded economy that translated into economic security for most of the federation's unions. While textile unions could not convince Meany or the AFL-CIO at this time of the dangers of import competition, they did win, through the seven-point plan, the ARA, and the TAA some executive and legislative improvements they hoped would nurture the industry back to health after the recessions of the late 1950s and the industry's general postwar downward trend.

These actions came together under a president who, in representing Massachusetts in the House and Senate between 1947 and 1961, knew all too well the toll of textile industry decline on workers and communities across the commonwealth. Kennedy's efforts did win the support of workers, textile executives, and organized labor. But his precarious balancing act often left constituencies less than fully satisfied. Just as textile labor did not get import quotas, industry executives welcomed the help of the seven-point plan yet warily eyed his actions on civil rights and were angered by his refusal to end the 8.5-cent subsidy on cotton exports (the ITAC suggested ending the subsidy, only to drop it after opposition from cotton farmers and the State Department).[114]

One person concerned about the future of the textile industry was Walter Trevillian, the head of Clemson University's School of Industrial Management and Textile Science. In August 1963 Trevillian had proposed to the federal government a three-year academic study to find ways to help the industry survive. Trevillian wanted to research greater technological innovations for the industry, which in turn could be applied to alleviate problems caused by wage gaps between textile workers in the United States and other nations. Trevillian envisioned a domestic textile industry that built on US competitive advantages through smaller plants that made greater use of technology. "The industry will face during the coming decade a challenge which it can meet only through dramatic technological progress," Trevillian wrote. "With increasing competition from abroad and with increasing costs at home, the industry must innovate in order to survive."[115]

Trevillian's proposal, focusing on the industry's future, might have made a good addition to Kennedy's seven-point plan. But fate tragically intervened seven days after the president's AFL-CIO address. During a two-day campaign trip to Texas, intended to boost his southern support heading into the 1964 elections, Kennedy met an assassin's bullet in Dallas's Dealey Plaza. Lost in the outpouring of shock and grief over the youthful president's death was the sudden end of his effort to save an industry with New England roots that a century of migration had transformed into a mainstay of the life and economy of the US South, a region whose historic loyalties to the Democratic Party he had desperately hoped to retain amid the maelstrom of the civil-rights struggle.

5

WINDS OF CHANGE

Trade Deals, Rising Imports, and Shifting Political Alliances, 1964–69

As the 1960s proceeded, the cotton textile industry was returning to health, thanks to the federal program begun in the Kennedy administration to assist it. In addition, an expanding domestic economy and military demands arising from the nation's escalating involvement in Vietnam contributed.

Yet, by the late 1960s, new challenges arose. Efforts to monitor textile and apparel imports broke down, leading to significant increases as more nations exported their products to the United States. With import competition from as far away as Asia and as close as the US-Mexico border, executives, workers, and politicians resumed their calls for import quotas.

For portions of the US labor movement, the late 1960s represented a turning point on trade. By 1967, various labor leaders, following the lead of their textile and apparel union counterparts, were questioning more sharply import competition and the aims of US trade policy. President Lyndon Johnson succeeded in fending off protectionist measures yet lost the ability to advance new trade policy. Furthermore, his refusal to impose quotas on textiles and apparel delivered textile executives, an important Democratic and southern constituency, to the Republican Party as Johnson's presidency ended.

Forging Ahead: LBJ and the Seven-Point Program

Johnson's sudden ascent to the presidency left him mere months to establish a legislative record of his own to make a convincing case for election to a full term in 1964. In his first weeks as president, Johnson, relying on political skills he gained in his congressional career, took action to move much of Kennedy's existing legislative program, chief among them the tax cut and civil-rights bills that Kennedy introduced in his last months in office.

One such bill was originally a part of Kennedy's seven-point plan. The bill was intended to help domestic textile producers compete with foreign imports by eliminating an 8.5-cent-per-pound disparity between the price domestic producers and the price their foreign counterparts paid for raw cotton. The "one-price cotton" bill was crucial for winning political support from textile interests, with whom the Johnson administration consulted as the bill was developed, and southern voters who might have qualms about Johnson's support of the Civil Rights Act of 1964.[1]

The lower prices essentially delivered an annual subsidy to the domestic textile industry worth an estimated $312 million, which could help them compete with imports. US consumers were expected to benefit as well from the measure. The Commerce Department estimated that lower raw cotton prices could save US consumers $500 million a year or more. In congressional testimony, manufacturers pledged to lower prices if the measure passed, in the process making their goods competitive with imports and more attractive to consumers.[2]

By the mid-1960s, the cotton textile industry was making a comeback after decades of overcapacity, outdated equipment, and recessions. Operating at just 75 percent of capacity in 1960, textile-industry production increased to 96 percent of capacity by 1965. Producers struggled to fill orders; some plants operated around the clock to meet demand; industry towns revived as job openings increased. Manufacturers built new factories or converted existing buildings—in one case, a bowling alley—into plants to get production going. Aides to Johnson marveled that the industry was more prosperous than ever; Robert Stevens, the president of J. P. Stevens, informed Johnson in late 1964 his company would open a new plant as a testimony to "our confidence in the American economy under your leadership." Other executives also noted the change of fortune. "In my 50 years in the industry, I've never seen a better year than this one," Cannon Mills President Charles Cannon said in 1965. "And only two years ago we were considered a sick industry."[3]

In testimony before the US Senate in 1965, J. M. Cheatham, a Georgia textile executive and ATMI officer, said the one-price law had increased domestic consumption of cotton by 800,000 bales, the largest one-year increase since the Korean War, and the Commerce Department estimated the industry anticipated investing $900 million on new plants and equipment in 1965. The recovery continued into 1966; by the middle of that year, industry prices and profit margins had increased 50 percent over the previous two years.[4]

With such promising results, goodwill between executives and the White House soared. Meeting with eight executives in 1965, an aide to Johnson reported back that the seven-point plan represented "a completely new and constructive era of business-Administration relationships" and that all, including customers, would reap the benefits.[5] Domestic and international efforts had yielded a sense of peace and optimism for the time being. But at home and abroad, changes were already underway that would upend the textile and apparel industries, in the process reshaping allegiances among businesses, lawmakers, and workers.

The revitalization generated by the seven-point plan appeared to give the textile and apparel industries new life, a point Johnson made as he sought reelection. "I am convinced that our program for textiles is in the best interests of all America," Johnson said during a campaign stop in Macon, Georgia, in October 1964. "I intend to pursue it to a successful conclusion." At that campaign stop, Johnson promoted the incentives under the seven-point plan—the STA and LTA, depreciation, and lower cotton prices for domestic manufacturers—as a path to an industry revival that included higher demand for products and higher wages for workers. Johnson vowed to monitor wool and cotton imports while continuing federal efforts to help the industry.[6]

As the decade and the Johnson presidency progressed, however, import quotas in the textile and apparel industries posed a growing problem. While both industries were healthy overall in the 1960s, downturns in one segment, region, or town could trigger repeated calls for quotas from labor, executives, and elected officials. Through it all, textile and apparel imports continued to grow—a development that scared many connected to the industries. While imports did affect individual businesses or sectors, at that time they never threatened to overwhelm any industry entirely. The calls for quotas left the Johnson administration in a difficult position. In the 1964 campaign, Johnson's advisers strenuously urged him not to mention import quotas. A move toward protectionism, while politically popular, would have negative effects, particularly discord with trading partners and a possible trade war. Domestically, if Johnson extended further protections to the two industries, he risked triggering demands from other industries seeking similar treatment. Yet, facing demands from a politically connected manufacturing sector that was vital to his (and his party's) electoral success, Johnson also could not avoid taking action. What ensued was a long, tense standoff over trade policy between the White House and workers, executives, and politicians connected to the textile and apparel industries, including claims and counterclaims on the state of the two industries. The standoff over two industries, employing 2.25 million people in the mid-1960s—one of every eight US manufacturing workers—was heavily overshadowed by the defining themes of Johnson's presidency: the escalating war in Vietnam and intensifying conflict over the direction of US society, as outlined by struggles over civil rights, poverty, and the economy.[7]

As the industry rebounded in the early and mid-1960s, amid an economic expansion that stretched from February 1961 to December 1969, the TWUA embarked on a new effort to organize southern textile workers while securing higher wages—goals the union hoped would bring the South in line economically with the rest of the nation. In early 1965 delegates from TWUA cotton and rayon industry locals met in New York to plan a strategy for winning higher wages in contract negotiations. With weekly textile workers' wages lagging behind those of other industrial workers by as much as $30 a week, the TWUA, as one joint board official put it, saw "the favorable conditions presently existing in the industry" as an opportunity to close that gap.[8]

By late 1965 and early 1966, the comity between textile executives and government officials began to show signs of strain. Despite the favorable treatment extended through the seven-point plan, executives continued to demand textile and apparel import quotas. The animosity grew as the Johnson White House countered that, while the one-price-cotton law increased industry profits, the Commerce Department's forecast of higher wages and lower prices had not materialized. "*This objective has been completely frustrated*," wrote Gardner Ackley, the chairman of the Council of Economic Advisers (CEA) (italics in original). Suspicion grew among White House aides that manufacturers were pocketing the industry subsidy the bill created, leading one aide to tell Johnson that the industry "no longer needs special help." At one point, contrary to calls for import quotas on textiles and apparel, one CEA member suggested the United States allow more imports, not fewer, to lower prices on consumer goods.[9]

In January 1966 the CEA reported that profit margins in the cotton textile industry, as measured by the spread between the cost of raw cotton and the price of cotton fabrics, increased 44 percent between mid-1964 and mid-1966, from 26 cents a pound to 38.75 cents a pound. The CEA also noted that a goal of the one-price cotton law, which reduced raw cotton prices by eight cents per pound in 1964 and another two cents in 1966, was to pass savings on to consumers. Later that month, Ackley confronted textile executives with the information in a meeting to discuss the state of the industry. When executives claimed strong demand had driven up prices, while industry benefits from the law were distributed through higher payrolls and greater capital investment, Ackley shot back that higher wages and greater investment had not cut significantly into mill profits and that textile manufacturers could have reduced prices by up to 20 percent without affecting profits. The disclosures, Ackley wrote, produced "a trace of embarrassment" among the executives in attendance.[10]

Despite government aid to the industry, the growth of textile and apparel imports was having a marked effect by the mid-1960s. The trade balance in textiles, for instance, had radically shifted. According to an industry group, the US textile industry in 1957 ran a trade surplus of $14 million. From there, the balance entered a deficit—from $36 million in 1958, it widened each year except for 1961, 1964, and 1967 until it reached $1.1 billion in 1968.[11]

Dramatic increases in synthetic textile imports, and the resumption of growth in cotton textile imports despite efforts to monitor international trade, forced textile labor and management to spend more energy on fighting imports. Yet this focus did not yield any broad, lasting alliance between management and labor—or even among the four textile and apparel unions—on the issue of slowing imports.

Uprising against Imports: The Kennedy Round Flap

As US negotiators made their way to Geneva, Switzerland, in late 1963 to negotiate the Kennedy Round of international trade agreements under the GATT, they knew they faced a daunting task in the challenge of textile and apparel imports. Developing nations were increasingly critical of the United States and other industrialized nations for using the LTA to restrict developing nations' textile and apparel exports and for failing to expand trade opportunities for less-developed countries. The US delegation realized that, with the growth in imports, especially in cotton textiles, it would have to be more circumspect in how it justified its restraints on imports and also it needed to encourage other developed nations to open up export markets for less-developed countries.[12]

Import growth continued to spell difficulty for the domestic textile industry. The improvement in the industry's fortunes masked high unemployment: in the first three quarters of 1963, unemployment rates in apparel (9.5%) and textiles (6.9%) both exceeded the national unemployment rate of 5.7 percent. Such high levels of joblessness also portended severe social and economic damage, as textile and apparel mills often represented a community's only source of factory employment.[13]

In addition to imports, mergers and consolidations were also wiping out jobs. Between 1947 and 1960, a Senate subcommittee reported, no fewer than 838 textile mills closed in the United States, throwing an estimated 229,000 employees out of work. During that period, employment in the textile industry fell by 440,000 workers, from 1.3 million in 1947 to 925,000 at the end of 1960. Industry employment plummeted 61 percent in New England, 47 percent in the Middle Atlantic states, and even 14 percent in the South.[14]

The consolidation continued in the 1960s with another 110 mergers and acquisitions, and executives expected the trend to continue. The remaining firms were more profitable and more productive. A textile firm in 1962 was 55 percent more productive than its counterpart a decade before, thanks to an increase in capital investment. Investment and economic recoveries after the recessions of the late 1950s drove industry profits higher: in 1957, all textile manufacturers recorded total profits of $248 million; by 1962, that figure had increased to $346 million.[15]

These rosy figures, however, obscured an ongoing crisis affecting the textile industry. After the textile industry hearings he chaired in 1958 and 1959, Senator John Pastore of Rhode Island would go on to lead a three-person Senate subcommittee, along with fellow Democrat Strom Thurmond of South Carolina and Republican Norris Cotton of New Hampshire, charged with studying problems in the domestic textile industry.[16]

The industry's increase in productivity and profitability masked several problems. Most of the gains in productivity came from lower employment after 1947. Some modernization had occurred, but the subcommittee found nearly two-thirds of the industry's machines were at least ten years old; more than one-fourth had been in operation for more than twenty years.[17]

Although the Senate committee blamed narrow profit margins and outdated depreciation schedules for the slow modernization, the implications were clear. The domestic textile industry, with a shrinking workforce and aging machinery, was trying to compete with nations that had rebuilt their textile sectors in the late 1940s and 1950s. Combining state-of-the-art machinery with wages that were a fraction of their US counterparts, nations like Japan, South Korea, Hong Kong, and Taiwan rapidly challenged US textile dominance. In 1948 imports equaled less than 1 percent of domestic cotton textile production, 1.7 percent of domestic wool textile production, and 1.2 percent of synthetic textile production. In 1960 imports had grown in all three categories to equal 8 percent of domestic cotton textile production, 5.4 percent of synthetic textiles, and 16 percent of wool textile production.[18]

The committee determined that the United States was "rapidly approaching a major turning point in the domestic textile industry" as more countries produced textiles for export, with an eye on the US market. In a call that inspired decades of protectionist action by labor and business, the committee recommended that the United States impose quotas on textile imports by country and category of textile goods. The imports the committee envisioned would be flexible, allowing import levels to increase as the domestic market grew.[19]

While other nations were building and retooling their textile sectors, the pace of mergers and consolidations among their US counterparts was more reflective of a maturing sector than a growing one. The changes sometimes even caught workers and union officials off guard. Such was the case in May 1965, when investor Warren Buffett acquired the Berkshire Hathaway textile chain, prompting Chairman Seabury Stanton's sudden resignation. The swift takeover surprised TWUA officials, who had been negotiating wage increases for Berkshire Hathaway workers in the company's headquarters of New Bedford, Massachusetts. "What is Buffet [*sic*] Enterprises? Is it a producing company, or a liquidating company?" TWUA's New Bedford joint board manager, George Carignan, asked in a hastily written letter to TWUA President William Pollock.[20]

Carignan's final question hinted at a practice that had occurred previously in New England—the rise of a conglomerate. Textron, which got its start as a Boston textile firm in 1923, became an industrial conglomerate in the 1940s. It produced parachutes for the war effort, then, after the war, shifted to domestic production, manufacturing a range of consumer goods such as lingerie and blouses. Yet Textron also contributed to the textile decline in New England in the early postwar period through closing and liquidating factories it deemed unprofitable. Like Textron, Berkshire Hathaway under Buffett would repeat the practice in the years after 1965, eliminating thousands of jobs.

Unlike Textron, though, Buffett's takeover of Berkshire Hathaway marked the rise of a new phase of capitalism in which conglomerates spread across business sectors and expanded their international reach. As some manufacturers struggled to compete with increasing imports using outdated equipment, Buffett used the cash reserves of the Berkshire Hathaway textile firm to branch into insurance, publishing, railroads, real estate, and basic materials.[21] Along the way, the conglomerate gathered massive amounts of capital to further extend its reach, driving explosive growth in its stock price. By May 11, 2015—fifty years after Carignan's frantic letter—one share of Berkshire Hathaway that Buffett first purchased for $7.50 in December 1962 had been transformed into one of the company's famous class A shares, closing at $219,550.[22]

Such shifts in corporate philosophy as personified by Buffett and the conglomerate model illustrated a new capitalist order that textile workers, their unions, and the industry began to face in the 1960s. The industry's increasing profitability didn't guarantee its survival. Instead, it made the industry attractive to financiers like Buffett, who could purchase the companies and use their cash reserves and profitable operations to generate capital to fuel more mergers and acquisitions. Another such textile manufacturer that would become a target in this new environment was Cannon Mills, the North Carolina producer of towels and bed linens. By 1967, Cannon's 21,100 employees made it the nation's fourth-largest textile manufacturer by employment, behind Burlington Mills, J. P. Stevens, and Deering-Milliken. Cannon boasted a 1967 after-tax profit of $13.8 million and a net worth of more than $200 million.[23] Cannon's profitability and net worth soon made the company ripe for takeovers by financiers who wanted access to its assets rather than its products.

The changes also pushed textile companies, especially privately held ones, into an arena where their operations were more likely to be directed by demands from the financial world than from families or tightly knit boards. Decisions once centralized and made by company chairmen in New Bedford and Kannapolis and Spartanburg were increasingly influenced and driven by events on (and demands from) Wall Street. The rise of conglomerates like Berkshire Hathaway, and the increasing globalization of textiles and garment manufacturing, together injected another degree of uncertainty into both industries.

The growing ethnic and racial diversity of the two industries also was a change to note in this period. A growing number of Puerto Ricans, African Americans, and Chinese workers were coming into the garment industry, supplanting ethnic Eastern Europeans, Italians, and native-born white Americans.[24] After the passage of the 1964 Civil Rights Act, and at the direction of the EEOC, textile companies finally began to hire African Americans in large numbers, adding to a workforce that included ethnic and native-born whites, Jews, Italians, and Eastern Europeans. Such changes increasingly diversified a workforce in which women were a majority in both industries. The dominance of women, and the growing ethnic and racial diversity in the industries, stood in direct contrast to the leadership of the four textile and apparel unions, which was dominated by men of ethnic European or native-born heritage.

But job discrimination against some groups, especially African Americans, still existed. "We have gone to these plants and Beg them to give us a Job *But* they say no oping [*sic*], come back later," a group of eighteen African American women from Calhoun, Georgia, wrote in a 1968 letter to Johnson, naming fifteen companies that had refused to hire them for two years. "Please send somebody down here to look into this Matter Before Some thing *bad* start to happen Down here. We are tire [*sic*] of Runing around for Nothing." A handwritten notation on the letter suggests the matter was referred to the EEOC.[25]

The Johnson administration and its trade negotiators were well aware of the opposition to lower tariffs in the textile and apparel industries, as well as the objections of less-developed countries over trade policy. In this environment, the administration sought to navigate a position between the two opposing forces, reflecting a policy from 1962, during early discussions of the LTA, when US negotiators sought to give other nations tariff reductions in exchange for extending its provisions to other exporting nations.[26]

The Johnson administration approached the Kennedy Round with the intention of using lower tariffs to not only promote trade but also shift "toward a system of trade preferences for less developed countries in the markets of the advanced nations" and in the process improve their trade prospects and encourage economic development. US negotiators intended to use their power under the TEA to reduce tariffs by as much as 50 percent, acknowledging they would need to demonstrate "a willingness to withstand domestic pressures."[27]

In the three years of negotiations for the Kennedy Round, from May 1964 to May 1967, cotton textiles were one of the most difficult sectors to navigate, alongside steel and chemicals.[28] By March 1967, negotiators were hurrying to finalize and ratify an agreement by the end of June, when Johnson's authority to negotiate trade deals under the TEA expired.

For US textile and apparel interests aside from cotton textiles, negotiations did not yield all they requested. When LTA negotiations began in November 1966, the ATMI asked for a five-year extension of the agreement, with its provisions extending to wool and synthetic textiles. Negotiators reached an agreement in principle on the LTA in the spring of 1967 that extended the pact for only three years and did not include wool and synthetic fabrics.[29]

Another provision gave the United States power to negotiate bilateral agreements with textile-exporting countries, in the process limiting imports but allowing for growth in the market. In a nod to the power of the domestic textile and apparel industries, which was "almost frantic" that negotiations would yield a substantial tariff reduction, US negotiators did not push for a full 50 percent reduction on cotton textile tariffs. Instead, negotiators agreed to reduce tariffs by an average of 20 percent, in keeping with other importing countries, whose tariff reductions on textiles were lower than the 35 percent tariff cut extended to industrial products overall. Wool textiles were exempted from tariff reductions, synthetic textile tariffs were reduced by 13 percent; chemical textiles, which were not facing any significant import threat, received the full 50 percent tariff reduction.[30]

When negotiations concluded in May 1967, negotiators had produced an agreement that reduced duties on roughly $8 billion worth of US industrial and agricultural exports. In exchange, the United States would reduce tariff levels on a similar volume of its imports.[31] Industries that had been stung by foreign competition, however—textiles, chemicals, steel, glass, and certain other industries—did not support the lower tariff levels set by the Kennedy Round and opposed the proposed agreement, claiming the United States had failed to remove other nontariff barriers that blocked US exports' access to foreign markets. The ATMI, through a spokesman, said the Kennedy Round would harm the industry because of "the virtual tripling of imports into this country since the Kennedy round talks began."[32]

Johnson signed the Kennedy Round agreement on June 30, 1967, mere hours before his negotiating authority lapsed. By then, the president was facing a backlash from industries, workers, and members of Congress angry at the tariff cuts in the agreement. Industry dissatisfaction with the Kennedy Round and its new tariff reductions drove a protectionist sentiment in Congress. No fewer than eighteen import-quota bills were introduced, a result of frustration with Johnson over the Kennedy Round deal and the Vietnam War; political maneuvering as members of Congress sought to position themselves favorably for the 1968 elections; and labor-industry cooperation in the steel industry. In 1967 the USWA ended its support of free trade and joined with much of the steel industry in calling for quotas to protect the industry from imports. Members of Congress introduced bills to impose import quotas on textiles, steel, chemicals, electronics, meat, dairy products, lead, zinc, and even mink skins.[33]

The import-protection bill with the widest scope came from Representative John Dent, a labor-friendly Pennsylvania Democrat. He introduced a highly popular bill that would allow the president to impose quotas on imports or raise tariffs on goods if the Labor Department determined that US workers were injured by imports that had been produced under conditions banned by the FLSA. It also allowed the president to waive minimum-wage requirements in industries affected by imports. It passed the House on an overwhelming 340–29 vote in September 1967 and became a target for opposition by exporters and supporters of free trade. It eventually died in a Senate committee.[34]

Several other bills addressed textile-import quotas, including three cosponsored by Republican Senator Edward Brooke of Massachusetts; another would establish textile-import quotas by statute.[35] But the most popular import-quota bill dealing with textiles came from Ernest F. "Fritz" Hollings and sixty-seven of his Senate colleagues. That bill sought to reduce imports of cotton, wool, and synthetic fibers from 2.7 billion square yards per year to 1.7 billion square yards per year. Senator Vance Hartke, an Indiana Democrat, sponsored another popular import-quota bill, which sought to tie steel imports to a fixed percentage of recent steel consumption in the United States.[36]

One article, in summarizing the larger import-quota bills before Congress that year, highlighted the growing divide over trade within the labor movement: "The AFL-CIO has consistently stood for freer trade and against protectionism although it is embarrassed currently by some of its constituent unions—particularly in steel, textiles and stone and clay products—who are beating the drums for protectionism." But protectionism was part of a larger, and more troubling, shift confronting the AFL-CIO leadership. Shortly after the 1966 midterm elections, the federation's Committee on Political Education commissioned a study of several thousand members in about a dozen AFL-CIO unions. The survey found diminishing support for unions among its own membership and also found that labor leadership and the rank and file were growing apart. Leaders were concerned about economic issues like expanding unemployment insurance and increasing the minimum wage and about social issues like fighting racial discrimination, but union members' concerns—taxes, crime, housing integration, and maintaining property values—had "a surprisingly 'conservative' cast"; some workers even expressed reservations about disclosing their union membership. The results so troubled Meany that he held the only full copy of the survey results, refusing to share it with other leaders within the federation.[37]

By October, Hartke and Senate Republican Leader Everett Dirksen of Illinois had combined several import-quota bills and were preparing to send the package through the Senate, setting the stage for a showdown with the White House. Members of Johnson's cabinet offered to testify in the administration's defense, and Secretary of State Dean Rusk also proposed a campaign in which senior administration officials spoke in favor of Johnson's trade policy. Rusk also envisioned "more visible and more vocal" support from leading exporters, importers, financiers, and shippers to "wake up the sleeping majority of American economic and political interests" whose futures might be jeopardized "if the more highly-organized minority of protectionist forces have the field to themselves."[38]

Rusk warned that import restrictions proposed in 1967 "pose a threat to our trade policy of an entirely different order of magnitude than we have had to face for many years." On steel and textiles alone, restrictions would affect 11 percent of total imports, nearly $3 billion total. "The combination of textile and steel pressures for trade restrictions, organized labor's disenchantment, and Congressional receptivity to pressure groups in an election-year adds up to an ominous conjecture," Rusk wrote. In addition to domestic dangers, such moves could encourage retaliation by trading partners while strengthening anti-US sentiment and forcing the United States to delay its proposed trade policy for less-developed countries "for a number of years."[39]

The ultimate goal of such a campaign, Rusk wrote, would be to show Congress that reversing its traditional trade policy "to placate one or more disaffected sectors" risked inflicting greater disapproval from a larger group of Americans who benefit from trade. "We also have to remind the Congress of the contribution of liberal trade policies to our own domestic prosperity."[40]

Johnson's exact response to Rusk's proposal is not known, but he was already at work to stop quota measures. The president was sympathetic to Hollings, who'd brought textile manufacturers to the Democrats' side in 1960 and faced a 1968 reelection campaign. But the president placed a roadblock in the path of Hollings's bill on October 4, when he and House Ways and Means Chairman Wilbur Mills, by previous agreement, asked the US Tariff Commission to conduct a study of the effect of imports on the textile and apparel industries. The Hollings bill came to a stop when Mills refused to hold hearings on any import-quota legislation, though Johnson would later say that "any action on textiles should await the results" of the Tariff Commission study.[41]

Later that month, Johnson dispatched Rusk and four other cabinet members to Capitol Hill in a single day to bat down the Dirksen-Hartke import quota package, arguing that protectionist measures would undercut the goal of expanding global trade. Johnson also bluntly laid down his marker on November 2: "I think those protectionist bills just must not become law," he told a convention of consumer groups in Washington. "And they're not going to become law as long as I am president." The declaration did stop most of the measures from moving through Congress, even as Dirksen asserted some import-quota bills would survive a veto. Johnson, true to his political nature, had already gathered dirt to use on import-quota supporters. In Dirksen's case, the White House used trade data to prepare talking points to show, if necessary, that Illinois stood to lose more from widespread trade restrictions than any other state.[42]

The White House succeeded in stopping the import-quota bills, but at a steep cost. The anger generated by the Kennedy Round agreement forced the Johnson administration to delay plans to renew the TEA. In renewing the TEA, the Johnson administration had also sought to help workers by easing Tariff Commission qualification criteria for workers and firms seeking TAA benefits. Five years after organized labor supported the TEA and the TAA program within it, the Tariff Commission had awarded no TAA benefits to workers or firms because the Tariff Commission used a strict criterion to determine eligibility. Applicants had to show that imports were the total and sole reason behind business closures or worker displacement to receive TAA benefits. In 1963 the Tariff Commission received and rejected the only case it received from the textile and apparel industries, a petition from a group of Alabama textile workers. By refusing to award TAA benefits to workers who had supported the program's creation, the Tariff Commission added to labor's frustrations at the results of its early 1960s support of lower trade barriers. The Johnson administration did introduce a TEA reauthorization bill in 1968, but it died in the House Ways and Means Committee.[43]

The backlash over the Kennedy Round also effectively ended a proposed major shift in US trade policy. After abiding by the most-favored-nation principle for nearly fifty years, the Johnson administration by the spring of 1967 was ready to propose a new system in which less-developed countries would have an advantage in world trade over developed nations.

The new trade policy would keep US exports going to Western Europe while addressing requests from more than one hundred poorer nations that wanted to boost their exports. It also sought to address and eliminate discrimination against poorer nations in trade, provide safeguards to US producers, and protect workers against injury. The State Department had also discussed the policy with "a number of key business, labor and public interest groups," including the US Chamber of Commerce, the National Association of Manufacturers, the AFL-CIO, the Council on Foreign Relations, the League of Women Voters, and the Brookings Institution. The AFL-CIO supported the plan with qualifications: all major developed countries should extend trading preferences to all developing countries; adequate safeguards should be offered to US workers; and the benefits of preferences given to developing countries should accrue to workers in those countries.[44]

The idea behind the proposal was to help poorer nations develop economically without disrupting the economies of wealthier nations. It also reflected a belief that new industries in less-developed countries, in general, were failing to compete with their more established counterparts in wealthier nations. And it was intended to respond to a growing dissatisfaction among less-developed countries with the most-favored-nation principle that fueled their dislike of trade policies developed through the GATT, which less-developed-country representatives felt put them at a disadvantage. Preferences for less-developed countries (in the form of immediate tariff cuts while tariff reductions were phased in for developed nations), sought to give poorer nations a head start toward free trade as developed nations pursued free trade "to the maximum extent possible." Between the summer of 1966 and February 1967, the US State Department solicited comment from senior administration officials to produce a new trade policy, which Johnson articulated at the Summit of the Americas, a gathering of the leaders of the Americas at Punta del Este, Uruguay, in April 1967.[45]

Despite the warm reception, the Johnson administration worried that the new plan to favor less-developed countries could lead to "possible injury to US industry and labor arising from increased imports from low-wage countries" and could require "additional safeguards and expanded adjustment assistance." While Johnson favored such efforts, he did not envision proposing new protections for labor or an expansion of TAA until 1968 or even early 1969—plans that were cut short on March 31, 1968, when Johnson, worn down by the Vietnam War, announced he would not seek reelection.[46]

An Urgent Need for Quotas: Labor Fights Textile Imports

After years of revitalization, a slight economic downturn in late 1966 and import growth renewed worries among textile workers and executives. "During a time when the economy is booming, we find ourselves out of work," the TWUA's Carignan declared in a letter to Johnson asking for "whatever corrective measures are needed" after Berkshire Hathaway, citing a lack of orders, announced a three-week shutdown over the last quarter of the year at its plants.[47] Berkshire Hathaway's president, Kenneth Chace, also wrote Johnson to mention one of the layoffs in October 1966, affecting 1,700 of the company's 2,300 workers, and urging action to limit textile imports.[48] TWUA locals in New Bedford, concerned about further job cuts at the city's last remaining large mill, sent twenty thousand postcards to the White House that fall urging action on imports, and the

New Bedford city council joined in with a December 1966 petition to Johnson urging import quotas.[49]

By early 1967, as imports continued their rapid increase and the downturn continued, the White House began to receive more resolutions and petitions urging import limits, higher tariffs, and additional help for the industry. "Mr. President, we should not permit foreign countries to sell their yarns in these United States to the detriment of our own people," wrote a North Carolina attorney.[50] Various UTWA locals sent identical petitions to Johnson urging the federal government to impose import quotas by textile categories and countries of origin and to renew the LTA while extending its provisions to wool and synthetic textiles. "Our textile workers are anxious to work, but with mills gradually closing, due to the cheap textile imports flooding the market, we do not want to add *our* workers to the unemployment lines, or poverty hand-out lists!" wrote a UTWA official from Beacon, New York.[51] A Tennessee UTWA local official warned of rapid growth in synthetic textiles, especially from Japan. "It is not hard to imagine that unless the importation of man-made textiles is controlled, we can expect a flood that could engulf this segment of the textile industry."[52]

In April 1967 William Pollock testified before a House committee that imports, especially of synthetic textiles, "have been growing by leaps and bounds" while inventories grew, orders declined, and nearly fifty thousand workers were laid off, and others were put on reduced schedules in what Pollock called, for the industry, "the greatest crisis since the fifties." To Pollock, imports were a large part of the slowdown. In 1961 imports took less than 5 percent of the domestic market; by 1966, the proportion had exceeded 10 percent. He urged the federal government to take unilateral action to protect textile and apparel jobs.[53]

That summer, after the announcement of a deal in negotiations on the Kennedy Round, UTWA members continued to protest. At a southern regional UTWA meeting in Atlanta in August 1967, 150 UTWA delegates, representing thousands of workers from West Virginia to Alabama, expressed their disappointment with the Kennedy Round agreement and called for import quotas on each country exporting to the United States and all categories of textiles. After the Atlanta conference, North Carolina UTWA members collected twenty thousand signatures on petitions and letters to Johnson and Representative Roy Taylor, whose Asheville district formed the epicenter of the UTWA effort, renewing the call for extending the LTA to wool and synthetic fabrics with quotas keyed to country and category.[54]

By February 1967, with imports increasing and prospects unlikely for import quota legislation, the UTWA, the oldest and smallest of the four textile and apparel unions, began to sketch out an anti-import campaign that involved textile employers, public officials, and leading figures in textile-producing communities.

The campaign was driven by concerns that the LTA was failing to stop import growth. Also, the United States faced import competition in textiles and apparel from eighteen nations in which textile workers earned no more than two-thirds the wages of their US competitors.[55]

The UTWA, which represented the majority of synthetic textile workers, was also particularly concerned about the import limits established by the LTA. Because import limits covered only cloth and apparel containing more than 50 percent cotton, similar products containing up to 50 percent of cotton were not. The potential for damage to the textile industry from imported synthetic products was tremendous.[56]

The UTWA campaign against imports began to capture the attention of the AFL-CIO. In December 1967, at the federation's seventh constitutional convention, foreign trade was one of the topics on the agenda for the nearly 950 conferees in attendance. President Johnson and five members of his cabinet—Secretary of State Dean Rusk; Labor Secretary W. Willard Wirtz; Attorney General Ramsey Clark; John Gardner, the secretary of health, education, and welfare; and Transportation Secretary Alan Boyd—addressed the convention, and Meany spoke of a strong, effective labor movement that "constituted and will continue to constitute the vital main force of the progressive movement in America." Having gained 1.5 million dues payers since the 1965 convention to reach 14.3 million members, Meany said that at no time within his memory was the labor movement "better equipped and prepared to deal with its problems and responsibilities in society than is the case today."[57]

Neither the UTWA's concern about imports nor its urgent call for actions to fight them, spurred the AFL-CIO to apply its influence on trade issues. At its 1967 convention, the federation issued a resolution on international trade that stated imports were disrupting domestic markets and industries and imposed "severe hardships on thousands of American workers" as the volume of world trade surpassed the $200 billion mark in 1966. Furthermore, the AFL-CIO did not call for import quotas and omitted trade from a fourteen-point list of domestic priorities. It did, however, propose that the LTA be effectively enforced and expanded to cover wool and synthetic textiles and apparel.[58]

UTWA members were also asked to consider resolutions on imports several months later at its seventeenth convention, planned for Miami Beach in May 1968.[59] There, Baldanzi made imports the central part of his keynote speech, arguing that the flow of textile imports, valued at $1 billion and coming from Taiwan, South Korea, the Philippines, Hong Kong, Japan, and others threatened the viability of the $60 billion domestic textile industry.[60]

Imports could not only threaten hard-won labor standards but also undermine antipoverty efforts and the recent desegregation of the industry. African

American workers had largely been shut out of many southern textile mills until the 1960s. Thanks to increased demands for workers in the mid-1960s and EEOC enforcement, mills were hiring new workers, including a large number of African Americans for the first time. Import growth risked the jobs of these new workers as mills cut production. "When you hurt furniture, garments, toy and shoe industries, as well as textile industries, you wipe out opportunities for people on the borderline of poverty to develop their skills," Baldanzi said.[61]

The UTWA delegates passed a resolution calling for control of cotton textile and apparel imports through "firm enforcement" of the LTA and the expansion of the LTA to include woolen and synthetic fibers, fabrics, and apparel. The resolution also stated that its support of expanding trade was intended to "promote job security and improved working conditions here and abroad."[62]

Meanwhile, as textile and apparel unions struggled to put import controls on the domestic agenda, imports continued to grow. In late 1968 the US Commerce Department reported that textile imports in the first ten months of 1968 reached 2.758 billion square yards equivalent (SYE), a 27 percent increase over the same period in 1967, with increases in cotton and synthetic textiles also. The trends, according to ATMI President Harold Whitcomb, the board chairman of Fieldcrest Mills, meant the United States was "fast becoming a basic supplier of raw materials and a purchaser of the manufactured goods. If this policy continues there is no way in the world to keep from exporting American jobs."[63]

While manufacturers were expressing concern over the increase in imports, Baldanzi was warning textile and garment union workers from other countries of the threat imports posed to living standards and jobs in industrialized nations. "The financial interests on a world-wide basis are establishing productive facilities in developing countries and in countries such as Hong Kong, Taiwan, Korea, Portugal and Mexico," Baldanzi told the 1968 gathering in Berlin, West Germany, of the Congress of the ITGWF, representing more than 3 million textile and garment workers in fifty-five affiliated unions in thirty-four countries. His remarks found support from international representatives, including those from Western European textile and garment unions. The ITGWF resolved to increase organizing efforts in less-developed nations, including new regional branches in Africa to monitor expanded textile production in Nigeria and Uganda.[64]

The 1968 Election: End of the Textile-Democratic Coalition

In January 1968 the Tariff Commission issued its report on the textile and apparel industries. Despite the worries of executives, workers, and elected officials about the growth of imports, the Tariff Commission found both the textile and the apparel industries relatively healthy amid an expanding domestic economy and a wave of industry consolidation stretching back to 1954. While individual companies might be affected by import competition, the Tariff Commission concluded that, as a whole, the textile and apparel industries were strong.[65]

Even after accounting for the slowdown in late 1966 and early 1967 that reduced textile production by nearly 2.9 percent and apparel production by 5.2 percent, both industries were doing well overall. Under an index of production used by the Federal Reserve Board that set 1957–59 production levels at 100, the production index for the apparel industry stood at 146.1 by August 1967 and 141.2 for the textile industry in September 1967. Between 1961 and 1966, annual pretax profit in the industry more than doubled: for textile manufacturers, from $589 million to $1.27 billion; for apparel manufacturers, from $331 million to $740 million.[66] Profit margins increased by more than one-third for the industries after the one-price-cotton law was enacted and continued to increase into 1966, even with raw cotton prices increasing and labor increases of 10 percent in 1963–64 and 9 percent in 1965.[67]

While the commission acknowledged a rapid growth of imports in textile products and apparel since 1961, it stopped short of calling imports a threat to the two industries. The growth of textile imports was uneven and "varies according to the market conditions" for different products, while apparel imports were a matter of retailers and wholesalers seeking to diversify their product lines for consumers. "In relatively few instances do imports appear to have been a major factor," the commission declared.[68]

The commission attributed a significant growth in imports between 1965 and 1966, from 1.3 billion SYE to 1.8 billion SYE, to Vietnam War buildup that increased demands for both military procurement and domestic supplies. To meet needs, the federal government gave Portugal, Colombia, Spain, Israel, and Brazil one-time allowances to export more textiles and apparel to the United States. It also accepted imports from Mexico that were not controlled by the LTA.[69]

The Johnson administration had anticipated the study's conclusions would anger textile and apparel executives, who would see it as "a device to stall and evade" the import quotas they sought. The administration also had to contend with a veiled threat from the industry in November 1967 that domestic textile companies might build plants abroad to counter import growth. The Tariff Commission study also worried officials in organized labor; several weeks after the study was released, the TWUA's Carignan highlighted the closure of a Berkshire Hathaway plant in Warren, Rhode Island. "Again, we find that because of a lack of strict regulations 450 persons have lost the opportunity of earning their living," Carignan wrote, urging Johnson to sign quota legislation on textiles.[70]

With support for quota legislation still high, and the Hollings quota bill pending in Congress, Mills stepped into the fray once more. Speaking before textile workers at a Greenwood, South Carolina, rally, Mills said he did not like import quotas but pledged nonetheless to find a solution. "I was not made chairman of the Ways and Means Committee to preside over the destruction of U.S. industry, and I do not intend to see the U.S. textile industry go down the drain," he said.[71]

Johnson also had to contend with Vice President Hubert Humphrey, who, in the wake of Johnson's decision not to run for reelection, was considering his own run for the presidency. In the preceding year, Humphrey had also taken an interest in the import issue and the textile industry. He suggested the White House back a compromise textile import quota bill from Hollings and Mills to blunt Hollings's push for import quotas and to stop the textile industry from joining other industries on quota legislation. But the White House rejected Humphrey's suggestion, considering quota legislation a "bad precedent" that could encourage other industries to follow suit. "The Administration continues to be opposed to any form of import quota legislation," a White House aide stated in response to a supporter of Johnson's trade policy. Shortly thereafter, Hollings's textile quota bill—first proposed as a standalone bill but then offered as an amendment to a bill that would have renewed the TEA—died in Mills's committee, with Johnson's blessing. Mills would threaten to introduce another textile quota bill in the summer of 1968, but the immediate danger had passed.[72]

Johnson's opposition to import quotas, over the objections of textile and apparel companies, workers, unions, and local officials, as well as groups like the Committee for a National Trade Policy and the League of Women Voters, marked the end of nearly a decade of collaboration between the Kennedy-Johnson administrations and textile manufacturers. In July 1968 Myer Feldman, a former White House aide, relayed to a Johnson aide that "the textile industry feels the President has let them down, that they have not had a friend in the White House since Kennedy." While Feldman pledged to "do what he can to bring pressure on the southern Democrats" in the fall elections, the switch was already in motion. In June 1968 Thurmond, now a Republican, had already secured a promise from GOP candidate Richard Nixon to pursue import quotas.[73] In a mirror image of their activity in 1960 with Hollings for the Kennedy campaign, in 1968, textile executives, spurred by Thurmond, did their part to deliver the presidency to Nixon.

In just over five years as president, Johnson steered a difficult course and won the larger battle against a protectionist trade policy. But, in the process, the backlash from the Kennedy Round agreement cost him the authority to negotiate further trade agreements and a chance to help import-affected workers and firms. Business's and labor's anxiety over the lower tariffs and relaxed trade barriers the Kennedy Round brought, meanwhile, reflected a shift in public views on trade. Despite decades of support for free trade from elected officials, most businesses, and organized labor, the positive reaction to the import quota bills in 1967 demonstrated a growing unease among large swaths of the general public about import growth since the end of the 1950s. Public support for limits on imports, a move that would have sharply reversed the goal of the trade bill Kennedy had sought in 1962, was not compatible with the efforts by the Kennedy and Johnson administrations to use trade as an instrument of Cold War policy to thwart Soviet engagement with the world. Supporters of import quotas were more concerned with domestic economics than international affairs; for them, limiting imports reflected a belief that the postwar economic prosperity many in the United States had enjoyed since World War II was under siege, if not in outright danger.

Public Displays of Discontent: Labor Becomes Increasingly Vocal

In addition to petitions and lobbying, the UTWA had expanded its efforts to fight imports, working alongside (but not with) other textile and garment unions, such as the TWUA, the ILGWU, and the ACWA. By 1969, the ACWA's in-house publication, *The Advance*, was urging ACWA members, locals, and joint boards to call Nixon and their senators and representatives and send letters and resolutions to elected officials and their local newspapers urging action to reduce imports. "Rising imports threaten jobs and standards in the textile and apparel industry, which employs 2½ million people, many of them members of minority groups, women, and others who won't find it easy to find other jobs," the ACWA warned. "The result could be more people on welfare, rising taxes—all the things this nation is trying to avoid." With imports continuing to grow at increasing rates, Baldanzi said industry survival against imports, not "high wages and profits," was of greater importance. "No one can really escape this problem anymore," he said in June 1969. "It is so serious that all workers—union and nonunion—chambers of commerce, civic clubs and other community organizations in every mill town and city must join our fight to exist."[74]

The new round of globalization in the garment and textile industry had long concerned Jacob Potofsky, the longtime ACWA president. Potofsky, a Russian immigrant and pocket maker at Hart Schaffner and Marx in Chicago, was all of nineteen years old when he witnessed the birth of the ACWA on New York's Lower East Side in 1914. A manager of his local board, Potofsky rose through the ranks to become an aide to ACWA President Sidney Hillman, then president after Hillman's death in 1946. Potofsky had called attention to the increase in imports in the late 1950s; now, a decade later, the rise in imports brought him into the spotlight once more.

By 1967, the ACWA had embarked on a small campaign, holding informational pickets outside stores selling imported clothing. The idea was to make shoppers aware of the threat to domestic jobs posed by cheaper, imported clothing. The ACWA had gained notice for the benefits it secured for its workers: better workplace conditions; pension and health benefits; cooperative housing, and even banking. But import competition threatened decades of ACWA accomplishments. "Years of scowling at the accelerating rate of imported clothing and apparel has been in vain," *Men's Wear* wrote in a 1969 profile. "And like a modern Moses with a close-cropped stubble of white hair, clipped goatee and moustache, Potofsky sees an increasing need to lead the industry out of potential import bondage."[75]

The trade and daily press were noticing the new globalization and the consternation it was causing for labor, manufacturers, and retailers. "It is theoretically possible to walk into a major department store stark naked and walk out fully—and inexpensively—clothed without buying a single American-made item," the *Los Angeles Times* declared in 1969, listing a wardrobe that could include Taiwanese underwear, a shirt from Hong Kong, an Italian suit, and a necktie from Thailand. "The significance goes much deeper. To the consumer, it can mean lower prices. To the retailer, higher markups. To American manufacturers, increased competition. To American labor, a threat of lost jobs."[76]

Manufacturers were in a dilemma: if they joined their unionized workforces in an unsuccessful fight against imports, they could risk losing business to cheaper manufacturers or even closing down. Or they could manufacture goods overseas, make greater profits, and risk having a union-led educational campaign, complete with informational pickets, at their front door. Some attempted to make peace with the unions. In March 1969 the Clothing Manufacturers Association of the United States, a trade group, adopted a resolution calling for "the orderly marketing of imports by men's, young men's and boy's tailored clothing by setting quotas by category and by country."[77]

Retailers were much less conflicted than their suppliers; they saw imports as integral to having "the freest of markets where we can buy at the lowest prices for our customers." They argued that unions had been given relief from import competition in the form of the TAA through the TEA, even as they acknowledged TAA benefits had yet to be disbursed. By tying TAA to the trade bill, retailers effectively turned the program into a justification for increasing imports and thereby potentially reducing industry jobs. Their acknowledgment that assistance had not reached workers was underscored by the Johnson administration's refusal to put forth a trade bill in 1967, which ended an administration proposal to ease the criteria workers and companies needed to qualify for TAA (rather than imports as the sole cause of job losses, imports as a single factor in job losses). "The trouble in the past is that there have been too many delays," said William Burston, a vice president of the National Retail Merchants Association, referring to the difficulties in extending TAA to workers and firms. "We say the machinery should be speeded up."[78] Left unsaid, however, was the acknowledgment that retailers' opposition to import quotas also contributed to the delay in getting TAA assistance to workers and firms.

Japan had been the focal point of import competition, mainly because of the increase in imports from that nation, but retailers who were shopping around for better bargains on apparel were turning to other locations by the late 1960s. One Los Angeles department-store executive said that Japan was still a good place for bargains, but with wages and prices increasing there, Taiwan and Korea were "coming along."[79] Meanwhile, two fashion writers who had toured Japan, Taiwan, Hong Kong, Thailand, Indonesia, Australia, New Zealand, and the South Pacific reported that the apparel industry in that region were combining tremendous gains in style and low wages, posing a threat to domestic manufacturers:

> The Orient and the Pacific are Janus-like in the realm of apparel[,] . . . *taking the low road in costs and the high road in fashion*. . . . A quick look-in to eye-witness the garment manufacturing endeavors in these diverse countries verified that the prices paid the apparel workers made it impossible for U.S. firms to compete—with the inevitable result that Americans will continue to lose their jobs if textile imports are not drastically curbed. (italics in original)[80]

Style gains and wages as low as nine cents an hour in South Korea and Taiwan, versus the $3 hourly wage a garment worker could make in Los Angeles, were "threatening the very life of American apparel firms and the day-to-day jobs of tens of thousands of needlecraft workers in this country," the fashion writers reported. They suggested some limit on imports—whether through voluntary agreements or legislation—or "garment manufacturers and workers in America are going to be severely jolted."[81]

Such shocks were already rippling through the US clothing industry. Import quality was improving, in part through new technology, and in other cases as US manufacturers imposed on-site quality controls in overseas plants. ACWA Vice President Howard Samuel estimated that synthetic clothing imports increased by 400 percent for the first nine months of 1969 over 1968, and clothing imports overall, valued at $2 billion in 1967, had increased 60 percent since then.[82]

From his offices overlooking Union Square in Manhattan, Potofsky saw imports posing challenges to his union's North American membership. These challenges largely came from Asia and Europe. But along the US-Mexico frontier, the rise of the Border Industrialization Program, more broadly known as *maquiladoras*, offered a new threat to US apparel jobs.

Mexico began the Border Industrialization Program in 1965 to attract US industry to a zone along the US-Mexico border. In 1968 alone, the *maquiladora* program had attracted 66 plants to the zone—more than half the 125 plants that had arrived since its start. AFL-CIO officials estimated *maquiladoras* had attracted twenty thousand US jobs to Mexico, and labor officials such as Nat Goldfinger, the federation's chief economist, believed the number could grow much larger—to as high as three hundred thousand jobs within the coming three years. "This has been a partly experimental, partly operational program so far, but within a short time it could really explode into a very serious problem," he said.[83]

Maquiladoras imported machinery, raw materials, or components for manufacturing without tariffs or restrictions as long as the plant's entire output was exported. US manufacturers who set up in the *maquiladora* zone and exported their output to the United States, meanwhile, only paid tariffs on the value added to the goods in Mexico—roughly wage costs that ranged between 30 and 40 cents per hour, a fraction of the $1.60 hourly minimum wage and the average $3.10 hourly manufacturing wage in the United States. In addition to the wage differential, Item 807 of the US tariff schedule provided an exemption for clothing that consisted of American-manufactured components assembled abroad without being altered in appearance or "advanced in value or improved in condition." Both factors contributed to a clothing boom in the late 1960s in the *maquiladora* zone, and by 1968 at least one US clothing maker was negotiating to make boys' shirts in Mexico.[84]

Labor and business traded arguments about the border program. The US Chamber of Commerce claimed US unions helped move US businesses to Mexico because their efforts to raise the minimum wage in the 1960s were "nearly bankrupting so many businesses that rely on unskilled labor."[85] The AFL-CIO executive council, in turn, blamed "greedy businessmen" for exploiting Mexico's desire for industrialization and creating a system that exploited Mexican workers. Critics such as Potofsky, who once fought shirt manufacturers fleeing industrial cities for rural, nonunion shops in Pennsylvania and the South, saw in *maquiladoras* a new form of runaway shops where workers and factories migrated south into Mexico. They wanted laws to boost US tariffs on imports and clearly label the country of origin on products. The ILGWU criticized *maquiladoras* as part of the growth in imports of garments that threatened the domestic industry; AFL-CIO President Meany appointed an ad hoc executive council committee to study *maquiladoras*. The ACWA met with the Confederación de Trabajadores de México, Mexico's largest labor federation, with an eye toward having US and Mexican unions jointly organizing plants in the *maquiladora* zone and negotiating higher wages. Potofsky, who wrote Johnson that the border program "could seriously undermine much of what this nation has so laboriously achieved in building the highest standard of living the world has ever seen," also held out the prospect of boycotting or picketing stores selling goods made in Mexico. "We don't propose to sit idly by and see our hard-won union standards undermined by some chiselers who want to get by on cheap labor," he said.[86]

While textile and garment unions supported import quotas, other observers were not so quick to agree. Arthur Gutenberg, a management professor at the University of Southern California, said automation would cause jobs to disappear, making imports less of a problem. In areas like garment sewing, nearly 60 percent of the market was automated, and labor dislocation was highly unlikely because sewing jobs were disappearing, especially on the East Coast.[87]

Textile executives, meanwhile, were blaming imports as part of the reason behind textile company failures and warned that more businesses would close without definitive action. "It's been the same thing year after year, with nothing but promises and mounting casualties in the domestic textile field," said one executive. The Northern Textile Association, producers, and a joint statement by the ACWA, ILGWU, TWUA, and UTWA showed growing desperation for congressional action if negotiations to persuade Japan to limit textile exports to the United States failed.[88]

As imports grew throughout the 1960s, the four textile and apparel unions differed in their responses. The UTWA, representing workers in synthetic textiles, where imports were growing fastest, was the most vocal about competition. In contrast, the much larger TWUA raised a number of issues: addressing import competition, raising wages, enacting more effective labor laws, and the difficult task of organizing southern textile workers.

As fashion styles and trends changed rapidly, and the use of synthetic fabrics came to supplant or even replace cotton and wool, the ILGWU and the ACWA took note. The ACWA, in particular, seeing the growth and spread of new international competitors from Mexico, the Caribbean, and Asia, began to deploy informational pickets and communicated with unions in other countries to find solutions to import competition.

Taken together, these actions represented a step forward in the battle against increasing imports to the United States. While their actions did lead the AFL-CIO to question the wisdom of US trade policy in 1967, the federation did not go any further then. Even the essential question of whether the textile and apparel industries were in trouble was itself up for debate. In early 1968, as the Tariff Commission study was released, an internal Labor Department report conducted at the request of Vice President Hubert Humphrey found the textile and apparel industries in good shape. With 2.4 million employees in about 33,000 establishments, the industries employed high percentages of women and semiskilled workers. The industries were of critical importance to Appalachian communities, the Southeast, and areas in which labor surpluses existed. Women made up 44 percent of textile and 80 percent of apparel workers. Nonwhite workers made up 8 percent of textile workers and 11 percent of apparel workers, after a rapid increase between 1962 and 1966.[89]

While textile employment fell 25 percent between 1947 and 1966, much of the decline had occurred by 1958; between then and 1966, the industry had maintained a relatively stable employment level, with employment growing between 1963 and 1966. Meanwhile, apparel employment grew 21 percent between 1947 and 1966, with changing fashion trends and population shifts responsible for the increase.[90]

The same could not be said for the industry's unions, particularly in southern textiles, according to the internal Labor Department report. Just 14 percent of the South's 226,650 cotton textile workers were unionized in 1965. Only 9 percent of the region's 18,409 wool textile workers belonged to a union, as did just 1 percent of the 76,907 southern synthetic textile workers. The greatest concentration of southern unionized textile workers was among the 31,651 workers in the dyeing and finishing sector, of whom 26 percent were unionized in early 1966.[91] At this critical moment, when unions and industry were fighting growing imports, the decades-long failure to organize southern textiles would prevent any meaningful successes in that fight.

Conclusion

The mid-1960s initially offered hope that better times were at hand in an industry long known for its instability. Implementation of President Kennedy's seven-point plan, the end of subsidies for raw cotton exports that had disadvantaged US producers, and greater demand for goods as US involvement in Vietnam deepened all contributed to a small boom of profitability in that period. Increasing consolidation and exposure to financiers like Warren Buffett held out the prospect that the industry would be swept into a modern conglomerate era.

But these changes existed alongside persistent evidence of an industry in crisis. The domestic textile industry was more productive but shrinking. Increases in textile workers' wages were slow and losing ground in comparison with their manufacturing sector counterparts, exposing how low unionization rates in the textile industry—particularly in the South—consigned workers to low wages. Mergers created larger firms, and the seven-point plan encouraged widespread modernization, but US textile manufacturers now competed with newly retooled foreign competitors, like Japan, who could always beat the Americans on labor costs. Meanwhile, other textile sectors were developing in nations with wages even lower than Japan's. In apparel, the continued development of a global apparel market posed additional challenges to domestic manufacturers, and the rise of Mexico's *maquiladora* program placed low-wage competition much closer to the United States than before.

Efforts to maintain the viability of the textile and apparel industries initially succeeded in strengthening an industry that had been troubled before World War II and that was showing signs of weakness again by the late 1950s. But demands for similar assistance to other industry segments then arose. The advantages given to the textile industry exposed serious general domestic and international divisions over trade. US workers, executives, and politicians repeatedly demanded protectionist measures that Johnson rebuffed, in part because of fears of retaliation by trading partners and growing backlash from less-developed countries, who felt they were being shut out of trading with the United States.

A sudden spurt in imports of cotton textiles in 1966 and 1967 coincided with increases in imports of other goods and the successful conclusion of the Kennedy Round of trade talks, leading to widespread calls from unions in a range of industries for import quotas on numerous products, including chemicals and steel, effectively forcing the Johnson administration to let its trade-negotiating authority expire and to shelve plans to implement its policy for less-developed countries. By the end of the Johnson presidency, textile manufacturers who played a key role in Kennedy's and Johnson's elections were now supporting Richard Nixon, and organized labor was beginning to question more earnestly the benefits of the trade policy the United States had followed since the 1930s.

Although far less visible than Vietnam and civil rights, trade was a defining issue for the Johnson presidency. In helping preserve jobs for the nation's largest manufacturing sector, he could not contain a conflict over imports that eventually took away a significant source of political support. He hoped to continue the tradition of lowering trade barriers by producing a new trade policy to aid less-developed countries, but he was overwhelmed by a backlash that erupted over the signing of the Kennedy Round of trade talks. Instead of a new trade policy, Johnson left office having lost the political support of executives and labor leaders, especially those in the textile and apparel industries, as they reevaluated the usefulness of the trade policy that the United States had been following for more than three decades.

As the nation's longest economic expansion to that point slowed to a stop in late 1969, US trade policy was at a crossroads. While the AFL-CIO continued to express its support of lower trade barriers, unions such as the ACWA and UTWA became more vocal in calling for import restrictions, in direct contrast to the federation's leadership. Textile and apparel unions, in addition to demanding controls on imports, also saw a need to give their workers and industries a chance to compete in a global marketplace. They saw protection of the textile and apparel industries as a way to preserve jobs for unskilled and low-skilled workers, offer manufacturing jobs to a diversifying workforce, and contribute to the economic vitality of communities and regions. Having seen the results of import competition after World War II—and in the spirit of those workers earlier in the twentieth century who questioned lowering tariffs—textile and apparel unions by the late 1960s were uniquely positioned to warn organized labor and the US public of the negative effects of the current trade policy and to fight for change.

6

FIGHTING TO WIN

Organized Labor and the Battle to Shape Trade Policy, 1969–70

In 1967 public dissatisfaction with the results of the Kennedy Round of negotiations combined with worries of greater import competition to spur a new skepticism about trade policy. But it did not lead to any new laws, as the attempts to pass import quota bills over Lyndon Johnson's objection show. Likewise, the increase in skepticism failed to shift the AFL-CIO's support of trade policy, despite demands from textile and apparel unions for greater import protections. Undaunted, unions continued to sound the alarm about the dangers of increases in imports to their industries, jobs, and communities. Seeking to educate the general public on the danger imports represented to their industries and workers, the ACWA began holding public demonstrations to warn consumers against buying imported goods.

Beginning in 1969 and continuing for years thereafter, nationwide import demonstrations at last forced the AFL-CIO to reconsider its long-standing support of trade policy, ushering in a period of rapid change by the federation on this issue. The protests dovetailed with efforts by incoming President Richard Nixon to make good on his August 1968 campaign promise to aid the textile industry; he had vowed to "effectively administer" the LTA and extend it to wool, synthetic, and blended textile products, which negotiators under President Johnson had failed to accomplish.[1] Whereas the events of previous decades highlighted the weakening and erosion of worker security, the late 1960s marked some slight reversal of fortunes: organized labor, feeling the pressure from unions in the needle trades and other industries under assault from imports, challenged the outcomes of US trade policy and began to examine labor's support of it. As workers in the textile and apparel industries vowed to protect their jobs, trade received renewed public scrutiny and protests gained momentum, putting pressure on the Nixon administration and Congress to intervene on imports.

The efforts of textile and apparel unions in this period to raise public awareness of import competition and to demand import quotas offers a glimpse, however brief, of what might have been possible had labor organizers throughout the twentieth century succeeded in organizing southern textile and apparel workers. The unions' efforts also illustrate the limitations of those southern organizing failures: protests did take place in the South, but most occurred in the Northeast, in the Midwest, and on the West Coast.

The trade protests, starting in 1967 by the UTWA and ACWA, branched out to the ILGWU and the TWUA by 1969 and 1970. To be sure, they were overshadowed by the staggering number of events in that tumultuous era: the Vietnam War, urban rebellion, the assassinations of Martin Luther King Jr. and Robert F. Kennedy, the violent protests accompanying the 1968 Democratic National Convention in Chicago, and, finally, Nixon's triumph on a law-and-order platform appealing to public fear about the direction of US society and the public's demands for less dissent.

Yet the debate on import competition, while obscured, was significant in its own right: the unease about trade policy expressed by leaders in import-sensitive industries like textiles, steel, and electronics finally moved the leadership of US organized labor away from categorizing the debate as a simple difference of opinion on trade and toward advocating a new trade policy that did not jeopardize swaths of the national economy. In doing so, the federation started a transformation of its views of trade that, by the mid-1970s, resembled its contemporary philosophy on the issue. After decades of being ignored or marginalized within the AFL-CIO, the shift finally gave voice to textile and apparel unions that had long warned of the negative effects of trade.

"We Do Not Intend to Surrender": The ACWA Informational Pickets

From the late 1950s, the ACWA had monitored the increases in imported clothing from Asia and Latin America. It had sought remedies in its 1961 boycott targeting imported cloth, and President Kennedy's response demonstrated the union's strength and capacity to take its message to the halls of power. By the end of the 1960s, the ACWA sought to educate the general public about imports through a campaign targeting retailers who sold imported clothing. It would build on a limited series of protests that some ACWA members had carried out in 1967.[2]

The ACWA educational campaign began on May 19, 1969, in midtown Manhattan. The union's first target was the flagship of Ohrbach's, a moderate-price department store, on West Thirty-Fourth Street across from the Empire State

Building. Members of ACWA's Union Label Department and its New York Joint Board crowded the sidewalks, handing out leaflets and gathering signatures on petitions. Others carried signs with messages for consumers: "Attention to the Public: Do Not Buy Imported Clothing Sold at Ohrbach's. Foreign made goods undermine the standards of the New York Joint Board."[3]

The ACWA's newspaper, *The Advance*, mixed denunciations of the rapidly increasing imports of garments and fabric with patriotic overtones, appeals to the union's history, and exhortations for further protest. "What was once a trickle that caused no alarm has become a flood that threatens our jobs; this flood threatens the very existence of an important American industry," read an editorial. "We have successfully fought the sweat shop here at home. We do not intend to surrender to this evil from overseas."[4]

Because Japan and Hong Kong were sources of much of the imported clothing and textiles, the fervor of the cause inspired racist charges and anti-Asian stereotypes. A picket at Shillito's department store in Cincinnati, for instance, featured ACWA members "dressed in coolie hats, robes and Chinese masks."[5]

Originally targeted on major cities, the ACWA campaign spread across the country after *The Advance* devoted a June 1969 issue to a special report on the threat imports posed to garment and textile jobs.[6] The following month, six thousand ACWA members from Fall River and New Bedford, Massachusetts, by mutual agreement between labor and management, participated in a two-and-a-half-hour work stoppage. Workers left their jobs to attend a rally in the Lincoln Park Ballroom in nearby North Dartmouth, where they asked the Nixon administration to limit apparel and textile imports. "Apparel imports from low-wage countries now are threatening our hard-earned American standard of living," ACWA New England director Joseph Salerno told the gathering, estimating that the textile industry had lost more than two hundred thousand jobs to import competition.[7]

In Ohio, members of the ACWA Cleveland Joint Board held informational pickets in July 1969, winning shoppers' sympathies and gathering petition signatures. At one store, police were called to disperse picketers. The arriving officers, however, met with "firm but polite resistance" from picketers who refused to leave, and the protest concluded without incident.[8]

As the educational campaign unfolded, the ACWA also kept the issue in the public view through political actions. In June 1969 Baltimore ACWA representatives Bessie McCullough, Helen Getz, and Rita Petti delivered to the White House and the Japanese embassy petitions with tens of thousands of signatures—by some counts as high as one hundred fifty thousand—from ACWA workers in New York City, Chicago, Los Angeles, Philadelphia, and Baltimore.

The petitions asked Japan to agree to voluntarily reduce its apparel exports to the United States. The ACWA also placed advertisements in the *New York Times* and the *Washington Post* asking the Japanese foreign minister to agree to regulation of textile imports entering the United States. The advertisements, recalling the US aid sent to help Japan recover after World War II, warned the growth of Japanese imports could cause US plant shutdowns and long stretches of unemployment for low-skilled workers. The advertisement warned that import quotas were possible unless Japan made a voluntary agreement to limit imports.[9]

In June 1969 Baldanzi, the ACWA's Jacob Potofsky, ILGWU President Louis Stulberg, and Sol Stetin, the TWUA secretary-treasurer, met with Commerce Secretary Maurice Stans after he completed a tour of Southeast Asia to learn of imports from the region. After a discussion with the four labor leaders on issues including trade and imports, Stans pledged to fight for the domestic industry but offered no specific commitments.[10]

The ACWA was not the only union in this period to carry out import protests. In May 1969 the UTWA's George Baldanzi rejected a request from Minoru Takita, the president of the Japanese Federation of Textile Workers (JFTW),

Three members of the Amalgamated Clothing Workers of America from Baltimore (left to right)—Bessie McCullough, Helen Getz, and Rita Petti—deliver petitions to White House deputy counsel Peter Flannigan urging reductions on apparel imports from Japan, 1969. (From *AFL-CIO News*, June 7, 1969. George Meany Memorial AFL-CIO Archives, University of Maryland–College Park.)

to support a JFTW resolution questioning whether the United States should limit textile imports. The resolution also asked the UTWA to oppose extending LTA provisions to synthetic and woolen textiles. "Our Union has made no secret of our position in this field," Baldanzi wrote in response. "Our support of world trade in textiles stops short of permitting any country to undermine our standards and threaten to destroy thousands of jobs through competition, which is based upon human exploitation." Baldanzi suggested that, rather than expecting the United States "to absorb an abnormal amount of imports," Japan needed to build its market "by increasing the standards of your own people so that they can be consumers as well as producers."[11]

Potofsky, the ACWA president, weighed in at the White House, arguing that slowing imports was as important as finding jobs for the unemployed. "Since our government is bending so much of its effort to augmenting job opportunities for the disadvantaged, it appears to us that everything possible should be done to make sure that rising import levels do not undermine existing job opportunities for the disadvantaged in an industry such as apparel manufacturing," he wrote.[12] Nixon responded on June 11 with a four-sentence letter that offered vague support for the textile unions' position. "The working future of those millions of Americans involved in the textile and apparel industry cannot be jeopardized," Nixon wrote. In a phrase that signaled backing away from his 1968 promise to Thurmond to enforce the LTA, Nixon promised to "work for solutions that will bring about the orderly flow of imports in the textile market."[13]

The ACWA would return to Capitol Hill later in the year; in September, fourteen members of the Chicago joint board visited Washington, speaking with Democratic members of the Illinois congressional delegation and bringing petitions containing twenty thousand signatures urging voluntary import curbs. The joint board also enlisted Esther Peterson, a longtime labor leader who headed the US Women's Bureau and served in the Kennedy and Johnson administrations, to aid their effort.[14]

Nixon's June statement of support for textile and apparel unions did not dispel those unions' growing concern about Nixon's proposal to use voluntary trade restrictions to regulate international trade. Events through the summer of 1969 appeared to validate their worries, especially as discussions with the Japanese bogged down. Potofsky and ILGWU President Louis Stulberg had already warned Stans on May 8 that, if negotiators could not reach a voluntary agreement with Japan to limit textile imports, the unions would urge Congress to pass import quota legislation.[15] After a meeting with the Japanese foreign minister on June 3, Stans said he believed the United States and Japan would resolve the issue and that they would explore it further in a Tokyo ministerial meeting later that summer that included Secretary of State William Rogers. Stans indicated he would continue efforts to negotiate voluntary agreements with Japan or open multilateral negotiations with other large textile-exporting nations to limit imports. If both options failed, Stans said he would be open to import quota legislation. His approach squared with one reporter's observations that a shift on trade was occurring within the labor movement: while labor was committed to free trade at least in theory, unions also wanted a slower flow of imports and spoke of mutually protecting US trade partners against "imperiled work opportunities and work standards."[16]

With little concrete evidence of support for import limitations from the Nixon administration, textile and apparel unions planned to continue anti-import campaigns. At a UTWA Southern Regional Conference in Atlanta in July, Baldanzi said the four unions would picket major stores and companies in New York and Chicago to protest imports. Baldanzi also expressed gratitude at the administration's response. "We are optimistic that we might get relief in Washington," he said, "and we may get it because Government officials are being bombarded with letters about imports, and the Republicans certainly want to be reelected in 1970 and 1972."[17]

The 150 delegates at the Atlanta gathering also approved most of a three-point plan for textiles that Baldanzi proposed to Nixon in February. Delegates approved calls for import limits and a $2 hourly minimum wage but rejected a third suggestion: a UTWA-operated worker-training program. In a stark reminder of labor's long-standing failure to organize southern textile workers, delegates opted instead for an organizing drive in hopes of unionizing "millions of unorganized workers."[18]

The Southern Regional Conference came at a time when more members of Congress were expressing concerns about the danger of imports to the US economy. Members such as Democratic Representatives John Dent of Pennsylvania, James Burke of Massachusetts, Al Ulmann of Oregon, John Blatnik of Minnesota, and William Dodd Hathaway of Maine spoke on the House floor in mid-1969 about the threat of imports. House Ways and Means Chairman Wilbur Mills also spoke out on imports: "Imports are growing so much more than the domestic market that we must have a slowing of import growth if a healthy fiber and textile economy is to be maintained in this country," he said.[19]

If Stans could not reach a multilateral agreement to reduce imports by the fall of 1969, Mills said, "there is no alternative but for the Congress to legislate on this subject before the end of the present session." Such a measure would impose import restrictions on wool, synthetic, and blended textiles to preserve those industries. Mills also saw import restrictions as a way to preserve employment options for minority groups and residents of depressed rural areas and to promote sales of agricultural, chemical, and mechanical products used in producing textiles.[20]

On July 22, the day the Apollo 11 crew concluded their historic two-day sojourn on the moon's Sea of Tranquility and began their return flight to Earth, the four apparel and textile union leaders asked Japanese ambassador Takeso Shimoda for help in convening an international conference to produce a voluntary restriction of imports from Japan. The leaders envisioned an agreement that would apply the LTA provisions to synthetic fabrics and apparel, but no conference came to fruition.[21]

By August 2, the ACWA campaign reached one of its largest targets: the Chicago flagship of the Marshall Field department store chain. In a city with special historic significance to the ACWA, and where suit makers like Hart Schaffner and Marx and other garment manufacturers still operated, the ACWA warily eyed Field's for offering Italian-made suits to customers. In the words of Chicago joint board manager Murray Finley, Field's was also known as "the largest retail importer of [men's and boys' apparel] in Chicago."[22]

Nearly 450 ACWA members descended on Field's location on State Street in the Loop to protest sales of imported men's and boys' clothing. Among the picketers was a leggy model, Ingeborg Day, who was captured by a newspaper photographer wearing a man's suit jacket arranged for crowd-stopping effect and carrying a sign that read "I go for a guy in a union suit."[23] The action won support from the Chicago Federation of Labor but also the enmity of Field's officials. Clarence Gregg, a senior vice president, refused to pull imported clothing from the stores, saying that move would deprive its customers of the right to independently choose merchandise, and he suggested the ACWA contact federal agencies to deal with imports instead of picketing stores.[24]

Going International: Pushing US-Japan Negotiations

As the year progressed, textile and apparel unions continued their effort to push US and Japanese negotiators, as well as their labor counterparts in Japan, to reach an agreement on limiting Japanese textile imports. In September 1969, as US and Japanese officials prepared to negotiate import levels, the ACWA, ILGWU, TWUA, and UTWA went on the offensive. As they did in May, the unions ran full-page advertisements in the *New York Times* and the *Washington Post* during the September 15–16 meeting in Washington.[25] The advertisements outlined the unions' arguments for voluntary import restrictions: a 439 percent increase in textile and apparel imports between 1958 and 1968; a 1,281 percent increase in synthetic and wool imports over the same period; 2.5 million US textile and apparel jobs at stake. A mutual agreement on textile imports, the unions argued, would help "prevent unemployment and business distress in the importing countries" as exporting nations "share the growth of domestic markets for textiles and apparel." Once again, the unions threatened to seek import quota legislation if no agreement was reached.[26]

The unions' advertisements did not find favor with some Japanese companies and unions, who expressed opposition in muted terms as discussions commenced.

"We question the wisdom of American union leaders in carrying out such a boycott," said an official for the Japanese Chemical Fibers Association. (The use of the term "boycott" exposed differences between American and Japanese labor representatives: while the ACWA saw their anti-import actions as part of an "educational campaign" to convince retailers and consumers to reject imports, Japanese labor officials saw these activities as a boycott.) Meanwhile, a minister with Japan's Ministry of International Trade and Industry simply characterized negotiations as being "in a very delicate stage."[27]

The JFTW urged discussions on imports between the AFL-CIO and the Japanese Confederation of Labor (Domei), of which the JFTW was an affiliate. The JFTW, too, said it would be disappointed if US unions implemented a boycott plan and said that it had proposed holding joint talks on imports in Hawaii with the ACWA, ILGWU, TWUA, and UTWA, only to be rejected.[28]

The unions' push also won the disapproval of the US State Department. A spokesman pointed out that the governments of the United States and Japan were holding discussions aimed at a "voluntary solution" to the import problem and that efforts by private groups, such as boycotts, were not welcome. "The Federal Government, rather than private groups, is responsible for assuring that foreign trade is not detrimental to our national interests," the spokesman said. The State Department's opposition ironically came the same day that the Commerce Department released figures underscoring the motivation for the import protest campaign: imports of synthetic-fiber textiles for the first seven months of 1969 totaled 898 million SYE, a 38 percent increase over the same period in 1968.[29]

The ACWA fired back. "I would say, in all candor, that in these matters the State Department is always likely to bring up the rear," said Howard Samuel, an ACWA vice president. "It is still motivated by the Cordell Hull kind of international trade theory, which was valid back in the 30s. The department is less aware of the economic problems that face our country. It really is inspired, almost entirely, by a desire to have a smooth and easy relationship with other countries." Samuel said the United States had become a target for imports the world over, and that imports of knitted sweaters, gloves, shirts, and slacks had cost two hundred thousand jobs in the textile and apparel industry since 1964.[30]

Turning the Ship: The AFL-CIO and Its Historic Positions on Trade

The work by textile and apparel unions to warn the public about imports finally began to show results with the rest of the AFL-CIO by 1969. Since the RTAA became law in 1934, unions in the AFL and, later, those in the CIO had voiced at least tacit support of US trade policy. In 1962 the AFL-CIO put forth its greatest support for lowering trade barriers in supporting Kennedy's TEA. That support was based in part on two principles. First, expanding trade would generate jobs for its constituent members and industries. Second, the United States, by building closer ties with its trading partners, could realize a Cold War goal of containing communism. The federation's support of international trade held through the 1965 biennial convention, when the AFL-CIO declared lower trade barriers would yield "a stronger U.S. in a stronger Free World" and urged lower trade barriers to preserve the nation's economic well-being.[31]

In its 1965 resolution on international trade, the AFL-CIO presciently proclaimed that trade would assume greater importance in coming years. "New problems of the 1960s have received too little consideration and study," the resolution read. "The question of U.S. investment abroad . . . needs realistic reassessment in relation to the balance-of-payments and the loss of jobs in the domestic economy."[32]

Delegates at the 1965 convention adopted a resolution that supported continuing the expansion of international trade but injected eleven conditions, including greater public and private efforts to expand exports; new criteria for relief under the TAA program; the development of international fair labor standards through multilateral negotiations; and the continuation of efforts to "work out multilateral international arrangements for the development of trade in industries highly sensitive to disruption by unfair competition," especially in other textile sectors not covered by the LTA. The resolution also called for identifying new efforts needed by 1967, when they anticipated a renewal of the TEA.[33]

By the time the AFL-CIO met in 1967, the tone on trade had indeed changed. The conclusion of the Kennedy Round had raised anger, and calls for import quotas came from unions in steel, glass, chemicals, and electronics. Suddenly, the AFL-CIO was pushed to defend its support of lower trade barriers, and trade supporters in labor were forced to reconcile that support with the effects of imports their counterparts in other industries were facing.

The federation's 1967 convention represented the beginning of a shift as delegates emphasized the need to police imports. While the total value of world trade approached $200 billion in 1966, of which the United States accounted for $30 billion in exports and $25 billion in imports, difficulties abounded. "Other nations have created or maintained barriers to trade, despite achievement of competitive prowess in world markets," read one convention resolution. "Major trading nations have established quotas, border taxes, variable levies and buy-national policies." The artificial barriers limited some US industries' exports. In other cases, barriers allowed foreign competitors to produce excess capacity, which they then tried to sell in the United States.[34]

The AFL-CIO resolution also highlighted the effects of imports on US industries and workers. "We cannot ignore the fact that rising imports have disrupted some domestic markets and resulted in adverse impacts on some industries," the resolution continued. While the nation's export surplus in 1967 had not substantially changed since 1960, the United States had become, in those years, a net importer of certain products, including steel, affecting thousands of industrial workers. Government and business policies had made the situation possible by accelerating the movement of private capital from the United States to other industrial nations and developing countries. The amount of capital invested abroad by US companies and private investors rose from $3.8 billion in 1960 to $8.7 billion in 1966, and US direct private investment abroad—typically less than $1 billion per year in the early 1950s—increased from $1.7 billion in 1960 to $3.5 billion in 1966.[35]

The AFL-CIO cited the STA and LTA, which limited cotton textile imports, and the Automotive Products Act of 1965, a free trade agreement between the United States and Canada that encouraged cross-border automobile manufacturing, as efforts in which the United States tried to promote international trade while preventing market disruptions. It called for expansion of trade that did not lend itself to "the promotion of private greed at public expense" or harming workers' wages or working conditions.[36]

Whereas the federation had included eleven suggestions for expanding international trade in 1965, it included sixteen in 1967, including efforts to fight nontariff barriers; investigation of flows of US capital and effects on international trade; greater federal enforcement of antidumping, antitrust, and other laws that applied to unfair international trade competition; multilateral negotiations to develop international fair labor standards; adopting an "effective and workable" TAA program; and effective enforcement of the LTA while extending its provisions to wool and synthetic fibers.[37]

The breakthrough for unions in textiles and apparel, as well as in other import-sensitive industries, finally came in 1969 at the federation's convention in Atlantic City, New Jersey. After campaigns by textile and apparel unions, and widespread calls for import quotas on a broad range of goods, the 1969 convention marked a major change on the federation's view of trade policy, as well as its undivided support for lower trade barriers. The change to a Republican administration may have contributed, but the AFL-CIO's position was more a result of the concerns about trade and the economy raised by a collection of unions in industries besides textiles and apparel than about electoral politics. In addition to promising to take protectionist steps to help the textile industry, Nixon had also aided labor in 1969 by finally making it easier for the US Tariff Commission to certify workers and companies for TAA benefits. The move ended a seven-year stretch after enactment of the TEA during which no firms or workers won TAA benefits. With the new qualification criteria, the Tariff Commission would certify TAA petitions in eighty-one cases between December 1969 and June 1973, covering more than thirty-seven thousand workers in twenty-eight states. Most of the early successful petitions came from the shoe and footwear industry as well as television and radio manufacturers. Twenty-three TAA petitions came from the textile industry; six of them were approved.[38]

On October 6, Potofsky, Stulberg, Baldanzi, and Pollock joined with AFL-CIO President Meany and leaders of six other unions to describe the devastation of imports on their respective industries. Their comments reflected a sobering realization that the landscape for US workers had drastically shifted. US technology and know-how alike were no longer constrained within its borders; companies were not tethered to a sovereign nation but were multinational enterprises endowed with the ability to shift production and capital more quickly to low-cost areas and export US jobs in the process. Meany continued to defend the federation's historical support of expanded world trade, but he sounded a note of caution, adding that "this expansion must be regulated in some way that will protect the jobs and the standards of American workers from further exploitation overseas."[39]

Potofsky pointed out that the rapid growth in apparel imports happened in the course of just over a decade. While the Kennedy administration's negotiation of the STA and LTA for cotton textiles had helped, Potofsky called on Nixon to include synthetic textiles and apparel in the LTA. "It is important to our industry, for the price of failure is unemployment and the erosion of our standards," he said. "It is important to the country, for the price of failure is working people out of work, a large number of them having no skills and no place to go except on the welfare rolls."[40]

In 1958 Stulberg had said 5 percent of all garments were imported, but the proportion had reached 19 percent in 1968 and was on pace to hit 25 percent by 1969. Like Potofsky, Stulberg saw imports as a threat to the working standards the ILGWU had built. He ended with a criticism of the stalled negotiations with Japan: "We need some attention on this problem or we are going to find the culture of America being imported from Japan, as well as American jobs being washed out."[41]

Baldanzi mentioned the threat imports posed to the textile industry and connected it to federal desegregation efforts. Continued increases in imports would threaten the jobs of 2.5 million workers in 33,000 plants nationwide. The loss of these jobs to imports, he warned, would also "shut off, particularly in the South and urban centers, the growing opportunity for employment of blacks, Spanish-Americans and many other minority groups."[42]

Potofsky, Stulberg, Pollock, and Baldanzi repeated their request for efforts, like the ongoing US-Japan negotiations, aimed at reaching a voluntary agreement to limit imports. If that failed, they vowed to pursue "appropriate legislation to check the flow of imports to our shores." Even with the support the textile and apparel unions received from their AFL-CIO colleagues, discussion of trade and imports worried some AFL-CIO leaders that the internal dispute might threaten relationships with non-Communist labor movements abroad.[43]

A Washington newspaper columnist captured the intensity of the moment at the AFL-CIO convention: "Labor leaders listened passively to resolutions on foreign policy, the Vietnam war, civil rights, education and political action. But they came to life only in discussing a convention statement on international trade." Ten unions used floor time to discuss the effect of imports on their organizations and their members; time constraints kept six additional unions from participating. The resolution on foreign trade adopted by the 1969 convention marked the first time the AFL-CIO as an organization repudiated its unconditional support of US trade policy. The federation condemned what it called the "continuing deterioration of the U.S. position in world trade" and called for new trade policies. The resolution urged lawmakers to revise the TEA and update other trade laws to "clearly state the objective of protecting jobs and labor standards."[44]

Five Arguments for Reexamining Trade Policy

The campaign to curb import competition led textile and apparel unions to develop several arguments about the negative effects of foreign competition on workers, communities, and industries. Where supporters talked about lower trade barriers in terms of the potential for future growth and jobs, textile and apparel labor unions spoke about negative changes wrought by import competition. They also sought to portray industry preservation as a means of facilitating social and economic changes under way. They argued that aiding the industry would help the private sector complement government efforts to alleviate poverty or preserve blue-collar occupations that could help their workers, and new populations, move closer to a middle-class living. In doing so, unions developed five arguments in favor of protecting textile and apparel industries from further import competition:

"Fair trade, not free trade": The AFL-CIO began to use this argument in its 1969 shift on trade policy. The reasoning behind the argument did not represent a rejection of free trade. Instead, it signaled the federation's historic support of trade policy while acknowledging the negative impacts of trade in seeking a constructive solution. The major components of the argument reflected a desire to bridge the divide on trade among its constituent unions. The phrase offered a

nod of acknowledgment to unions and members in industries like textiles, steel, and electronics, who sought to limit imports, while preserving the federation's historic commitment to trade policy. The phrase also signaled its support of unions in industries that benefited from increases in trade, like Teamsters near the ports on both coasts. The argument represented the federation's new position on trade: keep the benefits but minimize its negative effects.

"Sweated" labor: This argument, generally put forth by ACWA President Potofsky, highlighted organized labor's historic role in the US garment industry to improve working conditions. Increased imports from nations placed domestic industry in direct competition with sweatshops in emerging nations without the protections offered by their American counterparts, threatening to undercut the historic and ongoing work by the ACWA and ILGWU of improving industry working conditions. The consumer played a role in this fight. By purchasing imported goods, their choices would support those newly developed textile sectors. hence the argument that "sweated" labor was undercutting American jobs and the informational pickets. While this argument typically applied more to garment factories than to textile mills, which were not "sweated," it is important to note that the definition of "sweatshop" was changing from its traditional definition of a workplace in which multiple workplace laws were violated. Over time, and influenced by factors such as neoliberal economics and immigration, "sweatshops" were redefined as mobile or temporary places in which workers could be profoundly exploited—all beyond the reach of laws to protect workers because those laws had not been updated to reflect new forms of abuse. The shifting definition of "sweatshop" offers another example of the disintegration of worker security following the New Deal.[45]

Preserving jobs for an increasingly diversified workforce: The UTWA's George Baldanzi put forth this argument in seeking protective measures to aid the industry. By the late 1960s, the textile industry was facing a concerted federal effort to integrate its workforce. The EEOC, created by the Civil Rights Act of 1964, responded to complaints of racial or sex discrimination in employment and sought to enforce equal opportunities in hiring and promotion in companies or industries with patterns of discrimination. Textiles, especially the southern branch of the industry, became one of the first industries the EEOC attempted to open in the 1960s—between 1962 and 1966, the proportion of African Americans in the textile industry rose from 4.8 percent to 8 percent. The textile industry was also segmented by gender. While women comprised nearly 45 percent of the textile workforce, women still held many of the lower-paying, low-skilled jobs and men held higher-level jobs or positions requiring technical training, such as loom fixers. In the garment industry, women comprised 80 percent of the workforce, while 11.1 percent were people of color, specifically African Americans and Latinos, with a growing presence in the workforce.[46] Here, too, labor unions sought to craft an argument that protecting the textile and apparel industry from imports would also protect sources of employment for women and people of color who were entering the industry.

By extension, this argument linked with the efforts by civil-rights groups to seek full employment policies for African Americans. In the last years of his life, Martin Luther King Jr. spoke of a "stage two" of the civil-rights movement that sought economic inclusion for poor people of all colors. A notable effort in this arena came in 1966—the proposed "freedom budget" from A. Philip Randolph and Bayard Rustin, with the help of Leon Keyserling, a former aide to President Franklin Roosevelt. The document envisioned spending $185 billion over ten years to improve infrastructure and the environment, provide better health care and education, and guarantee a living wage while providing full employment to counter job discrimination. The freedom budget was widely praised and supported by labor, clergy, and even some business groups. But it was issued during Lyndon Johnson's War on Poverty and escalation of the Vietnam War; consequently it received no political support in Congress.[47] While the freedom budget was intended to generate prosperity through public investment, efforts to protect the textile industry, proponents argued, would keep the private sector involved by maintaining jobs and opportunities for workers escaping poverty.

Wages not welfare: This argument, generally reflected on the protest signs that ACWA, ILGWU, and TWUA members carried on their informational pickets, reflected a benefit of protecting textile and apparel industries: keeping the industries from being overwhelmed by imports would prevent their collapse and would stave off higher government expenditures for unemployment insurance, welfare, and other public assistance. The phrase also reflected a dignity about work and sought to remind the public that their choices as consumers not only affected the vitality of these industries but also affected the social safety net their taxes helped support.

Preserving communities' vitality: Finally, the decentralized nature of the textile and apparel industry meant its unions represented members in numerous large population centers, such as New York, Chicago, Baltimore, Philadelphia, and Los Angeles. But workers were also found in small towns across the United States, from the West Coast through the Midwest, from the deep South through Appalachia and into New England. The geographic range of the industries provided a powerful incentive to politicians from city halls to Capitol Hill. Protecting the industry against imports, which threatened the jobs of union and nonunion workers alike, would also preserve local economies nationwide. The UTWA sought to seize on this connection, making this argument repeatedly before Congress and at union conventions.

As the debate over trade intensified within the labor movement, at the White House, in Congress, and among business leaders, textile and apparel unions would repeatedly use variations of such arguments to call for further import limits.

Where the AFL-CIO had discussed trade as an issue in its 1965 and 1967 conventions, the trend continued in 1969. That year, convention delegates adopted no fewer than nine resolutions dealing with the effect of international trade on domestic workers and industries. Aspects of these resolutions addressed the shortcomings of the TAA, the rise of the *maquiladora* system along the US-Mexico border, runaway flag shipping—the use of inadequately trained crews on substandard vessels by shipping companies to escape a nation's taxes and regulations—and the "dollar gap" calculation, under which foreign nations operating under the Bretton Woods system could accumulate dollars and exchange them for gold from US reserves.[48]

One of the longest resolutions concerned the use of US direct foreign investment, licensing arrangements, and patent agreements to effectively export US technology and jobs. Direct foreign investment by US companies had expanded from $3.8 billion in 1960 to $10.7 billion in 1968, creating a landscape in which US companies with international subsidiaries could "juggle production, employment, prices, profits, shipping, technology, patents and national currencies across boundary lines and oceans, to build world-wide concentrations of economic power in various industries."[49] The federation, concerned with the effect of using federal expenditures to develop technology—only to spend more money to address "adverse impacts on communities and job opportunities" when that technology was exported and then reimported by way of cheaper products that eliminated domestic jobs—called for the federal government to "adopt and put into effect measures to supervise and regulate the outflows of private American capital." Delegates also asked Congress to pass legislation to oversee the operations of US-based international companies and to repeal Section 807 and similar provisions of the US Tariff Code that set low tariffs on goods such as those produced through the *maquiladora* program.[50]

ILGWU delegates to the convention offered a resolution asking the federal government to check the relocation of US firms across the Mexican border; demanding a repeal of Section 807; and the passing of new laws to ensure that "every product assembled abroad be fully labeled as to the country of . . . assembly."[51] The ILGWU requests came as Mexican officials increasingly urged US garment firms to relocate in order to benefit from Mexican tariffs, tax inducements, and wages that delegates characterized as "appallingly low. . . . A Mexican worker after a day's toil barely receives what an American garment worker earns for a single hour's work." Between 1965 and 1968, the ILGWU reported, apparel imports from Mexico increased twentyfold, with imports in 1969 increasing at a rate nearly double that of 1968.[52]

Delegates and officials with the four textile and apparel unions filed a resolution stating their concern about the increase in imports. Total imports of textiles and apparel had increased 438 percent in the past decade, cotton product imports were up 235 percent, and wool and synthetic fibers had increased 1,281 percent. The increases threatened the 2.5 million workers in the textile and apparel industries and employment opportunities for a workforce increasingly composed of racial and ethnic minorities and reliant on jobs not requiring previous training or experience, as well as the "major or the only source of manufacturing employment" in far-flung communities. A separate resolution from the Illinois State AFL-CIO claimed that textile imports had displaced more than four hundred thousand jobs since 1964. And the AFL-CIO Industrial Union Department, in a further resolution, noted that textile imports more than doubled in four years—from 1.5 billion SYE in 1964 to 3.3 billion SYE in 1968. The negative balance of trade in textiles and apparel in 1968 alone cost the US economy more than $800 million.[53]

The textile and apparel union delegates' resolution repeated their request that import controls under the LTA be extended to wool and synthetic fibers. They asked for a further renewal of the LTA beyond its expiration in September 1970. Finally, they asked Congress to impose legislative import quotas on textiles and apparel if the Nixon administration could not obtain voluntary restrictions with other nations.[54]

The AFL-CIO's momentous shift on trade still generated a what-have-you-done-for-me-lately response from some quarters. "Although gratifying, it is a little surprising that labor has waited so long to take up arms against this sea of import troubles. Some of us have been pleading for a realistic trade policy, and saying the same things, for quite a few years," wrote a columnist for *Leather and Shoes*, who further characterized labor's slow response to trade problems as the result of an effective snow job by those who supported lower tariffs. "We have been shouted down by the internationalists in industry and banking, who have not hesitated to misrepresent our position as advocating a banning of imports and a 'turning back of the clock' on trade. . . . One can expect, and even hope[,] that with rising [unemployment] likely in the coming months, labor will become even more militant on the import problem."[55]

Raising "a Flag of Distress": New Actions against Imports

Although Meany and other labor leaders who supported the current trade policy proclaimed that the AFL-CIO was not embracing protectionism in seeking a reevaluation of the benefits and costs of trade, other labor leaders began to question the virtues of free trade at a time when imports were increasing in many manufacturing sectors and domestic manufacturing employment was declining. A new, more assertive labor militancy on trade was coming to the fore, building on several events: growing support for import quotas in response to the Kennedy Round agreement, the informational pickets by unions like the UTWA's and the ACWA's, and finally, the AFL-CIO shift.

The protests came at a time when unions in steel, chemicals, and electronics, under pressure from imports, began posing the same questions and arguments on trade that their contemporaries in the needle trades had made for years. Some union support of trade rested on the principle that it favored workers: as the worker is also a consumer, the theory went, imports kept prices down and guarded the worker's purchasing power. But an economic shift had occurred that left Americans scrambling to catch up: a growing number of managed economies worldwide encouraging exports and discouraging imports; greater US investments abroad; and a larger number of multinational companies. "Just as the boss in the front office has called for government to protect his plant from low-wage foreign competition, now labor in general is asking the same help to insulate jobs from the same threat," a reporter for the *Washington Post* observed in early 1970. Labor hostility to imports "has spread to glass, steel, shoes, ceramics and tile, maritime, meat processing, electrical equipment, electronics and many other industries."[56]

Import protests continued into the fall of 1969 while negotiations with the Japanese dragged on. On October 29, in Los Angeles, several thousand ACWA and ILGWU garment workers marched out of their factories and up to the May Company's downtown store at Eighth Street and Broadway, carrying signs with messages such as "Imports at May Co. Mean Lost Jobs for L.A. Apparel Workers" and "Attention Shoppers: Please Don't Buy Imported Clothing Sold at May Co." Demonstrators spent more than an hour in front of the store, passing out handbills, explaining the impact of imports from low-wage countries on their jobs and calling for protections.[57]

"How does a U.S. worker compete with sub-standard conditions?" asked Sam Schwartz, manager of the ILGWU's Los Angeles Dress and Sportswear Joint Board. "Can we go back to a standard of living that comparable to ours is practically abject slavery? . . . Establish controls and quotas so that there is equity and logic and sanity governing imports."[58] Harry Block, the manager of ACWA's Southern California Joint Board, encouraged federal action to limit imports in order to protect the nation's textile and apparel jobs.[59]

Amid the rising number of protests, the ACWA's General Executive Board weighed in. On November 19, the board called import competition a threat to the gains the union had achieved in its fifty-five years: a higher standard of living for workers, elimination of the sweatshop, and old age and illness protections. It also saw imports as a threat to an industry that was becoming a principal source of employment for minority, low-skill, and women workers, putting many at risk of going on welfare "at the very time that our country is making a determined and costly effort to provide jobs for those already on welfare." The board joined the chorus of labor voices asking for a reduction of imports through voluntary efforts or legislation and, while admitting Americans could not compete with workers earning as little as eight cents an hour, demanded concrete measures to prevent the destruction of the nation's textile and apparel industries.[60]

While warmly received in some quarters, the unions' campaign against imports also drew some objections. One Midwestern newspaper editorialized that efforts to limit imports could ultimately harm consumers by forcing them to pay higher prices to assist US manufacturers. While some US workers might benefit in the short term, the newspaper wrote, import quotas meant they stood to lose in the long run amid competition with low-wage workers.[61]

The spring of 1970 brought a renewed scrutiny of trade and more widespread import protests, as observers hoped for a positive outcome of the US-Japan negotiations. In March of that year, the AFL-CIO's Industrial Union Department hosted what it billed as the first conference of trade unionists to discuss world trade and its implications for the loss of US jobs. The Industrial Union Department's Special Conference on International Trade, held in Washington, came at a time when the Consumer Price Index for all items posted a 6.1 percent increase between 1968 and 1969, the largest twelve-month increase in inflation recorded since November 1951, during the Korean War.[62]

The Industrial Union Department conference occurred as John Pastore, the Rhode Island senator—whose hearings in the late 1950s and early 1960s documented import growth in textiles, urged federal action to aid the industry, and helped drive the push for import quotas—criticized the Nixon administration for lacking "a workable program to protect US industry and US jobs from low-wage imports." Pastore's comments, made at a Miami Beach, Florida, meeting of the National Board of the Coat and Suit Industry, a labor-management board for the industry, were responding to an administration bill intended to make it easier for workers and industries to qualify for TAA benefits, one of the measures the Johnson administration was forced to scrap in 1967 and 1968. Pastore said the TAA proposal was akin to "paying for embalming fluid after you're dead." Further, with textiles representing $1 billion of Japan's $1.5 billion trade surplus with the United States in 1969, Pastore suggested Nixon and federal agencies take stronger, proactive actions on imports, especially in getting Japan to voluntarily reduce its textile exports to the United States.[63]

The Industrial Union Department, which comprised approximately sixty international union affiliates, decided to hold its imports conference because "we thought it was about time that we took a fresh look at foreign trade as it affects the economy and its workers," said Industrial Union Department administrative director Jacob Clayman. "This is the first time that the trade union movement has raised the flag of distress on this issue but it is about time."[64]

Clayman cited several examples: a doubling of textile imports between 1965 and 1969; a nearly 50 percent increase in the value of electronics imports, from $1.3 billion in 1968 to $1.9 billion in 1969; shoe imports rising from 10 million pairs in 1966 to 176 million in 1968, and job losses in the glass, ceramics, steel, and automotive industries. Multinational corporations were another issue the conference intended to examine. While producing between $150 billion and $200 billion worth of goods in 1968, behind only the United States and the Soviet Union in terms of output, Clayman said their production did not benefit foreign workers through higher wages or domestic consumers through lower prices. Only producers and financiers were benefiting.[65]

The trade conference drew six hundred members from forty-five international unions, representing what the *Textile Challenger* called "almost a roll call of U.S. industry—steel, electronics, textiles, apparel, glass, shoes, pottery, meat processing, maritime and so on." AFL-CIO secretary-treasurer Lane Kirkland told attendees that imports were "a problem of the entire trade union movement—not just the problem of some workers. It's a problem of the entire U.S. and that's the way we intend to handle it."[66]

In his keynote address to the conference, I. W. Abel, both head of the Industrial Union Department and president of the USWA, said the challenge for the fight against imports was finding new answers in a new economic landscape, where the rise of new economies, capital flight, international sharing of technology, and multinational corporations had reshaped trade issues. It was no longer a question of free trade and protectionism. "You cannot cling to the trade practices of the past while utilizing all the technologies of the future," added Elizabeth Jager, the AFL-CIO's trade expert.[67]

AFL-CIO research director Nat Goldfinger also drew attention to the presence of the multinational corporation, calling it a special concern in tracking the export of US investments and jobs because such organizations were not tied to sovereign laws or national boundaries. Multinational corporations held about $100 billion in assets, with total annual sales exceeding that amount, and were responsible for about 25 percent of both exports and imports in the United States. Yet such trade, which Goldfinger believed included "the exporting of U.S. technology," was considered company transactions rather than international trade.[68]

A point of contention arose in the conference over protections for labor in the TEA. Richard Gardner, a professor at Columbia Law School who helped write the GATT, argued that an escape clause in the law gave US workers the protections they needed against imports. When he asked why the US labor movement did not use the clause, ILGWU research director Lazare Teper responded that the complex barriers to securing trade adjustment for workers amounted to "burial insurance"—in other words, the worker would only receive a benefit, nowhere near replacing the worker's lost income, long after the job was gone. In order to certify workers or companies for TAA, the Tariff Commission had to successfully find that rising import levels cost workers their jobs or injured firms, that imports were a major factor in causing unemployment or injury, and that rising imports were caused "in major part" by tariff cuts—the last being most difficult finding to reach. As a result, the Tariff Commission received only seven petitions for TAA benefits between 1962 and 1969 and rejected all seven, said Meyer Bernstein, the USWA's international affairs officer. The rejections, coming as imports increased through the 1960s, dried up support among labor for the very program it had conceived and fought to create. Even when the Tariff Commission in late 1969 adopted new criteria that made TAA certifications more likely, the results were not encouraging for labor. In granting TAA petitions in three separate cases involving about six hundred steelworkers in California and Pennsylvania, workers received fewer benefits than requested—a lump sum equivalent to 65 percent of their average weekly wage, minus any unemployment compensation they received.[69]

On the issue of trade policy, Howard Samuel of the ACWA argued that non-tariff barriers to trade that other nations were using against the United States—such as tax policies, foreign quotas, import licenses, national preference laws, and foreign exchange controls—also needed to be addressed. "Anyone who talks free trade today is no longer echoing the economic liberalism of Cordell Hull and the 1930s," he said. Samuel's observations reflected a new reality of trade in the late 1960s: the world had changed, and the United States no longer enjoyed the economic dominance it had experienced in the aftermath of World War II. If US industries were to remain viable, and workers employed, the nation's trade policy needed to reflect those changes.

Conferees suggested remedies to fight against imports, including labeling foreign products, revising tariff schedules, regulating foreign imports, enacting antidumping laws, regulating the export of capital, and more adequate TAA for US workers. Another suggestion was to adopt international fair labor standards, a goal of the ILO. Jager pointed out that problems in international trade would most likely be resolved by Congress and the White House.[70]

"It's Happening Too Late": The March 1970 Work Stoppage

As awareness of import competition grew, so did activism among textile and garment workers. Leaders and the rank and file of those unions continued to conduct informational picketing and distribute leaflets to customers at major retail outlets that sold imported textiles and clothing from low-wage countries. The unions also used British Prime Minister Harold Wilson's January 1970 visit to the United States to raise awareness to the challenge they faced on imports. Seizing on Hong Kong's colonial relationship with Great Britain, the unions sponsored advertisements in newspapers showing that imports from Hong Kong, where wages were about 27 cents an hour, had increased significantly between 1962 and 1969: 55 percent for cotton textile goods, 359 percent for woolen goods, and 2,353 percent for man-made and synthetic fibers. The ads urged Wilson to negotiate a reduction of Hong Kong's exports to ease the erosion of US textile and garment jobs.[71]

The unions' educational campaign of 1969 and 1970 against textile and apparel imports hit its high-water mark on March 19, when garment and textile workers engaged in one of the nation's largest labor protests. Across the country, two hundred thousand ACWA members walked off the job in an authorized work stoppage to hold import protest marches. The action "drew enthusiastic support and flowery oratory from governors, senators, state legislators and community leaders," the *Washington Post* reported in recounting the protests. "It was one of the most respectable strikes the nation has seen."[72] While workers were upbeat about taking action, others, such as a woman in Doylestown, Pennsylvania, wondered why it took so long. "It feels good to get out here and protest," she said. "But I'm afraid it's happening too late. This should have happened several years ago."[73]

The one-day nationwide work stoppage was part of the ACWA's continual call for restrictions on imports of textiles and apparel. Unlike work stoppages to highlight unfair labor practices, this one, occurring in locations where the union had contracts with manufacturers, was designed to focus attention on the increase of textile and apparel imports from Japan and other low-wage countries. While US workers earned an average of $2.30 an hour, the ACWA said their counterparts in Korea (7 cents an hour) and Japan (37 cents an hour) earned far less. The union also found low wages among garment makers in Spain (35 cents an hour) and Italy (54 cents an hour). Protests focused on Japanese imports because the country was responsible for much of the import growth in the 1960s and because it was the target of negotiations with the Nixon administration, although wages there were higher than in nations like South Korea.[74]

The ACWA held demonstrations in numerous cities nationwide, including Knoxville, Tennessee; Los Angeles; Atlanta; Baltimore; Chicago; and Pawtucket, Rhode Island. TWUA members joined the ACWA protests in at least two towns—Pawtucket and Manchester, New Hampshire. In New York, an estimated twenty-five thousand ACWA members—including shipping clerks, cutters, and sewing machine operators—marched a circuitous route in Manhattan that stretched between Fifteenth Street and the Garment District. Among

Key officers of the Amalgamated Clothing Workers of America, including ACWA President Jacob Potofsky (left) and ACWA Vice President Bessie Abramowitz Hillman (right) lead a mass march in New York City, March 20, 1970. An estimated 250,000 workers nationwide participated in marches to protest the growth of clothing imports and their threat to domestic apparel jobs. (Photo by Sam Reiss. ACTWU Photographs, Kheel Center for Labor-Management Documentation and Archives, Cornell University Library, Ithaca, New York.)

them were Potofsky; Bessie Abramowitz Hillman, an eighty-year-old ACWA vice president; and Louis Hollander, a seventy-two-year-old manager of the New York Joint Board; all had been among the ACWA organizers at its founding in 1914. The rise in imports, particularly from Japan, had made the nation a target for sharp criticism and defiance from protest participants. "We will not permit Japan to commit another Pearl Harbor in the clothing industry," Hollander said during the march.[75]

Such nationalistic sentiment, whether directed at Japan or at low-wage nations in general, was also reflected in the Baltimore protest march, combining the argument for import controls with the larger societal anxiety that Americans felt at that time about foreign competition. As marchers proceeded down Baltimore Street, a photographer captured two women bearing protest signs. The first sign

Clothing workers march in the New York import protest parade, March 20, 1970. (Photo by Sam Reiss. ACTWU Photographs, Kheel Center for Labor-Management Documentation and Archives, Cornell University Library, Ithaca, New York.)

reflected the more immediate need for low-skilled workers facing job loss from foreign competition: "This is my job. This is my country. This is the only trade I know." The second sign conveyed both a longstanding resentment of the nations whose exports were increasingly challenging US products and a perception that the import challenge was the end result of US efforts to lower trade barriers and build a new postwar order: "We rebuilt you. We fed you. We defend you. You want my job now."[76]

For the most part, marchers were focused on immediate concerns, such as receiving shorter work hours as imports reduced demand for their products. Maria Locada, a sewing machine operator in a Nineteenth Street shop in Manhattan, described erratic work schedules that combined a few days of work with one to two weeks of layoff. Such schedules made raising families and covering bills quite difficult. "The trouble is I work three days and then I'm off three weeks," said buttonhole worker Francisco Gonzales. "How do you take care of six kids

While the 1970 import protest marches offered workers an opportunity to take action, they also surfaced resentment, xenophobic stereotypes, and frustration over the postwar economic challenge the United States faced from other nations, as suggested by these Baltimore marchers' signs. (Photo by William Hotz, [Baltimore] *Evening Sun*, used by permission of Baltimore Sun Media. All rights reserved.)

in that kind of a job?" Added Brooklyn tailor James Greene, "People are losing their jobs because of the imports of cheap clothing, but the politicians don't do anything. Unless the growing problems of the working man are corrected, I'm afraid things are going to get out of hand."[77]

Rallies connected to the work stoppage attracted thousands of garment workers in other garment centers, such as Philadelphia. There, more than twenty-five thousand ACWA members, a significant proportion of them African American, joined mayor James H. J. Tate and other union leaders in a rally on Independence Mall. Union leaders claimed that imports of textiles from Japan, Korea, Taiwan, and Hong Kong had eliminated two hundred thousand jobs in the clothing industry, mainly among members of minority groups. "When they start laying people off, black and brown people are the first to go," said Bernie Dinkin, a business agent for ACWA Local 170 in Philadelphia. He warned that the low wages and prices that made imports attractive to consumers had led one Center City clothing manufacturer to close its shop, and he warned that more would likely follow. "I'll tell you right now that when we start walking the streets, Nixon is going to have hell to pay," Dinkin said. "About 50% of the members of our local are already working three- and four-day weeks because there's not enough work for them. The situation is desperate."[78]

Another Local 170 business agent, Eddie Davis, warned the Nixon administration to take action on imports to protect garment workers' jobs. "These are people who are already having a tough time making ends meet," Davis said. "These are mostly women with families making anywhere from $1.95 an hour to $4.50 an hour. This industry is the largest employer of minority people in Philadelphia, and we can't allow it to go down the drain."[79]

The health of the textile and apparel industries was of particular concern to its workforce, which was largely female and rapidly diversifying. Here, a group of African American ACWA members participate in a Philadelphia import protest march, ca. 1971. (Photo by Standard Photo Service Company, ACTWU Photographs, Kheel Center for Labor-Management Documentation and Archives, Cornell University Library, Ithaca, New York.)

In city after city, union members and politicians joined in rallies to call for protection against imports. Maryland Governor Martin Mandel and Baltimore Mayor Thomas J. D'Alessandro III spoke to an estimated 5,500 workers and ACWA international vice president Samuel Nocella told the Baltimore audience that suits manufactured in Taiwan could sell for $12.75 in the United States, slightly less than the $14 in labor costs alone to manufacture the suit domestically. In Chicago, Mayor Richard J. Daley joined roughly five thousand ACWA members at the Civic Center Plaza, where he echoed the union's call for regulating imports and noted that controlling imports would protect the jobs of workers in the city's clothing industry, including large numbers of minorities. Thomas Faul, the Chicago Federation of Labor secretary-treasurer, added his own condemnation of "the attack of low wage competition on the jobs of American workers."[80]

In San Francisco, industry executives also participated. The Clothing Manufacturers of America, a trade group for apparel makers, endorsed the ACWA campaign, and ATMI President Charles Meyers expressed his concern about the threat posed by low-cost imports. Although unions and textile manufacturers had not historically joined forces to fight imports, Meyers's statement was a signal that the two groups were beginning to see eye to eye on the issue of import competition.[81]

A 1970s Philadelphia import protest march takes ACWA members past Independence Hall. (Photo by Standard Photo Service Company, ACTWU Photographs, Kheel Center for Labor-Management Documentation and Archives, Cornell University Library, Ithaca, New York.)

The stoppage in Los Angeles was relatively small by comparison with the protests in New York, Chicago, Philadelphia, and Baltimore, involving about three thousand workers. But the *Los Angeles Times*, in its reporting of the ACWA protest, made clear—despite a glaring error—how aware the public was becoming of the shift the AFL-CIO was making on trade policy: "U.S. unions were once among the most ardent champions of free trade and low tariffs, and frequently denounced conservative manufacturers and politicians who were pressing for high tariff barriers to 'keep the foreigners out,'" it stated, ignoring labor support of high tariffs in some industries, including textiles and apparel, during the late nineteenth and early twentieth centuries. "Today, the unions officially support a broad interchange of goods around the world, but more and more of them are urging the erection of tariff barriers or some form of quotas to keep out foreign made products."[82]

A reporter for the *Wall Street Journal*, in documenting the ACWA demonstration, noted a call by the International Union of Electrical Workers for a cabinet-level agency to deal with international trade, shoe workers' picketing the White House over shoe import levels, and even calls from the Screen Actors Guild for subsidies to produce domestic films, and it reflected on the increasing urgency with which labor was viewing imports and trade: "After more than 30 years of strong support for US free trade policies, labor men have begun a major campaign to steer the nation onto a more protectionist course," he reported.[83]

For decades from the 1930s onward, textile and apparel unions had long been a voice in the wilderness on trade policy. Members of the rank and file, and some midlevel officials, had expressed concerns about imports, only to be countered by leaders in government, business, and even some of their labor counterparts extolling the benefits of free trade. In the process, textile and apparel unions' arguments about the downsides of trade policy were minimized or brushed aside. But by early 1970, workers and unions in other industrial sectors experienced similar import competition and joined textile and apparel workers in a growing chorus of voices challenging trade policy.

Enter the Chairman: Import Quotas Come to Capitol Hill

If the protests over imports generated optimism that import limits were imminent, stalled negotiations between the United States and Japan served to dash those hopes just as quickly. Through the spring of 1970, frustration mounted as negotiators failed to reach an agreement. Japan refused to agree to voluntary import quotas; to make matters worse, competing demands from US labor and business interests further strained talks. While US unions and the federal government wanted voluntary import curbs, domestic textile producers favored scrapping talks altogether; they wanted import quota legislation from Congress. They were opposed by Japanese textile unions and an ad hoc organization of roughly sixty US multinational corporations that called itself the Emergency Committee for American Trade (ECAT), which supported lower trade barriers.[84]

After months of discussion and more than a hundred meetings and negotiating sessions, Japan ended negotiations with the State Department in March 1970. Commerce Secretary Stans called the move a "negative reply" and a "major disappointment." The Nixon administration later announced it would not object if Congress took action to restrict textile exports. In this manner, Nixon could still take a step toward fulfilling his 1968 campaign promise to back a protectionist measure that could help the textile industry. While negotiations were under way, the administration had not written its own bill; now that the talks had collapsed, "there will have to be a legislative solution," an administration official said.[85] Congressional action also raised the potential for quotas or other restrictions on woolen and synthetic goods—which the UTWA's Baldanzi and other textile labor leaders had advocated—as well as restrictions on imports of cotton textiles and apparel to correct the shortcomings of enforcement of the LTA in managing the flow of textile imports.

With talks ended, Wilbur Mills—who had been described as "an old liberal trade advocate in the tradition of Cordell Hull who has battled the protectionist"—changed course. In 1967 and 1968, Mills had helped Lyndon Johnson by blocking import quota legislation; as recently as 1969, Mills had hoped for a negotiated agreement to limit textile imports, rather than legislation. But with negotiations ended, Mills introduced a trade bill, which he had proposed to UTWA delegates in Atlanta the previous summer, that would impose import quotas on textiles and shoes. The trade bill joined a crowded legislative agenda for Mills that included a major expansion of Social Security benefits and Nixon's Family Assistance Plan, an effort to provide a basic income to all Americans.[86]

At the time, the Commerce Department was officially noncommittal on a trade bill; it simply wanted to help domestic industries improve the rapidly eroding US balance-of-payments position, which had had a net surplus for the United States since 1893. Under pressure from the Americans to negotiate a deal limiting textile imports, the Japanese, by ending talks, essentially dared the United States to impose trade restrictions through legislation. With the introduction of the Mills bill, the Nixon administration hoped to use it as a club to lower some trade barriers against US exports imposed by the Japanese and the EEC.[87]

As Congress moved toward debating the Mills bill, the US textile and apparel industry again confronted signs of decline. In the first months of 1970, a trade publication reported, textile and apparel imports were rising at a faster rate: from 3.6 billion SYE in 1969, early trade data showed imports on pace to reach 4 billion SYE in 1970. Employment was dropping in the manufacturing sector that was, at once, the largest employer in the rural United States and in New York City. In the fifteen months since the start of 1969, employment in the textile and apparel industries was down 65,000 workers, to 1,395,000. Worse, textile employment was continuing to lag all US manufacturing. Between 1959 and 1969, overall industrial employment in the nation increased by 31.5 percent, eight times as high as in textiles. And while the US trade balance was still in surplus in 1970, the textile industry had run a trade deficit since 1957. Since 1959, the textile trade deficit had increased sevenfold, reaching $1.37 billion in 1969, with Japanese imports accounting for $540 million, or more than one-third of that year's deficit. Industry capital spending, which in the mid-1960s had risen sharply as a result of the seven-point plan, dropped 23 percent between 1966 and 1970, from $820 million to $630 million.[88]

By 1970, however, the Mills bill and the activism of the four textile and apparel unions offered a ray of hope for the textile and apparel industry and organized labor. After decades of supporting lower trade barriers, the US labor movement had finally, if painfully, begun to realize that trade was not a universal panacea and that, to survive, US workers needed to navigate a new global environment featuring the broad availability of technology, capital flight, and multinational corporations—all of which US corporations embraced widely in the postwar era. At this moment, after decades of being in the overwhelming minority on trade policy, textile and apparel unions were in the vanguard of helping save US industries from import competition. More important, they raised a salient point through their reminder that lowering trade barriers was not always beneficial. Trade had a downside, too—which politicians and business leaders tended to ignore unless confronted with the loss of jobs, companies, or tax revenue. Textile industry suffering drew attention to the need for policies to help workers, communities, and businesses affected by trade.

Textile and apparel unions had brought the downside of trade into the spotlight, spurred by their competition with imports produced by *maquiladoras* and foreign workers earning as little as 8 cents an hour and the refusal of industrializing nations like Japan to accede to US trade demands, and despite their differences with manufacturers and other unions. By mobilizing their members and the general public, they educated millions of Americans about the rising tide of imports and prodded them to think about the economic and social consequences of buying cheap garments manufactured by low-wage labor. As Congress prepared to debate the Mills bill, the unions' attitude on imports was reflected in a defiant declaration by the ACWA's General Executive Board: "We do not intend to permit the fruits of 55 years of struggle and sacrifice to be washed away; we bring to the struggle against imports the same determination and energy we brought to all the struggles of the past. And we intend to win."[89]

Conclusion

Between 1967 and 1970, the public demonstrations against imports by textile and apparel unions helped bring trade policy into the public consciousness more firmly. More important, their concerns, along with similar worries voiced by unions in other manufacturing sectors, finally convinced the AFL-CIO in 1969 to go beyond acknowledging a difference of opinion on trade. In that critical year, with trade deficits in the textile industry reaching $1 billion and the United States facing dwindling surpluses in its balance of trade, the federation finally began to rethink its decades-long support of Cordell Hull's philosophy of reciprocal trade. The federation agreed to reconsider its position and called for a trade policy that did not undermine domestic industries, an approach that fit well with calls for limiting imports of textiles, steel, electronics, pottery, and other goods.

Labor protests complemented ongoing efforts to ask Congress for import quota legislation, a call the Pastore Committee had made in the early 1960s. The demonstrations appeared to add to growing demands for protection of import-sensitive industries from unrestricted import competition. In addition, textile executives felt they had an ally in Richard Nixon, who, in 1968, in a move mirroring that of John F. Kennedy in 1960, had pledged to the textile industry to curb imports. Nixon's pledge helped shore up the southern vote for him, and he won support that thwarted George Wallace's 1968 independent presidential bid. Labor could also take heart in the 1970 decision by House Ways and Means Chairman Wilbur Mills to introduce an import quota bill after he had held up such legislation for several years. With public attention galvanized, organized labor rethinking its position on trade, and elected officials appearing to be receptive to some form of protection for US industry, textile and apparel labor continued what it believed would be a successful campaign to save the industry.

7

LABOR STRIKES OUT

The Mills Bill, Burke-Hartke, and the Trade Act of 1974

Nearly two decades after noticing increases in imports, and amid a growing trade deficit in textiles, the rising protests by textile and apparel unions drove a growing public awareness of the economic threat of imports. Their efforts finally convinced the AFL-CIO in 1969 to reconsider its unconditional support of the kind of trade policy the US had espoused since the 1930s—a policy that benefited farmers and exporting industries yet left other industries increasingly susceptible to foreign competition.

Encouraged by both the federation's shift and their protests, textile and apparel unions continued to press Congress and the Nixon administration for import quotas. Unions in import-sensitive industries saw the early 1970s as a brief window of opportunity, and they placed their hopes on two import-protection measures in Congress. But the window quickly closed in the face of opposition from multinational firms and an economic decline that forced Nixon to contemplate generating jobs through trade. The turnaround was quick: by 1974, workers who in 1970 had expected to secure protectionist legislation were instead fighting a new proposal to reduce trade barriers. Despite winning several pieces of major legislation in this period, labor's defeats on trade marked a continuation of the decline in the movement's influence in general, textile and apparel unions' influence in particular. Leaders in unions like the ACWA, ILGWU, TWUA, and UTWA had to contemplate how to maintain their relevance in an era of decreasing union density. The trade-issue defeats also ensured that the domestic textile and apparel industry would continue to decline, alongside other manufacturing sectors, and left them vulnerable to growing deindustrialization.

America's Changing Economic Landscape

The early 1970s marked the end of a quarter-century of overall—but not evenly distributed—prosperity after World War II. The administrations of Richard Nixon and Gerald Ford struggled with surging unemployment, budget deficits, and growing inflation that sapped the nation's economic vitality. In 1971 alone, Nixon abandoned fixed rates of currency exchange (established at the Bretton Woods Conference during World War II) to stop an outflow of dollars; imposed wage and price controls in an attempt to contain inflation; and devalued the dollar to make US exports more affordable. By the end of 1971, additional economic challenges were evident: the United States recorded its first overall trade deficit since 1888, and the annual domestic textile trade deficit widened, exceeding $2 billion for the first time.[1]

The economic decline of this period severely hampered Nixon's goal of realigning US presidential politics as a counter to the 1930s formation of the New Deal political coalition. In his 1968 presidential campaign, Nixon sought the support of southern textile executives, as he had unsuccessfully attempted in 1960. By June, Nixon had secured the support of South Carolina Senator Strom Thurmond, the onetime Democrat and 1948 state's rights presidential candidate who now stood poised to help the Republican Party make inroads in the South. While Thurmond already backed Nixon for his military and defense policies, Nixon had pledged to aid the textile industry, which represented 40 percent of South Carolina's manufacturing jobs, by promising to enforce the LTA and to seek voluntary restrictions on textile exports to the United States.[2]

Thurmond used Nixon's telegram to build GOP support in the region, effectively splintering the Democratic Party's conservative southern wing, which was expected to support former Alabama Governor George Wallace. (In a bit of irony, Wallace's campaign on the prosegregation American Independence Party ticket represented an updated version of Thurmond's 1948 candidacy.) By supporting Nixon, Thurmond also paved the way for southern textile executives to end their historic allegiance to Democrats and join the GOP. The political shift of southern textile executives, resistant to racial integration and wary of most government involvement, was a consequence of their unease with federal efforts to end racial discrimination in industry hiring.[3]

As Democrats fractured over issues of race, cultural politics, and the Vietnam War, Nixon had difficulties of his own in building a political coalition. The economy entered a recession in December 1969, and the nation's deteriorating trade position also revealed a loss of US dominance in the global economy. Confronted with inflation, high interest rates, tightening credit, stock market declines, and the fall of the dollar, Nixon had to scramble for answers or risk damaging his party's prospects in the 1970 midterm elections, not to mention his own reelection chances in 1972.[4]

Nixon's nominal support for free trade and his simultaneous push to negotiate a restriction of textile imports from Asia offered an example of how Nixon was often guided by political instinct rather than policy considerations. To complicate matters further, economic policy was not Nixon's strong suit, and he was not inclined to advocate for corporations, despite needing their political and financial support. His dislike of businessmen and Eastern elites often displayed his working-class California roots. Though he also ridiculed labor leaders—"they're short sighted, partisan, hate Nixon personally," he once said—Nixon admired labor leaders like George Meany for their perseverance, even though the AFL-CIO's backing of Hubert Humphrey nearly cost him the 1968 election.[5]

As previous presidents had realized, Nixon could not advocate textile import quotas without risking similar demands from other industries with stronger corporations and unions, such as steel. To avoid this particular danger, Nixon referred to protective measures for textiles as a "special case" needing attention. Politically, seeking protection for textiles was as lucrative as it was dangerous: it was an investment that, if successful, could increase Nixon's support in the South and splinter the New Deal political coalition by highlighting workers' economic interests. Instead of focusing on improving workers' conditions or organized labor's fortunes, Nixon intended to put workers' economic interests second to "their allegedly superior moral backbone and patriotic rectitude." In short, Nixon's labor agenda sought to drive a wedge between organized labor and the Democratic Party. Trade was one of the areas in which Nixon aimed to accomplish those aims. If Nixon could bring labor within his coalition and make gains in the South, his New Majority would be within reach.[6]

Simultaneously, Nixon's interest in imposing import quotas on textiles, starting with negotiations with Japan in 1969 at the behest of unions like the ACWA, would be joined by an influential member of Congress who toyed with—and briefly attempted—a 1972 presidential run: House Ways and Means Chairman Wilbur Mills. The Arkansas Democrat had long been considered a free trader and opposed to import quotas, but Mills's introduction of import quota legislation in 1970 represented a change of position that hinted at a play for the very southern and labor base Nixon sought. Mills would switch positions during his brief campaign on other issues, such as revenue sharing and increasing Social Security benefits while cutting the taxes that funded the program. Ultimately, the push for import quotas in 1970 was as much about a battle between a sitting president preparing for reelection and a committee chairman not afraid to use his power as it was a battle over globalization involving organized labor and multinational corporations.[7]

A Continuing Downward Spiral: The US Textile Industry

In addition to increasingly ominous conditions for the US economy, shakeouts continued to affect the US textile industry. The (New York) *Daily News Record* reported in 1971 that New England lost forty textile mills to closure the previous two years, one of the largest waves of closures the industry had sustained in the region. In the South, at least fifty textile mills closed during the same period. Combined, the closures eliminated more than one hundred thousand jobs. One of the largest New England closures came in New Bedford, Massachusetts. Four years after TWUA officials were surprised by Warren Buffett's 1965 takeover of Berkshire Hathaway, the company closed its box loom division in New Bedford, eliminating 1,100 jobs. Another company shuttering New England plants in 1970 was West Point Pepperell, which eliminated 900 jobs in closing a sheeting division in Biddleford, Maine. Meanwhile, J. P. Stevens and Company eliminated 1,608 jobs at plants in Tilton and Franklin, New Hampshire, and in the Massachusetts cities of Dracut, North Andover, Easthampton, Littleton, and Lowell.[8]

The growing economic instability inspired textile and apparel unions and their allies to fight back. On three occasions between 1970 and 1974, they joined fights in Congress over trade legislation. The first came in 1970, when they backed the Mills bill, which aimed to impose quotas on certain imports, including textiles, over opposition from multinational corporations and other supporters of lower trade barriers. The second came in 1972 and 1973, over a bill by Representative James Burke and Senator Vance Hartke that would have lowered import levels for manufactured goods, including textiles. Finally, textile and apparel trade unions joined much of organized labor in opposing the Trade Act of 1974, which granted the Executive Branch fast-track authority to negotiate multilateral trade agreements. The Trade Act marked a watershed for the AFL-CIO, which before 1969 proclaimed a full-throated defense of US open-trade policy. By 1974, it was opposing the Trade Act—the first time the federation opposed a measure to lower trade barriers. Coming at a time of greater public consternation about imports and the erosion of US jobs and wages, the unions drew public support from concerned allies and opposition from supporters of lower trade barriers in government and business.

Organized labor's push to reevaluate trade policy and fight further efforts to lower trade barriers showed the degree to which concerns about foreign trade had captured the nation's imagination as more people became affected. The actions of textile and apparel workers in seeking protectionist measures in the 1960s and 1970s showed that they, too, were "at the center of the New Deal compact between capital and labor" as well as "the economic crises and reconstructions of the 1970s and 1980s," as Judith Stein described in her analysis of the domestic steel industry and its role in civil rights, economic change, and the decline of New Deal political coalition. Yet labor's failure to transform that public awareness about import competition into new policies that would help protect industries from imports illustrated the movement's political weakness at a time when service and financial sectors had supplanted manufacturing in economic importance. Ironically, the failures to stop measures to lower trade barriers occurred as organized labor secured advancements in health and economic security for more US workers.[9]

The conflict between Cold War and economic goals evident in helping other nations reconstruct their steel manufacturing sectors and encouraging steel imports to maintain vital and strategic US alliances also played out in the textile industry, if on a less prominent scale. Also, the protectionist fights of the 1970s show that the New Deal political coalition, damaged by the strains of civil-rights issues and Vietnam, was further unraveled by the domestic effects of foreign policy and trade—an observation in line with Stein's argument that New Deal liberalism died "because Democratic elites did not devise a modernization project compatible with the interests of their working-class base."[10]

Many of the sins Stein attributed to late 1970s Democrats in Congress and the administration of President Jimmy Carter can also be visited on the administrations of Gerald Ford and Richard Nixon. Both Nixon and Ford vowed to fight inflation and promote balanced budgets and, to the chagrin and opposition of most segments of organized labor, promoted growth through lower trade barriers. For Nixon, however, a growing economy would prove secondary to early 1970s austerity policies intended to control inflation.[11]

The growing corporate resistance in the 1970s to organized labor's push for protectionism aligns with sociologist Mark Mizruchi's observation that business elites were in the midst of a decades-long transformation in which an interest in issues of importance to their firms—especially the weakening of labor and lower regulation—replaced interest and involvement in any role addressing societal needs.[12] But another force was emerging in the debate over trade. Multinational corporations, many American-based but with international operations, joined to block the effort by unions and allied individuals to counter the effects of imports and capital mobility on US industry and jobs.[13]

Seen one way, the push by multinationals can be interpreted as support for the international trade regime that had been in place during the postwar era. More likely, its timing places the corporate response to the battle between free trade and protectionism at the point of an important shift of business behavior. In the period of turmoil and transition that marked the 1970s and 1980s, the long-standing willingness of business elites to act as moderate entities willing to engage organized labor on some level (an assertion that excludes a significant swath of domestic textile and apparel manufacturers) and display some form of leadership and vision on societal problems—even if it was driven by motives other than altruism or civic-mindedness—was giving way. Over time, as corporations became more powerful, they were increasingly more likely to focus on their own needs than to exercise their power to address community or societal problems.[14]

The growth of corporate power, and the manner in which companies wielded it, eventually overwhelmed the voice of labor—yet another consequence of unions' weakened state after the New Deal. The near-total control of operations acquired by southern textile manufacturers and runaway apparel companies in shutting out unions offered a prototype for the use of power by US corporations. The rise of corporate power and decline in workers' power—all indicated by Taft-Hartley, the weakness of the NLRB, and a business climate in which fines for labor law violations and court cases over labor rights were seen as the cost of shutting out unions—further transformed an increasing number of businesses into global entities detached from their local roots and in which workers had virtually no power.

The Mills Bill: Labor's Import Campaign Reaches Capitol Hill

Fresh off the March 1970 work stoppage that put two hundred thousand apparel workers into city streets nationwide, the ACWA leadership felt confident. Textile and apparel unions had the attention of the US public; politicians in Washington, after years of labor protest on imports, were taking up the unions' mantle and talking of imposing import quotas on textiles and clothing. Heartened by these developments, the ACWA hinted more was to come. The stoppage and educational campaign were "from every point of view an outstanding success," ACWA President Jacob Potofsky and Secretary-Treasurer Frank Rosenblum reported to the ACWA General Executive Board in April 1970. "The work stoppage must be not the end but the beginning of an intensified program of activities to obtain the kind of security against imports that we need." Both Potofsky and Rosenblum promised to continue their consumer education campaigns and add a legislative campaign for import quotas. Shortly thereafter, Mills introduced a bill that would impose import quotas on textiles, apparel, and footwear starting January 1, 1971. While heartening to labor, significant opposition was already building. The chief international economist, in a letter to Federal Reserve Chairman Arthur Burns, warned that the Mills bill, if enacted, "would be the most important backward step in post–World War II industrial policy."[15]

As promised, ACWA members repeatedly voiced their opposition to imports over the course of the year. At the ACWA convention in Atlantic City that May, some of the fifteen hundred delegates staged demonstrations during proceedings in support of resolutions on trade, at one point halting proceedings for ten minutes. They circled the floor with placards reading "Save Our Jobs," "Don't Import Unemployment," "We Want Wages Not Welfare," and "Bring Back Our Boys, Not Ready-Made Clothes"—a reference to the ACWA's decision to oppose the Nixon administration's policy in Vietnam and Cambodia, in a break with Meany and the AFL-CIO leadership. In a reprise of the threatened 1961 boycott, the ACWA authorized its members to stop cutting Japanese cloth if textile import regulation failed. "If Congress won't act, we are going to stop cutting Japanese textiles," thundered ACWA Vice President Murray J. Finley. Later that year, the ACWA eyed an expanded "vigorous anti-import campaign" aimed at the nation's leading department stores and considered a program of political pressure against members of Congress who were reluctant to support the Mills bill. By the end of the year, ACWA members would shadow a nationwide tour of a Korean garment trade show and set up informational pickets about low-wage apparel from Los Angeles to New York. The defiance was reflected in a speech by ACWA Vice President Sam Nocella, who raised more economic nationalistic sentiments by calling Japan a nation that "has decided to invade the clothing industry of the U.S." Describing the futility of negotiations with the Japanese, Nocella said, "After trying for five years to get a voluntary agreement with the Government of Japan, which is the principal importer or exporter into this country, we have failed, and we now have to do something else. . . . I am wondering who won the war anyhow, us or Japan."[16]

When hearings began on the Mills bill (H.R. 16920) in May 1970, the ACWA, ILGWU, TWUA, and UTWA offered testimony describing the increase in competition and requesting import quotas. Although other US industries, such as pottery, steel, and electronics, faced import competition, Mills—who had introduced the bill with an eye toward a 1972 presidential bid—originally limited the import quotas to textiles, apparel, and footwear. The maneuver served as a direct overture to labor and voters in New England, the Mid-Atlantic, and the South aligned with those particular industries. It also reflected the reluctance of Mills, who had long supported free trade, to offer broader protections for a wider range of industries.

A survey by the ACWA showing imports of all products to be regulated by the Mills bill climbed between the first half of 1969 and the first half of 1970. Imports of suits and sport coats increased 71 percent, from 1.4 million in the first half of 1969 to 2.4 million in the first six months of 1970. Imports of trousers increased 5.9 percent overall, but the increase was more pronounced for wool trousers (57.8%) and synthetic fabrics (23.29%). Shirt imports increased 42.2 percent during the first half of 1970, the ACWA found, adding that imports displaced as many as 250,000 domestic textile and apparel workers.[17]

A particularly impassioned plea for the bill came from the UTWA's George Baldanzi, who described a trade crisis in need of a "fundamental overhaul of U.S. trade policy."[18] Baldanzi argued that US trade policy and import competition were both "escalating economic blight at home and abroad." While global competition undercut US workers' wages and threatened their jobs, workers elsewhere gained access to jobs but without protections their US counterparts had sought and received. Further, trade policy was striking at vulnerable manufacturing industries, like textiles and apparel. Citing Labor Department statistics, Baldanzi pointed out that textile workers earned an average weekly wage of $97.69, about three-fourths of the $132.40 an average US manufacturing worker earned and less than half the $196 the Labor Department estimated was necessary for an urban family of four to maintain an adequate standard of living. "We cannot hide the grim fact that textile workers are in an intolerable situation," Baldanzi said. He warned further that corporate leaders like IBM's Arthur Watson were all too willing to believe that a growing number of Americans with more than a high school education justified eliminating entire domestic manufacturing sectors. "We do not accept this kind of economic thinking that many jobs should be farmed out to the low-wage areas around the world," he said. "The price that this nation is paying now, and will have to pay in the future with this kind of approach, is not hard to envision."[19]

While Baldanzi focused on the human cost of trade policy in vulnerable industries, the ACWA, TWUA, and ILGWU made statistical cases to bolster their respective arguments. Potofsky argued that the textile and garment industry's survival was at stake because "we cannot compete with wages of eight cents an hour in South Korea or even 37 cents an hour in Japan." The ACWA, while committed to international trade, supported the Mills bill as a way to encourage "orderly trade, without inequities or harmful effects on any of the countries involved."[20]

Stulberg, meanwhile, observed that apparel imports, only 4 percent of total domestic apparel production in 1956, had reached 22 percent by 1969. Despite the administration of agreements like the STA and LTA, the level of cotton textile imports was 65 percent higher in 1969 than in 1962; during that period, imports of cotton, wool, and synthetic garments had all more than tripled. As a percentage of total domestic production by product, imports now comprised 11 percent of all playsuits and up to 72 percent of sweaters. "These figures reflect the invasion we have had to face up to now, but they are only a prologue of things to come unless this flood is dammed," he wrote.[21]

Pollock asked committee members to keep in mind that "what we are talking about here are 2½ million Americans" whose livelihood depended on the vitality of the textile and apparel industries. In 1969, he told the committee, thirty-two mills were closed, eliminating more than eight thousand jobs, and in the

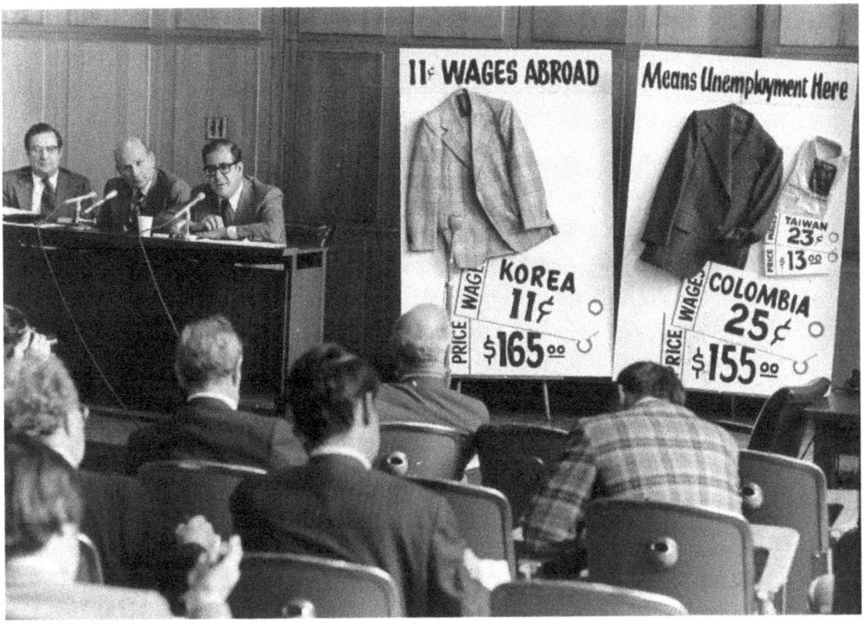

Anti-import protests succeeded in raising awareness of how lower wages for international workers and lower prices for imports threatened domestic manufacturing jobs. At this news conference, participants make connections between imports and domestic unemployment. (George Meany Memorial AFL-CIO Archives, University of Maryland–College Park.)

first four months of 1970, he cited imports as the chief factor in another nine plant closures that eliminated fifteen hundred jobs. And Andrew Biemiller, the AFL-CIO legislative director, added testimony bolstering the viewpoint of the textile and apparel trade unions. Calling economic policies that made sense in the 1930s and 1940s "utterly unrealistic" in the 1970s, Biemiller argued new developments in international trade—including growing investment by US firms in foreign subsidiaries and foreign governments that restricted the entry of US exports—had rendered traditional concepts of trade and protectionism "outdated and increasingly irrelevant."[22] Biemiller's testimony suggested that the AFL-CIO, while sharing the concerns of its member unions troubled by imports, was neither ready to embrace protectionism nor abandon the benefits of a higher volume of trade. Rather, his comments indicated a need for a balance in trade policy that preserved its benefits while helping those who were affected.

Other observers saw the need for protections in terms of jobs and potential effects on the exchange of goods. On May 20, South Carolina's lieutenant governor, John West, testified that despite a decade-long push by the Palmetto State for economic diversification, textiles and apparel still comprised two-thirds of the state's industry. The growth in import levels between 1964 and 1969, moreover, translated into 2,400 lost textile jobs in the state from January 1969 to February 1970. And those lost jobs were not just an economic problem. "The layoffs added to the racial problem," West said, "because black workers were hit the hardest." Nationally, the import increase "represented the displacement of well over a quarter of a million US textile and apparel jobs," said ATMI President Donald McCullough. But he did not believe Japan would retaliate on import curbs in the Mills bill through lower purchases of raw materials.[23]

A New Force Emerges: Multinationals and the Fight over the Mills Bill

While textile and apparel trade unions felt they had a good chance to secure passage of the Mills bill, they met with strong opposition from an alliance of multinational corporations, which wanted no restrictions on trade that could jeopardize their overseas entities. Multinationals and the US Chamber of Commerce opposed the Mills bill; the chamber warned of retaliation "swiftly invoked by foreign governments" if import quotas were enacted. Other opponents predicted a rise in artificial trade barriers or higher inflation as a result of fewer imports if the bill passed.[24]

The heart of the opposition to the Mills bill came from a coalition of dozens of multinational firms. The Emergency Committee for American Trade (ECAT) was founded in late 1967 as Congress and the Johnson administration battled over import quotas when the Kennedy Round concluded. ECAT opposed import quotas and was committed to supporting the nation's trade policy. It counted among its leadership executives of some of the nation's largest manufacturers, banks, and merchandisers, including IBM's Watson, David Rockefeller of Chase Manhattan Bank, Robert Kirkwood of F. W. Woolworth Co., and Ford Motor Company Chairman Henry Ford II. ECAT members were not shy about moving jobs abroad, as its spokesman, Continental Can President Ellison Hazard, admitted in a 1970 speech. As part of its opposition to the Mills bill, ECAT sent a delegation to Japan to support US trade policy; while there, ECAT leaders made sure to inform the Japanese that its corporations counted operations in twenty-two districts of members of the House Ways and Means Committee. With its organization, range of executives, and global reach, ECAT had an advantage over its labor rivals in voicing its opposition to import quotas.[25]

To one ECAT official, the Mills bill represented an overzealous effort by Congress to provide protectionism; it further offered evidence that the Nixon administration's attempt to fulfill a campaign pledge to the textile industry had spun out of control. While limited to textiles, apparel, and shoes, the official noted in the summer of 1970, the bill's provisions could be extended to other industries: steel, automobiles, dairy, meat, electronics. "And this is an election year," the ECAT official said. "By the time the lobbyists get through and the Senate acts on this bill it's going to look like a Christmas tree."[26]

Other critics argued that Nixon needed to negotiate with the Japanese and avoid measures like the Mills bill. "Japan's aggressive marketing of textiles in the United States is in part responsible for the strong protectionist sentiment on Capitol Hill, and Mr. Nixon himself is not without culpability," the *St. Louis Post-Dispatch* editorialized. Additional opposition in the form of congressional lobbying came from Europe, Latin America, and Japan. Lobbyists joined government leaders and ministers from abroad, bypassing domestic channels and competing with US lobbyists as they together turned Congress into an international bazaar on trade policy. One Washington law firm representing Japanese trade interests disclosed it received the bulk of its financing from the Japanese government. Nelson Stitt, an attorney representing the US-Japan Trade Council, told the House Ways and Means Committee he suspected many witnesses were "substantially financed from abroad" but had not disclosed their activities to the Justice Department, as required.[27]

By the summer of 1970, Congress and the Nixon administration appeared to be on the same page with regard to the Mills bill, reflecting labor's success in convincing congressional leaders and the general public of the need for some form of import protection. In June 1970, after negotiations with Japan's Ministry of International Trade and Industry in Washington collapsed after only three days, Stans, the commerce secretary, told the Ways and Means Committee the administration supported the Mills bill as "the only means presently available for solving this problem."[28]

With the bill's prospects good, the tensions between business and labor intensified. One labor newspaper urged readers and members to continue sending messages of support for the bill. The AFL-CIO began sharing opposition research on corporations opposed to import quotas "on the pretense they want to strengthen U.S. firms in world trade." Not to be outdone, the ECAT ran a full-page advertisement in the *Washington Post* under the headline "Congress: Please Don't Declare a World Trade War." Biemiller, the AFL-CIO's legislative director, attacked the advertisement as illustrating how US and Japanese interests were opposing workers' interests. Thirty-two of the fifty-one signatory firms in the advertisement had ownership in Japanese firms, "many producing the same goods abroad they once produced in the U.S." Further, the companies owned foreign affiliates in 108 nations and were financially involved with companies in Mexico, Taiwan, Hong Kong, South Korea, and elsewhere. The signatories had no altruistic interest on trade, Biemiller charged, and were not promoting a growth in trade. Rather, their goal was to continue importing products made with cheap labor to compete with US-made goods at similar or "slightly lower" prices. The immediate effect was lost US jobs. "Eventually, the loss is the entire American standard of living," he said.[29]

Despite ECAT's efforts, the Mills bill survived with mandatory quotas on textiles, apparel, and shoes intact. On August 13, the Ways and Means Committee reported the bill on a 17–7 vote. Stans called the measure "a remarkable piece of work" and called concerns that the bill would provoke an international trade war "a lot of nonsense." Other observers, such as Paul McCracken, the chairman of Nixon's Council of Economic Advisers, saw the bill as a nod to the reality of failed negotiations on Japanese textile imports. Committee opposition to the bill came from a handful of junior members in both parties, such as Republican Jerry Pettis of California and Democrats Sam Gibbons of Florida, William J. Green of Pennsylvania, and James Corman of California. Opposing members, in a breach of the committee protocol of deference to Mills, or at least of dissenting privately, denounced the bill as "restrictive, ill-timed and provincial" and "a backward step for America and the world."[30]

Opposition to the Mills bill did not kill the measure in the committee, but it did delay further action until after the 1970 midterm elections. Despite lobbying from labor, the bill sat in the House Rules Committee until House leadership agreed to take up the bill after the election. The delay was a cause for concern—in postelection sessions, members were less likely to follow their constituents' wishes as elections were another two years off—but other developments encouraged supporters. In reporting the bill to the full House, the Rules Committee disallowed amendments on the floor, in keeping with a tradition that trade and tax legislation be voted up or down without amendment. In the Senate, a supporter—Ernest Hollings—announced he would attempt to move the bill through the upper chamber, most likely as an amendment to a separate bill. Meanwhile, opponents such as the Committee for a National Trade Policy were marshaling their forces to fight the Mills bill. "This bill in the context of 1970 is worse than Smoot-Hawley in the context of 1930," executive director John Hight wrote in an October 1970 invitation to allies to a strategy session after the election. "We cannot permit it to happen."[31]

"The Job You Save May Be Your Own": Workers Sound Off on Imports

While Congress debated imports and trade policy in the fall of 1970, constituents were also speaking out about the impact of imports. To workers, imports meant closed factories and fewer jobs for making a living; to consumers, imports meant a declining amount of domestic goods they could buy. In a letter to Democratic Senator Thomas J. McIntyre of New Hampshire, one of his constituents, Evelyn Erickson, of Farmington, described how imports led her factory owner to declare bankruptcy. She wrote of fears of her factory closing and losing her home at the age of sixty-three, all because of import competition. She offered to educate Nixon with a hometown tour of closed factories, unemployed workers, and import-filled stores. "In watching President Nixon, he impresses me as being wrongly informed about imports," Erickson wrote. "I *know* we need trade but I hate to give up *my* job for them to prosper and we know Japan is prospering at our expense. It would seem the President is more anxious to protect them than to help us Americans."[32]

As the debate on trade continued in the 1970s, the toll on domestic textile and apparel plants continued. In early 1971, Beaunit Mills, a rayon and polyester producer, closed its Bemberg division in Elizabethton, Tennessee, wiping out five hundred jobs. Six months later, another Beaunit plant, in Childersburg, Alabama, closed after operating in the red for six years because import competition increased and demand decreased, taking a thousand more jobs with it. The closures angered UTWA President Baldanzi. "If we had been able to pass a reasonable bill in the last Congress setting low-wage import quotas, as urged by organized labor, these jobs could well have been saved," he said in response to the closures.[33]

Import concerns led to more visible demonstrations from labor. Members of the UTWA's Midwestern Council printed up and distributed black, yellow, and white fifteen-inch bumper stickers with the phrase "Buy American—the Job You Save . . . May Be Your Own." The council also started a petition drive urging import quotas to protect workers in industries where imports affected their jobs. UTWA members began to lower the US flag to half-staff at plants closing from import competition. And ACWA members continued their informational pickets, targeting retailers and urging consumers not to buy imported goods.[34]

The unions' activism throughout 1970 was not enough to assure the Mills bill's survival, despite its promise in the House. After the midterm elections, it passed the House, 215–165, only to be ensnared in a series of filibusters in the Senate, along with legislation Nixon sought to fund his Family Assistance Plan (the brainchild of economist Milton Friedman). The Mills bill halted in the Senate when Russell Long, the Louisiana Democrat who chaired the Senate Finance Committee, attempted to pair the Mills bill and the Family Assistance Plan with another measure increasing Social Security benefits. Long faced opposition from moderate and liberal senators who did not like the method of packaging controversial bills with more popular ones to move them through the Senate. In the House, Mills rejected the package, telling both Senate leadership and the White House he would consider only individual bills, although his committee had passed each of the three measures. In response, Long refused to take up the Mills bill as an individual measure, killing it.[35]

In early 1971, the bill appeared to have new life. Mills vowed to take it up after measures to increase Social Security and welfare benefits. The Nixon administration had also pledged its support. Unions like the UTWA, sensing victory on import legislation was close, marshaled their forces once more. The deteriorating domestic economy also seemed to indicate favorable conditions for a trade bill. The gross national product declined for the first time in twelve years; unemployment reached 6 percent in December 1970, and observers were wondering whether the Nixon administration would pursue an economic stimulus.[36]

Yet again, the bill's prospects would clash with political and international developments. Mills reintroduced his trade bill but also enlisted an intermediary to begin back-channel negotiations with the Japanese to limit textile exports. In early March, the Japanese Textile Federation agreed to limit exports for three years, holding the growth in textile exports to 5 percent in the first year and 6 percent each of the following two years. The ATMI rejected the deal, which was less restrictive than a proposed export restriction deal that collapsed in December 1970. Nixon, initially hoping the industry would embrace the deal, was advised to accept it. But when Thurmond criticized the deal as "totally inadequate," Nixon backed away; he also criticized Mills for meddling in foreign policy. Chastened by the rejections of both Nixon and the textile industry, Mills withdrew his bill, blaming the textile industry for willingly rejecting the negotiated agreement: "Those greedy bastards . . . will not get *any* quota legislation passed until a voluntary agreement is given a fair chance," he told Nixon aide Pete Peterson. The administration then made unsuccessful attempts to reach similar voluntary export agreements on textiles with Korea, Taiwan, and Hong Kong.[37]

The Nixon-Mills struggle over imports—and by extension its implication for the 1972 presidential election—halted momentum for import quotas. It also damaged prospects for the Mills bill to get through Congress in the face of opposition from Nixon (who wanted import quotas only in the "special case" of textiles) and from multinational corporations (who saw quotas as threatening their business model and US trade policy). But other observers hated the agreement: Baldanzi said the deal, if it established 1970 as the baseline year for restrictions, would allow a total 40 percent increase in Japanese imports. George Meany called it "altogether unsatisfactory" and vowed the federation would instead seek import quotas for textiles and apparel and other industries "in which there is a loss of American jobs due to market disruption or the activities of American multinational corporations." And the House Textile Committee, an informal bipartisan caucus of no fewer than 150 southern representatives, opposed the Mills deal and continued demanding import quota legislation. Nixon relented and called for an import quota bill, but Mills's refusal ended the possibility for such legislation.[38]

As part of Nixon's wage and price controls imposed in August 1971 as part of his New Economic Plan (NEP), the president opted to take a hard line on imports from Asia. He threatened to impose unilateral quotas on Japanese textile imports, using language from a 10 percent surcharge on imports to declare a national emergency and call for efforts "to strengthen the international economic position of the U.S." By mid-October, Japan, Hong Kong, Taiwan, and South Korea all agreed to similar import quotas limiting growth to 5 percent per year for synthetic fabrics and 1 percent per year for wool. The import growth levels were based on a baseline import level of 900 million square yards for synthetic fabrics and 50 million square yards for wool.[39]

At first glance, Nixon had appeared to win the economic battle with Japan while keeping alive his political quest for a New Majority. "The U.S. has not bargained hard for a better position in world trade, the goddamn State Department hasn't done the job," Nixon groused afterward, reflecting on US approaches to world trade over the previous twenty-five years. "We're changing the rules of the game." Through these imposed import limits, Nixon expected to secure some labor support (by imposing protectionist quotas), attract financial and political support from textile executives (who otherwise might back Mills or George Wallace), and further hearten southern voters (who might like Nixon's refusal to back busing for school integration), building the GOP's foothold in the region. But textile executives, who had given about $430,000 to Nixon's reelection campaign by April 1972, wondered whether the deal was too late—or came with too many concessions—to help their industry. As imports continued to increase, the delay in reaching a deal meant a larger baseline from which import restrictions would be calculated. Furthermore, exporters responded to the import surcharge by lowering prices to help US retailers offset it. And the expiration of the surcharge in late December wiped out any remaining price advantage on domestic goods.[40]

For labor, however, the collapse of the Mills bill and any legislative effort to impose quotas again illustrated labor's weakness in influencing the trade debate. Textile and apparel unions, and their counterparts in other manufacturing sectors, would need a new approach to challenge the impacts of trade on their respective workers and industries. They would need it to address the growing influence of multinational corporations—a prominent foe of labor on trade issues and part of a new postindustrial economy that elites were quick to embrace.

Beyond Import Quotas: Labor Targets Multinational Corporations

In July 1971 the AFL-CIO held a Washington conference on jobs in which workers and unions voiced even stronger opposition to imports and their intention to fight import competition. In the run-up to the conference, Baldanzi argued for labor cooperation across industrialized nations to counter the actions of multinational corporations. In an address to the New Jersey AFL-CIO convention at Atlantic City, Baldanzi argued that US corporations had invested about $60 billion in overseas operations, with $16 billion of that amount coming in 1970 alone. "There is no case on record where they have attempted to raise the standards of the people who work for them," Baldanzi said. "They joined with the native capitalists in the exploitation of their workers and they bring the product back to sell it to the US market at US prices—and destroy our jobs in the process."[41]

At the special jobs conference in July 1971, labor mustered its most united voice to that date in challenging imports, which were blamed for the loss of five hundred thousand jobs in the three years preceding the conference. USWA president I. W. Abel and the head of the AFL-CIO's Industrial Union Department said union members and other US workers had faced dwindling numbers of jobs because of imports. "We simply cannot continue to export American jobs and American expertise and maintain our living standards under the rules of the game of international trade as they are played today. It's as simple and as frightening as that," he said. Unions in various manufacturing sectors—steel, electronics, shoes, rubber, and pottery—joined to discuss trade problems caused by imports. Unaware of the back-channel negotiations by Mills, union representatives urged action of the Mills bill, which was expected to occur shortly after hearings on legislation to introduce national health insurance.[42]

The ACWA's Potofsky sounded a note of defiance, offsetting the gloom other attendees expressed, by reminding them of the union's historical work to eliminate sweatshops and low wages like those offered by foreign competitors. "We cannot compete with 9 cents an hour—and we don't want to try to compete," he said. "It took us years to overcome sweatshop conditions in this country, and we don't intend to allow the sweatshop to return on the back of low-wage workers."[43]

Though import problems had existed for years in the textile industry, AFL-CIO President Meany accused the Nixon administration of worsening the national economy through sharp increases in the cost of living and five million workers unemployed while hundreds of thousands more had exhausted their unemployment benefits. "The state of the economy is just plain lousy," he said. "We are here because we are just plain fed up. We are here because we are concerned about jobs and about the shortage of jobs, about the various ways jobs are being made to disappear." Meany estimated the economy needed at least two million new jobs annually to steady unemployment rates, with another 2.5 to 3 million jobs each year to reduce unemployment—"more than were created in any year in the 1960s."[44]

Meany may have been late to realize the calls by textile and apparel trade unions and labor in other import-sensitive industries to reevaluate US trade policy. Even so, his observations on the nation's economic position in the 1960s and 1970s hint at a deep understanding of the challenges facing the country at the conclusion of its post–World War II economic boom. In counterpoint to his younger, and more socially liberal, labor movement colleagues, Meany was among those calling for solutions to problems caused by increases in automation and industrial decline long before those ideas reached the mainstream. His support for expansionary economic policies and wariness of multinational corporations were as far-reaching and forward-thinking as his staunch anticommunism, and concomitant views on the Vietnam War, placed him in the depths of the Cold War and as his views on organizing unorganized workers and racial and gender equity in the labor movement marked him as an anachronistic, retrograde leader. His finely tuned understanding of where the nation was headed economically at that particular moment, and the depth of his knowledge about the challenges facing the nation and the role labor could play in addressing those challenges, sharply contrast with his shortcomings in other areas.

A Worsening Balance of Trade and the Search for Answers

The fight over import quotas and trade came as the United States faced yet another effect of its decades-long push to lower trade barriers. In February 1971 Stans told the Joint Economic Committee that the surplus in the nation's balance-of-trade surplus, reaching $5 billion to $6 billion in the early 1960s, had dipped below $1 billion in 1968. While the surplus reached $2.7 billion in 1970, Stans said continued deterioration was expected. The largest shift in the trade balance came in the category of manufactured products that included textiles and apparel—thanks in part to lower labor costs, a $1.1 billion annual surplus in that category in 1957 had, by 1970, turned into an annual $6.1 billion deficit. Stans expected the trend to continue because the United States lacked a technology advantage in that category and because imports would grow faster than anticipated while export growth would lag expectations. By the end of 1971, the nation would record its first trade deficit since 1888; just four months later, the deficit reached its second-highest level ever.[45]

The ACWA responded by staging at least two protests to raise awareness of the effect of imports on their jobs. On May 19 it held an import protest rally in Washington featuring a caravan of ACWA members from two dozen cities nationwide. The ACWA also continued import protests outside department stores, winning concessions in the process. In the summer of 1971, Local 125 of ACWA, representing clothing workers in southern Connecticut, and the New York Joint Board brought protesters to department stores such as Alexander's, E. J. Korvette, and Klein's, where ACWA members handed out flyers urging consumers not to buy imported goods. All three retailers agreed to limit their sales of imported clothing as a result. Laborers applied political pressure as well. In October 1971 the AFL-CIO's Industrial Union Department held a one-day "Save Our Jobs" rally in Washington, at which unionists were encouraged to discuss the impact of imports on their jobs with their elected representatives.[46]

Despite these efforts, the growth in apparel imports continued. Imports of suits, sport coats, wool suits, jackets, and synthetic suits and jackets all increased by more than 60 percent in the first half of 1970 over the corresponding period a year earlier. Meanwhile, the number of US workers making tailored clothing fell from 120,400 in 1969 to 112,900 in 1970. The ACWA argued that if the imported items had been made domestically, the nation's ranks of textile and apparel workers would have increased by 250,000.[47]

While imports commanded the attention of the textile industry and organized labor, trade issues in the Nixon administration mingled with the collapse of the Bretton Woods system of fixed currency exchange, which had guided international monetary policy and supplies since 1944. In the spring of 1971, West Germany, Switzerland, and France left the Bretton Woods system, strengthening their respective currencies and exchanging their dollar reserves for gold. In August 1971, Nixon, acting on the advice of Federal Reserve Chairman Arthur Burns, Treasury Secretary John Connally, and Paul Volcker, the undersecretary for international monetary affairs, decided to break up the Bretton Woods system, ending the practice of allowing nations to exchange their dollars for gold. Nixon had previously opposed controls on wages and prices, but he reversed course when faced with rising inflation, unemployment, and balance-of-trade deficits.

On August 15, Nixon imposed his NEP in an effort to create jobs, halt inflation, and protect the dollar from speculation. The policy, also known as the Nixon Shock, instituted an immediate ninety-day freeze on wage, price, and rent levels; a 10 percent cut in foreign economic aid; a $4.7 billion cut in fiscal 1972 federal budget levels; and a six-month deferment of a pay increase for federal employees. Two additional measures were aimed at reducing the nation's trade deficit and an overvalued dollar: a temporary 10 percent surcharge on most imports and a suspension of the dollar's convertibility into gold. The latter move marked the end of US participation in the Bretton Woods system by establishing a floating dollar value in world markets.[48]

In the final three years of his presidency, Nixon pursued a neo-mercantilist economy that included quotas on textile and apparel imports. His attempt at mercantilism was short-lived, however, and, after his reelection in 1972, he sought to increase US exports and jobs by embracing trade as a tool of domestic economic policy rather than of foreign affairs. In the process, Nixon continued to play for the support of organized labor as part of his political coalition, a task that suddenly ended as Nixon was swept up in the Watergate scandal. Yet Nixon's downfall contained elements the New Right would use during the 1970s to rise to ascendance. Poor economic performance, public anxieties over the economy, and a steep recession in 1974–75 (caused by Nixon's failure to tame inflation) fed a view that business alone, and not government policies, contributed to economic prosperity. Economic downturns and public anxiety, in turn, opened the door to pro-business policies, lower domestic spending, and tight monetary policy—all of which the New Right adopted.[49]

This chapter's review of the interplay between labor and Congress, as well as between labor and the Nixon administration on trade, engages an issue completely missing from Robert Collins's book on the political economy of postwar economic growth. Nixon's shift from a neo-mercantilist to a supporter of lower trade barriers by 1973 moved him from seeing trade less as a part of Cold War foreign policies and more as a policy of domestic economic growth. It also represents his version of what Collins describes as Nixon's "full-blown growth liberalism" amid the economic pressures of the 1970s. Nixon's reversal represents what Collins calls an attempt to match foreign and domestic policies with expectations for more growth without generating unemployment, inflation, or stagflation.[50]

Multinational firms began to oppose organized labor on many trade issues, part of the shift of political elites and segments of the Democratic Party who began to avoid labor-oriented policies by the early 1970s. Those shifts led a growing number of white-collar, professional workers and elites to see finance and multinational enterprise, rather than domestic manufacturing, as a key driver of economic growth. Those views intensified as labor suffered its defeats on trade legislation in the early 1970s and was mirrored in public opinion that similarly saw finance and free trade, rather than manufacturing and managed trade, as the wave of the future.[51]

Finally, the defeat unions endured in their campaign for import quotas and trade barriers is a development not fully addressed by other observers of the decline of the US textile and apparel industry. The failed effort to shift US trade policy in the late 1960s and early 1970s—all as workers and union officials interacted with leaders at the highest levels of government—illustrates textile and apparel trades' relatively weak position within the US labor movement, as well as the weakness of both the labor movement within the New Deal political coalition and the political coalition itself. The difficult fight also illustrated the problems rooted in textile and apparel trade unions' failure to join forces in fighting import competition and in resolving decades-long disputes, as well as their collective failure to establish any meaningful presence in the US South. Labor's losses on trade in the early 1970s set the stage for the continued decline of the textile and apparel industry, as well as of US manufacturing in general.[52]

Nixon's Nationalist Neo-mercantilism and the NEP

Nixon's NEP was part of a "nationalist conception of U.S. interests" in trade, as Allan Matusow described it. But political considerations still held priority; Nixon would continue to seek import protections for textiles, in order to fulfill his political ambitions of bringing the South into his New Majority. Elsewhere, Nixon intended to lower trade barriers and aggressively produce exports to generate domestic employment. Nixon hoped that doing so would stave off what European trading partners were calling an American nightmare, in which competing nations combined technology and low wages to push US-made goods out of domestic and international markets.[53]

The impetus for Nixon's reversal on trade came from Peter Peterson, an up-and-coming executive at Bell and Howell and an acquaintance of George Shultz, Nixon's labor secretary, who found his way into the administration as an assistant for foreign economics in January 1971. Peterson's tenure in the White House lasted less than a year before he moved to the Commerce Department, driven out by Nixon's paranoia about leaks and his suspicions about Peterson's ease in navigating Washington's social scene.[54]

Yet three months after joining the White House staff, Peterson wrote a confidential memorandum on the state of US competitive decline that jolted Nixon into action. Published later that year as a two-volume report, Peterson described a US economy lagging in productivity, in economic growth, in investment, and in its share of export trade. Warning of rapidly declining superiority in the world economy, Peterson urged the nation to both challenge unfair conduct among its trading partners and institute an industrial policy for the domestic economy. The report, which also argued the United States could create between sixty and eighty thousand new jobs for each $1 billion in exports it generated, helped Nixon see a connection between trade and domestic politics. In a July 1971 conversation with Peterson, Nixon said the country needed to use trade policy "as an instrument of our domestic policy, e.g. jobs," rather than as a part of foreign policy. Nixon repeated Peterson's findings to his staff, members of Congress, labor leaders, and others, even as academic economists scored the report as "mercantilist fantasy" because it flew in the face of centuries of study of international trade. Using classical economic theory, Herbert Stein—a member of Nixon's Council of Economic Advisers—argued that a nation's export trade existed to satisfy consumer wants, not to create jobs. Other critics said imports were necessary because they drove down prices, saving money for US consumers.[55]

The criticisms did not deter Nixon or certain of his aides, who saw a political benefit. A crusade to boost exports, even without results in time for the 1972 elections, would help Nixon with factions of the labor movement that were more open to trade and equated exports with job growth. Aide H. R. Haldeman believed Nixon could win labor "by showing an interest in protecting their jobs." Connally also believed Nixon could reach organized labor "especially on the issue of jobs and particularly, on the American position in the world economy, i.e. our trade relations. On that issue, labor will be our strongest ally."[56]

Less than a month after announcing his NEP, Nixon outlined its principles in an address to Congress. He called for "a new prosperity without war and without inflation" that would help the economy transition from a war footing as the country wound down its involvement in Vietnam. Mixed among calls to reorganize the federal government, reform welfare, and impose budget cuts and delay federal pay raises was an admission that the United States no longer occupied a dominant position in world trade. Nixon bowed to the new reality, citing challenges in a world that had been reshaped in the previous quarter-century, during which the balance between the United States and the rest of the world had changed drastically. "Fifteen years ago, a prominent world statesman . . . commented to me that world trade was like a poker game in which the United States held all the chips, and that we had to spread them around so others could play," Nixon said. "It is no longer true today. We have generously passed out the chips. Now others can play on an equal basis—and we must play the game as we expect and want them to do."[57]

Even as his administration had sought in its early years to limit textile and apparel imports through voluntary agreements, and though he had promised to pursue import quotas on textiles and apparel, Nixon signaled a course reversal on trade, warning against trade isolationism and calling for continued engagement with the world. "We cannot remain a great nation if we build a permanent wall of tariffs and quotas around the United States," he said. "We cannot live behind a wall that shuts the rest of the world out. If we were not a great power, we would not be the America we know. If we do not stay a great power, the world will not stay safe for free men."[58]

The economic challenges Nixon mentioned to Congress were already a reality for millions of Americans; for them, a precarious hold on employment and economic security was all too familiar. Their challenging economic reality, shaped in part by international competition, domestic unemployment, and a sense that the nation's postwar economic boom was over, produced unsettling reminders. "The war in Vietnam belongs to the past,—nobody talks about it anymore," Ann Fleming, an Elmira, New York, housewife, wrote in a letter to Meany. "The main problem in this country now is the unemployment."[59]

Fleming reflected on the anxiety she felt when her husband, a Westinghouse engineer laid off two days after Nixon announced the NEP, could not find a job:

> My husband went to the Employment Agency, nothing. Then he went to a private agency, they told him, the companies are flooded with resumes from engineers, from all over the country. He went to college for 4 years, now nobody wants him. I am so depressed, that I see only one way out of this situation; to turn on the gas in the kitchen. . . . This world belongs to the rich only. The poor people have to fight for their every day life, till they die. . . . What kind of life is this, if we have to worry about tomorrow, if we are going to have money to buy food?[60]

Fleming's concern about unemployment dovetailed with the proliferation of imported goods that were just as good as, or better than, their US counterparts. "You are a very powerful man Mr. Meany, isn't there anything you can do about this? To stop the imports from Japan, Germany, Taiwan, Korea, Hong Kong etc.?" she wrote. "If you Mr. Meany and President Nixon would get together, and figure out something how to stop the imports, we would have more jobs. If the people have jobs, then we shouldn't have any inflation either." Yet, as a consumer, Fleming also found cheap imports difficult to resist. "About a month ago I bought myself four bluses [*sic*] imported from Hong Kong, they were $1 a piece," she wrote, referring to a price tag and label from one of the blouses she included in the letter. "That's why our people don't have jobs in this country. This should be stopped."[61]

Burke-Hartke: Organized Labor's Second Try for Import Quotas

While Nixon shifted toward an export campaign to generate jobs as part of the NEP, the president had to contend with dissatisfaction from organized labor. The wage and price controls negated increases won through collective bargaining agreements, further fraying relations with Nixon.[62]

The UTWA criticized the import surcharge as inadequate to stop textile imports from Asia and repeated their call for "firm, fair and adequate quotas" on textile and apparel imports.[63] In contrast with its stance on Asian imports, the union asked the administration to remove the import surcharge on Canadian imports, characterizing the surcharge as harmful to the nation's largest trading partner.[64]

Members of the UTWA's executive council, meeting in New York, called for import quotas as the solution to protecting jobs and manufacturing in the US textile industry. "The crisis in the textile industry has reached proportions unparalleled in our history, and the threat of utter extinction of the industry faces us today," the council declared. It further blamed imports as well as the ability of multinational corporations to exercise "their manipulation of international investment, their exploitation of people, and their growing control of the channels of commerce" as contributing to "the daily exportation of jobs and technologies, of plants and equipment." The council also criticized Nixon's import surcharge as "far too small a barrier to stem so great a tide of cheap textile and apparel imports."[65]

At the AFL-CIO's ninth biennial convention in 1971, import competition was as strong an issue as it had been in recent years, yet the federation devoted more attention and effort to criticizing Nixon's economic plan. Though there were no legislative or policy successes on import competition to speak of, the AFL-CIO could point to a 1970 Industrial Union Department conference on the crisis in international trade, which attracted more than five hundred delegates from forty unions calling for action from the White House and Congress.[66] The only other action, besides the AFL-CIO conference on jobs in July 1971, was a report by Baldanzi and Charles Feinstein, president of the International Leather Goods, Plastics and Novelty Workers Union, designed to call attention to the "detrimental impact upon the job opportunities of American workers that has been created by foreign imports of all kinds of manufactured goods."[67]

In September 1971, in testimony to the Senate Finance Committee on the international aspects of the NEP, Volcker urged new attention to the issue of world trade. He suggested the United States needed a "complete and convincing elimination of our deficits" that included realigning exchange rates, assuring fair competition in world markets, and rebuilding a trade surplus. But others, such as O. R. Strackbein, the president of the Nation-Wide Committee on Import-Export Policy, called for limiting imports. Proposals to help businesses through investment credits, he argued, did little to address import competition. "With the establishment of ceilings on import-harassed products we could remove other trade barriers, even the tariff, and thus overcome foreign objection to our insistence on preserving our system against destruction," he said.[68]

Frustrated with mounting job losses caused in part by trade and the failure to win import quota legislation, labor and its congressional allies mounted yet another push for import quotas. This time, their hopes lay with a trade quota bill first proposed in September 1971. Sponsored by two Democrats, Massachusetts Representative James Burke and Senator Vance Hartke of Indiana, their Foreign Trade and Investment Act would bear their last names, Burke-Hartke. The Nixon administration vehemently opposed the bill during its short-lived existence on Capitol Hill in 1972 and 1973. For its entire existence, however, Burke-Hartke was part of trade policy negotiations between the administration and the AFL-CIO.[69]

Burke, a native Bostonian, and Hartke, from a small southern Indiana town, seemed worlds apart but shared similarities. Both served in World War II—Burke in a counterintelligence unit attached to an infantry division; Hartke, in the US Coast Guard and Navy as a seaman. The two shared an interest in politics and government: Hartke was a county prosecutor and mayor of Evansville before entering Congress; Burke served in the Massachusetts general court and the state house. Both were elected to Congress in 1958 and served into the 1970s: Burke retired in 1978, two years after Hartke lost a reelection bid to Republican Richard Lugar. Between 1963 and 1977, Burke represented the Massachusetts Eleventh Congressional District, the same seat held by John F. Kennedy from 1947 to 1953. Hartke also had higher political aspirations, mounting a short-lived presidential campaign in 1972. Burke, meanwhile, organized a "Draft Mills for President" movement in 1971, inspiring Wilbur Mills's short-lived presidential campaign. The constituents of both knew job losses because of imports. In Hartke's Indiana, the steel industry was declining and mounted its own late 1960s campaign against imports; Burke was well versed in the decline of the Massachusetts textile and shoe industries. Hartke attempted to aid the latter in 1970 when he joined independent Senator Harry Byrd of Virginia and Democratic Senator Albert Gore of Tennessee to keep an import quota on shoes in the Mills bill.[70]

Developed with the aid of the AFL-CIO's legislative department, Burke-Hartke was designed to prevent both the outflow of capital from the United States and the influx of imported goods, some of which came from US multinationals. Beginning in the mid-1960s, according to critics in organized labor and some economists, the combination of technology and capital from wealthy nations combined with the cheap labor of poor nations to shift jobs out of the United States for the purpose of maximizing profits. The shift to cut labor costs meant that only a fraction of consumer goods for the US market were manufactured domestically by the early 1970s. Supporters of offshoring, including ECAT, cited a study of seventy-four multinationals that claimed direct foreign investment helped save or create 600,000 domestic jobs. Another promultinational study, conducted by the US Chamber of Commerce and surveying 121 companies, claimed the companies created 771,000 jobs between 1960 and 1970. The AFL-CIO, meanwhile, claimed global corporations cost 500,000 jobs in the United States between 1966 and 1969. While disputes continued over multinationals' effect on domestic employment and manufacturing, others noticed worsening effects for workers. For instance, jobs created in corporate headquarters did not offset the loss of an equal number of manufacturing jobs.[71]

The lower wages offered in countries outside the United States undermined labor's bargaining power, allowing multinationals to push wages down when they transferred operations abroad. "Increasingly, unions have forgone increases or even accepted wage reductions in order to induce a company not to relocate abroad," wrote two analysts of multinationals' activities. Capital mobility, they observed in 1974, was challenging labor's relative immobility, with one particularly

Senator Vance Hartke, D-Ind., addresses members of the National Conference of Motion Picture and Television Unions lobbying Congress on the Burke-Hartke trade bill. The anti-import measure, backed by organized labor, drew significant opposition from domestic and multinational corporations. (Photo from *AFL-CIO News*, May 19, 1973. George Meany Memorial AFL-CIO Archives, University of Maryland–College Park.)

frightening result: the earlier trend toward greater income equality in the United States "has ground to a halt. . . . The exodus to Taiwan, Singapore and Mexico over the past 10 years has complicated the employment crisis in the United States, particularly for blue collar workers."[72]

Burke-Hartke was intended to reduce imports by imposing quotas across a range of products threatened by import competition. More important, though, it also aimed to limit capital mobility by changing the tax regulations governing foreign investment by US multinational corporations. One such proposal would eliminate a provision from the 1954 tax act that allowed US companies with overseas subsidiaries to pay taxes only on the profit it repatriated. Instead, Burke-Hartke would subject a US multinational's corporate income to US income taxes in the year it was earned, regardless of where it was earned—blocking multinationals from deferring taxes on overseas earnings until they were repatriated.[73]

Labor leaders supported Burke-Hartke as a way to fight imports. The bill, Andrew J. Biemiller told the House Foreign Affairs Subcommittee on Foreign Economic Policy, "is to save threatened industries and to eventually enable hard-hit producers to regain domestic production and re-employ workers idled by the imports." Meanwhile, some textile labor leaders saw Burke-Hartke as an opportunity to regulate multinationals as well. "Much of what we choose to call 'foreign competition' has, in a very real sense, been 'domestic competition,'" Baldanzi said in a speech to members of the AFL-CIO Maritime Trades Department. "Much of it has come from the very companies which used to employ your members but which have exported your jobs abroad and kept the profits for themselves."[74]

With the debate over imports continuing amid a slowing economy, the introduction of Burke-Hartke, after the failure of the Mills bill, continued to buoy organized labor's hopes of securing import quotas. But they would have to overcome resistance from multinationals, the very businesses that political leaders and prominent thinkers were equating with the future of the US economy.

Labor versus Business: Burke-Hartke and the Battle over Imports

As organized labor saw in Burke-Hartke a possible solution to import competition, the nation's business community began to fight it. A tax attorney, answering a questionnaire from the National Association of Manufacturers (NAM), wrote that the most effective position against Burke-Hartke would be to point out that the bill would be more likely to reduce domestic manufacturing tied to exports than to increase domestic manufacturing. "I do not think that the prospect of increased tax burden on US manufacturers will tend to defeat Burke-Hartke; a demonstration that the enactment of that bill would not lead to a greater employment here might," the attorney wrote.[75] In response, the NAM's Edward Sprague agreed that "the *most pertinent and effective information* that the business community could develop in terms of combating Burke-Hartke type of legislation would be whatever negative effects it would have on U.S. employment" (emphasis in original).[76]

Corporations were most concerned about the effects of parts of the bill that would require corporations to include the earnings of controlled foreign subsidiaries in their income, regardless of whether the earnings were distributed to shareholders or held by the corporation. Another section of the bill that concerned business would reduce business write-offs of their US tax liabilities by eliminating a tax credit for US-based businesses that paid taxes on their overseas operations to other nations.[77]

Under Burke-Hartke, the survey found, the combined foreign and US corporate income tax rate on earnings of foreign subsidiaries would approximate 72 percent, assuming an effective foreign income tax rate of 40 percent and a 10 percent tax on dividends. A survey of corporations belonging to the NAM's international taxation subcommittee, which included companies like Pfizer, Xerox, Mobil Oil, Inland Steel, US Steel, Goodyear, and Chrysler, found foreign subsidiaries would pay most earnings to their parent company to finance tax payments under the bill if enacted, which they argued could hinder efforts to increase employment. "In my opinion, the Dow Jones average would fall 300 points if Mr. Mills were stupid enough to report this bill out of Ways and Means," one chief executive officer wrote in response.[78]

Whereas the AFL-CIO argued that Burke-Hartke would aid the economy by encouraging domestic employment (saving union jobs) and pushing the nation's trade balance into surplus, businesses were prepared to counter with arguments that Burke-Hartke would isolate the domestic economy from the rest of the world and accelerate US manufacturing decline. They believed Burke-Hartke would increase corporate tax rates and reduce earnings, reducing the amount of money available to pay dividends, invest in operations, and modernize and expand domestic facilities. As for the balance-of-payments issue, businesses argued that any short-term advantage for the United States would turn unfavorable as lower foreign exports and sales reduced foreign investment, ultimately reducing the earnings corporations could repatriate from abroad.[79]

The bill's arrival came as the nation's trade deficit continued to increase. A $700 million trade deficit recorded for the month of April 1972 alone, representing one-third of the trade deficit for the whole previous year, seemed to validate Stans's 1971 warning that the trade deficit would continue to deteriorate. While the *Christian Science Monitor* argued that mostly temporary problems lay behind the growing trade deficit—an improving domestic economy was generating more exports and increasing consumption of goods, for instance—it posited long-range issues still needed resolution. Unfortunately, one area that needed attention, reform of tax benefits given to US firms in the postwar years, was tied in with Burke-Hartke, which the *Christian Science Monitor* opined contained protectionist elements putting the legislation "in the class of the notorious Smoot-Hawley Act of 1930."[80]

In December 1972 the NAM announced, in a presentation at Washington's International Club, the results of a survey of eighty-three US corporations with foreign subsidiaries on the bill. Respondents said Burke-Hartke would hurt domestic employment by jeopardizing the jobs of 3 million Americans whose work depended on exports and "certainly trigger an international trade war" by limiting imports. The bill's restrictions on technical interchanges and licensing would erode US leadership in technology. Finally, US direct foreign investment would widen the nation's balance-of-payments gap by reducing earnings that corporations remitted back to the United States. The firms surveyed also paid a higher proportion of taxes on foreign income (50%) than on their domestic income (44.5%), reinvested an average of 47 percent of their after-tax remitted earnings in domestic plants, equipment, and research and development, and had an additional $4.5 billion available through remittances for domestic facilities—an amount large enough to create or maintain more than two hundred thousand US jobs at $22,000 per job. Enacting Burke-Hartke, the NAM said, could force US multinationals to close or reduce their foreign operations, jeopardizing $800 million in dividend income for stockholders and pensioners among the companies surveyed. It could also worsen the nation's balance of payments, reducing US exports and likely increasing imports. Finally, it warned, the bill's tax provisions would threaten US companies' foreign subsidiaries and risk making the country "a second-rate economic power."[81]

J. Stanford Smith, a General Electric vice president, denounced the Burke-Hartke proposals as measures that "would impede the competitiveness of US industry and turn the clock backward to the tragic days of Smoot-Hawley." Republican Representative Bill Frenzel of Minnesota, meanwhile, argued the United States could not trade with the rest of the world while simultaneously shutting out other nations. "It is distressing to see big labor apparently retrenching from a traditional free trade position," he said. "I believe the answer is not to build a wall around our country and thereby deny to future generations the advantages of our participation in international competition." Instead of helping the United States compete better internationally, he said, Burke-Hartke would take the nation back to an older, isolationist era and "ultimately [would place] all of the U.S. in the wagon box and buggy whip industries. It is literally a declaration of willingness to drop out of the world."[82]

Other opponents of Burke-Hartke, in addition to the multinational corporations represented by the NAM, were ECAT, the US Chamber of Commerce, and the Committee for a National Trade Policy. They argued that the tax changes, import quotas, and other provisions would harm multinationals and hinder the international flow of capital and technology. Still other opponents were in industries that benefit from the expansion of exports, banks, and the National Foreign Trade Council. At least one union—the UAW, which had left the AFL-CIO in 1968 when it broke with Meany over the Vietnam War—decided to oppose Burke-Hartke. The bill's provisions—imposing quotas on all imports, denying international use of US-developed technology, and reliance on import quotas, not TAA benefits, to help displaced workers—shocked Nat Weinberg, the UAW's director of special projects and economic analysis. Though Weinberg favored some Burke-Hartke provisions, such as its closing of tax loopholes that encouraged US corporations to shift production abroad, "the guts of the bill . . . would be disastrous, in my opinion, if it were to be enacted," he wrote.[83]

The UAW's opposition also relied on the union's confidence that the automobile industry would export more cars abroad, benefiting its members in the process. In reality, though, recessions, oil shocks, and a flood of Japanese imports, all at a time when Detroit automakers misjudged consumers' car-buying preferences, would reverse the UAW's fortunes by the end of the 1970s. Such splits over Burke-Hartke were not uncommon. In another union outside the AFL-CIO, the Teamsters, Burke-Hartke divided its locals by geography: members of locals in the inland industrial states, which were aware of their fellow laborers' tribulations with import competition, tended to support the measure. Teamsters locals on the coasts, however, opposed Burke-Hartke, with an eye toward additional jobs transporting goods from ports, a benefit of lower trade barriers and an increase in trade.[84]

In opposing Burke-Hartke, the UAW opted to seek TAA funding at levels that its president, Leonard Woodcock, said would allow the entry of imports from less-developed countries "without harm to American workers." Woodcock wanted assistance at a level similar to what Congress gave the nation's passenger railroad employees in 1971 when it consolidated the passenger railroads to form Amtrak: up to six years of full pay for laid-off workers, plus reimbursement for moving expenses and losses on home sales for relocating workers.[85]

Other opponents, like Minnesota Democratic-Farmer-Labor Representative Donald Fraser, said the bill "would do great damage to our nation's economy and to our foreign relations." Trading partners had already indicated they would retaliate against US products if the United States imposed import quotas or tariffs; such a move would lead to a trade war, undermining the national economy and increasing unemployment. Fraser believed a combination of a better TAA program and lower trade barriers would help the most, by giving workers who lost their jobs through import competition an opportunity to find new work.[86]

Supporters and opponents of Burke-Hartke eyed each other warily as Congress prepared to move the measure. "Union labor is presently engaged in a massive program to secure definite commitments to support this bill from present senators and congressmen as well as prospective new 1972 candidates," read a missive to employees of the Honeywell Corporation. "They claim overseas manufacturing by subsidiaries of U.S. companies represents an export of jobs and technology causing unemployment in this country." The company argued that multinationals were engaged in overseas manufacturing "to be competitive in the overseas market place" and that such activities made an increase in exports possible. Instead of adopting proposals like Burke-Hartke, Honeywell suggested, the executive branch should negotiate with trading partners, using "judicious and selective use of import quotas and other economic measures" to reduce trade barriers.[87]

Others sent letters to Senator Hartke voicing their opposition. "Nobody can deny that the U.S. today faces a series of circumstances which must be addressed straightforwardly and solved," wrote Robert Malott in a letter to Hartke, listing inflation, unemployment, and deficits in the balance of trade and balance of payments. Malott, whose FMC Corporation exported agricultural and food equipment, felt that Burke-Hartke ran counter to the best interests of the nation and most US consumers. "I think it is extremely dangerous to generalize and leave an impression that American multi-national companies are either the source of the problem or that they generally operate contrary to the interest of the United States in maintaining a world competitive position," he wrote. Malott argued that the United States needed "new, more equitable, selected trade understandings" with major trade partners to even out the nation's balance of payments.[88]

A. Carl Kotchian, the president of Lockheed Aircraft Corporation, also set down his opposition to the bill in a letter to Hartke. "The expansion of trade, investment, and technical exchange which has contributed to the welfare of the United States and other nations since World War II would be replaced by retaliation and contraction," Kotchian wrote.[89]

Course Reversal: Nixon, Lower Trade Barriers, and the Trade Act of 1973

As organized labor and business squared off over Burke-Hartke, Nixon's NEP encountered problems as its wage and price controls and currency devaluations failed to stop inflation and made the dollar vulnerable to currency speculation similar to that which preceded the policy in 1971. Trade flows also played a role in currency speculation: the growing deficits in the US balance of trade and balance of payments with Japan and West Germany had once again given both nations a large supply of dollars. The US trade deficit had increased to more than $6.4 billion during 1972, and the balance-of-payments deficit had not rebounded in the country's favor, as had been expected. Furthermore, the international community harbored lingering doubts about Nixon's wage and price controls.[90]

Nixon had planned to put his New Majority into action again in the 1972 elections and, on balance, accomplished that objective with organized labor. Nixon had antagonized George Meany and the AFL-CIO with his opposition to both Burke-Hartke and the Mills bill, as well as with his decision to impose wage and price controls. Yet, with Meany still supportive of US efforts in Vietnam, the AFL-CIO remained neutral in the election rather than support the Democratic candidate, antiwar Senator George McGovern of South Dakota. By offering no endorsement, the federation's member unions divided between the building trades, many of whom endorsed Nixon, and industrial unions, including the TWUA, ACWA, and ILGWU, which endorsed McGovern.[91]

Nixon had instituted wage and price controls in the hopes of stimulating the economy and removing an obstacle to his reelection campaign; he sought a macroeconomic policy that would generate growth without inflation. By early 1973, just as revelations of a June 1972 burglary at the Watergate Hotel set in motion the scandal that ended Nixon's presidency, another issue had surfaced. A boom in production had generated explosive growth in consumer spending and demand for raw materials; prices outstripped controls. Inflation would reach higher levels in 1973, driven by excess domestic demand and worldwide commodity shortages (food, then oil). In response, the Nixon administration imposed another round of wage and price controls in January 1973.[92]

A month later, Nixon reversed course on his 1969 declaration that no round of trade negotiations would proceed on his watch. Over the course of 1973, more than eighty nations conducted trade negotiations, the first since the Kennedy Round. The United States could not participate; the Johnson administration had allowed presidential authority to negotiate trade deals lapse in the backlash to the 1967 Kennedy Round agreement.

The Nixon administration had opened the door to revamping trade policy in late 1972. It had entertained proposals that included giving the president new authority to negotiate trade deals with other nations, as well as a revised TAA program that would qualify workers and industries for benefits more easily. Most important, Nixon's plan included a feature he hoped would soften the impact of foreign imports while adhering to the philosophy of lower trade barriers. The proposal envisioned allowing the president to raise tariffs for five years on imported goods to a level high enough to allow the affected domestic industry to compete. During the five-year period, the tariff would be lowered gradually to its original level, giving the affected industry time to find ways to compete or, if necessary, to end production altogether. Nixon also wanted authority to negotiate trade agreements, which Congress could approve or reject within ninety days. If Congress did not take action, the agreement would automatically take effect after the ninety-day period. Nixon hoped the flexible approach of raising and lowering tariffs, as well as the fast-track authority extended to the president, would lessen the need for the fixed, across-the-board quotas envisioned in Burke-Hartke.[93]

On February 12, 1973, while announcing a third devaluation of the dollar amid a new round of currency speculation, Treasury Secretary George Shultz said Nixon would send Congress "proposals for comprehensive trade legislation" that would grant the Executive Branch fast-track authority and the power to raise or lower tariff and nontariff barriers, as needed, to protect US interests. Much of the immediate reaction to the Shultz announcement focused on the dollar devaluation, however, and not on the trade bill. Newly installed ACWA

President Murray Finley, who replaced Jacob Potofsky upon his retirement in 1972, argued the devaluation illustrated the need for passage of Burke-Hartke: "It has become obvious that the band-aid solution to our monetary problems a year ago did not work," he said. "All it did was to make easier the export of U.S. capital through multinationals." Other unions who had sought import quotas, such as the International Union of Electrical, Radio, and Machine Workers, concurred with Finley.[94]

The devaluation announcement and Nixon's pursuit of a trade bill was part of an approach by the administration to ease the nation's trade and payments deficits. It sought a currency devaluation to even out the nation's balance of payments with Japan and West Germany, believing such a move would eventually inflate prices and wages, stimulate demand for workers, and eventually reduce unemployment. Simultaneously, lower trade barriers could drive growth in US exports, reducing the nation's deficit in its overall balance of trade.[95]

For the Nixon administration, a new trade bill would help produce growth by generating additional exports and creating jobs. Lower trade barriers would ease US exports into new markets; a revised tariff policy could give industries time to compete under temporary tariff raises, and workers affected by imports could take advantage of a revamped TAA to retrain for new careers. The policy could wind up benefiting workers, as well as industries, both exporters and those challenged by imports, and it would likely help Nixon politically heading into the 1974 midterm elections. A revised trade policy would continue Nixon's neomercantilist policies of the early 1970s, but it did not bode well for textiles and other industries facing stiff import competition. Even if the Nixon administration's tariff policy had been exercised as envisioned, domestic textile and apparel producers would likely have not been able to compete with their foreign counterparts. The only likely path out would have been a drastic embrace of automation—an effective restructuring of the industry that would have jeopardized thousands of jobs as a result of technological upgrades and not import competition.

In the week after Shultz's announcement of a new trade bill, Nixon took his case for the legislation to the annual AFL-CIO convention in Florida in a push to win their support. The stop was the first for Nixon in his campaign for a trade bill and also represented a gesture of respect to Meany and the federation for Meany's remaining neutral in the 1972 election. While the chief industrial unions, including the USWA, the United Rubber Workers, and the textile and apparel trade unions, still supported Burke-Hartke, Meany indicated the AFL-CIO was open to amending Burke-Hartke to include some of Nixon's proposals.[96]

On April 10, Nixon sent the trade bill to Congress, which he said called for the most important changes in trade policy since the TEA. The bill included new authority to negotiate trade agreements, which were needed for the United

States to participate in the Tokyo Round of trade negotiations under the GATT, and fast-track authority to negotiate trade agreements with other nations, to counter the proliferation of export subsidies, antidumping duties, quotas, and discriminatory bilateral agreements that had appeared since the conclusion of the Kennedy Round in 1967.[97]

Nixon asked Congress to grant the executive branch five years' authority to enter trade agreements, to continue or modify existing duties, impose additional duties, and continue existing tariff treatment. Unlike the authority granted in the RTAA and the TEA, which allowed tariff reductions of up to 50 percent from levels established by Smoot-Hawley and the RTAA, respectively, Nixon proposed that the legislative branch could raise or lower tariff levels to whatever level was desired. Nixon also called for liberalizing eligibility criteria for TAA and easing import-relief procedures.[98]

Nixon's proposal to reduce trade barriers, coming less than three years after he pledged to aid textile workers in their quest for import quotas, particularly rankled George Meany, who still supported Burke-Hartke. "The proposals provide no specific machinery to regulate the flood of imports and, indeed, some would increase the amount of damage to US employment and industrial production," Meany answered on April 11 when asked for his reaction to Nixon's introduction of the bill.[99]

Yet Meany's indignation masked a growing realization that Burke-Hartke, the vehicle the AFL-CIO had developed in hopes of protecting industries through a combination of import quotas and tax restrictions on multinational corporations, was effectively dead. By the time Nixon introduced his bill, Wilbur Mills, the Ways and Means committee chairman who supported textile quotas in his 1970 effort to outflank Nixon, had resumed his long-standing support of lower trade barriers. Mills embraced many of the president's proposals in a March 21 speech to members of the House. In rejecting the broad, fixed quotas of Burke-Hartke, Mills instead vowed to push for presidential authority to raise or lower tariffs and impose quotas. He also vowed to support Nixon's request for fast-track authority. Nixon's visit to the AFL-CIO signaled his willingness to negotiate over legislation sought by labor, such as an increase in the minimum wage that had stalled in Congress in 1972 and a revamped TAA program. In exchange, however, the AFL-CIO would have to drop its support of Burke-Hartke and favor Nixon's trade bill. While the president certainly had political goals in mind—notably, at least acquiring labor's neutrality in the 1974 midterm elections—securing passage of the trade bill came first.[100]

Business groups like the NAM, which opposed Burke-Hartke, now began to push for the trade bill. The NAM seized on the testimony the AFL-CIO provided to the House Ways and Means Committee in the spring of 1973, when it declared the Trade Reform Act was worse than no bill at all. "Organized labor has already declared its active opposition to this legislation and will campaign against it in committees and on the House floor, seeking to kill the bill outright or substitute Burke-Hartke provisions for it," a NAM official wrote in a memorandum urging the association's legislative coordinators to seek "the largest possible favorable vote" on the trade bill in Ways and Means.[101]

The trade bill moved slowly in the House during the spring and summer of 1973, amid ongoing economic stabilization efforts and as hearings on the Watergate incident got under way. A NAM survey of the members of the political landscape that the trade bill faced revealed a lack of in-depth support among industry and labor. Survey respondents demonstrated little, if any, understanding of how the trade bill would affect trade negotiations, dollar devaluations, or foreign policy issues. They also could not explain the difference between the trade bill and Burke-Hartke. In addition, congressional support for the trade bill was thin, prompting government officials to seek the business community's support to get the measure passed.[102]

The negotiations with labor, Mills's support of the Nixon trade bill, and the president's characterization of the need for more trade agreements to increase US exports galvanized support for the trade bill among the business community and in Congress. It also spelled the end of the line for Burke-Hartke and its supporters' hopes that reining in multinationals and imposing across-the-board import quotas could give import-sensitive US industries like textiles more space to compete against imports. On July 16 Burke-Hartke died in the Ways and Means Committee when the committee defeated, 17–7, an amendment to add Burke-Hartke to the Nixon trade bill.[103]

With Burke-Hartke dead, the developing Watergate scandal, international events, and commonplace legislative wrangling continued to slow the progress of the Trade Reform Act. By the end of August 1973, the bill had stalled over disagreements on how to pay for an expanded TAA program and how much trade negotiation authority the Executive Branch should receive; labor opposition to the bill and Mills's poor health also contributed to the delays.[104]

By October, action on the trade bill was delayed at the Nixon administration's request over a sensitive issue about the bill. Senator Henry "Scoop" Jackson, a conservative Democrat from Washington state, and Representative Charles Vanik, an Ohio Democrat, sought to block the Soviet Union from receiving most-favored-nation trading status unless it allowed Soviet Jews to emigrate to Israel. The administration feared the Jackson-Vanik amendment, as it was known, would complicate multilateral peace talks after the October 1973 Yom Kippur War. The Soviet Union was involved in those talks, and the Nixon administration did not want the amendment passed as part of the trade bill at the same time the Soviets' participation would be needed to ease tensions among Israel, Egypt, Syria, and other Middle East nations.[105]

After Nixon asked the House to suspend floor debate and a final vote on the Trade Reform Act, a NAM official, Nicholas Hollis, warned its legislative coordinators to watch for action from labor against the bill. "Organized labor, which has grown increasing[ly] hostile toward the Trade Bill, can be expected to intensify its efforts to defeat this legislation," Hollis wrote. In addition, a close vote in the House on the trade bill might revive Burke-Hartke by encouraging its supporters to place the measure into the Senate version of the trade bill. A delay in the bill could also jeopardize interest in multilateral trade and monetary negotiations and undermine efforts to develop "more effective industry/government planning for trade talks." Nearly a month later, Hollis warned that labor was seeking to divide the trade bill's supporting coalition and deliver "no" votes from at least 40 percent of the House.[106]

On December 11, 1973, the House passed the Trade Reform Act of 1973 by a vote of 272–140. Republicans voted 160–19 for the bill and Democrats opposed it by a 112–121 margin. The floor debate on the bill was especially heated, with opponents like Representative John Dent—the Pennsylvania Democrat who in 1967 had sought to link imports with the FLSA—noting the historic nature of the opposition. Dent said the AFL-CIO had opposed the Trade Act because "the labor movement, for the first time in its history since 1926, has decided that free trade is not good for the American people." He continued, "If this bill were good, if it were to create jobs, would labor be against it today? They could not; they would not. They know what they are doing." Upon the bill's passage, Dent warned of dire consequences. "They will either repeal it in the next five years or this nation will become virtually dependent for its livelihood on foreign products." Burke, meanwhile, warned the Trade Act "would encourage the President to take almost any action he chooses to encourage manufactured imports and will . . . lead to the erosion of America's industries."[107]

The House-passed trade bill started off slowly in the Senate in early 1974. Because it contained no provisions to regulate either imports or multinational corporations, the measure was derided as "worse than no bill at all" by much of organized labor. As the bill progressed in Congress, and the Watergate scandal and congressional hearings culminated in Nixon's resignation on August 9, the nation's economic situation worsened. Economic conditions were particularly dismal for labor: while the wage and price controls of Nixon's NEP were finally lifted in April, prices outstripped wages as double-digit inflation set in. While wages in the first year of major union contracts in 1974 increased 9.8 percent (as compared with 5.8% in 1973), 1974 saw a record 9,500 strikes, with large work stoppages in textiles, mining, shipbuilding, and the chemical industry. The BLS found average worker compensation increased 8.7 percent in 1974, but when inflation was factored in, average compensation actually *declined* by 2.1 percent. It was the first such decline recorded by BLS since it began keeping statistics in 1947.[108]

There was one bright spot about imports in textiles and apparel: international negotiators reached an agreement governing the international trade in synthetic and woolen textiles. After the bluntly negotiated bilateral agreements in 1971 by which Hong Kong, Japan, and South Korea agreed to voluntarily limit their wool and synthetic textile exports to the United States, Asian producers shifted their textile exports away from the United States and to Europe. In 1973 textile-producing nations embarked on a new round of multilateral negotiations to govern the global wool and synthetic textile trade. The resulting agreement, formally called the Arrangement regarding International Trade in Textiles but colloquially named the MFA, finally extended the provisions of the 1962 LTA governing the cotton textile trade to wool and man-made fibers. The MFA restricted the growth of foreign textile imports in the United States to 6 percent a year, with a limit of 24 percent in any given year after borrowing quota amounts from other years. The MFA took effect in January 1974, after which the United States negotiated eighteen bilateral agreements with textile-exporting nations by 1977 in an effort to control access to the US market. But just as the LTA faltered in the mid-60s in its mission of protecting the United States from cotton textile imports, the same fate befell the MFA as textile production continued to shift to less-developed nations. Also, the MFA failed to satisfy nations that were net importers, who believed the agreement's provisions to limit exports were too lenient. Conversely, exporting nations believed the same provisions limiting the growth of exports were too harsh.[109]

Approval of the MFA was a bright spot in an otherwise gloomy domestic economic picture. Unemployment, which hovered around 5 percent during 1973 and the first half of 1974, rose to 7.2 percent by the end of the year as the economy entered a recession that threatened to be the deepest since the Great Depression. Unemployment by the end of 1974 reached 8.6 percent in the manufacturing sector and 8.3 percent in the wholesale and retail trade sector. Financial and service jobs were somewhat insulated from the downturn, with 5.6 percent unemployment; the rate for white-collar workers was just 4.1 percent. The unemployment increase began in late summer, as Vice President Gerald Ford succeeded Nixon upon the latter's resignation. In response to requests for relief from labor leaders, Ford released money to start a public-service-job program under CETA.[110]

Ford also quickly resolved the question about the emigration of Soviet Jews to Israel, which had clouded a proposal to extend most-favored-nation trading status to the Soviet Union. On August 15, 1974, less than a week after assuming the presidency, Ford reached a compromise on the Jackson-Vanik amendment allowing the denial of most-favored-nation trading status to countries that did not allow Jews to emigrate.[111] The Ford administration would allow the Jackson-Vanik amendment, which was especially popular in both houses of Congress and among supporters of Israel, to stand as part of the trade bill, while Secretary of State Henry Kissinger negotiated an agreement with Soviet Foreign Minister Andrei Gromyko that allowed at least sixty thousand Jews to emigrate from the Soviet Union. In exchange, Jackson and Vanik, meanwhile, would allow the trade bill to proceed in the Senate, and the Soviet Union would receive most-favored-nation trading status, a goal of businesses seeking access to the Soviet market.[112]

Organized Labor in 1974: A Turning Point

While 1974 revealed a dismal economic landscape for labor, its political fortunes were somewhat mixed. Labor did see gains at the ballot box in 1974; a concentrated political turnout campaign combined with dissatisfaction with the Watergate scandal and the economy to boost Democratic majorities in both houses of Congress. Organized labor also scored two significant legislative wins in that year. The first, a minimum wage increase, had died in Congress in 1972 and was vetoed the following year.[113] In April 1974 Nixon had signed a minimum wage increase into law that raised the minimum wage for farmworkers and nonfarmworkers to $2.30 an hour. The new law also added 7 million workers to minimum-wage coverage, including domestic workers. In a bit of irony, the minimum wage increase was aided by the high inflation evident during 1974: during floor debate on the measure, members conceded inflation was already taking place. As a result, a higher minimum wage could offset the effects of inflation by narrowing the growing gap between wages and prices.[114]

On Labor Day, September 2, President Ford signed into law ERISA, the first federal effort to establish minimum standards for private pension plans. The measure was designed to protect the private pensions of 23 million workers. The product of seven years' legislative work, unions and other supporters had fought for such protections in response to the loss of pensions at the hands of dishonest employers, as well as in corporate bankruptcies and mergers. Under ERISA, a worker who was eligible for a pension would be guaranteed to receive the pension regardless of whether the worker stayed with the same company until retirement. The law also created the Pension Benefit Guaranty Corporation (PBGC), a federal insurer of terminated pension plans. Labor had sought language in the bill making pensions portable—in other words, allowing workers to move their pension benefits to new employers when they changed jobs. But no portability provisions survived congressional negotiations after opposition from business groups.

Without portability, workers under ERISA could not build pensions across employers when they changed jobs. They also had to leave their pension benefits in the hands of their former employers, risking the possibility that those employers might use the money for other purposes. In the case of the North Carolina firm Cannon Mills, the pension fund became a source of cash that the textile manufacturer's new owner, David Murdock, used to fund corporate takeovers. He later terminated the pension fund, replacing deposits with annuities backed by junk bonds. In 1991 the insurer offering the annuities collapsed, and thousands of workers immediately saw their pensions drop by 30 percent. Had ERISA allowed pension portability, millions of US workers could have moved their pensions when they switched jobs, protecting their retirement funds as they grew over the course of their careers. Portability also might have made companies less attractive to financiers who conducted the corporate raids and mergers that were commonplace in the 1980s. In addition to the loss of the portability feature, ERISA took effect as the nation's manufacturing base was shrinking. Over time, as more companies used bankruptcy as a tool to evade pension responsibilities, the PBGC came under increasing stress as pension liabilities mounted.[115]

Despite winning a higher minimum wage and securing coverage under FLSA for 7 million workers and gaining some measure of protection for 23 million private pensioners, the Trade Reform Act represented a key setback for organized labor on trade policy. Just five years earlier, in 1969, the AFL-CIO finally began to question its decades-long support of US trade policy, after decades of protest from workers and unions in industries that realized the costs, rather than the benefits, of global trade. The labor movement's quest to challenge trade liberalization since then had gained attention, if not results. Labor had attempted to secure import quotas in the Mills bill in 1970, in the vetoed minimum wage law in 1972, and in Burke-Hartke in 1972 and 1973. Now, unable to secure mandatory import quotas in the Trade Reform Act, the AFL-CIO ended its long-standing support of free trade and opposed the bill as it moved through the Senate.

During the year, as Jackson-Vanik slowed action on the trade bill, the AFL-CIO and textile and apparel unions opposed the bill because they felt it did not adequately protect US employment in the manufacturing sector. Labor faced off against business and the Nixon and Ford administrations, which still needed authority to participate in the Tokyo Round of trade negotiations, scheduled to begin in February 1975. Even after losing their chance at passing Burke-Hartke, the textile and apparel unions continued to urge some degree of protection for their industries. As action on the trade bill continued in the waning months of 1974, organized labor returned to protest. Two days after the midterm elections, the AFL-CIO policy council declared the Trade Act "worse than no legislation at all" because it failed to protect industries especially sensitive to import competition.[116]

On Veterans' Day, 1974, with the trade bill moving again in committee, more than 125,000 ACWA members walked off the job to protest imports, just as they had in the import campaigns of 1970 and 1971. In a pamphlet documenting the marches that took place nationwide that day, ACWA President Finley and Secretary-Treasurer Jacob Sheinkman outlined the workers' motivations: "They were protesting short work weeks, reduced work days, lower earnings. They were protesting the growing number of plant closures and bankruptcies in their industries. They were protesting the loss of jobs when it is becoming more and more difficult to find a job." The pamphlet outlined yet another resolution on imports passed by the ACWA in October 1974 decrying oil shocks, trade deficits, and multinational behaviors. It concluded with a call for ACWA members to urge the Ford administration to reject the trade bill and embrace more protectionist measures, a plea with which many members complied. Meanwhile, the ACWA ran advertisements urging consumers not to buy imported apparel.[117]

By 1974, the ACWA had planned a Veterans' Day campaign to place its members in front of retail stores, where they would once again urge consumers not to purchase imported clothing. This time, South Korea—which had replaced Japan as the nation's largest single source of imported clothing—was the nation of specific interest. To the ACWA, image and participation were as important as the message of economic devastation at the hands of imports they wished to convey: "It is vitally important that Americans everywhere . . . are impressed with our unity and determination to guard our jobs and our standards from further deterioration from low-wage imports."[118]

Later that month, as the Senate prepared to take up the Trade Act, organized labor urged action against it. "The message should be loud and clear: *kill this bill as it stands*, because it is a threat to American jobs, and Connecticut jobs in particular," John J. Driscoll, the president of the Connecticut AFL-CIO, urged in a letter to state affiliates and union representatives. "If we do not stop it, this bill will further erode the jobs and industries already hit badly such as steel, apparel, chemical and allied products, rubber, shoes, stone, clay and glass, auto, aircraft, and electronics," he wrote, adding that the bill "would only increase imports" that had cost, by the AFL-CIO's estimate, more than 5 million domestic jobs.[119]

The efforts by labor and others who hoped to force a reconsideration of trade policy were for naught. With the Jackson-Vanik amendment and Soviet emigration issue resolved, the Trade Act's path to passage was much clearer after the midterm elections. Ford continued to press the need for passage of the Trade Act. "It is essential to the future of the United States' trade policy and that of the world as well," he said in a December 3 speech to the American Conference on Trade. "The health of our domestic economy and the strength, the very structure, of our international economic relations are involved."[120]

On the Senate floor, the Jackson-Vanik amendment was added to the bill, and senators also rejected a protectionist amendment, offered by Senator McIntyre of New Hampshire, that would have limited the president's authority to reduce tariffs and duties. McIntyre had offered the amendment to provide a minimal level of protection for industries suffering from high import levels, like the New England footwear industry. Though McIntyre's amendment lost, the Senate did approve four amendments aimed at offering some minimal level of protection against imports, rather than import quotas. One such amendment came from John Pastore, the Rhode Island Democrat whose hearings since 1958 on the state of the nation's textile industry had contributed to the growing call for import quotas. Pastore's amendment excluded a number of categories of goods from receiving duty-free treatment, including textiles and apparel, watches, footwear, some electronic and steel articles, and manufactured glass products.[121] After a cloture vote that represented the last chance to stop the Trade Act, the Senate passed it, 77–4, on December 13. The handful of opposition from organized labor supporters and conservatives in the Senate was not enough to block the bill, and the lopsided vote hinted mostly at the timing of the vote, between a midterm election and the end of the congressional session.[122]

As was the case with his House counterpart, James Burke, Vance Hartke provided one of the "no" votes on the trade bill, alongside Democratic Senator James Abourezk of South Dakota, the only Arab American in the Senate, and Republican Senators Jim McClure of Idaho and Lee Metcalf of Montana. Hartke said the Trade Reform Act endorsed "the same type of unchanged policies which have been a failure in the past" and listed nine shortcomings he found with the bill, including the failure to stop the export of US jobs, capital, and technology. "It is my belief that the present trade bill continues worn-out economic philosophy, and it is an element which is driving us fast down the highway toward the destruction of the western economic system," he said.[123]

Six days later, a conference committee produced a compromise between the House and Senate versions that gave the Executive Branch the authority for five years to enter trade agreements with other nations to reduce, adjust, or eliminate tariff and nontariff trade barriers. Instead of mandatory trade quotas, the bill required the president to impose temporary quotas and import surcharges for up to 150 days when the United States faced large balance-of-payments deficits with other nations. The compromise also upgraded the president's special representative for trade negotiations (a position originally created in the TEA) to cabinet status and gave the representative responsibility for handling trade agreements. Furthermore, the Trade Act reorganized and renamed the Tariff Commission to the US International Trade Commission. It also relaxed the TAA eligibility criteria for workers and industries, allowing the trade commission to determine whether import competition constituted a substantial cause of injury to firms or workers, allowing more workers and firms to qualify for assistance.[124]

The conference report returned to both houses of Congress on December 20, where the House approved it, 323–36, and the Senate cleared the report for Ford's signature, 72–4. One of the votes for the trade bill came from Massachusetts Senator Edward Kennedy, whose brother had transitioned from protecting industries to promoting greater trade liberalization in his time in Congress and the White House. Ford signed the bill into law on January 3, 1975.

Conclusion

The Trade Reform Act had appeared to be the conclusion of an initial salvo by the US organized labor movement in its quest to make trade work for its members who were concerned that imports would eliminate their industries. In the case of textile unions, which would continue to press for protections against imports, their activism would never again reach the levels it attained between 1969 and 1974, as their numbers and political influence steadily declined. The efforts of the

President Gerald Ford signs the Trade Act of 1974 into law, January 3, 1975. The bill was enacted over the bitter opposition of labor; it marked the first time the AFL-CIO had opposed a trade measure since its 1955 merger. (Photo by David Hume Kennerly, White House Photographic Office Records, Gerald R. Ford Presidential Library, Ann Arbor, Michigan.)

ACWA, UTWA, ILGWU, and TWUA, however disjointed, did indeed reflect a growing concern among textile and garment workers that postwar prosperity in the United States was quickly ending, trapping millions of Americans without a secure economic footing.

As was the case in the late 1930s, when laborers hoping to hold on in the depths of the Great Depression opposed Cordell Hull's crowning accomplishment of a trade agreement with Great Britain under the RTAA, laborers saw in world trade in the 1960s and 1970s a threat of imports undercutting the tenuous gains that industrial workers had made in the intervening decades. While union leaders of the 1930s, occupied with establishing a broad industrial union movement, showed little concern about trade, their counterparts in the 1970s were well versed in recognizing the costs of the activities of multinational corporations, expanded international trade, and capital mobility.

Organized labor in both periods had shown it could secure some form of broad-based economic security. In 1938 it came in the form of the FLSA, incorporating the eight-hour day that had been a goal of US unions since the 1860s. In 1974, despite a recession and double-digit inflation, labor won an increase in the minimum wage and helped make 7 million more workers, including domestics, eligible for its coverage. And through ERISA, organized labor secured federal pension protections for 23 million US workers. Those successes, unfortunately, were soon overshadowed by the passage of the Trade Act of 1974, defeating organized labor's bid for legislation that would promote trade while protecting US jobs and industries from import competition. Labor's skepticism of the aims and benefits of trade failed to produce meaningful industry protections or an adequate response to the local effects of trade in a global environment. Their failure to overcome business and lawmaker support for lower trade barriers would set the stage for the near-total disappearance of the domestic textile and apparel industries. As recently as the 1960s, the industries together employed one of every seven US manufacturing workers; in 1973, they employed 2,380,400 nationwide. From that level, employment fell and, by November 2020, it stood at just 183,000—a 92.3 percent decline.

EPILOGUE

Where Do We Go from Here?

The 2016 election highlighted deeply rooted problems with US trade policy: its preference for new economic sectors and a belief that a growing economy will simply compensate the decline of old sectors; a push for trade deals, even as trading partners bend or break trade laws with impunity; a vast inability to aid workers and communities affected by import competition; and a growing social divide between an overclass that benefited financially from trade deals, while their working-class counterparts struggled from the hollowing out of local economies. The election results produced a cruel irony: the candidate who seemed to best articulate the concerns of some working-class voters was the person least able to deal with and address those concerns.

Can a balance be reached that promotes trade and helps workers? The national experience with industrial decline—both with the textile and apparel industries after World War II and much other US manufacturing from the 1960s onward—demands that policy makers and businesses must stop thinking of trade only in terms of generalized benefits like lower costs for consumers or higher corporate profits. They must also take into account the experience of workers and communities who bear the costs of trade policy—think job losses or community disinvestment—and act accordingly.

At the federal level, as US economic might is being challenged more intensely by China, the European Union, and other developed nations, it only makes sense that the United States begin to seriously articulate an industrial policy. Some degree of planning is needed to bring about a policy that creates new and innovative businesses and economic opportunities while helping communities and workers alike adjust to changing conditions.

For decades, ideas put forth to help workers, such as the ARA or TAA, have been ridiculed, underfunded, and scorned as unnecessary government intervention into private enterprise. The result, however, is a system that serves only businesses—who play localities against each other and then depart once their tax incentive is used up, or once they can find a cheaper source of labor—at the expense of workers and governments. In past decades, the practice of awarding tax incentives has yielded grotesque results, such as the multistate competitions in the 1990s for automobile plants operated by Bayerische Motoren Werke (BMW) and Mercedes-Benz. In the 2010s competitions for Boeing and Amazon yielded tax breaks for highly profitable companies and jeopardized states' ability to pay for basic services without tax increases. In the case of Amazon, more than one hundred cities and localities, for the chance at being one of twenty final contenders for its second location, willingly signed nondisclosure agreements and assembled incentive and benefit packages for a company that paid no taxes on $11 billion worth of income in 2018 and that was run by a CEO worth more than $165 billion. Tax incentives also led cities, counties, regions, and states to raid each other for businesses, as demonstrated by the recently concluded "Battle of State Line Road" between Kansas City, Kansas, and Kansas City, Missouri. A rethinking of the local side of trade policy must take place, and that rethinking must lead to the development of a system of economic development that is more equitable among business, government, and workers.

A new manufacturing policy must include an acknowledgment that trade policy creates losers as well as winners and must work to alleviate the negative impacts of job loss—through the development of new technologies and industries that can draw workers from declining sectors, or through a revised, expanded TAA program that fully replaces workers' wages while they retrain for new jobs. In order to pay for any such program, governments at the state and local levels must seriously give thought to ending the arms race of providing companies with ever-larger subsidies and tax breaks to locate or maintain their operations. A meaningful trade and investment policy might take those incentives and invest them in workers, rather than businesses, to ensure the continued presence of a skilled, educated workforce.

Another reform that needs to be adopted is the strengthening of the voice of organized labor. Since the passage of the Taft-Hartley Act in 1947, organized labor in the United States has largely been playing defense. Only in the twelve years between passage of the Wagner Act of 1935, an era that included concessions to labor during World War II that allowed wartime production to continue unimpeded, and enactment of Taft-Hartley, has the US organized labor movement had the right to grow without significant restraints. Despite the restrictions imposed since Taft-Hartley, workers nevertheless played a key role in alerting members of the public to conditions such as the impact of imports and competition on their jobs. The increasing inequality of wealth since the mid-1970s is no surprise to those who have marked the decline in organized labor's power since the mid-1950s. In the first decades of the twenty-first century, workers painfully aware of low pay, unsatisfactory work conditions—especially during the COVID-19 pandemic—and growing pay gaps began turning to unions as a means of securing economic stability, even among teachers in states where public-sector unions are barred or public workers have no rights to strike. If income inequality is to be reduced further, labor needs a more powerful voice, ideally through a revision of labor laws that place no unnecessary barriers before workers who want to form a union. Such a revision might also guarantee union recognition, dues checkoffs, and contracts reached through the traditional collective-bargaining process or binding arbitration. The balance of power between labor and capital must be recalibrated in order to give workers a stronger voice, which can be used to articulate and call for a more equitable trade policy.

The United States is at a crossroads with its trade policy unlike any other since the New Deal. It no longer enjoys the dominance it experienced in the quarter-century after World War II. Instead, at a time where much of the rest of the world is playing by the rules and multilateral organizations created under US influence to avoid the conflicts of World War II, the United States itself attempted during the Trump presidency to replace its policy with a nationalist isolationism. Proponents foresaw a return to prosperity in such a move, but the more likely outcome would have been that the world would beat the United States at its own game, ironically using the tools that Americans created as part of the era of lowering barriers to world trade. Under the Biden administration, the nation has begun to embrace a more worker-friendly trade policy, moving away from the isolationist bent of the Trump years.

Just as Cordell Hull envisioned trade policies that sought to break down geographical barriers, the United States now must commit to a trade policy that promotes a broader prosperity for its citizens, especially those who are most vulnerable to economic change, and exchanges fear of the world for a willingness to take its rightful place alongside—not before or after—the nations of the world. In a nation where inequality, paired with a long legacy of racial discrimination, has created a dual economy that threatens to separate Americans by race as much as by wealth, and in a world of many different cultures and nationalities, it is foolish to develop a trade policy driven by racist populism or fear of other nationalities or countries.[1]

A trade policy that delivers broad-based economic growth and prosperity, instead of benefiting economic elites, will aid in narrowing economic divides. Furthermore, a policy that attacks inequality while delivering economic growth will serve as a form of social insurance. Broad-based economic stability can avert further radicalism of the sort that has surfaced in Latin America and the Middle East, which has grown among segments of the US white working class in recent years. Such economic stability could also promote a class consciousness that would make it difficult, if not impossible, for opportunistic politicians to win political support using demagoguery masquerading as populism.

A renewed commitment to a policy that helps workers affected by trade, while benefiting companies and governments, could help the United States build a new economy that works better for all, encourages stability for workers, promotes profitable operations for businesses, and delivers a steady, growing economy that sustains governments at all levels.

The trade policy the United States has followed since 1934 was designed to increase international harmony and decrease the potential for conflict. The time has come to develop a trade policy that does the same for the country, in the spirit of the workers who protested for "wages not welfare" and economic stability in the face of globalization and deindustrialization. A trade and economic development policy in which workers, businesses, and governments hold responsibilities and enjoy equal benefits could go a long way toward ensuring domestic tranquility and promoting the general welfare. If this nation is to realize that goal, it will take workers, first and foremost, fighting to create an economy that takes their considerations into account and ensures they share in the resultant prosperity. When workers, businesses, and governments repair the fraying fabric of US trade policy, the United States will be closer to creating an economy that yields broad-based prosperity for all and social stability to counter the ongoing radicalization under way. Our survival as a nation depends on it; all we need is the courage to act.

NOTES

Abbreviations

Catholic Univ.	American Catholic History Research Center and University Archives, Catholic University of America, Washington, DC
Clemson	Special Collections and Archives, Clemson University Libraries, Clemson, South Carolina
Eberly	Eberly Family Special Collections Library, Paterno Library, Pennsylvania State University, University Park, Pennsylvania
FDR Library	Franklin D. Roosevelt Library, Hyde Park, New York
Ford Library	Gerald R. Ford Presidential Library, Ann Arbor, Michigan
FRED	Federal Reserve Economic Data, Federal Reserve Bank of St. Louis
Hagley	Hagley Museum and Library, Wilmington, Delaware
Hornbake	Special Collections and University Archives, Hornbake Library, University of Maryland, College Park
JFK Library	John F. Kennedy Presidential Library and Museum, Boston
Kheel Center	Kheel Center for Labor-Management Documentation and Archives, Martin P. Catherwood Library, Cornell University, Ithaca, New York
LBJ Library	Lyndon B. Johnson Presidential Library, Austin, Texas
LC	Library of Congress, Washington, DC
Meany Archives	George Meany Memorial Archives, National Labor College, Silver Spring, Maryland (Now the George Meany Memorial AFL-CIO Archive, Special Collections and University Archives, Hornbake Library, University of Maryland, College Park)
NA	National Archives II, College Park, Maryland
NARA	National Archives and Records Administration, Washington, DC
NSF	National Security File
Reuther Library	Walter P. Reuther Library, Archives of Labor and Urban Affairs, Wayne State University, Detroit

RG	Record Group
Rubenstein	David M. Rubenstein Rare Book and Manuscript Library, Perkins Library, Duke University, Durham, North Carolina
SHSW	State Historical Society of Wisconsin, University of Wisconsin, Madison
SLA	Southern Labor Archives, Special Collections and Archives, Georgia State University Library, Atlanta
WEB Du Bois	Special Collections and University Archives, W. E. B. Du Bois Library, University of Massachusetts, Amherst
WHCF	White House Central Files
WHSF	White House Subject Files

Introduction

1. US Bureau of Labor Statistics, Civilian Labor Force Level and All Employees, Manufacturing; FRED, https://fred.stlouisfed.org.

2. Ibid.

3. Remarks by Alfred Eckes, "Congressional Briefing on the History of U.S. Trade Policy," National History Center, June 29, 2018.

Chapter 1. From Free Trade to Populism

1. US Bureau of Labor Statistics, *Industries in Alphabetical Order*, www.bls.gov/iag/tgs/iag_index_alpha.htm; 1973 figures in Timothy J. Minchin, "Decline of the Textile and Apparel Industry and Deindustrialization in the South," in *Life and Labor in the New New South*, ed. Robert H. Zieger (Gainesville: University Press of Florida, 2012), 260; 2019 figures from FRED.

2. Evelyn Dubrow, "Draft Speech on History of MFAs," n.d. (1981), box 28, folder 23, International Ladies' Garment Workers' Union (ILGWU) Political Department Records #5780/103, Kheel Center for Labor-Management Documentation and Archives, Martin B. Catherwood Library, Cornell University, Ithaca, New York [hereafter, Kheel Center].

3. Vinod K. Aggarwal, *Liberal Protectionism: The International Politics of the Organized Textile Trade* (Berkeley: University of California Press, 1985), 123–82; Richard L. Rowan and Robert E. Barr, *Employee Relations Trends and Practices in the Textile Industry* (Philadelphia: University of Pennsylvania, Wharton School, Industrial Research Unit, 1987), 20–21.

4. Cynthia D. Anderson, *The Social Consequences of Economic Restructuring in Textiles: Change in a Southern Mill Village* (New York: Garland, 2000), 40.

5. Martin Wolf, Hans Hinrich Glismann, Joseph Pelzman, and Dean Spinanger, *Costs of Protecting Jobs in Textiles and Clothing* (London: Trevor-Hobbs, 1984), 144; Cynthia Anderson, *Social Consequences*, 47; Rowan and Barr, *Employee Relations Trends*, 14–16, 22.

6. Cletus E. Daniel, *Culture of Misfortune: An Interpretive History of Textile Unionism in the United States* (Ithaca, NY: ILR, 2001), 273–78.

7. Timothy J. Minchin, *Don't Sleep with Stevens! The J. P. Stevens Campaign and the Struggle to Organize the South, 1963–80* (Gainesville: University Press of Florida, 2005), 166–67.

8. Daniel, *Culture of Misfortune*: 278–79; Minchin, *Don't Sleep*, 179–84.

9. Judith Stein, *Pivotal Decade: How the United States Traded Factories for Finance in the Seventies* (New Haven, CT: Yale University Press, 2010), 51–73.

10. Mark Mizruchi, *The Fracturing of the American Corporate Elite* (Cambridge, MA: Harvard University Press, 2013); Marc Levinson, *An Extraordinary Time: The End of the Postwar Boom and the Return of the Ordinary Economy* (New York: Basic Books, 2016); Lawrence Mishel and Julia Wolfe, *CEO Compensation Has Grown 940 Percent since 1978* (Washington, DC: Economic Policy Institute, 2019).

11. Minchin, "Decline," 263–64; J. Stein, *Pivotal Decade*, 176–90; Joseph Hower and Joseph McCartin, "Marshall's Principle: A Former Labor Secretary Looks Back (and Ahead)," *Labor* 11, no. 4 (Winter 2014): 100–104.

12. Barry Bluestone and Bennett Harrison, *The Deindustrialization of America: The Decline of Basic Industry* (New York: Basic Books, 1982); manufacturing data from FRED.

13. Minchin, "Decline," 263–64; Douglas Irwin, *Clashing over Commerce: A History of US Trade Policy* (Chicago: University of Chicago Press, 2017), 574–86. For more on Reagan firing air-traffic controllers, see Joseph McCartin, *Collision Course: Ronald Reagan, the Air Traffic Controllers, and the Strike That Changed America* (Oxford: Oxford University Press, 2011), 328–58.

14. McCartin, *Collision Course*, Gary Mucciaroni, *The Political Failure of Employment Policy, 1945–1982* (Pittsburgh, PA: University of Pittsburgh Press, 1990); Benjamin Collins, *Trade Adjustment Assistance for Workers and the TAA Reauthorization Act* (Washington, DC: Congressional Research Service, 2018), 12.

15. US Congress, Office of Technology Assessment, *The U.S. Textile and Apparel Industry: A Revolution in Progress*, Special Report OTA-TET-332 (Washington, DC: US Government Printing Office, 1987), 32–33, 81–82; Minchin, "Decline," 264–65; Irwin, *Clashing*, 579–83.

16. Gary Clyde Hufbauer, Yee Wong, and Ketki Sheth, *US-China Trade Disputes: Rising Tide, Rising Stakes* (Washington, DC: Institute for International Economics, 2006), 30–32; Helene Cooper and John Harwood, "The GATT Vote: Trade Winds: GATT Raises Stakes in U.S. Political Battle for Middle-Class Voter," *Wall Street Journal*, December 2, 1994; Irwin, *Clashing*, 621–22, 644–53; "All Employees, Textile Mills," US Bureau of Labor Statistics data retrieved from Federal Reserve Economic Data (FRED), Federal Reserve Bank of St. Louis, https://fred.stlouisfed.org/series/CES3231300001; "All Employees, Apparel," US Bureau of Labor Statistics data retrieved from FRED, Federal Reserve Bank of St. Louis, https://fred.stlouisfed.org/series/CES3231500001; data analyzed by author. Congress in late 1994 approved the US membership in the WTO, which replaced the GATT at the beginning of 1995, against the objections of the textile industry and executives such as Roger Milliken, who opposed a 40 percent cut in overall tariff levels contained in the Uruguay Round agreement.

17. Denis Audet and Raed Safadi, eds., *A New World Map in Textiles and Clothing: Adjusting to Change* (Paris: Organization for Economic Co-operation and Development, 2004), 93–94; Ellen Israel Rosen, *Making Sweatshops: The Globalization of the U.S. Apparel Industry* (Berkeley: University of California Press, 2002), 119–52.

18. Daniel, *Culture of Misfortune*, 279. UNITE merged again in 2004 with the Hotel Employees and Restaurant Employees International Union to form UNITE HERE (Union of Needletrades, Industrial, and Textile Employees and Hotel Employees and Restaurant Employees).

19. Cynthia Anderson, *Social Consequences*, 39; Minchin, "Decline," 266–67; Audet and Safadi, 94; Irwin, *Clashing*, 631–43; B. Collins, *Trade Adjustment Assistance for Workers*, 12.

20. Employment and Training Administration, US Department of Labor, "The Worker Adjustment and Retraining Notification Act," Fact Sheet, August 4, 1988, https://www.doleta.gov/programs/factsht/warn.htm.

21. Irwin, *Clashing*, 643, 656–60.

22. Ibid., 662.

23. Ibid., 663–67.

24. "Expanded Lobbying Group Calls on Bush for Help," *Textile World* 153, no. 8 (August 2003), 14; Hufbauer et al., *US-China Trade Disputes*, 29–32; "U.S. and China Reach Textiles Deal," *Washington Post*, November 8, 2005.

25. Irwin, *Clashing*, 667–68.

26. Ibid.

27. Guy Standing, *The Precariat: The New Dangerous Class* (London: Bloomsbury, 2011).

28. FRED; Barry Bluestone, "Deindustrialization and Unemployment in America," in *Deindustrialization and Plant Closure*, ed. Paul Staudohar and Holly Brown (Lexington, MA: D. C. Heath, 1987), 4–6.

29. Jerry Adler, "The Rise of the Overclass," *Newsweek*, July 30, 1995.

30. David Rohde, "Ted Turner Plans a $1 Billion Gift for U.N. Agencies," *New York Times*, September 19, 1997.

31. Anand Giridharadas, "The Elite Charade of Changing the World," episode 233, *New York Library Talks Podcast*, September 23, 2018, https://www.nypl.org/blog/2018/09/21/winners-take-all-tk; Giridharadas, *Winners Take All: The Elite Charade of Changing the World* (New York: Knopf, 2018).

32. Giridharadas podcast.

33. Ibid.

34. Patton Garriott, "Race Trumps Class? Whiteness, Social Class and the 2016 Presidential Election," *SES Indicator*, January 2017, https://www.apa.org/pi/ses/resources/indicator/2017/01/race-class; Arlie Russell Hochschild, *Strangers in Their Own Land: Anger and Mourning on the American Right* (New York: New Press, 2016). Political scientist Steven Miller and scientist Nicholas Davis, meanwhile, are developing research into whether a correlation exists between racial intolerance and support for authoritarianism—a correlation that could be built, in part, on feelings of lost economic status. For more, see Chauncey Devega, "Are White People Ready to Bail on Democracy? These Researchers Say the Danger Is Real," *Salon.com*, August 2, 2018, https://www.salon.com/2018/08/02/are-white-people-ready-to-bail-on-democracy-these-researchers-say-the-danger-is-real/.

35. Select Committee on Intelligence, US Senate, *Russian Active Measures Campaigns and Interference in the 2016 U.S. Election*, Senate Report no. 116–290 (Washington, DC: US Government Printing Office, 2019).

36. Barack Obama, speech to the Democratic National Convention, Philadelphia, July 27, 2016, https://abcnews.go.com/Politics/full-text-president-barack-obamas-2016-democratic-national/story?id=40949231.

37. B. Collins, *Trade Adjustment Assistance for Workers*, 12–13.

38. Stan Greenberg, James Carville, and Erica Seifert, *Inside the GOP: Report on Focus Groups with Evangelical, Tea Party, and Moderate Republicans* (Washington, DC: Democracy Corps, 2013), 2–3; see also Carol Anderson, *White Rage: The Unspoken Truth of Our Racial Divide* (London: Bloomsbury, 2016).

39. "Boehner Must Navigate around Senate, Obama—and Tea Party," *National Journal*, November 3, 2010; National Conference of State Legislators, "2010 Election: Legislature Party Control Switch," accessed December 12, 2021, http://www.ncsl.org/research/elections-and-campaigns/2010-legislature-party-control-switch.aspx.

40. Carol Anderson, *One Person, No Vote: How Voter Suppression Is Destroying Our Democracy* (London: Bloomsbury, 2018).

41. Joan C. Williams, "What So Many People Don't Get about the U.S. Working Class," *Harvard Business Review*, November 10, 2016.

42. Alfred E. Eckes Jr., *Opening America's Market: U.S. Foreign Trade Policy since 1776* (Chapel Hill: University of North Carolina Press, 1995), 202.

43. In the 2012 presidential election, African American voting rates exceeded that of non-Hispanic whites for the first time since the US Census began measuring that statistic in 1980 (66.6 percent vs. 64.1 percent). In 2016, by comparison, non-Hispanic white voting rates increased to 65.3 percent while African American voting rates dropped to 59.6 percent. Furthermore, the share of African American voters decreased from 12.9 percent in 2012 to 11.9 percent in 2016 while the share of white voters remained steady (73.7 percent in 2012 and 73.3 percent in 2016)—indicating the influence of factors like voter ID laws and lack of voter enthusiasm (Thom File, "Voting in America: A Look at the 2016 Presidential Election," *Census Blogs*, US Census Bureau, May 10, 2017, https://www.census.gov/newsroom/blogs/random-samplings/2017/05/voting_in_america.html).

44. W. E. B. Du Bois, *Black Reconstruction in America* (New York: Oxford University Press, 2007), 573–74.

45. B. Collins, *Trade Adjustment Assistance for Workers*, 12–13; Rick Perlstein, "Exclusive: Lee Atwater's 1981 Interview on the Southern Strategy," *The Nation*, November 13, 2012, https://www.thenation.com/article/archive/exclusive-lee-atwaters-infamous-1981-interview-southern-strategy/.

46. Robert B. Horwitz, "Culture Trumps Class," *Contexts* 16, no. 2 (2017): 14–15.

47. George Packer, "Head of the Class: How Donald Trump Is Winning Over the White Working Class," *New Yorker*, May 8, 2016; Horwitz, "Culture," 14.

Chapter 2. Clashing Aims

1. Griffin's Steering Committee on the Anglo-American Trade Treaty ran no fewer than six weekly newspaper advertisements in early 1938 criticizing the UK trade agreement. Activism in Lawrence included speeches, radio addresses, and resolutions from

civic groups opposing the agreement that drew the attention of local, state, and federal politicians ("When They Let Down the Tariff Bars They Let Down Your Pay!," *Evening Tribune* [Lawrence, MA], February 2, 1938; "Our Industries Compete with the World," *Evening Tribune*, February 9, 1938; "Trade Treaties Can Hit Us in 17 Ways!," *Evening Tribune*, February 12, 1938; "Is Industrial Stagnation the Price of 'World Peace,'" *Evening Tribune*, February 18, 1938; "Save American Industry!," *Evening Tribune*, February 26, 1938; "It's a Costly 'World Peace' That Banishes America's Smile of Confidence!," *Evening Tribune*, March 5, 1938).

2. "400 to Speak at Inquiry on British Trade; Committee Hearing on Reciprocal Treaty to Start March 14," *Washington Post*, March 7, 1938.

3. Walter Griffin, Stenographer's Minutes of the Hearing before the CRI in Connection with the Negotiations of a Reciprocal Trade Agreement with the United Kingdom of Great Britain, vol. 2, p. 189, March 14–15, 1938, RG 364 (Records of the Office of the U.S. Trade Representative), box 323, folder "U.K. Volume 2," National Archives II, College Park, MD [hereafter, NA]; "Protest Lower Tariff; N.E. Congressmen Declare for Increased Protection," *Evening Tribune*, March 14, 1938; "Employees' Group to Oppose Treaty," *Evening Tribune*, March 14, 1938; "Congressman Connery Registers His Protest," *Evening Tribune*, March 14, 1938; "Off for Capital Tonight; Local Delegation to Protest Lowering of Tariff," *Evening Tribune*, March 14, 1938; Frank O'Hearn, "Mayor Griffin Voices Protest of Lawrence; Tells Committee City Fearful of Trade Pact Result," *Evening Tribune*, March 15, 1938; "Encouraged," *Evening Tribune*, March 18, 1938; "Mayor Carries Protest to White House Today; Discusses Proposed Pact with President's Son," *Evening Tribune*, March 17, 1938.

4. When enacted in 1935, the Social Security Act covered only about 31 percent of the US workforce. But it excluded 27 percent of white workers, 65 percent of African American workers, and 66 percent of "others"—a designation including Native American, Latino, and Asian workers. The disproportionate exclusion of various racial and ethnic groups, and the uneven application of coverage for groups like farmworkers and domestics, led to contentious arguments about whether the Social Security Act was racist in nature (Ira Katznelson, *Fear Itself: The New Deal and the Origins of Our Time* [New York: Liveright, 2013], 252–60; Larry DeWitt, "The Decision to Exclude Agricultural and Domestic Workers from the 1935 Social Security Act," *Social Security Bulletin* 70, no. 4 [2010], https://www.ssa.gov/policy/docs/ssb/v70n4/v70n4p49.html).

5. Nelson Lichtenstein, "From Corporatism to Collective Bargaining: Organized Labor and the Eclipse of Social Democracy in the Postwar Era," in *The Rise and Fall of the New Deal Order 1930–1980*, ed. Steve Fraser and Gary Gerstle, 122–52 (Princeton, NJ: Princeton University Press, 1989); Mizruchi, *Fracturing*, 81–108, 180–221.

6. Employment figures from "All Employees, Manufacturing," US Bureau of Labor Statistics data retrieved from FRED, Federal Reserve Bank of St. Louis, https://fred.stlouisfed.org/series/MANEMP; "All Employees, Textile Mills," US Bureau of Labor Statistics data retrieved from FRED, Federal Reserve Bank of St. Louis, https://fred.stlouisfed.org/series/CES3231300001; "All Employees, Apparel," US Bureau of Labor Statistics data retrieved from FRED, Federal Reserve Bank of St. Louis, https://fred.stlouisfed.org/series/CES3231500001; data analyzed by author.

7. Cordell Hull, *Memoirs of Cordell Hull* (New York: Macmillan, 1948) 21–22, 81–84; Michael Butler, *Cautious Visionary: Cordell Hull and Trade Reform, 1933–1937* (Kent, OH: Kent State University Press, 1998), 2–3, 7–8.

8. Butler, *Cautious Visionary*, 1–11.

9. Ibid., 10–13.

10. Eckes, *Opening America's Market*, 90–96; Irwin, *Clashing*, 348–55, 371–73.

11. Thomas McMahon, "Report of International President," in UTWA, *Third Biennial and Twenty-Seventh Annual Convention*, September 10–14, 1928, Great Northern Hotel, New York (New York: UTWA, 1928), 16.

12. Robert Elliot Chiles, *The Revolution of '28: Al Smith, American Progressivism, and the Coming of the New Deal* (Ithaca, NY: Cornell University Press, 2018), 157–80.

13. Butler, *Cautious Visionary*, 15–16; Franklin Roosevelt, "I Pledge You—I Pledge Myself to a New Deal for the American People," July 2, 1932, in Franklin Roosevelt, *The Public Papers and Addresses of Franklin D. Roosevelt*, ed. Samuel I. Rosenman, vol. 1, *The Genesis of the New Deal, 1928–1932* (New York: Random House, 1938), 656–57.

14. Butler, *Cautious Visionary*, 4–5, 8–11.

15. Roosevelt, "Campaign Address on Agriculture and Tariffs at Sioux City, Iowa, September 29, 1932," in Roosevelt, *Public Papers and Addresses*, 1: 768–69; Roosevelt, "Campaign Address on Reciprocal Tariff Negotiations (excerpts), Seattle, Washington, September 20, 1932," in Roosevelt, *Public Papers and Addresses*, 1: 723–26. Quotations: "brought the Government to a state of financial distress" in Franklin Roosevelt, "The Candidate Discusses the National Democratic Platform, Radio Address, Albany, NY, July 30, 1932," in Roosevelt, *Public Papers and Addresses*, 1: 660–61; "financial, industrial, agricultural, and commercial leadership," in Democratic Party Platforms, 1932, Democratic Party Platform Online, *The American Presidency Project*, ed. Gerhard Peters and John T. Woolley, https://www.presidency.ucsb.edu/node/273214.

16. Roosevelt, "National Democratic Platform," in Roosevelt, *Public Papers and Addresses*, 1: 664–65; Butler, *Cautious Visionary*, 16.

17. Butler, *Cautious Visionary*, 1–2, 5–6, 10–11; "Hull, Cordell," *Biographical Directory of the United States Congress, 1774–Present*, http://bioguide.congress.gov/scripts/biodisplay.pl?index=H000940.

18. Butler, *Cautious Visionary*, 6–8, 15; Hull, *Memoirs*, 352–53 (quote).

19. Franklin Roosevelt, "First Inaugural Address, March 4, 1933," Presidential Speeches, Miller Center, https://millercenter.org/the-presidency/presidential-speeches/march-4-1933-first-inaugural-address (quotes); Irwin, *Clashing*, 417; Butler, *Cautious Visionary*, 15–16, 27–28, 39–48, 83–93; Hull, 352–53. Raymond Moley, an undersecretary of state and Brain Trust rival of Hull, repeatedly undercut Hull's authority during the London conference. Moley resigned in August 1933; he later became a bitter opponent of the New Deal and a critic of liberalism (Butler, *Cautious Visionary*, 39–40, 51–79; Raymond Moley, *After Seven Years* [New York: Harper and Brothers, 1939]).

20. Butler, *Cautious Visionary*, 104–5; Hull, *Memoirs*, 358–59. In the 1920s, Hull and McClure developed the MFN principle contained in the RTAA (Butler, *Cautious Visionary*, 14; Eckes, *Opening*, 93–96).

21. *Reciprocal Trade Agreements: Hearings on H.R. 8430*, before the Committee on Ways and Means, U.S. House of Representatives, Seventy-Third Congress, second session, 51 (March 8, 1934) (testimony of Henry Wallace, Secretary, U.S. Department of Agriculture).

22. Franklin Roosevelt, Statement on Reciprocal Trade Pact, June 12, 1934 (Roosevelt quote), FDR Family, Business, and Personal Papers, box 42, folder 39, FDR Library; Butler, *Cautious Visionary*, 93–96; Hull, *Memoirs*, 357 (Hull quote); Thomas Ferguson, "Industrial Conflict and the Coming of the New Deal," in Fraser and Gerstle, *Rise and Fall*, 18; Katznelson, *Fear Itself*, 261–64.

23. Adolf A. Berle, "America Embarks on a New Trade Policy," *New York Times*, August 26, 1934.

24. Solomon Fabricant, *Manufacturing Output 1929–1937* (Cambridge, MA: National Bureau of Economic Research, 1940), 5.

25. Timothy W. Vanderburg, "Cannon Mills: A Case Study in Southern Industrialization" (PhD diss., Mississippi State University, 2001), 25–26; John G. Winant, *Report of the Board of Inquiry for the Cotton Textile Industry to the President* (Washington, DC: US Government Printing Office, 1935), 1.

26. Janet Irons, *Testing the New Deal: The General Textile Strike of 1934 in the American South* (Urbana: University of Illinois Press, 2000), 49–56.

27. Irons, *Testing*, 50–51, 56–57.

28. Irons, *Testing*, 64–67.

29. Irons, *Testing*, 57–62; Hugh Johnson, Administration of N.R.A., in folder "Saturday Evening Post Articles 6/30/34, 7/7/34, 7/14/34, 7/21/34 on NRA," container 5, Hugh Johnson Papers, FDR Library.

30. Irons, *Testing*, 66–68; H. M. Douty, "Recovery and the Southern Wage Differential," *Southern Economic Journal* 4, no. 3 (January 1938): 314–20; Winant, *Report*, 2.

31. Irons, *Testing*, 72–74.

32. ACWA, "A New Deal for the Clothing Workers," n.d. [ca. 1933], box 12, folder 37 (Leaflets 1933–), MSS1 (ACWA, Local 125 Papers) [hereafter, Local 125 Papers, WEB Du Bois], Special Collections and University Archives, W. E. B. Du Bois Library, University of Massachusetts, Amherst [hereafter, WEB Du Bois].

33. ACWA, "Workers of the Standard-Romper Company," Pawtucket, RI, n.d. [ca. 1934], box 12, folder 37 (Leaflets 1933–), Local 125 Papers, WEB Du Bois.

34. James Hodges, *New Deal Labor Policy and the Southern Cotton Textile Industry, 1933–1941* (Knoxville: University of Tennessee Press, 1986), 61; Robert Parmet, *The Master of Seventh Avenue: David Dubinsky and the American Labor Movement* (New York: New York University Press, 2005), 85–97; Steve Fraser, *Labor Will Rule: Sidney Hillman and the Rise of American Labor* (New York: Free Press, 1991), 292–93.

35. Irons, *Testing*, 38–42; Hodges, *New Deal Labor Policy*, 86–90; Parmet, *Master of Seventh Avenue*, 113–14; Winant, *Report*, 2–4.

36. J. C. Atchison, "Strike Signal Flashed to Locals in Tense Ceremony," and United Press International, "U.S. Labor Board Starts Attempt for Peace in Cotton Textile Mills," *Daily News Record* (New York), August 31, 1934; Cletus Daniel, *Culture of Misfortune: An Interpretive History of Textile Unionism in the United States* (Ithaca, NY: ILR, 2001), 47;

Hodges, *New Deal Labor Policy*, 107–10; Irons, *Testing*, 112–55; John A. Salmond, *The General Textile Strike of 1934: From Maine to Alabama* (Columbia: University of Missouri Press, 2002), 45–80; F. Ray Marshall, *Labor in the South* (Cambridge, MA: Harvard University Press, 1967), 166–68.

37. Winant, *Report*, 3–5, 12–13; Irons, *Testing*, 156–60; Hodges, *New Deal Labor Policy*, 86–126; US Bureau of Labor Statistics, *General Textile Strike, September 1934* (Washington, DC: US Bureau of Labor Statistics, 1935), 6–7; Roosevelt, *Public Papers and Addresses*, 3: 404; Dewey Fleming, "Textile Labor Board Named by President," (Baltimore) *Sun*, September 27, 1934.

38. William Lockwood, *The Economic Development of Japan: Growth and Structural Change, 1868–1938* (Princeton, NJ: Princeton University Press, 1954), 3–13, 86, 102, cited in US Tariff Commission, *Postwar Developments in Japan's Foreign Trade* (Washington, DC: US Tariff Commission, 1958), 6; RG 364, box 289, folder "Japan—Misc. releases clippings," NA.

39. *Cotton Textile Industry: Message from the President of the U.S. Transmitting a Report on the Conditions and Problems of the Cotton Textile Industry* (Washington, DC: US Government Printing Office, 1935), 1–3, 7–18, 24–28 [hereafter, *Roper Commission Report*].

40. *Roper Commission Report*, 100–101; Lockwood, *Economic Development of Japan*, 64–65.

41. Testimony of Claudius Murchison, Stenographer's Minutes of the Hearing before the CRI in Connection with the Negotiations of a Reciprocal Trade Agreement with Czechoslovakia, October 25–29, 1937, vol. 1, 63, RG 364, box 318, folder "Czechoslovakia—Miscellaneous Material, October 25–29, 2937," NA [hereafter, Czechoslovakia Hearing Minutes]; memorandum of conversation between Secretary Hull and the Japanese ambassador, Mr. Hiroshi Saito: Trade, June 20, 1934, reel 30, Cordell Hull Papers, Manuscript Division, LC [hereafter, Hull Papers].

42. Letter from Franklin Roosevelt to James Curley, June 23, 1936. Official Files Collection 61, box 4, folder "Tariff Matters 1933–1945 T-V," FDR Library.

43. "Textile Exporters to Protest Trade Treaty with Cuba," *Daily News Record* (New York), August 28, 1934.

44. Summary of Information Received, "Report of the CRI in Connection with the Negotiations of a Reciprocal Trade Agreement with France and Its Colonies, Dependencies, and Protectorates Other Than Morocco: In Two Parts, August 1935," part 1, 3–4, RG 364, box 252, unsorted, NA.

45. "Henry G. F. Lauten," *New York Times*, May 28, 1951; Testimony of Henry G. F. Lauten, Stenographer's Minutes of the Hearing before the CRI in Connection with the Negotiations of a Reciprocal Trade Agreement with Haiti, October 15, 1934, 34–36, RG 364, box 319, folder "Haiti—October 15, 1934," NA.

46. Letter from William DeMin, Stenographer's Minutes of the Hearing before the CRI in Connection with the Negotiations of a Reciprocal Trade Agreement with Colombia, October 16, 1934, 79–83, RG 364, box 315, unsorted, NA.

47. Butler, *Cautious Visionary*, 42–45, 121; memorandum of conversation between Secretary Hull and the Japanese ambassador, Mr. Matsuji Debuchi: Reciprocity Negotiations,

August 10, 1933; Informal and personal message from Mr. Hirota, Minister for Foreign Affairs, as telegraphed to Mr. Saito, the Japanese Ambassador, February 21, 1934; memorandum of conversation between Secretary Hull and the Japanese ambassador, Mr. Hiroshi Saito: Commercial Treaty, May 10, 1934; memorandum of conversation between Secretary Hull and the Japanese ambassador, Mr. Hiroshi Saito: Trade, June 20, 1934; memorandum of conversation between Secretary Hull and the Japanese ambassador, Mr. Hiroshi Saito, Tuesday, February 19, 1935, at 10:30 a.m.: Japanese Trade in South and Central America; all in reel 30, Hull Papers.

48. "Roosevelt Signs the Wagner Bill as 'Just to Labor,'" *New York Times*, July 6, 1935; National Labor Relations Board, "1935 Passage of the Wagner Act," https://www.nlrb.gov/about-nlrb/who-we-are/our-history/1935-passage-of-the-wagner-act.

49. "The CIO," n.d. [1937], box 11, folder 25, John Brophy Papers [hereafter, Brophy Papers], American Catholic History Research Center and University Archives, Catholic University of America, Washington, DC [hereafter, Catholic Univ.]. The initial CIO unions, in addition to the UMWA, ILGWU, ACWA, and UTWA, were the International Typographical Union; the Oil Field, Gas Well and Refinery Workers; the United Hatters, Cap and Millinery Workers; and the International Union of Mine, Mill and Smelter Workers.

50. Radio Address of John L. Lewis, president of the UMWA, over the Red Network of the National Broadcasting Company, Thursday, December 31 [1936], box 11, folder 24, Brophy Papers.

51. "From Union News Service," n.d. (ca. 1937), box 12, folder 16, Brophy Papers; "Staple Print Cotton Prices Up on Threat of Higher Labor Costs," *Wall Street Journal*, March 5, 1937; "American Woolen a First Objective," *New York Times*, March 11, 1937.

52. Textile Workers' Organizing Committee, "U.S. Is for US!," n.d. [ca. 1937], box 12, folder 37 (Leaflets 1933–), Local 125 Papers, WEB Du Bois; Bernard Kilgore, "Wagner Decisions May Open Way for Broader Industrial Regulation," *Wall Street Journal*, April 13, 1937. The *Jones and Laughlin* case removed obstacles to CIO organizing, although workers still experienced rulings that outlawed the sit-down strikes that spread from the automotive industry to other industries in 1937, deadly violence against strikers, and the CIO's failure to organize Ford Motor Company and "Little Steel"—the smaller steel companies that competed with U.S. Steel. On these matters, see "Labor Day Statement by John Brophy, Director of the CIO" (September 5, 1938), box 18, folder 25, Brophy Papers; Robert Zieger, *The CIO 1935–1955* (Chapel Hill: University of North Carolina Press, 1995), 42–65; and "From Union News Service," box 12, folder 16, Brophy Papers.

53. "C.I.O. Textile Unit Names A. S. Nance," *Atlanta Constitution*, March 20, 1937; "Textile Agents Launch Campaign in 8 Dixie States," *Atlanta Constitution*, April 4, 1937; Zieger, *CIO*, 74–76.

54. TWOC, "Progress in the South," TWOC newsletter for regional directors, October 15, 1937, box 10, folder 23, CIO Papers, Catholic Univ.

55. "C.I.O. Moves Next into Textile Area," *New York Times*, March 5, 1937; "C.I.O. Union Organized to Fight Green A.F.L. Group," *Washington Post*, March 10, 1937; "C.I.O. Begins Drive in Textiles Today," *New York Times*, March 19, 1937; CIO, "The CIO," Brophy Papers; Zieger, *CIO*, 75.

56. TWOC, "From Union News Service," n.d. [ca. 1937], box 12, folder 16, Brophy Papers; TWOC, newsletter for regional directors, April 17, 1937; June 1, 1937; June 15, 1937; June 30, 1937; August 18, 1937; September 11, 1937; and October 15, 1937; all in box 10, folder 23, CIO Papers, Catholic Univ.

57. "CIO Textile Unit Names A. S. Nance"; "Textile Wages Raised as CIO Launches Drive," *Wall Street Journal,* March 20, 1937; Zieger, *CIO,* 75–76; Hodges, *New Deal Labor Policy,* 154–66; Edwin Camp, "Klan Drive Is Seen as a Fight on C.I.O.," *New York Times,* October 31, 1937; Louis Stark, "Lewis Sets C.I.O. against Any 'Deals' for Bridges Group," *New York Times,* November 17, 1938.

58. Committee for Industrial Organization, "The Committee for Industrial Organization," n.d. (ca. 1937), box 11, folder 25, Brophy Papers; "Membership of CIO Affiliated Unions," n.d. (ca. 1937), box 12, folder 3, Brophy Papers.

59. Zieger, *CIO,* 77–78. A prime example of a militant union influenced by radical politics was Local 22 of the Food, Tobacco, Agricultural and Allied Workers of America, which is best known for organizing African American workers at R. J. Reynolds Tobacco Company in the 1940s. Local 22 moved beyond collective bargaining at R. J. Reynolds to organizing other tobacco workers and building an African American political base in Winston-Salem, North Carolina (Robert Korstad, *Civil Rights Unionism: Tobacco Workers and the Struggle for Democracy in the Mid-twentieth-century South* (Chapel Hill: University of North Carolina Press, 2003).

60. US Department of State, "Negotiation of Trade Agreement with Czechoslovakia Contemplated," May 6, 1937, RG 364, box 286, folder "May 6, 1937—Negotiation of Trade Agreement with Czechoslovakia Contemplated."

61. Irons, *Testing,* 10.

62. Zieger, *CIO,* 76; Marshall, *Labor in the South,* 171.

63. Daniel, *Culture of Misfortune,* 106–24, 127; John Brophy, "A Draft Speech for Delivery at Boston, November 19, 1937," box 19, folder 37, Brophy Papers; letter from Lionel Jubinville and Edward Canasse, Local 157, TWOC (Holyoke, Massachusetts), to John L. Lewis, February 6, 1938; memorandum from John L. Lewis to John Brophy, February 8, 1938; letter from Mary Taccone, Secretary, Joint Board, TWOC (Providence, Rhode Island), to John Brophy, February 10, 1938; letter from Francis Gorman, UTWA, to Emil Rieve, acting chairman, TWOC, February 8, 1938; letter from Francis Gorman, UTWA, to John Brophy, February 9, 1938; letter from Rieve to Manuel Silva, Rayon Twisters and Yarn Finishers Local 1644, UTWA (New Bedford, Massachusetts), February 10, 1938; all in box 23, folder 47, Brophy Papers; Marshall, *Labor in the South,* 171.

64. Alan Brinkley, *The End of Reform: New Deal Liberalism in Recession and War* (New York: Knopf, 1995), 30.

65. Claudius Murchison, "American-Japanese Cotton Goods Agreement," *Journal of Marketing* 2, no. 4 (April 1938): 273–74; Butler, *Cautious Visionary,* 121–22; "Japanese Quotas for Textiles Vary," *New York Times,* January 23, 1937; "An Agreement with Japan," *New York Times,* January 28, 1937. Murchison, a former economics professor and Commerce Department official who was a member of the US delegation negotiating the agreement, by early 1937 also represented textile manufacturers as president of the CTI; in that capacity, he appeared repeatedly before the CRI to oppose tariff reductions on cotton textiles. The

Hull Papers contain no formal mention of the gentlemen's agreement in communications with Japan or the domestic textile industry.

66. The average exchange rate in 1937 was roughly US$4.94 to £1. Using that calculation, the value of British clothing imports in 1937 represented 21.5 percent of the value of US exports.

67. Merle Vincent, "Imports of Women's Coats, Suits and Dresses from England" [memorandum to David Dubinsky], October 5, 1937, box 81, folder 4, ILGWU-David Dubinsky, President's Records, 1932–1966, Kheel Center.

68. Testimony of US Representative Edith Nourse Rogers, Czechoslovakia Hearing Minutes, vol. 1, 7–9, RG 364, box 318, folder "Czechoslovakia—Miscellaneous Material, October 25–29, 1937," NA.

69. Testimony of US Representative George Bates, Czechoslovakia Hearing Minutes, vol. 1, 37–39, RG 364, box 318, folder "Czechoslovakia—Miscellaneous Material, October 25–29, 1937," NA.

70. Testimony of Claudius Murchison, Czechoslovakia Hearing Minutes, vol. 1, 64; testimony of J. G. Johnson, Czechoslovakia Hearing Minutes, vol. 1, 112–13; both RG 364, box 318, folder "Czechoslovakia—Miscellaneous Material, October 25–29, 1937," NA.

71. US Tariff Commission, "Effect of Trade Agreement Reductions on Tariff Levels in the U.S.," (Washington: US Tariff Commission, 1945), RG 364, box 5, unsorted, NA; testimony of Claudius Murchison, "U.K. Hearing Minutes" [hereafter, UK Hearing Minutes], March 1938, RG 364, box 324, folder "U.K. Volume 4," 388, NA.

72. Letter from Leonard Sherman, Frank Waterworth, and Edwin Buthmann, Ayer Mills, American Woolen Company, Lawrence, Massachusetts, to James Roosevelt, March 7, 1938, Official Files Collection 61, box 4, folder "Tariff Matters, 1933–1945: W-Z," FDR Library.

73. "Summary of Information Received by CRI concerning United Kingdom," March 1938, RG 364, box 257, folder "U.K.-C.R.I. Hearings," NA; Griffin, Stenographer's Minutes; CRI, "United Kingdom Hearings Open March 14," March 7, 1938, RG 364, box 257, folder "U.K.-C.R.I. Hearings," NA.

74. Murchison, UK Hearing Minutes.

75. Testimony of John Clark, UK Hearing Minutes, RG 364, box 324, folder "U.K. Volume 4," 457, NA.

76. Testimony of Fred Steele, UK Hearing Minutes, RG 364, box 324, folder "U.K. Volume 4," 475–76, NA.

77. Testimony of Solomon Barkin, UK Hearing Minutes, RG 364, box 259, vol. 4, 1525–26, folder "United Kingdom, Volume 7," NA; Fraser, *Labor*, 297; "Summary of Information Received by CRI concerning United Kingdom," March 1938, RG 364, box 257, folder "U.K.-C.R.I. Hearings," NA; Testimony of M. J. Flynn, UK Hearing Minutes, RG 364, box 323, folder "U.K. Volume 2," 376–89, NA; Lyle Cooper, "The Tariff and Organized Labor," *American Economic Review* 20, no. 2 (June 1930): 210.

78. Testimony of M. J. Flynn, UK Hearing Minutes, RG 364, box 259, vol. 2, 383–88, folder "United Kingdom, Volume 7," NA.

79. Statement of Francis Gorman, March 8, 1938, box 461, folder 1597, UTWA Papers, Southern Labor Archives, Special Collections and Archives, Georgia State University

Library, Atlanta [hereafter, SLA]; telegram from David Dubinsky to M. J. Flynn, March 14, 1938; telegram from Flynn to Dubinsky, March 14, 1938; and ILGWU, "Resolution Adopted by the General Executive Board of the ILGWU on Reciprocal Trade-Agreements Program," February 5, 1940; last three in ILGWU-Dubinsky Records, box 81, folder 4, Kheel Center; letter from [John Green], AFL, to Charles Forney, Princess Anne Clothespins, Inc., January 15, 1940, RG 21, AFL Legislation Department Records, box 51, folder 33, George Meany Memorial AFL-CIO Archives, Hornbake Library, University of Maryland–College Park [hereafter, Meany Archives].

80. US State Department, "The Trade Agreement with the United Kingdom, Signed November 17, 1938" (Washington, DC: US Government Printing Office, 1938), 88–92, RG 364, box 294, folder "The Trade Agreement with the United Kingdom, Signed November 17, 1938," NA.

81. Letter from Adolf Berle to David Dubinsky, February 2, 1940; letter from Dubinsky to Berle, February 5, 1940; ILGWU, "Resolution Adopted by the General Executive Board," February 5, 1940; "Garment Workers Back Hull Pacts," *New York Times*, February 6, 1940; "For a Fuller 'Dinner-Pail,'" *New York Times*, February 7, 1940; "Labor's Stake in More Trade," *Memphis Press-Scimitar*, February 26, 1940; letter from Matthew Woll to Senator Patrick Harrison, March 20, 1940; all in ILGWU-Dubinsky Records, box 81, folder 4, Kheel Center.

82. Claudius Murchison, CTI, "Planning in Manufacturing Industries," address to National Industrial Conference Board, May 26, 1943, in Accession no. 1057, series 1, box 18, vol. 89.12, National Industrial Conference Board Papers, Hagley Museum and Library, Wilmington, Delaware.

83. Douty, "Recovery"; "Textile Raise Is Foreseen," (Baltimore) *Sun*, January 12, 1945.

84. Zieger, *CIO*, 121–22, 141–45.

85. Zieger, *CIO*, 144–46; Nelson Lichtenstein, *Labor's War at Home: The CIO in World War II* (New York: Cambridge University Press, 1982), 82–86; Daniel, *Culture of Misfortune*, 137; W. H. Lawrence, "President Sets Up Labor Peace Plan That Bars Strikes," *New York Times*, December 24, 1941; "War Labor Board to Prevent Strikes Ordered by F.D.R.," *Atlanta Constitution*, January 13, 1942; Fraser, *Labor*, 452.

86. Daniel, *Culture of Misfortune*, 138; Steven Fraser, "The Good War and the Workers," *American Prospect*, September 20, 2009.

87. Daniel, *Culture of Misfortune*, 138–41; Zieger, *CIO*, 145.

88. Daniel, *Culture of Misfortune*, 141–44; Lichtenstein, *Labor's War*, 210–12; Zieger, *CIO*, 170–77.

89. Fraser, *Labor*, 452–53.

90. "Truman Orders Seizure of Gaffney Co.'s Plants," (Baltimore) *Sun*, May 29, 1945; Harry S Truman, "Executive Order 9559: Authorizing the Secretary of War to Take Possession of and Operate the Plants and Facilities of the Gaffney Manufacturing Company," May 28, 1945, "Executive Orders Disposition Tables; Administration of Harry S Truman," National Archives and Records Administration, Washington, DC [hereafter, NARA], http://www.archives.gov/federal-register/executive-orders/1945-truman.html#9559.

91. "Seized Properties Returned by U.S.; Owners of 16 Plants Are Reported Complying Generally with WLB Orders," *New York Times*, September 13, 1945; Joseph Loftus,

"Truman Orders 24 Seized Concerns Returned 'as Soon as Practicable,'" *New York Times,* August 26, 1945; Harry S Truman, "Executive Order 9603," "Executive Orders Disposition Tables; Administration of Harry S Truman," NARA, http://www.archives.gov/federal-register/executive-orders/1945-truman.html#9603.

92. "Descendants of Revolutionary Strike for a Year; Textile Workers Battle Odds at Gaffney, S.C.," *PM,* September 1, 1946; "Admits Loss in 26 Months Old Walkout," *Gaffney Ledger,* July 17, 1947; Timothy J. Minchin, *What Do We Need a Union For? The TWUA in the South, 1945–1955* (Chapel Hill: University of North Carolina Press, 1997), 71–81.

93. "Reciprocal Trade Agreements," House Ways and Means Committee, Seventy-Third Congress, second session, March 8, 1934 (Washington, DC: US Government Printing Office, 1934), 2–3, 12; "Extension of the Reciprocal Trade Agreements Act," HWMC, Seventy-Sixth Congress, third session, January 11, 1940 (Washington, DC: US Government Printing Office, 1940) 1–3, 4, 14, 32 (quote on 1); "Extension of the Reciprocal Trade Agreements Act," House Ways and Means Committee, Seventy-Eighth Congress, first session, April 12, 1943 (Washington, DC: US Government Printing Office, 1943), 4–6; "1945 Extension of Reciprocal Trade Agreements Act," Senate Finance Committee, Seventy-Ninth Congress, first session, May 30, 1945 (Washington, DC: US Government Printing Office, 1945), 5–7.

Chapter 3. New Challenges

1. Gerald Mayer, *Union Membership Trends in the United States* (Washington, DC: Congressional Research Service, 2004), 11.

2. Letter from Harry S Truman to Sidney Hillman, October 20, 1945, box 86, folder 45 (Harry S Truman, 1941–46), ACWA Records, no. 5619, Kheel Center; David Brody, "The Uses of Power I: Industrial Battleground," in *Workers in Industrial America,* ed. David Brody (Oxford: Oxford University Press, 1980), 175–76.

3. Letter from Seabury Stanton, Hathaway Manufacturing Co., to Ray Murdock, US Senate Subcommittee on Labor-Management Relations, October 20, 1950, in box 271, folder "Textile Industry Correspondence/TWUA Printed Material, 1950–51," CIO Organizing Papers ("Operation Dixie Papers–North Carolina"), David M. Rubenstein Rare Book and Manuscript Library, Perkins Library, Duke University, Durham, North Carolina [hereafter, Rubenstein].

4. "The Textile Industry in the Postwar Era," TWUA report, n.d., in MSS 129A, file 7A, folder "Inter-office Memos 1948, Jan–April," TWUA Papers, SHSW.

5. Research Department, TWUA, "The Nation's Most Prosperous Industry," January 1948, 2–6, series 3, box 6 (Bound Notebooks 1945–1949), FS 100 (Solomon Barkin Papers) [hereafter, Barkin Papers], WEB Du Bois.

6. Letter from John Schenck to employees, October 13, 1948, box 80, folder "Cleveland Mill & Power Co., Lawndale, N.C., 1948," Operation Dixie Papers–North Carolina, Rubenstein.

7. Anonymous letter to president, (Textile) Workers Union of America, August 12, 1946, in box 120, folder "Textile Industry Report, May 1946," Operation Dixie Papers–South

Carolina, Rubenstein; "The Bible and the Working Man," CIO pamphlet (1945), box 88, folder "Leaflets, Cannon Mills, Concord & Kannapolis," Operation Dixie Papers–North Carolina, Rubenstein. For an overview of the Operation Dixie campaign, see Barbara S. Griffith, *The Crisis of American Labor: Operation Dixie and the Defeat of the CIO* (Philadelphia: Temple University Press, 1988). Initial postwar prosperity was not the only obstacle to organizing textile workers in this period. Feuds between the TWUA and the UTWA continued, fueled in this period by a disastrous 1951 strike at Virginia's Dan River Mills. For more, see Minchin, *What Do We Need a Union For?*, and Daniel, *Culture of Misfortune*. While Operation Dixie's failures centered on textiles, its organizing efforts rippled out to encompass other unions involved in organizing, civil rights, and political activities, such as the Food, Tobacco, Agricultural and Allied Workers of America–CIO (FTA). For more on the FTA and its work, see Korstad, *Civil Rights*. Elizabeth and Ken Fones-Wolf reexamined Operation Dixie through the views of clergy and the use of religion in *Struggle for the Soul of the Postwar South: White Evangelical Protestants and Operation Dixie* (Urbana: University of Illinois Press, 2015).

8. TWUA, "Economic Security Program," May 23, 1947, MS 134, box 6, folder 68, TWUA New Bedford Joint Board Records, 1942–1981, WEB Du Bois. The resolution was issued days before the abolition of the Office of Price Administration, which had been controlling wages and consumer prices during World War II and into 1946.

9. Stanton letter to Murdock, October 20, 1950.

10. "Why Mills Close—Naushon Story," *Textile Labor*, April 17, 1948; "Demand U.S. Probe of Textron; Nashua Shutdown Is Slated," *Textile Labor*, September 18, 1948.

11. White House news release, August 9, 1949, MS 134, box 3, folder 30, TWUA New Bedford Joint Board Records, 1942–1981, WEB Du Bois.

12. Letter from George Carignan, New Bedford Joint Board, to Everett Kassalow, CIO, August 31, 1949; letter from Kassalow to Carignan, September 9, 1949; both in MS 134, box 3, folder 30, WEB Du Bois.

13. "Re: Unemployment in Massachusetts' Textile Centers–June 1950," memorandum from Barkin to Rieve et al., August 25, 1950, in MS 129A, file 7A, box 15, folder "Inter-office Memos 1950," TWUA Papers, SHSW.

14. Minchin, *What Do We Need a Union For?*, 152. In 1952 Baldanzi bolted to the UTWA, deepening the rift between the two unions (Daniel, *Culture of Misfortune*, 255–56).

15. Daniel, *Culture of Misfortune*, 168–69, 186–206; Solomon Barkin, interview by James A. Cavanaugh, MSS 467, tape 662A, cassette 7, side 2, TWUA Oral History Project, TWUA Papers, SHSW.

16. Stanton letter to Murdock, October 20, 1950; Solomon Barkin, statement to the Subcommittee on Labor-Management Relations, United States Senate, December 7, 1950, both in Operation Dixie Papers–North Carolina, box 271, folder "Textile Industry Correspondence/TWUA Printed Material, 1950–51," Rubenstein.

17. US Congress, Joint Committee on the Economic Report on the Textile Industry as a Depressed Industry (statement of Solomon Barkin, of TWUA Research Department, January 27, 1955), 1, 5, box 9 (Bound Notebooks, 1954–1955), Barkin Papers, WEB

Du Bois; "1955: Forecasts' Cheery Glow Is Pale in Textiles," *Textile Labor*, January 8, 1955; Bernard Nossiter, "Slump in Textiles: An Industry Goes 'Soft,'" *The Nation*, January 22, 1955. For decades, Barkin was a leading advocate for textile labor, turning down an offer to serve as assistant labor secretary under Truman. For examples, see the letter from Solomon Barkin to Walter Reuther, January 19, 1953, and the letter from Reuther to Barkin, January 26, 1953; both in box 8 (Bound Notebooks 1952–1953), Barkin Papers, WEB Du Bois.

18. Emil Rieve, TWUA, "Ninth Biennial Convention Call," n.d. (1956), MS 134, box 6, folder 67, WEB Du Bois.

19. William Pollock, "An Industry That's Sick," *American Federationist*, April 1958, in RG98-002, box 61, folder 1 (Textile Industry 1937–1986), Meany Archives.

20. Ibid.

21. Conference of New England Governors, *New England Textiles and the New England Economy: Report by the New England Governors' Textile Committee to the Conference of New England Governors*, November 5, 1959, II-3, MS 134, box 1, folder "New England Textile Study 1957–1959," WEB Du Bois.

22. The potential for pursuing an anticommunist agenda abroad during the Cold War was of particular interest to CIO unions. See Robert H. Zieger, *The CIO, 1935–1955* (Chapel Hill: University of North Carolina Press, 1995): 267–78. In addition to the Marshall Plan, several aid programs guided development in Asian nations, particularly Japan, China, and India.

23. Letter from William Green, AFL, to Anthony Valente, UTWA, September 7, 1950, in box 368, folder 99, UTWA Papers, SLA; letter from G. Warren Morgan, ECA, to Jack LeFevre, UTWA, November 28, 1950; letter from Curtis Anderson, ECA, to Anthony Valente, UTWA, March 29, 1951; letter from Bert Jewell, ECA, to Anthony Valente, UTWA, June 30, 1950; last three in box 367, folder 78, UTWA Papers, SLA.

24. Letter from Bert Jewell and Clinton Golden, ECA, to Anthony Valente, UTWA, March 7, 1950, box 367, folder 78, UTWA Papers, SLA.

25. Letter from Anthony Valente, UTWA, to William Green, AFL, October 4, 1950; letter from Maurice Tobin, US Department of Labor, to Green, September 27, 1950; both in box 368, folder 99, UTWA Papers, SLA.

26. Letter from Helen Hamilton Woods, ECA, to Anthony Valente, UTWA, July 7, 1950, box 367, folder 78, UTWA Papers, SLA.

27. "Hoffman Praises U.S. Help to Europe; E.C.A. Head Says Marshall Plan Has Done Much to Allay Fear of Communism," *New York Times*, June 23, 1950.

28. Letter from Anthony Valente, UTWA, to Helen Woods, ECA, July 6, 1950, box 367, folder 78, UTWA Papers, SLA.

29. Letter from Anthony Valente, UTWA, to George Baldanzi, UTWA, July 9, 1953, box 362, folder 23, UTWA Presidents' Correspondence, UTWA Papers, SLA; letter from Valente to Lewis Conn, UTWA, July 9, 1953, box 365, folder 51, UTWA Papers, SLA; memorandum from S. M. Justice, US Department of Labor, Bureau of Apprenticeship, "Industrial Training Assignment in Iran," July–November 1952, box 374, folder 168, UTWA Papers, SLA.

30. The average hourly wage for manufacturing workers in 1953 ranged between $1.60 and $1.66, according to US BLS data; the $3,390 figure assumes a forty-hour workweek over fifty-two weeks. For the range of hourly manufacturing wages, see Federal Reserve Bank of St. Louis, "Average Hourly Earnings of Production and Nonsupervisory Employees: Manufacturing," https://research.stlouisfed.org/fred2/data/AHEMAN.txt.

31. Letter from Valente to Baldanzi, August 5, 1953; letter from Baldanzi to Valente, July 20, 1953, both in box 362, folder 23, UTWA Presidents' Correspondence, UTWA Papers, SLA; letter from Conn to Valente, July 11, 1953, box 365, folder 51, UTWA Papers, SLA.

32. Sol Stetin, interview by James A. Cavanaugh, MSS 467, tape 648A, cassette 7, side 1, TWUA Oral History Project, TWUA Papers, SHSW.

33. "'60 Was a Great Textile Year—for Importers," *Textile Bulletin*, June 1961.

34. Figures compiled from *Textile Hi-Lights*, the quarterly economic publication of the American Textile Manufacturers' Institute (ATMI), 1968–69 to 1975. The group, formerly the American Cotton Manufacturers' Association (ACMA), was renamed the American Cotton Manufacturers' Institute (ACMI) in 1949 and the ATMI in 1962.

35. TWUA Research Department report for activities during period of January 1950 through May 1950, MSS 129A, file 7A, box 15, folder "Research Bulletins 1950–1951," TWUA Papers, SHSW.

36. Ibid.

37. "Re—Textile Production," memorandum to Rieve from Barkin, September 20, 1950; TWUA Research Department, "Production of Broad Woven Fabrics, 1948 and 1950," both in MSS 129A, file 7A, box 15, folder "Inter-office Memos 1950," TWUA Papers, SHSW.

38. Emil Rieve, TWUA, "Statement to the CRI concerning Possible Tariff Concessions on Textile Items in the Negotiation of Reciprocal Trade Agreements," June 1, 1950, 1, 10–13, box 7 (Bound Notebooks 1950–1951), Barkin Papers, WEB Du Bois.

39. Memorandum by the chairman of the Interdepartmental Committee on Trade Agreements (Corse) to the president, August 20, 1952, document 394.31/8–2052, in *Foreign Relations of the U.S., 1952–1954, General: Economic and Political Matters*, vol. 1, part 1, FRUS1, https://history.state.gov/historicaldocuments/frus1952–54v01p1/d32; memorandum by the assistant secretary of state for Far Eastern affairs (Robertson) to the assistant secretary of state for economic affairs (Linder), April 30, 1953, document 394.31/4–3053, FRUS1, https://history.state.gov/historicaldocuments/frus1952–54v01p1/d43; the ambassador in Japan (Murphy) to the Department of state, January 20, 1953, document 394.31/1–2053, FRUS1, https://history.state.gov/historicaldocuments/frus1952–54v01p1/d39; memorandum by the assistant secretary of state for economic affairs (Waugh) to the secretary of state, November 17, 1954, document 394.31/11–1754, FRUS1, https://history.state.gov/historicaldocuments/frus1952–54v01p1/d64.

40. Allyn McIntyre, Pepperell Manufacturing Company, "The Sales Outlook for 1957" (address to the Conference Board), September 21, 1956, in *Proceedings of the 369th Meeting of the Conference Board* . . ., National Industrial Conference Board Records, 1916–1985, accession no. 1057, box 65, vol. 446, Hagley Museum and Library, Wilmington, Delaware [hereafter, Hagley].

41. Jackson Spears, Burlington Industries, "The Ten Years' Sales Outlook" (address to the Conference Board), September 23, 1955, in "Proceedings of the 360th Meeting of the Conference Board," National Industrial Conference Board Records, 1916–1985, accession no. 1057, box 59, vol. 381, Hagley.

42. Memorandum to Rieve, TWUA, from Barkin, TWUA (draft of letter to M. Takita), May 3, 1956; memorandum from Pollock, TWUA, to Barkin, TWUA, September 26, 1956; memorandum from Barkin to Pollock, October 8, 1956; all in MSS 129A, file 7A, box 17, folder "Research 1956," TWUA Papers, SHSW.

43. Barkin, TWUA, memorandum to Rieve, TWUA, May 3, 1956, MSS 129A, file 7A, box 17, folder "Research 1956," TWUA Papers, SHSW.

44. Letter from George Carignan, New Bedford Joint Board, TWUA, to "Dear Member," n.d. (1956), MS 134, box 5, folder 61, WEB Du Bois.

45. Spears, "Ten Years' Sales Outlook."

46. McIntyre, "Sales Outlook for 1957."

47. "New England Textiles and the New England Economy: Report by the New England Governors' Textile Committee to the Conference of New England Governors," November 5, 1959, II-1, MS 117 (J. William Belanger Papers), box 1, folder "New England Textile Study 1957–1959," WEB Du Bois.

48. "New England Textiles," I-2–I-3.

49. Timothy J. Minchin, *Empty Mills: The Fight against Imports and the Decline of the U.S. Textile Industry* (Lanham, MD: Rowman and Littlefield, 2013), 8.

50. Stetin, TWUA, interview by Cavanaugh, MSS 467, tape 648A, cassette 7, side 1, TWUA Oral History Project, TWUA Papers, SHSW; Barkin, TWUA, interview by Cavanaugh, MSS 467, tape 662A, cassette 4, side 2, TWUA Oral History Project, SHSW.

51. Executive Council, TWUA, Resolutions on "Textile Tariffs" and "Inter-union Cooperation," March 1960, TWUA New Bedford Joint Board Records, MS 134, box 4, folder 38 (1960 TWUA Resolutions), WEB Du Bois; Stetin interviews by Cavanaugh, MSS 467, tape 648A, cassette 7, side 1, cassette 11, side 2, and cassette 12, side 1, TWUA Oral History Project, SHSW; TWUA, "A Cooperative Program: ILGWU-ACWA-TWUA," October 28, 1959; and "Cooperation: ACW-ILG-TWUA," January 22, 1962; both in MSS 396, box 634, folder "Areas of Cooperation, TWUA, ILGWU & ACW, 1960–1962," TWUA Papers, SHSW.

52. Stetin interview by Cavanaugh, cassette 11, side 2, TWUA Oral History Project, TWUA Papers, SHSW.

53. Stetin interview by Cavanaugh, cassette 12, side 1, TWUA Oral History Project, TWUA Papers, SHSW.

54. Memorandum from Barkin to Pollock, August 9, 1956, in MSS 129A, file 7A, box 17, folder "Research 1956," TWUA Papers, SHSW.

55. "CIO History of Progress" (1955 flyer), MS 134 (TWUA, New Bedford Joint Board Records, 1942–1981), box 3, folder 30, WEB Du Bois; Barkin interview by Cavanaugh, tape 3, side 2, TWUA Oral History Project, TWUA Papers, SHSW; Minchin, *Don't Sleep*; Daniel, *Culture of Misfortune*, 254–81.

56. Rieve, letter to Serraino, July 11, 1950, in MSS 129A, file 7A, box 15, folder "Inter-office Memos 1950," TWUA Papers, SHSW.

57. Barkin memorandum to Rieve, n.d., MSS 129A, file 7A, box 16, folder "Research, 1953," TWUA Papers, SHSW.

58. McIntyre, "Sales Outlook for 1957."

59. *CQ Almanac*, Eighty-Third Cong., second sess., 265–72; Claudius Murchison, *King Cotton Is Sick* (Chapel Hill: University of North Carolina Press, 1930), 135–38, 145.

60. Letter from Walter Robertson, Department of State, to Rush Dickson, American and Efird Mills, December 29, 1955, box 14, folder "ACMI/ATMI," Cannon Mills Records, Rubenstein.

61. Letter from Roger Milliken, Deering-Milliken, to Charles Cannon, Cannon Mills, January 20, 1956; letter from Cannon to Robert Jackson, ACMI, June 29, 1956; letter from F. S. Love, ACMI, to Cannon, July 2, 1956; all in box 15, folder "ACMI/ATMI," Cannon Mills Records, Rubenstein; Cynthia Anderson, *Social Consequences*, 37.

62. Memorandum from Barkin to Pollock, June 19, 1956; memorandum from Barkin to Victor Canzano, July 17, 1956; both in MSS 129A, file 7A, box 17, folder "Research 1956," TWUA Papers, SHSW.

63. Memorandum from Barkin to John Chupka, May 4, 1956, MSS 129A, file 7A, box 17, folder "Research 1956," TWUA Papers, SHSW.

64. Aggarwal, *Liberal Protectionism*, 51–53; H. Richard Friman, *Patchwork Protectionism: Textile Trade Policy in the U.S., Japan, and West Germany* (Ithaca, NY: Cornell University Press, 1990), 98–99.

65. Friman, *Patchwork Protectionism*, 100–101, 103; Aggarwal, *Liberal Protectionism*, 53–71, 77–78.

66. William Pollock, TWUA, "An Open Letter to the Managers of the Textile Industry" (TWUA advertisement), February 4, 1959, in MS 134 (TWUA, New Bedford Joint Board Records, 1942–1981), box 4, folder 47, WEB Du Bois.

67. ACMI, "Resolution: American Foreign Trade Policy," March 28, 1953, box 14, folder "ACMI/ATMI," Cannon Mills Records, Rubenstein.

68. Solomon Barkin, supplemental statement to Twentieth Century Fund and the National Planning Association, "American Imports," report of the Committee on American Imports (Twentieth Century Fund, 1955), 1–2, box 9 (Bound Notebooks, 1954–1955), Barkin Papers, WEB Du Bois.

69. McDonald proposed the TAA idea to President Dwight Eisenhower's Commission on Foreign Economic Policy (CFP) as a domestic parallel to the technical and financial assistance the United States offered other nations. The commission rejected McDonald's proposal, declaring that "no matter how great our sympathy may be for the problems of a displaced worker, or those of a business with a shrinking volume, this is but one phase of a much larger problem" (William Batt Jr., "Adjustment of Workers Displaced by Import Competition," December 9, 1953, box 58, folder 12 [Office Files—Foreign Economic Policy Staff Reports, 1953], USWA Legislative Department Records, USWA Papers, Eberly Family Special Collections Library, Paterno Library, Pennsylvania State University,

University Park, Pennsylvania [hereafter, Eberly]; memorandum from David McDonald to the CFP, December 28, 1953; CFP, "Outline of a Plan to Adjust Workers Affected by Increased Imports," latter two both in box 82, folder 12 (CFP, 1953/08–1954/01), USWA President's Office Records (David McDonald Records), USWA Papers, Eberly.

70. Resolution on "Area Redevelopment," TWUA Executive Council resolutions, March 1960, MS 134 (TWUA, New Bedford Joint Board Records, 1942–1981), box 4, folder 38 (1960 TWUA Resolutions), WEB Du Bois; Barkin interview by Cavanaugh, cassette 8, side 1, TWUA Oral History Project, TWUA Papers, SHSW; Roger Davidson, "Eisenhower and Depressed-Areas Legislation, 1955–1961," 11–28, accessed 12/16/2021, https://www.american.edu/spa/ccps/upload/Davidson-paper.pdf.

71. John Pastore biography, "Biographical Directory of the US Congress," bioguide.congress.gov/search/bio/P000100.

72. Committee on Foreign and Interstate Commerce, US Senate, "Problems of the Domestic Textile Industry," February 4, 1959 (Washington, DC: US Government Printing Office, 1959), 2–8.

73. Committee on Foreign and Interstate Commerce, "Problems of the Domestic Textile Industry," 9–14.

74. Memorandum from Canzano to TWUA Locals, Joint Boards and Staff, February 27, 1959, in box 3, folder 33 (1959–60 Correspondence), MS 134 (TWUA, New Bedford Joint Board Records, 1942–1981), WEB Du Bois.

75. Statement of the AFL-CIO Executive Council on Foreign Economic Policy, February 8, 1958, RG 13–005, box 1, folder 10 (AFL-CIO Economic Policy Committee 1958/01–1958/02), Meany Archives.

76. Executive Board, TWUA, "Resolution: Textile Tariffs," March 7, 1960, MS 134 (TWUA, New Bedford Joint Board Records, 1942–1981), box 4, folder 38 (1960 TWUA Resolutions), WEB Du Bois.

Chapter 4. New Domestic and International Frontiers

1. Letter to "Dear Friend" from Kennedy for Congress Committee, n.d. (1946); flyer from Kennedy for Congress Headquarters, both in box 94, folder "Labor: Minority Report, 14 April 1947," House of Representatives Papers [hereafter, HR Papers], JFK Pre-presidential Papers, John F. Kennedy Presidential Library and Museum, Boston [hereafter, JFK Library].

2. Telegram from JFK to Francis X. Morrissey, April 16, 1947, box 94, folder "Labor: Minority Report, 14 April 1947," HR Papers, JFK Library.

3. "Statement of Congressman John F. Kennedy," Surplus Manpower Committee Panel, March 27, 1951, box 93, folder "Massachusetts Commerce Speech Materials," HR Papers, JFK Library.

4. "Speech by Congressman John F. Kennedy before Massachusetts State CIO Industrial Union Council, 13th Annual Convention," December 7,1951, box 96, folder "Labor, Massachusetts CIO Industrial Union Council, December 7, 1951," HR Papers, JFK Library; John F. Kennedy, "Let's Fight for New England!," August 8, 1952, box 93, folder "Massachusetts Commerce Speech Materials," HR Papers, JFK Library; John F. Kennedy,

"Labor's Role in the Days Ahead," n.d., box 93, folder "Labor Speeches, Folder 2," HR Papers, JFK Library.

5. "Textiles," statement of John F. Kennedy, n.d. (1952); Research Department, TWUA, "Outline of Report on the New England Textile Industry," March 17, 1950; both in box 94, folder "New England Industry: Speeches and Materials," HR Papers, JFK Library.

6. Election data for 1946 and 1952 Massachusetts US Senate races: 1946, http://www.ourcampaigns.com/RaceDetail.html?RaceID=147415; 1952, http://www.ourcampaigns.com/RaceDetail.html?RaceID=83027.

7. "Major Legislative Efforts of Senator John F. Kennedy 1953–1957," December 30, 1957, in MS 134 (TWUA, New Bedford Joint Board Records, 1942–1981), box 4, folder 46, WEB Du Bois.

8. "An Open Letter to Our National Candidates," *America's Textile Reporter*, September 8, 1960.

9. Letter from JFK to Robert Stevens, August 8, 1960, and letter from Stevens to Kennedy, July 18, 1960, both in box 13, folder "Campaign Materials: Textiles (1 of 2)," Myer Feldman Personal Papers [hereafter, Feldman Papers], JFK Library. Feldman was a campaign aide and later served in Kennedy's White House staff. See also letter from A. Paul Kitchin to Robert Kennedy, JFK's brother, September 27, 1960; letter from Robert Kennedy to Kitchin, October 10, 1960; letter from Jack Childers to Kitchin, August 24, 1960; and letter from Jack Childers, executive vice president, to Fellow Employees, Erlanger Mills, Inc., n.d., all in box 13, folder "Campaign Materials: Textiles (1 of 2)," Feldman Papers; "All Those Clothes Coming In from Hong Kong and Japan Are Causing Problems," *U.S. News and World Report*, September 19, 1960.

10. "Draft Statement," n.d., in box 13, folder "Campaign Materials: Textiles (1 of 2)," Feldman Papers.

11. Letter from Ernest Hollings to JFK, August 26, 1960; letter from Kennedy to Hollings, August 31, 1960; letter from Robert Jackson to American Cotton Manufacturing Institute Members, August 31, 1960; all in box 13, folder "Campaign Materials: Textiles (1 of 2)," Feldman Papers.

12. Letter from Hollings to Myer Feldman, September 9, 1960; letter from Hollings to Feldman, Kennedy for President Headquarters, October 20, 1960, both in box 13, folder "Campaign Materials: Textiles (1 of 2)," Feldman Papers.

13. Bridges's plan was originally published in the *Boston Sunday Herald* on October 16, 1960. See also the letter from the textile publisher Frank Bennett to David Hackett, assistant to Kennedy, Kennedy for President Headquarters, October 18, 1960, in box 13, folder "Campaign Materials: Textiles (1 of 2)," Feldman Papers.

14. James Patterson, *Grand Expectations: The United States, 1945–1974* (New York: Oxford University Press, 1996), 458–59.

15. Patterson, *Grand Expectations*, 465.

16. Michael Beschloss, *The Crisis Years: Kennedy and Khrushchev, 1960–1963* (New York: HarperCollins, 1991), 48.

17. Robert Caro, *The Years of Lyndon Johnson: The Passage of Power* (New York: Knopf, 2012), 176–84.

18. US Department of Commerce, *Census of Manufacturing: 1947 Indexes of Production* (Washington, DC: US Government Printing Office, 1952); US Department of Commerce, *Annual Survey of Manufacturers 1961* (Washington, DC: US Government Printing Office, 1964).

19. "U.S. Foreign Trade in Manufactures of Cotton, Man-Made Fibers, and Wool," tables from Bureau of the Census Reports FT-120, FT-420, in "Statement by Noel Hemmendinger on Behalf of the U.S.–Japan Trade Council," testimony to the Special Committee to Study the Domestic Textile Industry, Senate Committee on Interstate and Foreign Commerce, January 16, 1962, box 945, folder "TA/Textiles 12-6-61–7-31-62," [hereafter, folder "TA/Textiles 12-6-61–7-31-62"], White House Central Files [hereafter, WHCF], JFK Library.

20. Taylor Branch, *Parting the Waters: America in the King Years 1954–63* (New York: Simon and Schuster, 1988), 271–87, 356–68.

21. Timothy J. Minchin, *Hiring the Black Worker: The Racial Integration of the Southern Textile Industry, 1960–1980* (Chapel Hill: University of North Carolina Press, 1999), 67–97.

22. Minchin, *Hiring the Black Worker*, 219.

23. Minchin, *Hiring the Black Worker*, 76–80. Textile executives, especially in the South, utilized a number of excuses for not hiring African Americans. The American Friends Service Committee, which operated a program to increase black employment in various fields, found the southern textile industry the most resistant to its efforts (Minchin, *Hiring the Black Worker*, 17–23).

24. Letter from Pollock to JFK, January 19, 1962, box 575, folder T, WHCF, JFK Library.

25. Stanley Ruttenberg memorandum, November 15, 1960, in RG 13–003, box 2, folder 17, Meany Archives.

26. Minutes of Economic Policy Committee meeting, January 4, 1961, RG 13–005, box 1, folder 12 (AFL-CIO Economic Policy Committee 1960/01–1962/10), Meany Archives.

27. Nat Goldfinger, AFL-CIO, to John McBride, Union Starch and Refining Company, Granite City, Illinois, August 21, 1962, RG 13–003, box 1, folder 62 (Meany, George, and Schnitzler, William, 1959–), Meany Archives.

28. Memorandum from Barkin to Pollock, TWUA, February 19, 1962, in letter from Barkin to Ruttenberg, AFL-CIO, February 23, 1962; both in RG 13–005, box 4, folder 54, Meany Archives.

29. Letter from Nathaniel Bradford to JFK, August 30, 1961, box 944, folder "TA/Textiles 7-12-61–12-5-61," WHCF, JFK Library [hereafter, folder "TA/Textiles 7-12-61–12-5-61"].

30. Letter from Truman Robinson to JFK, April 12, 1961, box 944, folder "TA/Textiles May 25, 1961," WHCF, JFK Library [hereafter, folder "TA/Textiles May 25, 1961"].

31. Letter from W. G. Gunter to JFK, July 3, 1961, Folder "TA/Textiles 7-12-61–12-5-61."

32. Letter from Margaret Summers to JFK, September 10, 1961, folder "TA/Textiles 7-12-61–12-5-61."

33. Letter from H. Clyde Hardy to JFK, June 30, 1961, folder "TA/Textiles 7-12-61–12-5-61."

34. Letter from Antone Viveiros to JFK, n.d., folder "TA/Textiles 12-6-61–7-31-62."

35. "Textile Study Set Up," *New York Times*, February 17, 1961; Myer Feldman to Bernard Brickman, Brickman Textile Co., February 26, 1961, folder "TA/Textiles May 25, 1961."

36. In November 1958, two TWUA locals struck the Harriet and Henderson Mills in Henderson, North Carolina, over an employee grievance procedure, closing the mills for three months. The millowners hired replacement workers; Hodges dispatched state troopers and the National Guard to protect the mill and replacement workers. The TWUA officially ended the strike in June 1961 (Daniel Clark, *Like Night and Day: Unionization in a Southern Mill Town* [Chapel Hill: University of North Carolina Press, 1997]).

37. "Statement by the AFL-CIO Executive Council on International Trade Policy," February 26, 1961, RG 20–003, box 15, folder 8, Meany Archives.

38. AFL-CIO Research Department, "AFL-CIO Looks at Foreign Trade: A Policy for the Sixties" (1961), 4–5; "AFL-CIO Looks at Foreign Trade," 74–82; both in RG 34–002, box 5, folder 21, Meany Archives.

39. Joint statement of George Meany and Minoru Takita, March 3, 1961, RG 20–003, box 16, folder 1, Meany Archives.

40. Letter from C. H. Borders to JFK, August 23, 1961, folder "TA/Textiles 7-12-61–12-5-61."

41. Letter from Carl Vinson to JFK, April 19, 1961; letter from George Andrews et al. to JFK, March 22, 1961; letter from G. Elliott Hagan et al. to JFK, March 20, 1961; telegram from Sam Ervin to JFK, March 17, 1961; letter from Ervin et al. to JFK, March 17, 1961; letter from Peter Garland to JFK, March 23, 1961; letter from Olin Johnston et al. to JFK, March 17, 1961; telegram from K. S. Tanner to JFK, March 20, 1961; letter from Jimmy Johnson to JFK, March 28, 1961; letter from Roger Milliken to JFK, April 6, 1961; letter from Truman Robinson to JFK, April 12, 1961; resolution "Saving the Textile Industry," n.d.; all in folder "TA/Textiles May 25, 1961."

42. "Major Legislative Efforts of Senator John F. Kennedy 1953–1957," December 1957, MS 134 (TWUA, New Bedford Joint Board Records, 1942–1981), box 4, folder 46, WEB Du Bois.

43. Letter from Senator John Pastore et al. to JFK, January 23, 1962; letter from Representative Carl Vinson to JFK, January 23, 1962, both in folder "TA/Textiles 12-6-61–7-31-62"; letter from Ervin to JFK, March 6, 1963, in box 944, folder "TA/Textiles 4-1-62–3-25-63," WHCF, JFK Library.

44. Statement of Jacob Potofsky, ACWA, March 9, 1961, folder "TA/Textiles May 25, 1961."

45. Ibid.

46. Letter from Jacob Potofsky to JFK, March 10, 1961; letter from Kenneth O'Donnell to Potofsky, March 16, 1961; memorandum from Mike Feldman to O'Donnell, March 20, 1961, all in folder "TA/Textiles May 25, 1961"; "Union Is Cancelling Its Plan to Boycott Japanese Textiles," *New York Times*, April 19, 1961.

47. "Union to Boycott Japanese Fabrics," *New York Times*, February 17, 1961; "Cooperation, ACW-ILG-TWUA," MSS 396, box 634, folder "Areas of Cooperation between TWUA, ILGWU and ACW 1960–1962," TWUA Papers, SHSW.

48. "Union Is Cancelling Its Plan to Boycott Japanese Textiles," *New York Times*, April 19, 1961.

49. "Memorandum on Textile Problems," December 11, 1961, folder "TA/Textiles 12-6-61–7-31-62."

50. The Freedom Rides triggered mob attacks, arrests, and a hastily brokered deal between the Kennedy administration and the governors of Mississippi and Alabama to prevent further violence. Publicity about the attacks on the Freedom Riders, who protested in bus and airport facilities between May and November 1961, forced the Kennedy administration to call for a "cooling-off period" and finally direct the Interstate Commerce Commission to desegregate interstate transportation (Branch, *Parting*, 412–50).

51. Letter from James Eastland to Myer Feldman, June 6, 1961, box 944, folder "TA/Textiles 5-26-61–7-11-61," WHCF, JFK Library [hereafter, folder "TA/Textiles 5-12-61–7-11-61"]; letter from William Jennings Bryan, Dorn et al. to JFK, March 17, 1961, folder "TA/Textiles May 25, 1961."

52. Letter from Carl Vinson to Feldman, June 7, 1961, and letter from Feldman to Vinson, June 9, 1961; both in folder "TA/Textiles 5-26-61–7-11-61."

53. Letter from Carl Vinson to JFK, June 22, 1961, and letter from John Pastore to JFK, June 22, 1962, both in folder "TA/Textiles 5-26-61–7-11-61."

54. Letter from JFK to Vinson, June 30, 1961, and letter from JFK to Pastore, June 30, 1961; both in folder "TA/Textiles 5-26-61–7-11-61."

55. Letter from Robert Stevens, J. P. Stevens and Co., to JFK, June 6, 1961; letter from Feldman to Stevens, June 9, 1961; letter from Frederick Dent, Mayfair Mills, to Feldman, June 21, 1961; letter from Feldman to Dent, June 23, 1961; all in folder "TA/Textiles 5-26-61–7-11-61."

56. Letter from W. Gordon McCabe to JFK, May 12, 1961; letter from Seabury Stanton to Myer Feldman, May 10, 1961; both in folder "TA/Textiles May 25, 1961."

57. "AFL-CIO Executive Council Statement on Recent Developments in International Trade Policy," October 12, 1961, RG20–003, box 16, folder 6, Meany Archives.

58. Ibid.

59. "Memorandum on Textile Problems," December 11, 1961, folder "TA/Textiles 12-6-61–7-31-62."

60. Ibid.

61. Letter from Myer Feldman to J. Spencer Love, Burlington Industries, Inc., December 14, 1961, folder "TA/Textiles 12-6-61–7-31-62."

62. TWUA Research Department, "Employment, Manhours, Production and Productivity of the Basic Textile Industry, 1947–58," in AFL-CIO Research Department, "AFL-CIO Looks at Foreign Trade: A Policy for the Sixties" (1961), 28–29, RG 34–002, box 5, folder 21, Meany Archives.

63. Martin Foil, Tuscarora Cotton Mill, to JFK, March 20, 1961, folder "TA/Textiles May 25, 1961."

64. "Textile Resolution Adopted by the Combed Yarn Spinners Association, Inc., March 3, 1961," and letter from J. R. Campbell, Executive Secretary, Combed Yarn Spinners Association, to JFK, March 8, 1961; both in folder "TA/Textiles May 25, 1961."

65. Letter from Graham Blaine to McGeorge Bundy, February 7, 1961, folder "TA/Textiles May 25, 1961."

66. Letter from Paul Daniels to JFK, May 29, 1961, folder "TA/Textiles 5-26-61–7-11-61." In the letter, Daniels refers to "Local Union #1344," TWUA operated Local 1344 at Waumbec Mills.

67. Letter from W. A. Edwards Jr. to JFK, May 30, 1961, folder "TA/Textiles 5-26-61–7-11-61."

68. Stanley Ruttenberg, transcript of "Labor News Conference," Mutual Broadcasting System, May 15, 1961, RG 20–003, box 16, folder 2, Meany Archives; Arlen Large, "Depressed Areas Aid Bill Is Signed, Poses Administrative Snarl Involving 7 Agencies," *Wall Street Journal*, May 2, 1961; James Patterson, *America's Struggle against Poverty 1900–1994* (Cambridge, MA: Harvard University Press, 1994), 127.

69. George Meany, speech to First Conference on World Trade of the IAM, November 29, 1961, RG 20–003, box 16, folder 7, Meany Archives.

70. Ibid.

71. Judith Stein, *Running Steel, Running America: Race, Economic Policy, and the Decline of Liberalism* (Chapel Hill: University of North Carolina Press, 1998), 29.

72. George Meany, speech to First Conference on World Trade.

73. Ibid.

74. Ibid.

75. George Meany, "Article for Philadelphia Inquirer," December 18, 1961, RG 13–003, box 1, folder 62, Meany Archives.

76. "AFL-CIO Executive Council Statement on Recent Developments in International Trade Policy," October 12, 1961, RG20–003, box 16, folder 6, Meany Archives.

77. Ibid.

78. Richard Mooney, "Trade War of '62 Building Up Fast; Maneuvering in Washington by the Protectionists and 'Liberals' Quickens," *New York Times*, November 27, 1961; Mooney, "Machinists Study Trade Problems; Chief Asks Curb on Business Expansion Abroad," *New York Times*, November 28, 1961; letter from A. J. Hayes, International President, IAM, to JFK, July 12, 1961; letter from Kenneth O'Donnell to A. J. Hayes, October 13, 1961; letter from Hayes to O'Donnell, October 18, 1961; all in box 575, folder I, WHSF, JFK Library.

79. Draft statement from JFK to A. J. Hayes, November 27, 1961, box 944, folder I, WHSF, JFK Library.

80. AFL-CIO, "The Common Market and the U.S." (1962 pamphlet), RG 34–002, box 6, folder 11, Meany Archives.

81. Ibid.

82. Ibid.

83. Ibid.

84. In the Internal Revenue Code of 1954, Congress established a worldwide system of taxation, in which the United States would tax the worldwide income of its nationals. But the code included a deferral provision in Sections 881 and 882, which allowed corporations to avoid paying taxes on income earned abroad until it was repatriated. Critics

have argued since that such provisions encouraged greater capital flight and deterioration of the domestic economic base; furthermore, attempts at reform have instead created a complicated system of international taxation in which both enforcement and compliance are difficult. See US Commission on Foreign Economic Policy (Randall Commission), *Report to the President and the Congress* (Washington, DC: US Government Printing Office, 1954), 14–23; Thomas E. Jenks, "Taxation of Foreign Income," *George Washington Law Review* 42 (1973–74): 538–39; Julie Roin, "The Grand Illusion: A Neutral System for the Taxation of International Transactions," *Virginia Law Review* 75, no. 5 (August 1989): 920; John F. Kennedy, "President's Special Message to the Congress on Taxation," H.R. Doc. no. 140, Eighty-Seventh Cong., first sess. (Washington, DC: US Government Printing Office, 1961), 6–7; and Daniel N. Shaviro, *Fixing U.S. International Taxation* (New York: Oxford University Press, 2014), 1–29.

85. AFL-CIO, "The Common Market and the U.S."

86. George Meany, speech to First Conference on World Trade of the IAM, November 29, 1961, RG 20–003, box 16, folder 7, Meany Archives.

87. Ibid.

88. Transcript of address by JFK to National Association of Manufacturers, Sixty-Sixth Annual Congress of American Industry, New York, NY, December 6, 1961, box 921, folder SP 3–23, WHSF, JFK Library; transcript of address by JFK to the Fourth Convention of the AFL-CIO, Miami Beach, Florida, December 7, 1961, box 921, folder SP 3–24, WHSF, JFK Library.

89. Address by JFK to National Association of Manufacturers, Sixty-Sixth Annual Congress of American Industry, New York, New York, December 6, 1961, box 921, folder SP 3–23, WHSF, JFK Library.

90. Ibid.

91. Ibid.

92. Ibid.

93. Letter from Carl Vinson to Lawrence O'Brien, January 4, 1962, box 944, folder "TA/Textiles 8-1-61–3-31-62," WHCF, JFK Library.

94. George Meany, testimony to Congress on TEA, March 19, 1962, RG 20–003, box 17, folder 2, Meany Archives.

95. Ibid.

96. Timothy W. Vanderburg, *Cannon Mills and Kannapolis: Persistent Paternalism in a Textile Town* (Knoxville: University of Tennessee Press, 2013), 149–56, 159–68; Charles Cannon, "Our Objective Is a One-Price System," *Textile Bulletin*, April 1963.

97. Statement of Carl Vinson, n.d., in letter from Vinson to Lawrence O'Brien, March 15, 1962; letter from Vinson to Robert Stevens, March 24, 1962; both in box 944, folder "TA/Textiles 4-1-62–3-25-63," WHCF, JFK Library.

98. Letter from Robert Jackson to Carl Vinson, April 4, 1962; letter from Vinson to Myer Feldman, April 6, 1962; both in box 944, folder "TA/Textiles 4-1-62–3-25-63," WHCF, JFK Library; "A.C.M.I. Spokesmen Review a Year's Hard Work at Association's Annual Meeting in Palm Beach," *Textile Bulletin*, May 1962.

99. While Meany and Walter Reuther testified before Congress in support of the TEA, other labor leaders, including George Baldanzi of the UTWA, James Carey of the

International Union of Electrical, Radio, and Machine Workers, Thomas Kennedy of the UMWA, and Sidney Zagri of the Teamsters supported the bill but expressed concerns about the effect of imports on manufacturing. Representatives of smaller unions, like Gerald Coleman of the United Hatters, Cap and Millinery Workers and Edwin Wheatley of the International Brotherhood of Operative Potters—as well as Frank Bennett, the publisher of *America's Textile Reporter*—opposed the bill. Bennett, in his opposition, repeated the argument that most-favored-nation status would extend to low-wage nations poised to undercut American textiles. See also US Congress, House, *Trade Expansion Act of 1962: Hearings on H.R. 9900*, Eight-Seventh Cong., second sess., Committee on Ways and Means (Washington, DC: US Government Printing Office, 1962), vol. 1, p. 1145 (Meany); vol. 3, p. 1506 (Reuther); vol. 3, p. 1713 (Kennedy); vol. 3, p. 2021 (Bennett); vol. 4, p. 2178 (Coleman); vol. 4, p. 2210 (Zagri); vol. 4, p. 2301 (Wheatley); vol. 4, p. 2392 (Carey); vol. 5, p. 2821 (Baldanzi).

100. "Trade, Progress and Prosperity" (AFL-CIO pamphlet), 1962, in RG 34–002, box 6, folder 11, Meany Archives.

101. Ibid.

102. Ibid.

103. George Meany, address to Thirty-First Convention, ILGWU, May 25, 1962, RG 20–003, box 17, folder 3, Meany Archives.

104. Ibid.

105. Statement of George Meany, AFL-CIO news release, June 20, 1962, RG 20–003, box 17, folder 3, Meany Archives.

106. "Policies to Make American Products Competitive in World Markets," Statement of George Harrison, White House Conference on National Economic Issues, May 22, 1962, RG 20–003, box 17, folder 3, Meany Archives.

107. Statement of George Harrison to Coordinating Council of Organizations on International Trade Policy, Conference on Trade Policy, May 17, 1962, RG 20–003, box 17, folder 3, Meany Archives.

108. Transcript of remarks by JFK and David McDonald, International President, USWA, September 7, 1962, box 575, folder U, WHCF, JFK Library.

109. Elizabeth Brenner, *The Trade Expansion Act of 1962*, Congressional Quarterly Special Report (Washington, DC: Congressional Quarterly, 1962), 5; US Congress, Senate, Committee on Finance, *Trade Expansion Act: Hearings on H.R. 11970*, Eighty-Seventh Cong., second sess. (Washington, DC: US Government Printing Office, 1962), 51–54, 76–78; David Richardson, "Trade Adjustment Assistance under the United States Trade Act of 1974: An Analytical Examination and Worker Survey," in *Import Competition and Response*, ed. Jagdish Bhagwati (Chicago: University of Chicago Press, 1982), 321–68.

110. John F. Kennedy, "Remarks upon Signing the Trade Expansion Act, October 11, 1962," American Presidency Project, https://www.presidency.ucsb.edu/documents/remarks-upon-signing-the-trade-expansion-act.

111. George Meany, "Article for Philadelphia Inquirer," December 17, 1962, RG 13–003, box 1, folder 62, Meany Archives.

112. "John F. Kennedy's Last Words to Labor," RG 34–002, box 7, folder 8, Meany Archives.

113. Ibid.

114. Sam Ervin to JFK, March 6, 1963, box 944, folder "TA/Textiles 4-1-62–3-25-63," WHCF, JFK Library. Ervin, a North Carolina Democrat, was also joined by longtime Cannon Mills President Charles Cannon, who opposed the "two-price cotton" system, created by subsidizing raw cotton exports, as harmful to the US textile industry (Vanderburg, *Cannon Mills*, 159–68).

115. Clemson College, "An Interdisciplinary Approach to the American Textile Problem," submitted to the U.S. Department of Commerce, Civilian Industrial Technology Division, August 1963, series 55, box 12, folder 16, School of Industrial and Textile Science, Office of the Dean, 1951–1975, Clemson University Libraries, Special Collections and Archives, Clemson, South Carolina [hereafter, Clemson].

Chapter 5. Winds of Change

1. Letter from Robert Jackson to LBJ, February 5, 1964; telegram from Bob Stevens to LBJ, February 5, 1964; letter from Myer Feldman to Bob Stevens, February 14, 1964; letter from Jackson to Feldman, February 19, 1964; telegram from Jackson to LBJ, April 10, 1964; letter from Jackson to Feldman, April 10, 1964; letter from Jackson to Lawrence O'Brien, April 14, 1964, all in name file A, box 138, folder "American Textile Manufacturers Institute," White House Central Files [hereafter, WHCF], Lyndon B. Johnson Presidential Library, Austin, Texas [hereafter, LBJ Library]; letter from Robert Stevens to Feldman, March 10, 1964, in name file S, box 565, folder "Stevens, Robert T.," WHCF, LBJ Library; memorandum from Jackson to Feldman, October 20, 1964, in Confidential File, box 2, folder "BE4/Industry (Textiles–Watches)," WHCF, LBJ Library.

2. "Combined Cotton and Wheat Programs Enacted," in *CQ Almanac*, Eighty-Eighth Cong., second sess. (Washington, DC: Congressional Quarterly, 1965), 98–100; US Congress, House, Committee on Agriculture, memorandum from Joseph Califano to LBJ, February 2, 1966, box 13, folder "TA6/Cotton (Executive)" [hereafter, "TA6/Cotton (Executive)"], WHCF, LBJ Library; "Revitalize the American Cotton Industry," House Report no. 366, Eighty-Eighth Congress, first sess., June 6, 1963 (Washington, DC: US Government Printing Office, 1963), 4–6; Richard Leger, "Textile Tonic: Cotton Bill, Boom Times Provide Best Year Yet for Oft-Ailing Industry," *Wall Street Journal*, November 29, 1965.

3. Memorandum from Christian Herter and George Ball to LBJ, June 18, 1964, box 47, folder "Trade—General, Vol. 1 [1 of 4]," National Security File, Subject File [hereafter, NSF], LBJ Library; letter from Robert Stevens to LBJ, December 14, 1964, name file S, box 565, folder "Stevens, Robert T.," WHCF, LBJ Library; Leger, "Textile Tonic."

4. Testimony of J. M. Cheatham to Senate Committee on Agriculture and Forestry, June 23, 1965, in "Food and Agricultural Act of 1965: Hearings before the Committee on Agriculture and Forestry, US Senate, Part 2" (Washington, DC: US Government Printing Office, 1965), 683–86; memorandum from Gardner Ackley to Joseph Califano, September 12, 1966, "TA6/Cotton (Executive)," LBJ Library.

5. Memorandum from Esther Peterson to LBJ, January 13, 1965, in BE4, box 14, folder "BE4/Textile-Executive," WHCF, LBJ Library.

6. "Statement by the President, Issued at Macon, Georgia, October 26, 1964," "TA6/Cotton (Executive)," LBJ Library.

7. Draft statement from LBJ on cotton textile imports, September 23, 1964; statement of LBJ on textile imports, September 26, 1964; memorandum from Dean Rusk and George Ball to LBJ, September 26, 1964; and memorandum from William Roth to Francis Bator, White House aide, and Myer Feldman, September 25, 1964; all in box 47, folder "Trade—General, vol. 2 [4 of 4]," NSF, LBJ Library.

8. TWUA, "America's Stake in the South," n.d. (ca. 1963), 1, MSS 396, box 634, folder "America's Stake in the South," TWUA Papers, SHSW; National Bureau of Economic Research, "US Business Cycle Expansions and Contractions," https://www.nber.org/research/data/us-business-cycle-expansions-and-contractions; New Bedford Joint Board, TWUA, news release to the New Bedford (MA) *Standard-Times*, n.d. (1965), MS 134, box 3, folder 26, WEB Du Bois.

9. Memorandum for the president, February 11, 1966, Confidential File, box 2, folder "BE4/Industry (Textiles–Watches)," WHCF, LBJ Library; memorandum from James Duesenberry to Joseph Califano, September 12, 1966, BE4, box 14, folder "BE4/Textile-Executive," WHCF, LBJ Library; memorandum from Gardner Ackley to Califano, September 12, 1966, in "TA6/Cotton (Executive)," LBJ Library; memorandum from Otto Eckstein to Califano, November 20, 1965; memorandum from Orville Freeman to LBJ, May 20, 1965; last two in GEN BE4, box 8, folder "BE4/C," WHCF, LBJ Library.

10. Memorandum from Gardner Ackley to Henry Fowler et al., January 29, 1966; memorandum from Melford Cleveland to Gardner Ackley, January 12, 1966; both in "TA6/Cotton (Executive)," LBJ Library.

11. The figures cited here come from an analysis of US Commerce Department data by the American Textile Manufacturing Institute. American Textile Manufacturing Institute, "U.S. Textile Trade," *Textile Hi-Lights*, September 1969 (Washington, DC: American Textile Manufacturing Institute, 1969): 26.

12. Memorandum from Benjamin Reed to McGeorge Bundy, December 19, 1963, in "TA6/Cotton (Executive)," LBJ Library.

13. Statement by US representative to the GATT, December 3, 1963, in "TA6/Cotton (Executive)," LBJ Library.

14. US Senate, Committee on Interstate and Foreign Commerce, "Problems of the Domestic Textile Industry (supplemental report)," March 14, 1961 (Washington, DC: US Government Printing Office, 1961), 5.

15. Clarence Newman, "Textile Comeback; More Efficient Plants, Mergers Help Industry to Increase Earnings," *Wall Street Journal*, March 3, 1964.

16. Thurmond would switch parties and become a Republican in 1964, out of dissatisfaction with the Civil Rights Act of that year; the move culminated a partisan shift that, for Thurmond, dated to his 1948 presidential candidacy on the States' Rights (Dixiecrat) ticket (Joseph Crespino, *Strom Thurmond's America* (New York: Hill and Wang, 2012), 165–84).

17. Committee on Interstate and Foreign Commerce, "Problems of the Domestic Textile Industry," 8–9.

18. Ibid., 11.

19. Ibid., 18–19.

20. Letter from Carignan to Pollock, May 10, 1965, MS 134, box 4, folder 42, WEB Du Bois.

21. Warren Buffett, "Berkshire—Past, Present and Future," in annual letter to shareholders, February 2015, 24–25, https://www.berkshirehathaway.com/SpecialLetters/WEB%20past%20present%20future%202014.pdf.

22. For the 1962 stock price, see "Warren Buffett bought his first Berkshire Hathaway shares for $7.50 each, 55 years ago today," CNBC.com, December 12, 2017, https://www.cnbc.com/2017/12/12/buffett-bought-berkshire-hathaway-shares-for-7-dollars-and-50-cents-each.html; for the 2015 stock price, see Nasdaq.com, https://www.nasdaq.com/market-activity/stocks/brk.a/historical; and e-mail from Warren Buffett, Berkshire Hathaway Corp., to author, February 23, 2022 (in author's possession).

23. Memorandum from George Perkel, TWUA research director, to Pollock, September 18, 1968, MSS 396, box 541, folder "Cannon Mills," TWUA Papers, SHSW.

24. Also included in this number are African Americans from the South and Caribbean immigrants, who started working in New York's garment industry at the end of World War I. See, for example, Janette Gayle, "'Invaders': Black Ladies of the ILGWU and the Emergence of the Early Civil Rights Movement in New York City," October 19, 2016, Gotham Center for New York City History, https://www.gothamcenter.org/blog/invaders-black-ladies-of-the-ilgwu-and-the-emergence-of-the-early-civil-rights-movement-in-new-york-city.

25. Petition from Helen Fain et al. to LBJ, July 16, 1968, General, PR (GEN PR), box 298, folder "PR14/ST10," WHCF, LBJ Library.

26. "Problems of the Domestic Textile Industry," 24.

27. "Chapter IX: International Economic Relations" in Administrative Histories, Department of State, box 3, folder "Chapter 9 (International Economic Relations): Overview and Section A" Intro, pp. 5–6, LBJ Library.

28. Ibid., 7, 18–25; "National Security Council Histories: The Kennedy Round Crisis," 13, in box 52, folder "Kennedy Round Crisis, April–June 1967, bk. 1, tabs 1–6," NSF, LBJ Library.

29. Statement from American Textile Manufacturers Institute, November 14, 1966, in GEN TA 6, box 24, folder "TA6/Textiles 11/22/63–2/10/67," LBJ Library; "Long-Term Arrangements between the U.S. of America and Other Governments," February 9, 1962, in "TA6/Cotton (Executive)," LBJ Library; "General Results of the Kennedy Round," tab 87, in National Security Council Histories: The Kennedy Round Crisis, box 52, folder "Kennedy Round Crisis, April–June 1967, bk. 1, tabs 54–96," NSF, LBJ Library.

30. Letter from Senator Richard Russell to LBJ, April 6, 1967, GEN TA 6, box 24, folder "TA6/Textiles 4/1/67–4/30/67," WHCF, LBJ Library; "Administrative History of Department of State," vol. 1: 25, Administrative Histories, Department of State, box 3, folder "Chapter IX (International Economic Relations) Overview and Section A," LBJ Library; memorandum from Francis Bator to LBJ, May 10, 1967, bk. 1, tabs 66 and 68a, box 52, folder "Kennedy Round Crisis, April–June 1967, bk. 1, tabs 54–96," National Se-

curity Council Histories: Kennedy Round Crisis, NSF, LBJ Library [Bator was special assistant to the president for national security affairs]; "General Results of the Kennedy Round," tab 87, in National Security Council Histories: Kennedy Round Crisis, box 52, folder "Kennedy Round Crisis, April–June 1967, bk. 1, tabs 54–96," NSF, LBJ Library.

31. "Johnson Hails Trade Accord; Tells Congress Pact Will Aid Participating Nations," (Baltimore) *Sun*, November 28, 1967.

32. Gerd Wilke, "Industries in U.S. Assail Tariff Cut; Kennedy Round Pact Leaves Some Non-duty Barriers, Producers' Groups Say," *New York Times*, May 17, 1967.

33. Kenneth Ross, "Fears 'Trade Anarchy' If Quotas Pass; U.S. Aid [*sic*] Warns of Retaliation," *Chicago Tribune*, November 9, 1967; John Averill, "Congress Revolt May Limit Foreign Imports; Political Expediency, Kennedy Round Pact Partly Responsible for Opposition," *Los Angeles Times*, October 23, 1967; Edwin Dale, "Timing Favors Protectionists," *New York Times*, October 29, 1967; "Summary of Major Import Quota Bills and Sponsors," *Washington Post*, October 29, 1967.

34. "House Unit Supports Bill to Curb Trade with Countries Employing 'Cheap Labor,'" *Wall Street Journal*, August 10, 1967; "Summary of Major Import Quota; "Dent Bill Called 'an Attempt to Welsh' on Tariff Cut Obligations," *Los Angeles Times*, October 27, 1967; "Defeat the Dent Bill," *Washington Post*, September 30, 1967.

35. Letter from Senator Edward Brooke to George Carignan, February 13, 1968, MS 134, box 3, folder 29, WEB Du Bois; letter from Carignan to Senator Edward Kennedy, July 26, 1967, MS 134, box 3, folder 28, WEB Du Bois.

36. "Summary of Major Import Quota Bills"; Frank Porter, "Textile Imports Study Is Ordered," *Washington Post*, October 5, 1967; Philip Dodd, "Dirksen Urges Congressional Vacation to Shed 'Ill Feeling,'" *Chicago Tribune*, November 15, 1967; Albert Sehlstedt, "Senate Gets Bill to Set Steel Quota," (Baltimore) *Sun*, October 17, 1967.

37. "Summary of Major Import Quota Bills"; James Gannon, "Divided Unions: Labor Leaders Alarmed by Diminishing Support among Rank and File," *Wall Street Journal*, July 6, 1967.

38. Memorandum from Dean Rusk to LBJ, October 10, 1967, in *Foreign Relations of the U.S., 1964–1968*, vol. 8, *International Monetary and Trade Policy* (Washington, DC: US Government Printing Office, 1998), 966–68. Quotes on 968, 967, 967, respectively.

39. Ibid. Quotes on 968.

40. Ibid.

41. Memorandum from Hubert Humphrey to LBJ, September 11, 1967; memorandum from William Roth to LBJ, September 18, 1967; and memorandum from Humphrey to LBJ, September 28, 1967; all in box 2, folder "BE4/Industry (Textiles-Watches)," Confidential File, LBJ Library; letter from LBJ to Glenn Sutton, October 4, 1967, and letter from Wilbur Mills to Sutton (acting chairman of the Tariff Commission), October 4, 1967, both in US Tariff Commission, *Textiles and Apparel: Report to the President on Investigation No. 332–55 under Section 332 of the Tariff Act of 1930* (Washington, DC: US Tariff Commission, 1968), 1: 122–23; Porter, "Textile Imports Study"; "Questions for President's Press Conference," November 17, 1967, NSF, Files of Edward Fried, box 2, folder "Chron Sept 1 1967–Nov. 30, 1967 [1 of 2]," LBJ Library.

42. Marjorie Hunter, "Dirksen Defiant on Import Curbs," *New York Times*, November 4, 1967; memorandum from Bob Hardesty to LBJ, October 20, 1967, box 10, folder "TA6—11/4/66 (Executive)," WHCF, LBJ Library.

43. Frank Porter, "Import Quota Plan Gets Wide Support," *Washington Post*, October 12, 1967; John Averill, "Top Aides of Johnson Warn on Import Curbs; President Sends Cabinet Panel Led by Rusk to Dampen Congressional Demands," *Los Angeles Times*, October 19, 1967; George Lardner, "Angry LBJ Vows to Veto Trade Curb," *Washington Post*, November 3, 1967; Robert Semple, "Johnson May Bar Any Import Curb," *New York Times*, November 3, 1967; Porter, "Textile Imports Study"; Norman Miller, "Backers of Import Curbs Prepare to Attack Administration's Program for Freer Trade," *Wall Street Journal*, September 26, 1967; Oswald Johnston, "Trade Measure Shelved for '67; White House Abandons Plan on Liberal Bill This Year," (Baltimore) *Sun*, December 1, 1967; Administrative History of Department of State, box 3, folder "Chapter IX (International Economic Relations) Overview and Section A," 53, LBJ Library; US Tariff Commission, *Textiles and Apparel*, 1: 44.

44. "Trade Policy—a Proposed Strategy for the U.S.," memorandum from George Ball to LBJ, August 15, 1966, in Administrative History of Department of State, Trade Preferences for Developing Countries, 7–12, in Administrative History of Department of State, box 3, folder "Chapter 9 (International Economic Relations) Sections B&C," LBJ Library.

45. Administrative History of Department of State, Section C, Trade Preferences for Developing Countries, 1–19, in box 3, folder "Chapter 9 (International Economic Relations) Sections B&C," Administrative History of Department of State [hereafter, AHDS, Trade Preferences], LBJ Library; "Trade Policy" memo.

46. AHDS, Trade Preferences, 4–6, LBJ Library; memorandum from Dean Rusk to LBJ, February 11, 1967, in AHDS, Trade Preferences, LBJ Library.

47. George Carignan to LBJ, September 28, 1966, GEN BE4, box 21, folder "GEN BE4/Textile," WHCF, LBJ Library.

48. Kenneth Chace to LBJ, October 21, 1966, GEN TA6, box 24, folder "TA6/Textiles 11/22/63–2/10/67," WHCF, LBJ Library.

49. Letter from George Carignan, TWUA, to Representative Hastings Keith, April 11, 1967; letter from Albert Pacheco, Alfred Barboza, and Charles Medeiros, Local 590, TWUA, to the editor, New Bedford (MA) *Standard-Times*, n.d. [1967], and letters from Carignan to Senators Edward Kennedy and John Pastore, March 3, 1967; all in MS 134, box 3, folder 28, WEB Du Bois; Ellen Gaughan to LBJ, December 23, 1966, in GEN TA 6, box 24, folder "TA6/Textiles 11/22/63–2/10/67," WHCF, LBJ Library.

50. Letter from Augustus Zellicoffer Jr. to LBJ, February 20, 1967, TA5 (Trade), box 14, folder "TA6/Cotton (General)," WHCF, LBJ Library.

51. Petition from Donald Timmons, UTWA Local 282 (Beacon, NY) to LBJ, April 15, 1967, in name file, box 18, folder "United, T," WHCF, LBJ Library.

52. Petition from Local 233, UTWA (Springfield, TN), March 1967, to LBJ, name file, box 18, folder "United, T," WHCF, LBJ Library.

53. Statement of William Pollock to General Subcommittee on Labor, Committee on Education and Labor, US House of Representatives, April 27, 1967, in GEN BE4, box 21, folder "GEN BE4/Textile," WHCF, LBJ Library.

54. "In Atlanta: Import Curbs, Pay Raise Asked," *Textile Challenger*, August 1967, 1; "A Call for Action: 20,000 North Carolinians Urge Broad Import Curbs; Petitions to Pres. Johnson Call for International Pacts on All Textiles," *Textile Challenger*, October 1967, 1.

55. "A Call to Action: UTW Urges Joint Effort to Curb Textile Imports," *Textile Challenger*, February 1967, 1.

56. Ibid., 3.

57. "AFL-CIO Meeting Sets Labor Policies for Critical 1968," *Textile Challenger*, February 1968, 1.

58. "AFL-CIO Convention Warns of Foreign Trade Dangers," *Textile Challenger*, February 1968, 1, 8; "International Trade, Resolution No. 207," *Proceedings of the Seventh Constitutional Convention of the AFL-CIO*, December 7–16, 1967 (Washington, DC: AFL-CIO, 1968), 578–80.

59. "17th UTW Convention Set for Miami Beach," *Textile Challenger*, April 1968, 1.

60. "UTW Convention Blasts Flood-Tide of Imports," *Textile Challenger*, June 1968, 1.

61. Ibid.

62. Ibid.

63. "Jobs Threatened: Textile Fibre Imports Spurt Up in 1968," *Textile Challenger*, December 1968, 1.

64. "World Textile Union Leaders Map Trade Import Program," *Textile Challenger*, December 1968, 1, 6.

65. In 1954 the United States had 8,070 textile mill producers and 31,372 apparel producers; by 1963, after a number of mergers and consolidations, 7,104 textile mill producers and 28,457 apparel producers remained (US Tariff Commission, *Textiles and Apparel*, 1: 23, 67).

66. US Tariff Commission, *Textiles and Apparel*, 1: 7, 83–85.

67. Ibid., 2: 54.

68. Ibid., 9–10, 69.

69. Ibid., 1: 47.

70. Memorandum from A. B. Trowbridge to Hubert Humphrey, September 21, 1967, in box 2, folder "BE4/Industry (Textiles-Watches)," Confidential File, LBJ Library (first quote); memorandum from Trowbridge to LBJ, November 29, 1967, BE4, box 4, folder "BE4/Textile-Executive," WHCF, LBJ Library; George Carignan to LBJ, February 7, 1968, in name file T, box 67, folder "TWUA," WHCF, LBJ Library (Carignan quote).

71. Memorandum from DeVier Pierson and Joseph Califano to LBJ, April 10, 1968, BE4, box 4, folder "BE4/Textile-Executive," WHCF, LBJ Library; Mills quote from "Rep. Mills Vows Action in Textile Import Threat," *Daily News Record* (New York), April 8, 1968.

72. Memorandum from Pierson and Califano to LBJ, April 10, 1968, BE4, box 4, folder "BE4/Textile-Executive," WHCF, LBJ Library; Barefoot Sanders to R. L. McNeill, May

9, 1968, in name file E, box 81, folder "ECAT," WHCF, LBJ Library; memorandum for the president, July 11, 1968, box 10, folder "TA6—11/4/66 (Executive)," WHCF, LBJ Library.

73. Memorandum from Mike Manatos to LBJ, July 2, 1968, BE4, box 14, folder "BE4/Textile-Executive," WHCF, LBJ Library; "Nixon Assures Thurmond on Textiles," *Washington Post*, August 22, 1968.

74. "What You Can Do to Help Stem Rising Tide of Imports," *The Advance*, n.d. (1969), box 10, folder 18 (Executive Board Correspondence, 1966–1969), Local 125 Papers, WEB Du Bois; "UTW Widens Battle against Low-Wage Textile Imports," *Textile Challenger*, June 1969, 1.

75. "ACW Flexes Its Muscles," *Men's Wear*, July 25, 1969.

76. Martin Rossman, "Do Apparel Imports Fit Market in U.S.?," *Los Angeles Times*, November 23, 1969.

77. "Resolution on Imports," *Association News Bulletin*, Clothing Manufacturers Association of the United States, March 3, 1969, box 303, folder "Imports 1969," ACWA Records, Kheel Center.

78. Rossman, "Do Apparel Imports Fit?"

79. Ibid.

80. Sally Roane and Frank Ackerman, "Faraway Fashion Foibles: Apparel Picture Clouded by Foreign Wage Scale," *Western Apparel Industry*, December 1969, 52.

81. Roane and Ackerman, "Faraway Fashion Foibles," 52–53.

82. Rossman, "Do Apparel Imports Fit?"

83. James P. Gannon, "Unions Plan Assault on Companies Lured by Mexico's Low Pay," *Wall Street Journal*, February 21, 1969.

84. Ibid.; "ILGWU Probes Boom in 'Offshore' Apparel," *Daily News Record*, July 21, 1970; "Oxford May Begin Output in Mexico of Boys' Shirts," *Daily News Record*, n.d. [1968]; undated clipping in letter from Jacob Potofsky to LBJ, October 14, 1968, in GEN TA6/Chemicals, box 14, folder "TA6/CI-CNZ," WHCF, LBJ Library.

85. Gannon, "Unions Plan Assault."

86. Ibid.; letter from Louis Stulberg to LBJ, June 13, 1968, and "Imports of Apparel and Textiles," report of Committee on Resolutions, ILGWU, May 28, 1968; both in name file I, box 27, folder "International Ladies Garment Workers Union," WHCF, LBJ Library; letter from Jacob Potofsky to LBJ, October 14, 1968, in GEN TA6/Chemicals, box 14, folder "TA6/CI-CNZ," WHCF, LBJ Library.

87. Rossman, "Do Apparel Imports Fit?"

88. "Textile Import Curbs Urged," *Chicago Daily News*, September 22, 1969.

89. Willard Wirtz, memorandum for the vice president, January 24, 1968; letter from Willard Wirtz to Harry McPherson, January 24, 1968, both Labor-Management Relations, box 9, folder "LA2 1/1/68–2/29/68," WHCF, LBJ Library; US Department of Labor, "The Textile-Apparel Labor Force: A Special Study" (Washington, DC: US Department of Labor, 1968), 2–16, Conditions-Employment-Unemployment, box 324, folder "Oversize Attachments," item 2054, WHCF, LBJ Library.

90. US Department of Labor, "Textile-Apparel Labor Force," 2–16.

91. Ibid., 117–18.

Chapter 6. Fighting to Win

1. "Nixon Assures Thurmond on Textiles," *Washington Post*, August 22, 1968. Nixon's pledge came in an August 21 telegram to Republican South Carolina Senator Strom Thurmond noted in the *Post*. In that telegram, Nixon alleged the Johnson administration had failed to protect the nation's textile industry in trade negotiations and had not done its part to ensure the LTA was enforced.

2. In 1967 ACWA members held protests at two Ohio department stores—Lazarus in Columbus and Rike's in Dayton—calling imports a threat to the state's estimated twenty thousand clothing workers. In March 1969 ACWA members in Cincinnati held a leaflet campaign at a third department store, Shillito's, to protest the sale of imported suits ("ACW Begins Drive on Shillito's over Hong Kong Suits," *Daily News Record* (New York), March 12, 1969; and Fred Robbins, "Clothing War Brewing Here," *Dayton Daily News*, April 6, 1967.

3. "'Dangerous Flood' of Imports Protested," *The Advance*, June 1, 1969; "ACW Launches Drive against Apparel Imports," *Daily News Record*, May 19, 1969; "Union Pickets Ohrbach's over Sale of Imports," *Women's Wear Daily*, May 20, 1969.

4. "A Growing Danger," Special Import Issue, *The Advance*, June 15, 1969.

5. "ACW Pickets Store for Selling Suits from Hong Kong," *Daily News Record* (New York), April 28, 1969.

6. "Threat to Our Jobs!" Special Import Issue, *The Advance*, June 15, 1969; "Unions Worried about Imports," *Johnstown* (PA) *Observer*, July 24, 1969.

7. "Union Workers to Protest Imports," *Fall River Herald News*, July 28, 1969; "Thousands Protest Import Policy," *Fall River Herald News*, July 30, 1969; "New World Wage Pacts Urged," *Boston Herald Traveler*, August 31, 1969.

8. "Consumers in Cleveland Support Amalgamated's Import Action," *The Advance*, August 1969.

9. "Clothing Workers Campaign for Cuts in Apparel Imports," *Galesburg* (IL) *Labor News*, June 26, 1969; "ACWA Carries Imports Fight to D.C.," Special Import Issue, *The Advance*, June 15, 1969; "An Open Letter to the Foreign Minister of Japan," Special Import Issue, *The Advance*, June 15, 1969; Richard Wightman, "ACW at White House Encouraged on Quotas," *Daily News Record*, June 4, 1969.

10. Wightman, "ACW at White House."

11. "UTW Widens Battle against Low-Wage Textile Imports," *Textile Challenger*, June 1969, 1, 10 (quotes on 10).

12. Reproduction of letter from Jacob Potofsky, president, ACWA, to Richard Nixon, n.d., in *The Advance*, July 1969: 9.

13. Ibid.

14. "Chicago Union Seeks Apparel Import Curb," *Chicago Tribune*, October 1, 1969; "Chicago Jt. Bd. Presses Case against Imports," *The Advance*, October 15, 1969.

15. "Apparel Unions Push Stans for 'Livable' Import Pact," *Daily News Record*, May 9, 1969.

16. "Stans, Aichi 'Friends' after Parley on Imports," *Daily News Record*, June 4, 1969; Ed

Townsend, "U.S. Unions Fidget over Import Flow," *Christian Science Monitor*, August 15, 1969.

17. "Unions to Picket Stores in Protest to Imports," *Daily News Record*, July 31, 1969.

18. "UTW Southern Conference Endorses Three-Prong Drive for Textile Job Security," *Textile Challenger*, August–September 1969, 1.

19. "More Solons Alarmed over Foreign Imports," *Textile Challenger*, August–September 1969, 5.

20. Ibid.

21. "Four Unions Ask Japan to Join Textile Talks," *New York Times*, July 23, 1969; "Unions Ask Japan's Aid on Imports," *Daily News Record*, July 23, 1969; "4 Union Heads Urge Japan Regulate Exports," *The Advance*, August 1969.

22. Pete Cakania, "Schultz Ducks Controversy on Imports," *Daily News Record*, May 27, 1969; "Amalgamated Sues Chicago Dailies on Refusal to Run Ad," *Advertising Age*, September 22, 1969.

23. "Union-Maid," *Fox River Labor News*, August 28, 1969.

24. "Clothing Workers Protest Field's Import Sales," *Chicago Sun-Times*, August 3, 1969; "Garment Workers Protest," *Chicago Tribune*, August 3, 1969; Pete Cakania, "ACW Targets Marshall Field Imports," *Daily News Record*, August 1, 1969.

25. "Unions Press Protest on Japan Goods," *Daily News Record*, September 4, 1969.

26. "U.S. Unions Warn Japan," *Daily News Record*, September 15, 1969; "When East Meets West," *The Advance*, October 1, 1969; "Nixon Urged to Help Curb Cloth Imports," *AFL-CIO News*, September 20, 1969.

27. "Japan Industry, Labor Hit U.S. Boycott Plan," *Daily News Record*, September 8, 1969. Though Japanese officials saw the US labor actions as a boycott, the ACWA called its activities part of an "educational campaign" to persuade retailers and the consuming public to fight imports.

28. Ibid.

29. "State Opposes Anti-imports Union Efforts," *Women's Wear Daily*, September 5, 1969; "U.S. Opposes Anti-Japanese Apparel Drive," *Daily News Record*, September 5, 1969.

30. Lloyd Schwartz, "ACW Sees Import Curbs Vital for U.S. Textile-Apparel Field," *Women's Wear Daily*, November 12, 1969.

31. "Resolution No. 192, International Trade," *Sixth Convention Proceedings, AFL-CIO, 1965* (Washington, DC: AFL-CIO, 1965), 1: 366.

32. Ibid., 1: 367.

33. Ibid., 1: 368–69.

34. "Resolution No. 207, International Trade," *Seventh Convention Proceedings, AFL-CIO, 1967* (Washington, DC: AFL-CIO, 1967), 1: 578–79.

35. Ibid., 1: 579–80.

36. Ibid., 1: 580.

37. Ibid., 1: 580–82.

38. Edwin Dale Jr., "New Rise in U.S. Imports Linked to Old Tariff Cuts," *New York Times*, November 10, 1969; "Nixon Proposes to Ease Access to Import Relief," *Wall Street Journal*, November 19, 1969; Edwin Dale Jr., "U.S. Benefits Set for Steelworkers Idled by Imports," *New York Times*, December 8, 1969; "Free Trade Posture Reaffirmed," *Los Angeles*

Times, November 20, 1969; Carroll Kilpatrick, "Nixon Seeks Lower Tariffs," *Washington Post*, November 19, 1969; Edwin Dale Jr., "President Urges Aid to Industries Hurt by Imports," *New York Times*, November 19, 1969; and "Tariff Agency Altering Criteria on Protection from Imported Goods," *Wall Street Journal*, November 5, 1969; "Retroactive Trade Protection Sought for Textiles, Apparel," 1; House Committee on Ways and Means, *Material Relating to Adjustment Assistance for Workers*, Ninety-Third Congress, first sess. (Washington, DC: US Government Printing Office, 1973), 1–27.

39. "Meany, Potofsky, 3 Presidents Protest the Rising Tide of Apparel, Textile Imports," *The Advocate*, October 15, 1969.

40. "Meany, Potofsky, 3 Presidents."

41. Ibid.

42. Ibid.

43. Townsend, "U.S. Unions Fidget."

44. Stanley Levey, "Labor Shedding Free Trade Pose," *Washington Daily News*, October 8, 1969; "AFL-CIO Demands Updating Tariff Regulations at Its 8th Convention," *The Advance*, October 15, 1969.

45. Jacqueline Hayes, "Toward a Redefinition of the U.S. Sweatshop," *Sanford Journal of Public Policy* 5, no. 2 (Spring 2014): 39–52.

46. US Department of Labor, "The Textile-Apparel Labor Force: A Special Study" (Washington: US Department of Labor, 1968), 27–33.

47. A. Philip Randolph Institute, *A "Freedom Budget" for All Americans: Budgeting Our Resources, 1966–1975, to Achieve "Freedom from Want"* (New York: A. Philip Randolph Institute, 1966).

48. "Resolution No. 11, Foreign Imports and International Competition"; "Resolution No. 207, U.S.-Mexican Economic Relations"; "Resolution No. 123, Runaway Flag Shipping"; and "Resolution No. 131, The Dollar Gap," all in *Eighth Convention Proceedings, AFL-CIO, 1969* (Washington, DC: AFL-CIO, 1969), 1: 257–62.

49. "Resolution No. 206, The Export of American Jobs," *Eighth Convention Proceedings, AFL-CIO, 1969* (Washington, DC: AFL-CIO, 1969), 1: 254–55.

50. "Resolution No. 206," 1: 255–56.

51. "Resolution No. 67, Runaways to Mexico," *Eighth Convention Proceedings, AFL-CIO, 1969* (Washington, DC: AFL-CIO, 1969), 1: 262–63.

52. Ibid., 262.

53. "Resolution No. 52, Imports of Textiles and Apparel," *Eighth Convention Proceedings, AFL-CIO, 1969* (Washington, DC: AFL-CIO, 1969), 1: 283; "Resolution No. 87, Competition of Foreign Imports," *Eighth Convention Proceedings, AFL-CIO, 1969* (Washington, DC: AFL-CIO, 1969), 1: 284; "Resolution No. 181, International Trade," *Eighth Convention Proceedings, AFL-CIO, 1969* (Washington, DC: AFL-CIO, 1969), 1: 287.

54. "Resolution No. 52," 284.

55. Merrill Watson, "Observations," *Leather and Shoes*, April 11, 1970.

56. Frank Porter, "Labor's Protectionist Shift," *Washington Post*, May 10, 1970.

57. "For Import Regulation," *Justice*, November 15, 1969; "Garment Workers Fight Rising Tide of Imports," *Los Angeles Citizen*, November 7, 1969.

58. "Los Angeles Protest Blasts Unchecked Garment Imports," *Justice*, November 15, 1969.

59. "Garment Workers."

60. "GEB Resolution on Imports," *The Advance*, December 1, 1969; "ACW Issues New Blast at Imports Rise," *Daily News Record*, November 21, 1969.

61. "Short-Sighted Campaign," *Watertown* (WI) *Times*, September 27, 1969.

62. "More Unions Join Fight against Imports," *Textile Challenger*, February 1970, 1; "Sharpest Rise since '51: Living Costs Continue to Soar as Workers' Real Income Drops," *Textile Challenger*, February 1970, 1.

63. "Pastore Asks Action," *Textile Challenger*, February 1970, 6.

64. "More Unions Join Fight," 1–6. Quote, p. 1.

65. Ibid.

66. "Unions Study Steps to Protect U.S. Workers in World Trade," *Textile Challenger*, April 1970, 7.

67. Ibid.

68. Ibid.

69. "Unions Study Steps"; Edwin Dale Jr., "New Rise in U.S. Imports Linked to Old Tariff Cuts," *New York Times*, November 10, 1969; Edwin Dale Jr., "U.S. Benefits Set for Steelworkers Idled by Imports," *New York Times*, December 8, 1969; "Tariff Agency Altering Criteria on Protection from Imported Goods," *Wall Street Journal*, November 5, 1969. Opinions on the number of rejected TAA cases between 1962 and 1969 varies: the USWA's Bernstein counted seven cases, while J. David Richardson counted six (Richardson, "TAA under the U.S. Trade Act of 1974: An Analytical Examination and Worker Survey" in *Import Competition and Response*, ed. Jagdish Bhagwati [Chicago: University of Chicago Press, 1982], 325–26).

70. "Unions Study Steps."

71. "More Unions Join Fight," 6.

72. Porter, "Labor's Protectionist Shift."

73. Joan Noblit, "Hundreds Join Protest March Here," *Daily Free Press* (Doylestown, PA), March 20, 1970.

74. Damon Stetson, "Clothing Union Is Planning a Stoppage over Imports," *New York Times*, March 17, 1970.

75. Damon Stetson, "Garment Workers Protesting Imports," *New York Times*, March 21, 1970; "Across-the-Board," *Textile Labor*, June 1970, 9.

76. William Hotz photograph of Baltimore ACWA protestors, (Baltimore) *Evening Sun*, March 19, 1970. The ACWA protest sentiments expressed in this photo, along with similar sentiments expressed in other protests and "Buy American" campaigns of this period, tapped into a tradition of economic nationalism extending back to the colonial era. Such campaigns also revealed long-standing prejudices. The ACWA protests surfaced anti-Japanese and anti-Asian sentiment, an example of which is demonstrated by the *Evening Sun* photo, or comparisons between Japanese imports and the Pearl Harbor attack that led the United States into World War II. Another example came with unions' opposition to the presence of traveling salesmen who measured US customers for suits

that were tailored in Hong Kong and shipped to them ("Another Hong Kong Firm Flees Information Picketline," *The Advance*, September 15, 1970; "Attention Shoppers: Are You About to Be Gypped?" *The Advance*, September 15, 1970; "Pittsburgh Bd. Bids City Curb Peddlers of Hong Kong Suits," *The Advance*, November 13, 1970; "ACW Shows Its 'Hospitality' to Hong Kong Peddler," *The Advance*, December 4, 1970; and "Hong Kong Salesman Did Not Make a Dime in Huntington, Pa.," *The Advance*, December 26, 1970). For more on prejudices within "Buy American" campaigns, see Dana Frank, *Buy American: The Untold Story of Economic Nationalism* (Boston: Beacon, 1999).

77. Stetson, "Garment Workers Protesting Imports."

78. Len Lear, "March against Japanese Textiles Is Joined by Mass of Black Workers," *Philadelphia Tribune*, March 21, 1970.

79. Ibid.

80. Stetson, "Garment Workers Protesting Imports"; "Daley, Union Label Asia Goods 'Unfair,'" *Chicago Tribune*, March 21, 1970.

81. Harry Bernstein, "Men's Clothing Workers Stage 1-Day Stoppage," *Los Angeles Times*, March 21, 1970.

82. Ibid.

83. Richard Levine, "'Free Trade' Fight: Unions, Fearful of Losing Jobs, Leverage, Implore Congress to Pass Import Quotas," *Wall Street Journal*, May 19, 1970.

84. Brendan Jones, "U.S. Trade Group to Hold Talks in Japan; Business Leaders to Urge End of Import Curbs," *New York Times*, March 9, 1970; "U.S. and Japanese Ask Trade Action; Business Groups Bid Tokyo to Liberalize Curbs," *New York Times*, March 17, 1970; Philip Shabecoff, "Trade Legislation Cited; Japan Is Pressed on U.S. Demands," *New York Times*, March 19, 1970; Herbert Koshetz, "Producers in Meeting; Textile Leaders Press for Curbs," *New York Times*, March 19, 1970; "U.S. Textile Plan Splits Japanese; Industry Rejects Curbs, but Government Backs Rein," *New York Times*, March 25, 1970.

85. Quoted in "Washington Scene," *Fashion Week*, May 25, 1970. Though Nixon's 1968 pledge did not receive widespread coverage, the issue of protecting the textile industry did surface during the election. See, for example, "Nixon Assures Thurmond"; Don Oberdorfer, "Nixon Hits HHH Tactics," *Washington Post*, October 16, 1968; Robert Donovan, "Nixon to Follow Middle of Road," *Los Angeles Times*, November 7, 1968; Arthur Schlesinger Jr., "A Skeptical Democrat Looks at President Nixon," *New York Times*, November 17, 1968; "Prospects for Trade Pact with Japan Dim," *Textile Challenger*, April 1970, 8.

86. Julian Zelizer, *Taxing America: Wilbur Mills, Congress, and the State, 1945–1975* (New York: Cambridge University Press, 1998), 312–46.

87. Porter, "Labor's Protectionist Shift"; "U.S. Textile Plan Splits Japanese."

88. "Washington Scene."

89. "GEB Resolution on Imports."

Chapter 7. Labor Strikes Out

1. "U.S. Textile Trade," *Textile Hi-Lites*, December 1973, 25. Richard Nixon's presidency occupied an economic crossroads between the end of the rapid growth characterizing

much of the post–World War II US economy, and the genesis of economic stagnation through much of the 1970s and early 1980s. For more, see Allan Matusow, *Nixon's Economy: Booms, Busts, Dollars, and Votes* (Lawrence: University Press of Kansas, 1998); Robert Collins, *More: The Politics of Economic Growth in Postwar America* (New York: Oxford University Press, 2000); Jefferson Cowie, *Stayin' Alive: The 1970s and the Last Days of the Working Class* (New York: New Press, 2010); Fred Block, *The Origins of International Economic Disorder: A Study of United States Monetary Policy from World War II to the Present* (Berkeley: University of California Press, 1977); Arthur F. Burns, *Inside the Nixon Administration: The Secret Diary of Arthur Burns, 1969–1974*, edited by Robert Ferrell (Lawrence: University Press of Kansas, 2010); Joanne Gowa, *Closing the Gold Window: Domestic Politics and the End of Bretton Woods* (Ithaca, NY: Cornell University Press, 1983); Diane Kunz, *Butter and Guns: America's Cold War Economic Diplomacy* (New York: Free Press, 1997); Robert Mason, *Richard Nixon and the Quest for a New Majority* (Chapel Hill: University of North Carolina Press, 2004); Herbert Stein, *Presidential Economics: The Making of Economic Policy from Roosevelt to Reagan and Beyond* (New York: Simon and Schuster, 1984); and Wyatt C. Wells, *Economist in an Uncertain World: Arthur F. Burns and the Federal Reserve, 1970–78* (New York: Columbia University Press, 1994).

2. "Nixon Assures Thurmond."

3. Matusow, *Nixon's Economy*, 120–22. Nixon also criticized the Kennedy and Johnson administrations for their handling of the industry program and promised to include wool and synthetic textiles in LTA import safeguards. As president, Nixon also ended his predecessors' practice of denying contracts to textile firms with a documented record of racial discrimination in hiring (Timothy J. Minchin, *Empty Mills: The Fight against Imports and the Decline of the U.S. Textile Industry* [Lanham, MD: Rowman and Littlefield, 2013], 55, and Minchin, *Hiring the Black Worker*, 30). Connections among Republican politicians and textile executives like Roger Milliken, Nixon's 1968 finance chairman, contributed to the growth of the New Right beyond its California origins, setting the stage for its 1980 breakthrough (Crespino, *Strom Thurmond's America*, 207–10, 226–27); Crespino, "Goldwater in Dixie: Race, Region, and the Rise of the Right," in *Barry Goldwater and the Remaking of the American Political Landscape*, ed. Elizabeth Tandy Shermer (Tucson: University of Arizona Press, 2013), 144–69; William Link, "Time Is an Elusive Companion: Jesse Helms, Barry Goldwater, and the Dynamic of Modern Conservatism," in *Barry Goldwater and the Remaking of the American Political Landscape*, ed. Elizabeth Tandy Shermer (Tucson: University of Arizona Press, 2013), 238–58; and Lisa McGirr, *Suburban Warriors: The Origins of the New American Right* (Princeton, NJ: Princeton University Press, 2001).

4. The National Bureau of Economic Research data indicate a recession began in December 1969 and ended in November 1970 (National Bureau of Economic Research, "US Business Cycle Expansions and Contractions," last updated 07/19/2021, http://www.nber.org/cycles/cyclesmain.html); Matusow, *Nixon's Economy*, 3–4.

5. Matusow, *Nixon's Economy*, 2–3.

6. Matusow, *Nixon's Economy*, 6; "Free Trade Posture Reaffirmed," *Los Angeles Times*, November 20, 1969. Quote in Jefferson Cowie, "Nixon's Class War: Romancing the New Right Worker, 1969–1973," *Labor History* 43, no. 3 (2002): 257–83.

7. Zelizer, *Taxing America*, 331–37. Zelizer argues that Mills, rather than campaigning from the start, encouraged speculation that he could defeat Nixon by beating him in several regions, including the South, and by appealing to several constituencies, including business, organized labor, and African Americans. Mills's 1972 campaign was short-lived, failing by March 1972. Yet, in contrast to his shortcomings as a presidential candidate, Mills exercised great power as House Ways and Means chairman from 1958 to 1974, writing tax legislation, recommending tariff levels, and doling out committee assignments. Mills was also known to hold up presidential requests in order to exact budgetary cuts—as he did with Lyndon Johnson's 1968 request for a 10 percent income tax surcharge—and gained enough power in Congress to rival the speaker of the House. See further Gregg Ramshaw, "Wilbur Mills—the Sympathy Slowly Fades," *Chicago Tribune*, December 8, 1974; Joseph Califano Jr., "Balancing the Budget, L.B.J. Style," *New York Times*, December 31, 1995.

8. "32 New England Textile Mills Shut Down in 1970," *Textile Challenger*, April 1971, 4.

9. J. Stein, *Running Steel*, 3.

10. J. Stein, *Running Steel*, 4–6.

11. J. Stein, *Pivotal Decade*.

12. Mizruchi, *Fracturing*, 139–91.

13. One of the first works to raise public awareness of the power of multinational corporations was Richard J. Barnet and Ronald E. Müller's *Global Reach: The Power of the Multinational Corporations* (New York: Simon and Schuster, 1974). Other works on the topic include Geoffrey Jones, *Multinationals and Global Capitalism: From the Nineteenth to the Twenty-First Century* (New York: Oxford University Press, 2005); Panos Mourdoukoutas, *The Global Corporation: The Decolonization of International Business* (Westport, CT: Quorum, 1999); John J. Reardon, *America and the Multinational Corporation: The History of a Troubled Partnership* (Westport, CT: Praeger, 1992); Alex Rubner, *The Might of the Multinationals: The Rise and Fall of the Corporate Legend* (New York: Praeger, 1990); Theodore Cohn, Steven McBride, and John Richard Wiseman, *Power in the Global Era: Grounding Globalization* (New York: St. Martin's, 2000); and Robert A. Pastor, *Congress and the Politics of U.S. Foreign Economic Policy, 1929–1976* (Berkeley: University of California Press, 1980).

14. Mizruchi, *Fracturing*, 1–21.

15. Pat Herold, "ACW Heats Up Coast Battle against Imports from Asia," *Daily News Record*, November 13, 1970; memorandum from Jacob Potofsky and Frank Rosenblum, ACWA, to members and managers, General Executive Board, April 7, 1970, box 10, folder 19 (Executive Board Correspondence, 1970–1972), Local 125 Papers, WEB Du Bois; Matusow, *Nixon's Economy*, 119–22; I. M. Destler, Haruhiro Fukui, and Hideo Sato, *The Textile Wrangle: Conflict in Japanese-American Relations, 1969–1971* (Ithaca, NY: Cornell University Press, 1979), 180–207.

16. William Brick, "Floor Fight May Stiffen ACW Anti-import Stand," *Daily News Record*, May 28, 1970; ACWA, General Executive Board Report and Convention Proceedings, Atlantic City, NJ, May 25–29, 1970, 345–48; Emanuel Perlmutter, "Potofsky, in Labor Split, Denounces War Policy," *New York Times*, May 25, 1970; Bill Brick, "ACW

Parley Confirms Fusing Ban Unanimously," *Daily News Record,* May 27, 1970; "Korean Garment Trade Show Gets Bad Review from the ACWA," *The Advance*, December 26, 1970; William Brick, "ACW Takes Hard Stand on Low-Wage Imports," *Daily News Record*, June 1, 1970.

17. "Need for Quotas Underlined by Climb of Imports in 1970," *The Advance*, October 1, 1970.

18. "Text of Baldanzi Testimony on Imports to U.S. Congress," *Textile Challenger*, June 1970, 3.

19. Ibid. In citing Watson, Baldanzi was referring to his December 1969 testimony to a congressional committee, in which Watson said the United States would "probably get out of" older industries because of expanded world trade (testimony of Arthur Watson, December 2, 1969, in Joint Economic Committee, *A Foreign Economic Policy for the 1970s* [Washington, DC: US Government Printing Office, 1970], 2–12).

20. "Textile and Apparel Union Leaders Ask Congress for Import Quotas," *Textile Challenger*, June 1970, 1.

21. Ibid., 7; Louis Stulberg, "To Regulate Imports" (letter to the editor), *New York Times*, April 27, 1970.

22. "Textile and Apparel Union Leaders," 7.

23. Pete Laine, "Textilists Lobby for Import Curb," *Charlotte Observer*, May 21, 1970.

24. "Multinational Firms Help Kill Trade Bill; New Drive Opens," *Textile Challenger*, February 1971, 1; "Textile and Apparel Union Leaders," 1.

25. Telegram from Arthur Watson to LBJ, November 15, 1967, in TA5 (Trade), box 10, folder "TA6—11/4/66—Executive," WHCF, LBJ Library; Gerd Wilcke, "Watson of I.B.M. Heads Group Opposing Import Quota Moves," *New York Times*, November 16, 1967; Brendan Jones, "Business Group Backs Free Trade," *New York Times*, March 17, 1968; Gerd Wilcke, "Nixon Is Expected to Uphold Trade Policies," *New York Times*, January 3, 1969; Robert Wright, "Business Leaders Back Free Trade," *New York Times*, August 14, 1969; Brendan Jones, "Mission Favors 'Orderly Trade': 'Confrontation' Opposed," *New York Times*, September 23, 1969; Brendan Jones, "World Trade War Brews: World Trade War Is Brewing as Congress Ponders Protectionist Measures," *New York Times*, July 19, 1970; "J. Frank Forster, 64, Is Dead; Was Chairman of Sperry-Rand," *New York Times*, July 3, 1972; "Would Export U.S. Jobs," *Textile Challenger*, February 1971, 1.

26. Frank Corrigan, "A Turn-around on Free Trade?" *Newsday*, August 24, 1970.

27. "Premier Sato and the Trade Bill," *St. Louis Post-Dispatch*, October 22, 1970; "Trade Bill Foes: Foreign Voices," *Textile Challenger*, February 1971, 1.

28. "Nixon Administration Backs Mills Bill on Import Quotas," *The Advance*, July 1970; "House Panel OK's Measure to Restrict Textile Imports," *Textile Challenger*, August 1970, 1.

29. "Let 'Em Know," *Textile Challenger*, August 1970, 1; "AFL-CIO Unmasks Firms Opposing Curbs on Imports," *Textile Challenger*, August 1970, 2.

30. "Sec. Stans Praises Apparel Quota Bill," *The Advance*, September 15, 1970; Frank Porter, "Trade Bill Hurdle Marked by Dissent," *Washington Post*, August 14, 1970.

31. Letter from John Hight, executive director, Committee for a National Trade Policy,

to Members of the Coordinating Council of Organizations on International Trade Policy, October 23, 1970, in UAW President's Office, Leonard Woodcock Files, box 12, folder 6 "Committee for a Nat'l Trade Policy, 1970–74," Walter P. Reuther Library, Archives of Labor and Urban Affairs, Wayne State University, Detroit [hereafter, Reuther Library]; "Import Bill Vote after Election," *Textile Challenger*, October 1970, 1.

32. "Human Side of Import Quotas Told Congress by a Worker," *Textile Challenger*, October 1970, 8.

33. "Imports Hit Beaunit, 1000 Lose Jobs," *Textile Challenger*, June 1971, 1.

34. "Sad Day in Talladega" (photograph), *Textile Challenger*, August 1971, 8; "Protest Low-Wage Clothing Imports" (photograph), *Textile Challenger*, August 1971, 8.

35. Frank Porter, "Opposition by Mills Dims Trade Legislation Prospects," *Washington Post*, December 17, 1970; John Finney, "The Order of the Day Was the Filibuster," *New York Times*, December 20, 1970; "Multinational Firms Help Kill Trade Bill; New Drive Opens," *Textile Challenger*, February 1971, 1.

36. "Multinational Firms Help Kill Trade Bill; New Drive Opens"; "U.S. Economy Failed to Increase in 1970," *Textile Challenger*, February 1971, 4.

37. Matusow, *Nixon's Economy*, 139–41; Destler et al., *Textile Wrangle*, 236–50, 251–66, 283–85. The deal of December 1970 collapsed in the final stage of negotiations as Congress took up the Mills bill.

38. "Japan Industry Maneuvers Imperil Textile Trade Bill," *Textile Challenger*, April 1971, 1; Ed Rogers, "Dixie Report," *Atlanta Daily World*, March 18, 1971; Richard Lyons, "New Englanders Set Hill Caucus," *Washington Post*, February 25, 1973.

39. Matusow, *Nixon's Economy*, 167–73; Destler et al., *Textile Wrangle*, 291–314; James Sterba, "Long Dispute Over: 10% Surtax Is Lifted for All on Wool and Synthetics," *New York Times*, October 16, 1971; Don Oberdorfer, "Japan Yields to U.S., Signs Textiles Curb," *Washington Post*, October 16, 1971; "U.S. Gives Japan Plan on Textiles; Tokyo Told to Accept Curbs or Face Quotas on Oct. 15," *New York Times*, October 1, 1971; Thomas Pepper, "Japan Will Limit Textile Exports; U.S. to Lift Tax," (Baltimore) *Sun*, October 16, 1971. The NEP language allowed Nixon to use the Trading with the Enemy Act of 1917 and the First War Powers Act, signed into law after Pearl Harbor, to regulate imports during wartime "or during any other period of national emergency declared by the President" (Destler et al., *Textile Wrangle*, 292–93).

40. John Pierson, "Nixon Agreement on Asian Textiles Sales Lays Claim for Southern Votes, Aid in '72," *Wall Street Journal*, October 18, 1971; Herbert Koshetz, "Those Textile Quotas: U.S. Industry Feels That Agreement Won't Curb Imports Much, after All," *New York Times*, October 19, 1971; Destler et al., *Textile Wrangle*, 318; Bernadine Morris, "The Import Surcharge—Fashion Industry Takes It in Stride," *New York Times*, October 4, 1971; "Textile Importers Will Get Refunds," *New York Times*, January 18, 1972. For more on Nixon's quest for a New Majority, see Matthew Lassiter, *The Silent Majority: Suburban Politics in the Sunbelt South* (Princeton, NJ: Princeton University Press, 2006), 232–75.

41. "Baldanzi Urges World Union Plan to Stop Corporate Exploitation," *Textile Challenger*, June 1971, 1.

42. "All Labor Joins UTW Campaign for Curb on Low-Wage Imports," *Textile Challenger*, August 1971, 1; "AFL-CIO Trade Plan," *Textile Challenger*, August 1971, 1.

43. "All Labor Joins UTW Campaign," 1.

44. Ibid.

45. US Congress, Joint Economic Committee, "The 1971 Economic Report of the President" (testimony of Maurice Stans) (Washington, DC: US Government Printing Office, 1971), pt. 1, 154; US Senate, Committee on Finance, "U.S. Trade and Balance-of-Payments Deficits," *Tables and Statistical Material on U.S. Balance of Trade and Balance of Payments*, December 1974 (Washington, DC: US Government Printing Office, 1974), 1; *Congressional Quarterly Almanac, 1972*, 437.

46. The ACWA rally participants came from Los Angeles, Salt Lake City, Denver, Kansas City, St. Louis, Minneapolis, Chicago, Little Rock, New Orleans, Atlanta, Knoxville, Cincinnati, Cleveland, Pittsburgh, Scranton, Allentown, Buffalo, Rochester, Boston, New York, Philadelphia, Baltimore, Washington, and Richmond (memorandum from Jacob Potofsky and Frank Rosenblum to General Executive Board Members, Clothing and Cotton Garment Managers, March 11, 1971, box 11, folder 30 [Import Protest March, 1970–1971], Local 125 Papers, WEB Du Bois); flyers from Alexander's August 1971 ACWA protest read "Enough Is Enough," "Unemployment for Sale," "Inside This Store They're Selling Unemployment," and "SAY NO! Put an American Back to Work," box 11, folder 30 (Import Protest March, 1970–1971), Local 125 Papers, WEB Du Bois; "Alexander's Agrees with ACW to 'Curtail' Imported Apparel; Joins 2 Other Chains in Move," *Advance*, August 1971; Bill Brick, "Alexander's and ACW Agree on Taport Sales," *Daily News Record*, August 16, 1971; memorandum from Jacob Potofsky and Frank Rosenblum, ACWA, to all Joint Boards and Locals, August 27, 1971, box 10, folder 19 (Executive Board Correspondence, 1970–1972), Local 125 Papers, WEB Du Bois.

47. "Imports—a Bigger Slice of the Pie," *Staff Letter News*, October 1970, box 11, folder 30 (Import Protest March, 1970–1971), Local 125 Papers, WEB Du Bois.

48. *Congressional Quarterly Almanac, 1971* (Washington, DC: Congressional Quarterly, 1972), 431. Under the Bretton Woods system, which was established in 1944, foreign currencies were fixed relative to the US dollar; the dollar, in turn, was pegged at a congressionally established price of $35 per ounce of gold. By the 1960s, the dollar was overvalued as foreign aid, military spending, and foreign investment created a surplus of dollars and the United States lacked enough gold to cover the dollars in circulation at the $35-per-ounce rate. As efforts to keep the system operating, the dollar became susceptible to runs in which foreign exchange traders sold dollars, expecting the United States to eventually devalue its currency. Nixon devalued the dollar under the NEP after one such run and amid evidence that the dollar's value was undermining the nation's position in foreign trade. In December 1971, the Smithsonian Agreement involving the Group of Ten (G-10) industrialized democracies formally devalued the dollar from $35 per ounce of gold to $38. See *Nixon and the End of the Bretton Woods System, 1971–1973*, Office of the Historian, US Department of State, https://history.state.gov/milestones/1969–1976/nixon-shock. For more on Nixon's economic policies, see R. Collins, *More*, 98–131, and Matusow, *Nixon's Economy*.

49. Matusow, *Nixon's Economy*.
50. R. Collins, *More*.
51. J. Stein, *Pivotal Decade*.
52. Minchin, *Empty Mills*.
53. Matusow, *Nixon's Economy*, 131.
54. Matusow, *Nixon's Economy*, 132.
55. Peter G. Peterson, *The United States in the Changing World Economy*, 2 vols. (Washington, DC: US Government Printing Office, 1971); Matusow, *Nixon's Economy*, 133–39.
56. H. R. Haldeman diary entry, June 27, 1971, quoted in Matusow, *Nixon's Economy*, 137; Connally quoted in Matusow, *Nixon's Economy*, 137.
57. Richard Nixon, "Address to the Congress on Stabilization of the Economy," September 9, 1971, American Presidency Project, https://www.presidency.ucsb.edu/documents/address-the-congress-stabilization-the-economy.
58. Ibid.
59. Letter to George Meany from Ann Fleming, September 1, 1971, RG1–038, box 35, folder 2, Meany Archives.
60. Ibid.
61. Ibid.
62. Nixon would receive a frosty reception from Meany and the AFL-CIO that fall at its convention in Bal Harbour, Florida, in part because of the effect of wage and price controls on wage increases won through contract negotiations (Matusow, *Nixon's Economy*, 160–62).
63. "UTW Council Raps Surcharge as Inadequate, Asks Quotas; Cites Growing Crisis in Textiles, Apparels," *Textile Challenger*, October 1971, 1.
64. "Union Asks Import Relief for Canada," *Textile Challenger*, October 1971, 1.
65. "UTW Council Raps Surcharge."
66. "Conglomerates and Imports," *Ninth Convention Proceedings, AFL-CIO, 1971* (Washington, DC: AFL-CIO, 1971), 1: 334–35.
67. George Baldanzi and Charles Feinstein, "Foreign Imports and U.S. Unemployment," *Ninth Convention Proceedings, AFL-CIO, 1971* (Washington, DC: AFL-CIO, 1971), 2: 365.
68. *Congressional Quarterly Almanac, 1971*, 377, 439.
69. Gerd Wilke, "Connally Opposes a Bill to Curb Imports; Treasury Chief Asserts U.S. 'Cannot Go Back to Protectionism,'" *New York Times*, January 22, 1972; Edwin Dale Jr., "Hartke Offers to Compromise on Controversial Legislation on Trade Quotas and Taxes," *New York Times*, January 27, 1973; Edwin Dale Jr., "Multinational Corporations in U.S. Set Job Pace in '60s," *New York Times*, February 15, 1972; Elizabeth Fowler, "U.S. Presses Demands," *New York Times*, March 3, 1972; Martin Waldron, "Nixon Aides Ask Support of Meany on Trade Plans," *New York Times*, February 15, 1973; Joseph Kraft, "A Cease-Fire with Labor?" *New York Times*, February 22, 1973.
70. Biographical information on Burke, "Biographical Directory of the U.S. Congress," https://bioguide.congress.gov/search/bio/B001092; biographical information on Hartke, "Biographical Directory of the U.S. Congress," https://bioguide.congress.gov/search/bio/H000297; Julian Zelizer, *Taxing America*, 331; Robert Walker, "Dip in Profits Is Worrying

Steel Men," *New York Times*, November 19, 1967; Warren Weaver Jr., "Panel Vote Keeps Quota on Shoes in Trade Bill," *New York Times*, December 2, 1970.

71. Edwin Dale Jr., "Multinational Companies in U.S. Set Job Pace in '60's," *New York Times*, February 15, 1972; Paul Jablow, "Meany Is Elated, but Labor Faces Delicate Task," (Baltimore) *Sun*, November 9, 1972; Richard Barnet and Ronald Müller, "Companies Go Abroad, and Jobs Go Along," *New York Times*, December 22, 1974. ECAT based its findings on the assumption that moving production to low-wage countries increased jobs for Americans because the labor-cost savings would produce domestic jobs in other areas, like services. If, conversely, manufacturers kept jobs in the United States, the wage differential between US workers and workers in low-wage nations would allow foreign competition to erode US manufacturers' market share.

72. Barnet and Müller, "Companies Go Abroad."

73. "President Rejects Corporate Tax Overhaul on Foreign Profit; Limited Change Sought," *Wall Street Journal*, April 11, 1973.

74. *Congressional Quarterly Almanac, 1972*, 487; "Retroactive Trade Protection Sought for Textiles, Apparel," *Textile Challenger*, December 1971, 3.

75. Letter from Henry Steiner to W. P. Gullander, May 1, 1972, Accession 1411, series 4, box 21, folder "Burke-Hartke," National Association of Manufacturers Records, Hagley [hereafter, NAM Records].

76. Letter from Edward Sprague, National Association of Manufacturers, to Henry Steiner, May 10, 1972, Accession 1411, series 4, box 21, folder "Burke-Hartke," NAM Records.

77. Minutes of the International Taxation Subcommittee Meeting, Sheraton-Four Ambassadors Hotel, Miami, April 5, 1972, Accession 1411, series 4, box 21, folder "Burke-Hartke," NAM Records.

78. Minutes of the International Taxation Subcommittee Meeting, Sheraton-Four Ambassadors Hotel, Miami, April 5, 1972, Accession 1411, series 4, box 21, folder "Burke-Hartke," NAM Records.

79. Ibid.

80. ". . . while trade deficit blooms," *Christian Science Monitor*, June 5, 1972.

81. Remarks by J. Stanford Smith, "Report on NAM Survey of the Impact on Multinational Corporations of Sections 102 & 103 of the Burke-Hartke Bill," International Club, Washington, DC, December 5, 1972. The surveyed group had total worldwide sales of $151 billion and $9.8 billion in after-tax earnings in 1971 (Accession 1411, series 4, box 21, folder "Burke-Hartke," NAM Records).

82. Remarks by J. Stanford Smith; Representative Bill Frenzel, "Burke-Hartke Bill Analysis," February 14, 1972, Accession 1411, series 4, box 21, folder "Burke-Hartke," NAM Records.

83. Memorandum from Nat Weinberg to Leonard Woodcock, October 7, 1971, in box 29, folder 8, "Imports, 1971," UAW President's Office, Leonard Woodcock Files, Reuther Library.

84. Christopher Lydon, "The Politics of Devaluation and Trade," *New York Times*, February 26, 1973.

85. Hobart Rowen, "UAW Points the Way," *Washington Post*, May 4, 1972.

86. Representative Donald Fraser to John Schlotz, March 16, 1972, Accession 1411, series 4, box 21, folder "Burke-Hartke," NAM Records.

87. Honeywell Corporation, "Issues and Position—Hartke-Burke Bill," December 22, 1971, Accession 1411, series 4, box 21, folder "Burke-Hartke," NAM Records.

88. Letter from Robert Malott to Senator Vance Hartke, June 14, 1972, Accession 1411, series 4, box 21, folder "Burke-Hartke," NAM Records.

89. Letter from A. Carl Kotchian to Senator Vance Hartke, May 12, 1972, Accession 1411, series 4, box 21, folder "Burke-Hartke," NAM Records.

90. James Reston, "Mr. Nixon Wins First Round," *New York Times*, February 21, 1973.

91. Matusow, *Nixon's Economy*, 214–16; Paul Jablow, "Meany Is Elated, but Labor Faces Delicate Task," (Baltimore) *Sun*, November 9, 1972; "Quite a Game of Golf," *Wall Street Journal*, September 18, 1972; Damon Stetson, "Garment and Auto Unions Endorse McGovern Drive," *New York Times*, August 16, 1972.

92. Matusow, *Nixon's Economy*, 219–21.

93. Joseph Kraft, "A Cease-Fire with Labor?" *Washington Post*, February 22, 1973; Philip Shabecoff, "President Plans to Seek 'Options' in Trade Talks," *New York Times*, February 20, 1973; Rowland Evans and Robert Novak, "A Major Shift in Trade Policy under White House Study," *Washington Post*, January 17, 1973; William Diebold Jr., "Are We Ready for New Trade Initiatives? America's Strategy Hampered at Home," *New York Times*, December 24, 1972; Leonard Silk, "Much at Stake in Trade and Money Talks," *New York Times*, September 5, 1973.

94. *Congressional Quarterly Almanac 1973*, Ninety-Third Cong., first sess., 1973, vol. 29 (Washington, DC: Congressional Quarterly, 1974), 225–27; Michael Jensen, "Reactions to Step Are Varied in U.S.; Economists and Many Big Companies Hail Move, but Importers Are Critical," *New York Times*, February 14, 1973.

95. Jensen, "Reactions to Step."

96. Kraft, "A Cease-Fire with Labor?"; Shabecoff, "President Plans to Seek 'Options.'"

97. *Congressional Quarterly Almanac, 1973*, 834–35, 42-A.

98. *Congressional Quarterly Almanac, 1973*, 834–35.

99. *Congressional Quarterly Almanac, 1973*, 836.

100. James Gannon, "Duty Calls: Nixon, Congress, Allies Get Set for Big Battle over U.S. Trade Policy," *Wall Street Journal*, January 4, 1973; Edwin Dale Jr., "Goals Appear to Be Similar to Nixon Ideas," *New York Times*, March 22, 1973; Carroll Kilpatrick, "President to Seek Trade Talk Powers," *Washington Post*, March 23, 1973.

101. Memo from Nicholas Hollis to Corporate Legislative Coordinators re: Trade Bill Action, September 28, 1973, Accession 1411, series 4, box 22 (General Administration Files), folder "Legislative Coordinator Correspondence," NAM Records.

102. "Inter-association Memorandum, Congressional Action on H.R. 6767," June 22, 1973, Accession 1411, series 4, box 22, folder "Trade Act 1973/1974," NAM Records.

103. Gannon, "Duty Calls"; Dale, "Goals Appear to Be Similar"; Kilpatrick, "President to Seek Trade Talk Powers"; "Import Curb in Trade Bill Rejected," *New York Times*, July 17, 1973; *Congressional Quarterly Almanac 1973*, 841.

104. National Association of Manufacturers, "International Economic Report," August 29, 1973, Accession 1411, series 4, box 22, folder "Trade Act 1973/1974," NAM Records.

105. "Mills Opposes Further Delay for Trade Bill," *New York Jewish Week*, November 21, 1973; Leslie Gelb, "The White House Now Urges Delay on Russian Trade," *New York Times*, October 30, 1973; Bernard Gwertzman, "Kissinger Given Trade Bill Delay," *New York Times*, October 12, 1973.

106. Memorandum from Nicholas Hollis to Corporate Legislative Coordinators re: Trade Bill Postponement, November 9, 1973; memorandum from Hollis to Corporate Legislative Coordinators re: Trade Bill Vote, December 4, 1973; both in Accession 1411, series 4, box 22 (General Administration Files), folder "Legislative Coordinator Correspondence," NAM Records.

107. *Congressional Quarterly Almanac, 1973*, 845. Despite concerns that the bill would harm import-sensitive industries, much of the coverage of the House's passage of the Trade Act of 1973 focused on the dispute between Congress and the Nixon White House over the Jackson-Vanik amendment (Edwin Dale Jr., "Credits to Soviet Barred as House Backs Trade Bill," *New York Times*, December 12, 1973).

108. "Trade Hearings Going On in Senate," *Amalgamated Action*, April 1974, box 11, folder 40, Local 125 Papers, WEB Du Bois; *Congressional Quarterly Almanac 1974*, Ninety-Third Cong., second sess. 1974, vol. 30 (Washington, DC: Congressional Quarterly, 1975), 235.

109. Cynthia Anderson, *Social Consequences*, 39; Aggarwal, *Liberal Protectionism*, 95–123, 136–41.

110. *Congressional Quarterly Almanac, 1974*, 235–36.

111. Richard Lawrence, "Passage of Trade Reform Bill Likely; Major Hurdle Cleared," *Journal of Commerce*, August 16, 1974.

112. Murray Seeger, "Accord Reached on Jewish Emigration," *Los Angeles Times*, October 19, 1974; Seeger, "Tenacity, New President Led to Trade Accord," *Los Angeles Times*, October 19, 1974; Gregg Ramshaw, "Jackson, Ford Agree on Soviet Trade, Jews," *Chicago Tribune*, October 19, 1974; "Congress Seen Passing Major Trade Bill as Soviets Agree to Increase Emigration," *Wall Street Journal*, October 21, 1974; Marilyn Berger, "Big Firms to Press Hill on Soviet Trade Benefit," *Washington Post*, September 16, 1973.

113. In his 1973 veto of minimum-wage legislation, Nixon had objected to provisions to increase the minimum wage twice in eight months, to $2.20 an hour, and argued the measure would increase unemployment and harm disadvantaged workers. The House of Representatives sustained Nixon's veto later that month (*Congressional Quarterly Almanac 1972*, Ninety-Second Cong., second sess., 1972, vol. 28 [Washington, DC: Congressional Quarterly, 1973], 361–64; and Richard Nixon, "Veto of the Minimum Wage Bill," September 6, 1973, American Presidency Project, https://www.presidency.ucsb.edu/documents/veto-the-minimum-wage-bill.

114. *Congressional Quarterly Almanac, 1974*, 239–43.

115. The Senate version of ERISA contained a voluntary portability program for companies to allow their employees to transfer their pensions when they changed jobs, but the House version had no similar provision, in part because of business opposition (*Con-*

gressional Quarterly Almanac, 1974, 238; John Morris, "Pension Reform Drive Gains as House Panel Supports a Bill to Protect Rights of Workers," *New York Times*, September 26, 1973; "Senate Votes to Overhaul Private Pensions but Limits Plans' Benefits to $75,000 a Year," *Wall Street Journal*, September 20, 1973; Mary Russell, "House Votes Pension Plan Reform Bill," *Washington Post*, March 1, 1974; Bruce Riblett, "Hodgson Claims Proposals for Portable Pension Unworkable," *Los Angeles Times*, April 19, 1973. For more on Cannon Mills and the loss of its pension funds, see Vanderburg, *Cannon Mills*, 199, and Nancy Peckenham, "Out in the Cold at Cannon Mills," *The Nation* 253, no. 8 (September 16, 1991), 298–302.

116. Edwin Dale Jr., "Trade Bill Is Due for Early Action; Long Pledges Closed-Door Study in Senate of Act 'within Several Weeks,'" *New York Times*, May 24, 1974; Richard Weintraub, "Trade Reform Bill Faces Crucial Test in Hill Panel Today," *Washington Post*, November 19, 1974.

117. Murray Finley and Jacob Sheinkman, ACWA Trade Act Pamphlet (1974), box 9, folder 3, Local 125 Papers, WEB Du Bois; "We're Worried about Jobs in America!" (ACWA advertisement), box 9, folder 3, Local 125 Papers, WEB Du Bois.

118. Murray Finley and Jacob Sheinkman, Memorandum to All Amalgamated Affiliates in the Apparel Industry, October 14, 1974, box 10, folder 20, Local 125 Papers, WEB Du Bois.

119. Letter from John Driscoll, Connecticut State Labor Council, AFL-CIO, to all affiliates and union representatives re: trade bill, November 26, 1974, box 10, folder 20, Local 125 Papers, WEB Du Bois.

120. *Congressional Quarterly Almanac, 1974*, 555–56.

121. *Congressional Quarterly Almanac, 1974*, 559–60.

122. Spencer Rich, "Senate Votes Long-Stalled Bill on Trade," *Washington Post*, December 14, 1974; Albert Hunt, "Sweeping Trade Bill Is Expected to Clear Conferees Soon, despite Key Differences," *Wall Street Journal*, December 16, 1974.

123. *Congressional Quarterly Almanac, 1974*, 558.

124. *Congressional Quarterly Almanac, 1974*, 554–55; Marilyn Berger, "Hill Panel Agrees on Trade Powers," *Washington Post*, September 15, 1973. President Jimmy Carter renamed the special representative for trade negotiations to US trade representative under a 1979 reorganization and Executive Order 12188 in 1980 (Office of the US Trade Representative, "History of the US Trade Representative," https://ustr.gov/about-us/history).

Epilogue

1. Peter Temin, *The Vanishing Middle Class: Power and Prejudice in a Dual Economy* (Cambridge, MA: MIT Press, 2017).

BIBLIOGRAPHY

Archival Sources

American Catholic History Research Center and University Archives, Catholic University of America, Washington, DC
Clemson University Libraries, Special Collections and Archives, Clemson, South Carolina
David M. Rubenstein Rare Book and Manuscript Library, Perkins Library, Duke University, Durham, North Carolina
Eberly Family Special Collections Library, Paterno Library, Pennsylvania State University, University Park, Pennsylvania
Franklin D. Roosevelt Library, Hyde Park, New York
Gerald R. Ford Presidential Library, Ann Arbor, Michigan
Hagley Museum and Library, Wilmington, Delaware
Hornbake Library, Special Collections and University Archives, University of Maryland, College Park
John F. Kennedy Presidential Library and Museum, Boston
Kheel Center for Labor-Management Documentation and Archives, Martin P. Catherwood Library, Cornell University, Ithaca, New York
Library of Congress, Manuscript Division, Washington, DC
Lyndon B. Johnson Presidential Library, Austin, Texas
National Archives and Records Administration, Washington, DC
National Archives II, College Park, Maryland
North Carolina, State Archives of, Raleigh, North Carolina.
Southern Historical Collection, Louis Round Wilson Library, University of North Carolina, Chapel Hill
Southern Labor Archives, Special Collections and Archives, Georgia State University Library, Atlanta
Walter P. Reuther Library, Archives of Labor and Urban Affairs, Wayne State University, Detroit

W. E. B. Du Bois Library, Special Collections and University Archives, University of Massachusetts, Amherst

Wisconsin, State Historical Society of, University of Wisconsin, Madison

References

A. Philip Randolph Institute. *A "Freedom Budget" for All Americans: Budgeting Our Resources, 1966–1975, to Achieve "Freedom from Want."* New York: A. Philip Randolph Institute, 1966.

AFL-CIO Research Department. *AFL-CIO Looks at Foreign Trade: A Policy for the Sixties.* Washington: AFL-CIO, 1961.

Aggarwal, Vinod K. *Liberal Protectionism: The International Politics of Organized Textile Trade.* Berkeley: University of California Press, 1985.

Anderson, Carol. *One Person, No Vote: How Voter Suppression Is Destroying Our Democracy.* New York: Bloomsbury, 2018.

———. *White Rage: The Unspoken Truth of Our Racial Divide.* London: Bloomsbury, 2016.

Anderson, Cynthia D. *The Social Consequences of Economic Restructuring in the Textile Industry: Change in a Southern Mill Village.* New York: Garland, 2000.

Audet, Denis, and Raed Safadi. *A New World Map in Textiles and Clothing: Adjusting to Change.* Paris: Organization for Economic Co-operation and Development, 2004.

Barnet, Richard J., and Ronald E. Müller. *Global Reach: The Power of the Multinational Corporations.* New York: Simon and Schuster, 1974.

Beschloss, Michael R. *The Crisis Years: Kennedy and Khrushchev, 1960–1963.* New York: HarperCollins, 1991.

Biographical Directory of the United States Congress. https://bioguide.congress.gov/.

Block, Fred L. *The Origins of International Economic Disorder: A Study of United States International Monetary Policy from World War II to the Present.* Berkeley: University of California Press, 1977.

Bluestone, Barry. "Deindustrialization and Unemployment in America." In *Deindustrialization and Plant Closure*, ed. Paul Staudohar and Holly Brown, 3–15. Lexington, MA: DC Heath, 1987.

Bluestone, Barry, and Bennett Harrison. *The Deindustrialization of America: Plant Closings, Community Abandonment, and the Dismantling of Basic Industry.* New York: Basic Books, 1982.

Board of Inquiry for the Cotton Textile Industry (Winant Board). *Report of the Board of Inquiry for the Cotton Textile Industry to the President.* Washington, DC: US Government Printing Office, 1935.

Branch, Taylor. *Parting the Waters: America in the King Years, 1954–63.* New York: Simon and Schuster, 1989.

Brenner, Elizabeth J. *The Trade Expansion Act of 1962.* Congressional Quarterly Special Report. Washington, DC: Congressional Quarterly, 1962.

Brinkley, Alan. *The End of Reform: New Deal Liberalism in Recession and War.* New York: Knopf, 1995.

Brody, David. *Workers in Industrial America: Essays on the Twentieth Century Struggle*. New York: Oxford University Press, 1980.

———. "The Uses of Power I: Industrial Battleground." In *Workers in Industrial America*, ed. David Brody, 173–214. New York: Oxford University Press, 1980.

Bureau of Labor Statistics, US Department of Labor. *General Textile Strike, September 1934*. Washington, DC: Bureau of Labor Statistics, 1935.

Burns, Arthur F. *Inside the Nixon Administration: The Secret Diary of Arthur Burns, 1969–1974*. Edited by Robert H. Ferrell. Lawrence: University Press of Kansas, 2010.

Butler, Michael A. *Cautious Visionary: Cordell Hull and Trade Reform, 1933–1937*. Kent, OH: Kent State University Press, 1998.

Caro, Robert A. *The Years of Lyndon Johnson: The Passage of Power*. New York: Knopf, 2012.

Chiles, Robert Elliot. *The Revolution of '28: Al Smith, American Progressivism, and the Coming of the New Deal*. Ithaca, NY: Cornell University Press, 2018.

Clark, Daniel J. *Like Night and Day: Unionization in a Southern Mill Town*. Chapel Hill: University of North Carolina Press, 1997.

Cohn, Theodore, Steven McBride, and John Richard Wiseman, eds. *Power in the Global Era: Grounding Globalization*. New York: St. Martin's, 2000.

Collins, Benjamin. *Trade Adjustment Assistance for Workers and the TAA Reauthorization Act of 2015*. Washington, DC: Congressional Research Service, 2018.

Collins, Robert M. *More: The Politics of Economic Growth in Postwar America*. New York: Oxford University Press, 2000.

Conference of New England Governors. *New England Textiles and the New England Economy*. Report by the New England Governors' Textile Committee to the Conference of New England Governors. Cambridge, MA: Conference of New England Governors, 1959.

Cooper, Lyle. "The Tariff and Organized Labor." *American Economic Review* 20, no. 2 (June 1930): 210–25.

Cowie, Jefferson. "Nixon's Class War: Romancing the New Right Worker, 1969–1973." *Labor History* 43, no. 3 (2002): 257–83.

———. *Stayin' Alive: The 1970s and the Last Days of the Working Class*. New York: New Press, 2010.

Crespino, Joseph. "Goldwater in Dixie: Race, Region, and the Rise of the Right." In *Barry Goldwater and the Remaking of the American Political Landscape*, edited by Elizabeth Tandy Shermer, 144–69. Tucson: University of Arizona Press, 2013.

———. *Strom Thurmond's America*. New York: Hill and Wang, 2012.

Daniel, Cletus E. *Culture of Misfortune: An Interpretive History of Textile Unionism in the United States*. Ithaca, NY: ILR, 2001.

Davidson, Roger H. "Eisenhower and Depressed-Areas Legislation, 1955–1961." Accessed December 20, 2021. https://www.american.edu/spa/ccps/upload/Davidson-paper.pdf.

Destler, I. M., Haruhiro Fukui, and Hideo Sato. *The Textile Wrangle: Conflict in Japanese-American Relations, 1969–1971*. Ithaca, NY: Cornell University Press, 1979.

Douty, H. M. "Recovery and the Southern Wage Differential." *Southern Economic Journal* 4, no. 3 (January 1938): 314–21.

Du Bois, W. E. B. *Black Reconstruction in America*. New York: Oxford University Press, 2007.

Eckes, Alfred E. Jr. *Opening America's Market: U.S. Foreign Trade Policy since 1776*. Chapel Hill: University of North Carolina Press, 1995.

Employment and Training Administration, US Department of Labor. "The Worker Adjustment and Retraining Notification Act: A Guide to Advance Notice of Closings and Layoffs." Fact Sheet. Accessed June 3, 2016. https://www.doleta.gov/programs/factsht/warn.htm.

Fabricant, Solomon. *Manufacturing Output 1929–1937*. Cambridge, MA: National Bureau of Economic Research, 1940.

Federal Reserve Bank of St. Louis. "Average Hourly Earnings of Production and Nonsupervisory Employees: Manufacturing." https://research.stlouisfed.org/fred2/data/AHEMAN.txt.

Ferguson, Thomas. "Industrial Conflict and the Coming of the New Deal." In *The Rise and Fall of the New Deal Order, 1930–1980*, edited by Steve Fraser and Gary Gerstle, 3–31. Princeton, NJ: Princeton University Press, 1989.

Ferrell, Robert, ed. *Inside the Nixon Administration: The Secret Diary of Arthur Burns, 1969–1974*. Lawrence: University Press of Kansas, 2010.

Fones-Wolf, Elizabeth, and Ken Fones-Wolf. *Struggle for the Soul of the Postwar South: White Evangelical Protestants and Operation Dixie*. Urbana: University of Illinois Press, 2015.

Frank, Dana. *Buy American: The Untold Story of Economic Nationalism*. Boston: Beacon, 1999.

Fraser, Steve. *Labor Will Rule: Sidney Hillman and the Rise of American Labor*. New York: Free Press, 1991.

———, and Gary Gerstle, eds. *The Rise and Fall of the New Deal Order, 1930–1980*. Princeton, NJ: Princeton University Press, 1989.

Friman, H. Richard. *Patchwork Protectionism: Textile Trade Policy in the U.S., Japan, and West Germany*. Ithaca, NY: Cornell University Press, 1990.

Giridharadas, Anand. *Winners Take All: The Elite Charade of Changing the World*. New York: Knopf, 2018.

Gowa, Joanne S. *Closing the Gold Window: Domestic Politics and the End of Bretton Woods*. Ithaca, NY: Cornell University Press, 1983.

Greenberg, Stan, James Carville, and Erica Seifert. *Inside the GOP: Report on Focus Groups with Evangelical, Tea Party, and Moderate Republicans*. Washington, DC: Democracy Corps, 2013.

Griffith, Barbara S. *The Crisis of American Labor: Operation Dixie and the Defeat of the CIO*. Philadelphia: Temple University Press, 1988.

Harrison, Bennett, and Barry Bluestone. *The Deindustrialization of America: The Decline of Basic Industry*. New York: Basic Books, 1982.

Hayes, Jacqueline. "Toward a Redefinition of the U.S. Sweatshop." *Sanford Journal of Public Policy* 5, no. 2 (Spring 2014): 39–52.

Hochschild, Arlie Russell. *Strangers in Their Own Land: Anger and Mourning on the American Right*. New York: New Press, 2016.

Hodges, James A. *New Deal Labor Policy and the Southern Cotton Textile Industry, 1933–1941*. Knoxville: University of Tennessee Press, 1986.

Hower, Joseph E., and Joseph A. McCartin. "Marshall's Principle: A Former Labor Secretary Looks Back (and Ahead)." *Labor* 11, no. 4 (Winter 2014): 91–107.

Hufbauer, Gary Clyde, Yee Wong, and Ketki Sheth. *US-China Trade Disputes: Rising Tide, Rising Stakes*. Washington, DC: Institute for International Economics, 2006.

Hull, Cordell. *The Memoirs of Cordell Hull*. New York: Macmillan, 1948.

Irons, Janet Christine. *Testing the New Deal: The General Textile Strike of 1934 in the American South*. Urbana: University of Illinois Press, 2000.

Irwin, Douglas A. *Clashing over Commerce: A History of US Trade Policy*. Chicago: University of Chicago Press, 2017.

Jenks, Thomas E. "Taxation of Foreign Income." *George Washington Law Review* 42 (1973–74): 537–56.

Jones, Geoffrey. *Multinationals and Global Capitalism: From the Nineteenth to the Twenty-First Century*. New York: Oxford University Press, 2005.

Katznelson, Ira. *Fear Itself: The New Deal and the Origins of Our Time*. New York: Liveright, 2013.

Kennedy, John F. "President's Special Message to the Congress on Taxation." H.R. Doc. No. 140, Eighty-Seventh Congress, first sess. Washington, DC: US Government Printing Office, 1961.

———. "Remarks upon Signing the Trade Expansion Act, October 11, 1962." American Presidency Project. https://www.presidency.ucsb.edu/documents/remarks-upon-signing-the-trade-expansion-act.

Korstad, Robert Rodgers. *Civil Rights Unionism: Tobacco Workers and the Struggle for Democracy in the Mid-twentieth-century South*. Chapel Hill: University of North Carolina Press, 2003.

Kunz, Diane B. *Butter and Guns: America's Cold War Economic Diplomacy*. New York: Free Press, 1997.

Lassiter, Matthew D. *The Silent Majority: Suburban Politics in the Sunbelt South*. Princeton, NJ: Princeton University Press, 2006.

Lawrence, Richard. "Passage of Trade Reform Bill Likely; Major Hurdle Cleared." *Journal of Commerce*, August 16, 1974.

Levinson, Marc. *An Extraordinary Time: The End of the Postwar Boom and the Return of the Ordinary Economy*. New York: Basic Books, 2016.

Lichtenstein, Nelson. "From Corporatism to Collective Bargaining: Organized Labor and the Eclipse of Social Democracy in the Postwar Era." In *The Rise and Fall of the New Deal Order 1930–1980*, edited by Steve Fraser and Gary Gerstle, 122–52. Princeton, NJ: Princeton University Press, 1989.

———. *Labor's War at Home: The CIO in World War II*. New York: Cambridge University Press, 1982.

Link, William. "Time Is an Elusive Companion: Jesse Helms, Barry Goldwater, and the Dynamic of Modern Conservatism." In *Barry Goldwater and the Remaking of the American Political Landscape*, edited by Elizabeth Tandy Shermer, 238–58. Tucson: University of Arizona Press, 2013.

Lockwood, William Wirt. *The Economic Development of Japan*. Princeton, NJ: Princeton University Press, 1954.

Marshall, F. Ray. *Labor in the South* . Cambridge, MA: Harvard University Press, 1967.

Mason, Robert. *Richard Nixon and the Quest for a New Majority*. Chapel Hill: University of North Carolina Press, 2004.

Matusow, Allen J. *Nixon's Economy: Booms, Busts, Dollars, and Votes*. Lawrence: University Press of Kansas, 1998.

Mayer, Gerald. *Union Membership Trends in the United States*. Washington, DC: Congressional Research Service, 2004.

McCartin, Joseph A. *Collision Course: Ronald Reagan, the Air Traffic Controllers, and the Strike That Changed America*. New York: Oxford University Press, 2011.

McGirr, Lisa. *Suburban Warriors: The Origins of the New American Right*. Princeton, NJ: Princeton University Press, 2001.

Minchin, Timothy J. "Decline of the Textile and Apparel Industry and Deindustrialization in the South." In *Life and Labor in the New New South*, edited by Robert H. Zieger, 258–88. Gainesville: University Press of Florida, 2012.

———. *Don't Sleep with Stevens! The J. P. Stevens Campaign and the Struggle to Organize the South, 1963–80*. Gainesville: University Press of Florida, 2005.

———. *Empty Mills: The Fight against Imports and the Decline of the U.S. Textile Industry*. Lanham, MD: Rowman and Littlefield, 2013.

———. *Hiring the Black Worker: The Racial Integration of the Southern Textile Industry, 1960–1980*. Chapel Hill: University of North Carolina Press, 1999.

———. *What Do We Need a Union For? The TWUA in the South, 1945–1955*. Chapel Hill: University of North Carolina Press, 1997.

Mischel, Lawrence, and Julia Wolfe. *CEO Compensation Has Grown 940% since 1978*. Washington, DC: Economic Policy Institute, 2019.

Mizruchi, Mark. *The Fracturing of the American Corporate Elite*. Cambridge, MA: Harvard University Press, 2013.

Moley, Raymond. *After Seven Years*. New York: Harper and Brothers, 1939.

Mourdoukoutas, Panos. *The Global Corporation: The Decolonization of International Business*. Westport, CT: Quorum, 1999.

Mucciaroni, Gary. *The Political Failure of Employment Policy, 1945–1982*. Pittsburgh, PA: University of Pittsburgh Press, 1990.

Murchison, Claudius T. "American-Japanese Cotton Goods Agreement." *Journal of Marketing* 2, no. 4 (April 1938): 272–77.

———. *King Cotton Is Sick*. Chapel Hill: University of North Carolina Press, 1930.

National Bureau of Economic Research. "US Business Cycle Expansions and Contractions." Last updated July 19, 2021. http://www.nber.org/cycles/cyclesmain.html.

National Labor Relations Board. "The 1935 Passage of the Wagner Act." https://www.nlrb.gov/about-nlrb/who-we-are/our-history/1935-passage-of-the-wagner-act.

Nixon, Richard M. "Veto of the Minimum Wage Bill." September 6, 1973. American Presidency Project. https://www.presidency.ucsb.edu/documents/veto-the-minimum-wage-bill.

Nossiter, Bernard. "Slump in Textiles: An Industry Goes 'Soft'." *The Nation* 180, no. 4 (January 22, 1955): 72–73.

Our Campaigns.com. "Massachusetts U.S. Senate" (1946 election results). Accessed December 20, 2021. http://www.ourcampaigns.com/RaceDetail.html?RaceID=147415.

———. "Massachusetts U.S. Senate" (1952 election results). Accessed December 20, 2021. http://www.ourcampaigns.com/RaceDetail.html?RaceID=83027.

Parmet, Robert D. *The Master of Seventh Avenue: David Dubinsky and the American Labor Movement*. New York: New York University Press, 2005.

Pastor, Robert A. *Congress and the Politics of U.S. Foreign Economic Policy, 1929–1976*. Berkeley: University of California Press, 1980.

Patterson, James T. *America's Struggle against Poverty, 1900–1994*. Cambridge, MA: Harvard University Press, 1994.

———. *Grand Expectations: The United States, 1945–1974*. New York: Oxford University Press, 1996.

Peckenham, Nancy. "Out in the Cold at Cannon Mills." *The Nation* 253, no. 8 (September 16, 1991): 298–302.

Peterson, Peter G. *The United States in the Changing World Economy*. Washington, DC: US Government Printing Office, 1971.

Reardon, John J. *America and the Multinational Corporation: The History of a Troubled Partnership*. Westport, CT: Praeger, 1992.

Richardson, David. "Trade Adjustment Assistance under the U.S. Trade Act of 1974: An Analytical Examination and Worker Survey." In *Import Competition and Response*, ed. Jagdish Bhagwati, 321–68. Chicago: University of Chicago Press, 1982.

Roin, Julie A. "The Grand Illusion: A Neutral System for the Taxation of International Transactions." *Virginia Law Review* 75, no. 5 (August 1989): 919–69.

Roosevelt, Franklin D. "Cotton Textile Industry: Message from the President of the United States Transmitting a Report on the Conditions and Problems of the Cotton Textile Industry, Made by the Cabinet Committee Appointed by Him" (Roper Commission Report). July 29, 1935. Washington, DC: US Government Printing Office, 1935.

———. "I Pledge You—I Pledge Myself to a New Deal for the American People." In *The Public Papers and Addresses of Franklin D. Roosevelt*. Edited by Samuel I. Rosenman. Vol. 1, *The Genesis of the New Deal, 1928–1932*. New York: Random House, 1938.

———. *The Public Papers and Addresses of Franklin D. Roosevelt*. Edited by Samuel I. Rosenman. Vol. 1, *The Genesis of the New Deal*. New York: Random House, 1938.

Rosen, Ellen Israel. *Making Sweatshops: The Globalization of the U.S. Apparel Industry*. Berkeley: University of California Press, 2002.

Rowan, Richard L., and Robert E. Barr. *Employee Relations Trends and Practices in the Textile Industry*. Philadelphia: University of Pennsylvania, Wharton School, Industrial Research Unit, 1987.

Rubner, Alex. *The Might of the Multinationals: The Rise and Fall of the Corporate Legend*. New York: Praeger, 1990.

Salmond, John A. *The General Textile Strike of 1934: From Maine to Alabama*. Columbia: University of Missouri Press, 2002.

Shaviro, Daniel N. *Fixing U.S. International Taxation*. New York: Oxford University Press, 2014.

Shermer, Elizabeth Tandy. *Barry Goldwater and the Remaking of the American Political Landscape*. Tucson: University of Arizona Press, 2013.

Standing, Guy. *The Precariat: The New Dangerous Class*. London: Bloomsbury, 2011.

Staudohar, Paul D., and Holly E. Brown. *Deindustrialization and Plant Closure*. Lexington, MA: D. C. Heath, 1987.

Stein, Herbert. *Presidential Economics: The Making of Economic Policy from Roosevelt to Reagan and Beyond*. New York: Simon and Schuster, 1984.

Stein, Judith. *Pivotal Decade: How the United States Traded Factories for Finance in the Seventies*. New Haven, CT: Yale University Press, 2010.

———. *Running Steel, Running America: Race, Economic Policy, and the Decline of Liberalism*. Chapel Hill: University of North Carolina Press, 1998.

Temin, Peter. *The Vanishing Middle Class: Power and Prejudice in a Dual Economy*. Cambridge, MA: MIT Press, 2017.

Truman, Harry S. "Executive Order 9559: Authorizing the Secretary of War to Take Possession of and Operate the Plants and Facilities of the Gaffney Manufacturing Company, Located at Gaffney, South Carolina." May 28, 1945. Executive Orders, Harry S Truman Library and Museum, https://www.trumanlibrary.gov/library/executive-orders/9559/executive-order-9559.

———. "Executive Order 9603: Termination of Possession of Certain Property Taken by the Government." Executive Orders, Harry S Truman Library and Museum. August 25, 1945. https://www.trumanlibrary.gov/library/executive-orders/9603/executive-order-9603.

US Bureau of Labor Statistics. *General Textile Strike, September 1934*. Washington, DC: US Bureau of Labor Statistics, 1935.

US Commission on Foreign Economic Policy (Randall Commission). *Report to the President and the Congress*. Washington, DC: US Government Printing Office, 1954.

US Congress. House. Committee on Ways and Means. *Extension of the Reciprocal Trade Agreements Act*. Seventy-Sixth Congress, third sess., January 11, 1940. Washington, DC: US Government Printing Office, 1940.

———. *Extension of the Reciprocal Trade Agreements Act*. Seventy-Eighth Congress, first sess., April 12, 1943. Washington, DC: US Government Printing Office, 1943.

———. *Tariff and Trade Proposals*. Ninety-First Congress, second sess., May 19, 1970. Washington, DC: US Government Printing Office, 1970.

———. *Material Relating to Adjustment Assistance for Workers.* Ninety-Third Congress, first sess., June 1973. Washington, DC: US Government Printing Office, 1973.

———. *Reciprocal Trade Agreements.* Seventy-Third Congress, second sess., March 8, 1934. Washington, DC: US Government Printing Office, 1934.

———. *Trade Expansion Act of 1962: Hearings on H.R. 9900.* Eighty-Seventh Congress, second sess. 6 vols., March 12–April 11, 1962. Washington, DC: US Government Printing Office, 1962.

US Congress. Office of Technology Assessment. *The U.S. Textile and Apparel Industry—a Revolution in Progress.* Special Report. Washington, DC: United States Congress, Office of Technology Assessment, 1987.

US Congress. Senate. Committee on Finance. *1945 Extension of Reciprocal Trade Agreements Act.* Seventy-Ninth Congress, first sess., May 30, 1945. Washington, DC: US Government Printing Office, 1945.

———. *Tables and Statistical Material on U.S. Balance of Trade and Balance of Payments.* Ninety-Third Congress, second sess., December 1974. Washington, DC: US Government Printing Office, 1974.

———. *Trade Expansion Act of 1962: Hearings on H.R. 11970.* Eighty-Seventh Congress, second sess. 4 vols. July 23–August 16, 1962. Washington, DC: US Government Printing Office, 1962.

US Congress. Senate. Committee on Interstate and Foreign Commerce. *Problems of the Domestic Textile Industry.* Supplemental report. Eighty-Seventh Congress, first sess., March 14, 1961. Washington, DC: US Government Printing Office, 1961.

US Department of Commerce. *Annual Survey of Manufacturers 1961.* Washington, DC: US Government Printing Office, 1964.

———. *Census of Manufacturing: 1947 Indexes of Production.* Washington, DC: US Government Printing Office, 1952.

US Department of Labor. *The Textile-Apparel Labor Force: A Special Study.* Washington, DC: US Department of Labor, 1968.

US Department of State. *The Trade Agreement with the United Kingdom, Signed November 17, 1938.* Washington, DC: US Government Printing Office, 1938.

US Department of State. Office of the Historian. *Nixon and the End of the Bretton Woods System, 1971–1973.* https://history.state.gov/milestones/1969–1976/nixon-shock.

US Tariff Commission. *Postwar Developments in Japan's Foreign Trade.* Washington, DC: US Tariff Commission, 1958.

———. *Effect of Trade Agreement Reductions on Tariff Levels in the United States.* Washington, DC: US Tariff Commission, 1945.

———. *Textiles and Apparel: Report to the President on Investigation No. 332–55 under Section 332 of the Tariff Act of 1930.* 2 vols. Washington, DC: US Tariff Commission, 1968.

US Trade Representative Office. "History of the United States Trade Representative." https://ustr.gov/about-us/history.

Vanderburg, Timothy W. "Cannon Mills: A Case Study in Southern Industrialization." PhD diss., Mississippi State University, 2001.

———. *Cannon Mills and Kannapolis: Persistent Paternalism in a Textile Town*. Knoxville: University of Tennessee Press, 2013.

Wells, Wyatt C. *Economist in an Uncertain World: Arthur F. Burns and the Federal Reserve, 1970–78*. New York: Columbia University Press, 1994.

Williams, Joan C. "What So Many People Don't Get about the U.S. Working Class." *Harvard Business Review*. November 10, 2016.

Winant, John G. *Report of the Board of Inquiry for the Cotton Textile Industry to the President*. Washington, DC: US Government Printing Office, 1935.

Wolf, Martin, Hans Hinrich Glismann, Joseph Pelzman, and Dean Spinanger. *Costs of Protecting Jobs in Textiles and Clothing*. London: Trevor-Hobbs, 1984.

Zelizer, Julian E. *Taxing America: Wilbur D. Mills, Congress, and the State, 1945–1975*. New York: Cambridge University Press, 1998.

Zieger, Robert H. *The CIO, 1935–1955*. Chapel Hill: University of North Carolina Press, 1995.

———, ed. *Life and Labor in the New New South*. Gainesville: University Press of Florida, 2012.

INDEX

JAMES C. BENTON is director of the Race and Economic Empowerment Project at the Kalmanovitz Initiative for Labor and the Working Poor at Georgetown University.

THE WORKING CLASS IN AMERICAN HISTORY

Worker City, Company Town: Iron and Cotton-Worker Protest in Troy and Cohoes, New York, 1855–84 *Daniel J. Walkowitz*

Life, Work, and Rebellion in the Coal Fields: The Southern West Virginia Miners, 1880–1922 *David Alan Corbin*

Women and American Socialism, 1870–1920 *Mari Jo Buhle*

Lives of Their Own: Blacks, Italians, and Poles in Pittsburgh, 1900–1960 *John Bodnar, Roger Simon, and Michael P. Weber*

Working-Class America: Essays on Labor, Community, and American Society *Edited by Michael H. Frisch and Daniel J. Walkowitz*

Eugene V. Debs: Citizen and Socialist *Nick Salvatore*

American Labor and Immigration History, 1877–1920s: Recent European Research *Edited by Dirk Hoerder*

Workingmen's Democracy: The Knights of Labor and American Politics *Leon Fink*

The Electrical Workers: A History of Labor at General Electric and Westinghouse, 1923–60 *Ronald W. Schatz*

The Mechanics of Baltimore: Workers and Politics in the Age of Revolution, 1763–1812 *Charles G. Steffen*

The Practice of Solidarity: American Hat Finishers in the Nineteenth Century *David Bensman*

The Labor History Reader *Edited by Daniel J. Leab*

Solidarity and Fragmentation: Working People and Class Consciousness in Detroit, 1875–1900 *Richard Oestreicher*

Counter Cultures: Saleswomen, Managers, and Customers in American Department Stores, 1890–1940 *Susan Porter Benson*

The New England Working Class and the New Labor History *Edited by Herbert G. Gutman and Donald H. Bell*

Labor Leaders in America *Edited by Melvyn Dubofsky and Warren Van Tine*

Barons of Labor: The San Francisco Building Trades and Union Power in the Progressive Era *Michael Kazin*

Gender at Work: The Dynamics of Job Segregation by Sex during World War II *Ruth Milkman*

Once a Cigar Maker: Men, Women, and Work Culture in American Cigar Factories, 1900–1919 *Patricia A. Cooper*

A Generation of Boomers: The Pattern of Railroad Labor Conflict in Nineteenth-Century America *Shelton Stromquist*

Work and Community in the Jungle: Chicago's Packinghouse Workers, 1894–1922 *James R. Barrett*

Workers, Managers, and Welfare Capitalism: The Shoeworkers and Tanners of Endicott Johnson, 1890–1950 *Gerald Zahavi*

Men, Women, and Work: Class, Gender, and Protest in the New England Shoe Industry, 1780–1910 *Mary Blewett*

Workers on the Waterfront: Seamen, Longshoremen, and Unionism in the 1930s *Bruce Nelson*

German Workers in Chicago: A Documentary History of Working-Class Culture from 1850 to World War I *Edited by Hartmut Keil and John B. Jentz*
On the Line: Essays in the History of Auto Work *Edited by Nelson Lichtenstein and Stephen Meyer III*
Labor's Flaming Youth: Telephone Operators and Worker Militancy, 1878–1923 *Stephen H. Norwood*
Another Civil War: Labor, Capital, and the State in the Anthracite Regions of Pennsylvania, 1840–68 *Grace Palladino*
Coal, Class, and Color: Blacks in Southern West Virginia, 1915–32 *Joe William Trotter Jr.*
For Democracy, Workers, and God: Labor Song-Poems and Labor Protest, 1865–95 *Clark D. Halker*
Dishing It Out: Waitresses and Their Unions in the Twentieth Century *Dorothy Sue Cobble*
The Spirit of 1848: German Immigrants, Labor Conflict, and the Coming of the Civil War *Bruce Levine*
Working Women of Collar City: Gender, Class, and Community in Troy, New York, 1864–86 *Carole Turbin*
Southern Labor and Black Civil Rights: Organizing Memphis Workers *Michael K. Honey*
Radicals of the Worst Sort: Laboring Women in Lawrence, Massachusetts, 1860–1912 *Ardis Cameron*
Producers, Proletarians, and Politicians: Workers and Party Politics in Evansville and New Albany, Indiana, 1850–87 *Lawrence M. Lipin*
The New Left and Labor in the 1960s *Peter B. Levy*
The Making of Western Labor Radicalism: Denver's Organized Workers, 1878–1905 *David Brundage*
In Search of the Working Class: Essays in American Labor History and Political Culture *Leon Fink*
Lawyers against Labor: From Individual Rights to Corporate Liberalism *Daniel R. Ernst*
"We Are All Leaders": The Alternative Unionism of the Early 1930s *Edited by Staughton Lynd*
The Female Economy: The Millinery and Dressmaking Trades, 1860–1930 *Wendy Gamber*
"Negro and White, Unite and Fight!": A Social History of Industrial Unionism in Meatpacking, 1930–90 *Roger Horowitz*
Power at Odds: The 1922 National Railroad Shopmen's Strike *Colin J. Davis*
The Common Ground of Womanhood: Class, Gender, and Working Girls' Clubs, 1884–1928 *Priscilla Murolo*
Marching Together: Women of the Brotherhood of Sleeping Car Porters *Melinda Chateauvert*
Down on the Killing Floor: Black and White Workers in Chicago's Packinghouses, 1904–54 *Rick Halpern*
Labor and Urban Politics: Class Conflict and the Origins of Modern Liberalism in Chicago, 1864–97 *Richard Schneirov*
All That Glitters: Class, Conflict, and Community in Cripple Creek *Elizabeth Jameson*
Waterfront Workers: New Perspectives on Race and Class *Edited by Calvin Winslow*

Labor Histories: Class, Politics, and the Working-Class Experience
Edited by Eric Arnesen, Julie Greene, and Bruce Laurie

The Pullman Strike and the Crisis of the 1890s: Essays on Labor and Politics
Edited by Richard Schneirov, Shelton Stromquist, and Nick Salvatore

AlabamaNorth: African-American Migrants, Community, and Working-Class Activism in Cleveland, 1914–45 *Kimberley L. Phillips*

Imagining Internationalism in American and British Labor, 1939–49 *Victor Silverman*

William Z. Foster and the Tragedy of American Radicalism *James R. Barrett*

Colliers across the Sea: A Comparative Study of Class Formation in Scotland and the American Midwest, 1830–1924 *John H. M. Laslett*

"Rights, Not Roses": Unions and the Rise of Working-Class Feminism, 1945–80
Dennis A. Deslippe

Testing the New Deal: The General Textile Strike of 1934 in the American South
Janet Irons

Hard Work: The Making of Labor History *Melvyn Dubofsky*

Southern Workers and the Search for Community: Spartanburg County, South Carolina
G. C. Waldrep III

We Shall Be All: A History of the Industrial Workers of the World (abridged edition)
Melvyn Dubofsky, ed. Joseph A. McCartin

Race, Class, and Power in the Alabama Coalfields, 1908–21 *Brian Kelly*

Duquesne and the Rise of Steel Unionism *James D. Rose*

Anaconda: Labor, Community, and Culture in Montana's Smelter City *Laurie Mercier*

Bridgeport's Socialist New Deal, 1915–36 *Cecelia Bucki*

Indispensable Outcasts: Hobo Workers and Community in the American Midwest, 1880–1930 *Frank Tobias Higbie*

After the Strike: A Century of Labor Struggle at Pullman *Susan Eleanor Hirsch*

Corruption and Reform in the Teamsters Union *David Witwer*

Waterfront Revolts: New York and London Dockworkers, 1946–61 *Colin J. Davis*

Black Workers' Struggle for Equality in Birmingham *Horace Huntley and David Montgomery*

The Tribe of Black Ulysses: African American Men in the Industrial South
William P. Jones

City of Clerks: Office and Sales Workers in Philadelphia, 1870–1920 *Jerome P. Bjelopera*

Reinventing "The People": The Progressive Movement, the Class Problem, and the Origins of Modern Liberalism *Shelton Stromquist*

Radical Unionism in the Midwest, 1900–1950 *Rosemary Feurer*

Gendering Labor History *Alice Kessler-Harris*

James P. Cannon and the Origins of the American Revolutionary Left, 1890–1928
Bryan D. Palmer

Glass Towns: Industry, Labor, and Political Economy in Appalachia, 1890–1930s
Ken Fones-Wolf

Workers and the Wild: Conservation, Consumerism, and Labor in Oregon, 1910–30
Lawrence M. Lipin

Wobblies on the Waterfront: Interracial Unionism in Progressive-Era Philadelphia
Peter Cole

Red Chicago: American Communism at Its Grassroots, 1928–35 *Randi Storch*
Labor's Cold War: Local Politics in a Global Context *Edited by Shelton Stromquist*
Bessie Abramowitz Hillman and the Making of the Amalgamated Clothing Workers of America *Karen Pastorello*
The Great Strikes of 1877 *Edited by David O. Stowell*
Union-Free America: Workers and Antiunion Culture *Lawrence Richards*
Race against Liberalism: Black Workers and the UAW in Detroit *David M. Lewis-Colman*
Teachers and Reform: Chicago Public Education, 1929–70 *John F. Lyons*
Upheaval in the Quiet Zone: 1199/SEIU and the Politics of Healthcare Unionism *Leon Fink and Brian Greenberg*
Shadow of the Racketeer: Scandal in Organized Labor *David Witwer*
Sweet Tyranny: Migrant Labor, Industrial Agriculture, and Imperial Politics *Kathleen Mapes*
Staley: The Fight for a New American Labor Movement *Steven K. Ashby and C. J. Hawking*
On the Ground: Labor Struggles in the American Airline Industry *Liesl Miller Orenic*
NAFTA and Labor in North America *Norman Caulfield*
Making Capitalism Safe: Work Safety and Health Regulation in America, 1880–1940 *Donald W. Rogers*
Good, Reliable, White Men: Railroad Brotherhoods, 1877–1917 *Paul Michel Taillon*
Spirit of Rebellion: Labor and Religion in the New Cotton South *Jarod Roll*
The Labor Question in America: Economic Democracy in the Gilded Age *Rosanne Currarino*
Banded Together: Economic Democratization in the Brass Valley *Jeremy Brecher*
The Gospel of the Working Class: Labor's Southern Prophets in New Deal America *Erik Gellman and Jarod Roll*
Guest Workers and Resistance to U.S. Corporate Despotism *Immanuel Ness*
Gleanings of Freedom: Free and Slave Labor along the Mason-Dixon Line, 1790–1860 *Max Grivno*
Chicago in the Age of Capital: Class, Politics, and Democracy during the Civil War and Reconstruction *John B. Jentz and Richard Schneirov*
Child Care in Black and White: Working Parents and the History of Orphanages *Jessie B. Ramey*
The Haymarket Conspiracy: Transatlantic Anarchist Networks *Timothy Messer-Kruse*
Detroit's Cold War: The Origins of Postwar Conservatism *Colleen Doody*
A Renegade Union: Interracial Organizing and Labor Radicalism *Lisa Phillips*
Palomino: Clinton Jencks and Mexican-American Unionism in the American Southwest *James J. Lorence*
Latin American Migrations to the U.S. Heartland: Changing Cultural Landscapes in Middle America *Edited by Linda Allegro and Andrew Grant Wood*
Man of Fire: Selected Writings *Ernesto Galarza, ed. Armando Ibarra and Rodolfo D. Torres*
A Contest of Ideas: Capital, Politics, and Labor *Nelson Lichtenstein*

Making the World Safe for Workers: Labor, the Left, and Wilsonian Internationalism *Elizabeth McKillen*

The Rise of the Chicago Police Department: Class and Conflict, 1850–1894 *Sam Mitrani*

Workers in Hard Times: A Long View of Economic Crises *Edited by Leon Fink, Joseph A. McCartin, and Joan Sangster*

Redeeming Time: Protestantism and Chicago's Eight-Hour Movement, 1866–1912 *William A. Mirola*

Struggle for the Soul of the Postwar South: White Evangelical Protestants and Operation Dixie *Elizabeth Fones-Wolf and Ken Fones-Wolf*

Free Labor: The Civil War and the Making of an American Working Class *Mark A. Lause*

Death and Dying in the Working Class, 1865–1920 *Michael K. Rosenow*

Immigrants against the State: Yiddish and Italian Anarchism in America *Kenyon Zimmer*

Fighting for Total Person Unionism: Harold Gibbons, Ernest Calloway, and Working-Class Citizenship *Robert Bussel*

Smokestacks in the Hills: Rural-Industrial Workers in West Virginia *Louis Martin*

Disaster Citizenship: Survivors, Solidarity, and Power in the Progressive Era *Jacob A. C. Remes*

The Pew and the Picket Line: Christianity and the American Working Class *Edited by Christopher D. Cantwell, Heath W. Carter, and Janine Giordano Drake*

Conservative Counterrevolution: Challenging Liberalism in 1950s Milwaukee *Tula A. Connell*

Manhood on the Line: Working-Class Masculinities in the American Heartland *Steve Meyer*

On Gender, Labor, and Inequality *Ruth Milkman*

The Making of Working-Class Religion *Matthew Pehl*

Civic Labors: Scholar Activism and Working-Class Studies *Edited by Dennis Deslippe, Eric Fure-Slocum, and John W. McKerley*

Victor Arnautoff and the Politics of Art *Robert W. Cherny*

Against Labor: How U.S. Employers Organized to Defeat Union Activism *Edited by Rosemary Feurer and Chad Pearson*

Teacher Strike! Public Education and the Making of a New American Political Order *Jon Shelton*

Hillbilly Hellraisers: Federal Power and Populist Defiance in the Ozarks *J. Blake Perkins*

Sewing the Fabric of Statehood: Garment Unions, American Labor, and the Establishment of the State of Israel *Adam Howard*

Labor Justice across the America *Edited by Leon Fink and Juan Manuel Palacio*

Frontiers of Labor: Comparative Histories of the United States and Australia *Edited by Greg Patmore and Shelton Stromquist*

Women Have Always Worked: A Concise History, Second Edition *Alice Kessler-Harris*

Remembering Lattimer: Labor, Migration, and Race in Pennsylvania Anthracite Country *Paul A. Shackel*

Disruption in Detroit: Autoworkers and the Elusive Postwar Boom *Daniel J. Clark*

To Live Here, You Have to Fight: How Women Led Appalachian Movements for Social Justice *Jessica Wilkerson*

Dockworker Power: Race and Activism in Durban and the San Francisco Bay Area
Peter Cole
Labor's Mind: A History of Working-Class Intellectual Life *Tobias Higbie*
The World in a City: Multiethnic Radicalism in Early Twentieth-Century Los Angeles
David M. Struthers
Death to Fascism: Louis Adamic's Fight for Democracy *John P. Enyeart*
Upon the Altar of Work: Child Labor and the Rise of a New American Sectionalism
Betsy Wood
Workers against the City: The Fight for Free Speech in *Hague v. CIO* *Donald W. Rogers*
Union Renegades: Miners, Capitalism, and Organizing in the Gilded Age
Dana M. Caldemeyer
The Labor Board Crew: Remaking Worker-Employer Relations from Pearl Harbor to the Reagan Era *Ronald W. Schatz*
Grand Army of Labor: Workers, Veterans, and the Meaning of the Civil War
Matthew E. Stanley
A Matter of Moral Justice: Black Women Laundry Workers and the Fight for Justice
Jenny Carson
Labor's End: How the Promise of Automation Degraded Work *Jason Resnikoff*
Toward a Cooperative Commonwealth: The Transplanted Roots of Farmer-Labor Radicalism in Texas *Thomas Alter II*
Working in the Magic City: Moral Economy in Early Twentieth-Century Miami
Thomas A. Castillo
Where Are the Workers? Labor's Stories at Museums and Historic Sites
Edited by Robert Forrant and Mary Anne Trasciatti
Labor's Outcasts: Migrant Farmworkers and Unions in North America, 1934–1966
Andrew J. Hazelton
Fraying Fabric: How Trade Policy and Industrial Decline Transformed America
James C. Benton

The University of Illinois Press
is a founding member of the
Association of University Presses.

University of Illinois Press
1325 South Oak Street
Champaign, IL 61820-6903
www.press.uillinois.edu